Networks
For
Networkers

Networks
For
Networkers:

Critical Issues in
Cooperative Library Development

**Edited by Barbara Evans Markuson
and Blanche Woolls**

Neal-Schuman Publishers, Inc.

Published by Neal-Schuman Publishers, Inc.
64 University Place
New York, New York 10003

Published outside North America by Mansell Publishing, 3 Bloomsbury Place, London WC14 2QA, England

This volume contains the proceedings of a Conference on Networks for Networkers and was prepared pursuant to Grant No. G007805130 from the Office of Education, U.S. Department of Health, Education and Welfare. The points of view and opinions do not necessarily represent official Office of Education position or policy.

Printed and bound in the United States of America.

Library of Congress Cataloging in Publication Data

Main entry under title:

Networks for networkers.

Includes index.
1. Library information networks—United States—Congresses. I. Markuson, Barbara Evans. II. Woolls, Blanche. III. Indiana. Dept. of Public Instruction.
Z674.8.N47   021.6'5   79-24054
ISBN 0-918212-22-7

British Library Cataloguing in Publication Data

Conference on Networks for Networkers,
Indianapolis, 1979
Networks for networkers.
1. Library information networks—United States—Congresses
2. Libraries—United States—Automation—Congresses
I. Title   II. Markuson, Barbara Evans
III. Woolls, Blanche
022'.9   Z674.8   80-40016

ISBN 0-7201-01599-X

Contents

PART IV: NETWORK GOVERNANCE AND
FUNDING

PART V: NETWORK USERS AND SERVICES

APPENDIXES

Foreword

Approximately ten years ago the Office of Education in conjunction with the American Library Association sponsored a conference to explore the implication of establishing library networks. While there was general agreement that networks should be encouraged, there was little in the way of practice and experience to provide guidance and direction for the future.

Over the past several years the concept of networks has become a fixture in the library and information world. Indeed, we have seen the spectacular growth of large systems such as OCLC, Inc., RLIN, and the Washington Library Network. There has been a prolific growth of various other statewide, regional, and multi-institution networks. The National Commission on Libraries and Information Science in its national plan called for a "nationwide network concept." It would be difficult to find a library or information service meeting, seminar, or conference which did not include networks on the agendas.

The "Networks for Networkers" conference brought together experts, proponents, operators, and evaluators to examine the present state of affairs and to suggest courses which deserve attention and deliberation. It was a propitious time to take stock of our progress, analyze successes and failures, and explore other thoughts.

The papers presented in this report are articulate, stimulating and purposeful. Hopefully, these papers together with the interaction of the many interested and affected parties who attended the conference will provide the perspective and stimulation for future planning.

The critical ingredient of the conference and this report was the outstanding and synergetic leadership provided by Barbara Evans Markuson, Phyllis Land, and Blanche Woolls. They and their colleagues deserve our gratitude.

Dick W. Hays, Associate Commissioner
Office of Libraries and Learning Resources
U.S. Office of Education

Preface

Networks and new technology are rapidly changing library and information services throughout this country. How this development evolves depends on the solutions to many critical issues. To enable a wide discussion of what networks have achieved and the issues that they raise, prior to the White House Conference on Libraries and Information Services, the U.S. Office of Education (Office of Library and Learning Resources) was interested in funding a network conference with a nationwide participation. We were interested and able to administer such a conference, and joining us were three other Indiana sponsors.

Funder and sponsors alike found a network conference in line with their institutional goals and objectives. The conference funder, Office of Libraries and Learning Resources of the United States Office of Education, over the years has sponsored research and development projects which helped pave the way for many of the network developments which were the subject of this conference. The Indiana Department of Public Instruction is committed to advancing the cause of public education and educational technology and the participation of school libraries in networking is in line with these goals. The Purdue University Libraries Audio-Visual Center, an early participant in library automation and an active supporter of library network development in Indiana, is committed to effective service to the academic community, a cause advanced by library networking. The Indiana University Graduate Library School provides a number of courses related to new technology and, through its research programs, has investigated aspects of national library programs and services. The Indiana Cooperative Library Services Authority (INCOLSA), as a multitype library network organization is committed to bringing network technology to all types of libraries, large and small, so that ultimately all libraries can participate in the benefits of technical development and library cooperation. In addition, INCOLSA agreed to take on the task of running the conference under the direction of Barbara Evans Markuson, Executive Director of INCOLSA, who served as Principal Investigator.

The National Advisory Committee helped us establish topics for commissioned papers and suggested potential authors. The Committee also developed the list of participants. The members of the Committee were James Barrentine, OCLC, Inc., Eileen Cooke, American Library Association, Joseph M. Dagnese, Purdue University Libraries/Audio-Visual Center, Keith Doms, Free Library of Philadelphia, Glyn Evans, State University of New York, Robert McClarren, North Suburban Library System, Lee Power, Federal Library Committee, Nettie Taylor, Maryland State Library Agency, and Alice Wilcox, Minnesota Interlibrary Telecommunications Exchange (MINITEX).

We chose the title, Networks for Networkers, to emphasize both the grass roots approach and the wide range of people who are involved in promoting the network environment. We wanted the authors to say what they thought without a built-in hidden agenda. We wanted lay and library representatives to speak out on what they thought were compelling network issues at this time—just as we enter the White House Conference era which may lead to change in legislation and program priorities. We saw network development as involving all types of networkers— library users; librarians from academic, special, school and public systems; state library agencies, state agencies for public instruction, library education, representatives from federal and national associations, and, last, but not least, directors and staff from the computer-based library networks and representatives of library consortia and cooperatives. All of these groups were represented at the conference.

As in all plans, some things came off well and some things not so well. These were, however, the minor irritations that fade quickly from memory. From the beginning we hoped for two things: a conference that would indeed boldly identify issues and a set of papers that would merit publication to allow a much wider audience than could be accommodated within the project budget. It was our good fortune to have achieved both of these goals.

All of the sponsors were gratified by the interest shown in this

conference and by the astounding array of talent that contributed to its success. Two men took time from extraordinarily busy
schedules to welcome the participants to Indiana and to join in
conference activities. We wish to acknowledge Harold Negley,
State Superintendent, Indiana Department of Public Instruction
and William Long, Chairman, Ways and Means Committee,
Indiana House of Representatives for their interest in and
support of this conference. To all of you who assisted and to all
who participated in the conference the sponsors express their
thanks. We hope that these people and those of you still to
participate through dissemination of these proceedings will
continue to work cooperatively to advance the cause of networking. Any errors in commission and omission during the conference and in this publication are regretted, but are, of course, our
responsibility.

> *Phyllis Land, Director*
> *Division of Instructional Media*
> *Project Director*

Introduction

From May 30 through June 1, 1979, there assembled in Indianapolis, Indiana, 136 official delegates, observers, guests, and speakers from the United States and the Virgin Islands. Of these participants, 21 were delegates or alternates to the then forthcoming White House Conference on Libraries and Information Services. Their purpose was to listen, ponder, discuss, argue, and make suggestions concerning the critical issues in library network development.

A number of social commentators are concerned that the United States is increasingly splintering into special interest groups vehemently arguing and aggressively lobbying for increasingly narrow cross-sections of the public. The combinations are endless: anthracite coal miners, retired teachers, independent truckers, wheat growers, rural women, mail order businesses, and on and on. Librarians have, in contrast, always tried to reach a consensus internally so as to provide a united front once their objectives have been identified. It is extremely important that library network proponents do not become, or become regarded as, a narrow special interest group. What must happen, instead, is that library network needs must be accommodated within whatever new library objectives are defined for the years ahead.

Library networks have introduced enormous change in a very short time. Change is not orderly. Myths, tradition, power struggles, failures, competition for funding and status, rumors, progress, and just plain confusion and uncertainty are all part of the process. This Conference presented an opportunity to discuss critical issues in networking; to recognize divergent views, opinions, and interests that must somehow, sometime, be accommodated if progress is to be made, and if change is to be intregated into the consensus process.

The papers published herein were prepared by authors who themselves, in microcosm, represent the professional stakeholders in network development: network directors and staffs, administrators of all types of libraries, library staff members, state agencies, library schools, library school students, foundations, and federal agencies. The participants added even more stakeholders including the most important group: library users.

The Conference allowed for five types of input. There were eight major theme papers prepared for oral delivery at the Conference, and twelve background papers which, while not presented orally, were distributed to Conference participants. All of these are published here. Also published here, and not distributed at the Conference, are the keynote speeches given by Don R. Swanson and Robert Wedgeworth. In addition, the staff has provided some supplementary material published here for the first time. Authors and speakers were given a brief outline to help minimize overlap, but no other guidelines were given and editing has been kept to a minimum, so that each presenter could deal as freely as possible with the assigned topic.

Inevitably, however, each Conference must limit the range of discourse. Topics selected principally address public policy issues. Topics discussed briefly or excluded entirely include: specific library functions that networks support (e.g., cataloging, acquisitions), the features of specific networks, the services that networks might provide specific interest groups such as research libraries or disadvantaged users, the administration and management of networks, the bibliographic control issues, resource development and delivery, educational programs for networking, and the role of publishers and the private sector. Also generally excluded were library cooperative endeavors outside computer-based networking.

While the list of topics that had to be excluded was long, there, fortunately, still remained a long list of critical issues to address. These included: the role of networks in the United States library system, the present and future technology of networking, governance and funding, the locus of network responsibility at each level of government, national information policy, and a broad look at users of networks. In addition to the issues identified by the formal presentations, Appendix A of these proceedings includes issues submitted by Conference discussion groups and a brief summary of a debate between Glyn Evans, Director of the SUNY Network and Roderick Swartz, State Librarian, Washington State Library on the topic: Role of State Libraries Versus Cooperatively Governed Networks.

The debate itself turned out to illustrate the potential of teleconferencing since one debator, Glyn Evans, was present, and one debator, Roderick Swartz, grounded by the DC-10 moratorium, was present vocally through the courtesy of equipment provided on very short notice by the Indiana Higher Education Telecommunications System.

About ten years ago, U.S.O.E. sponsored a network conference which is cited later in these proceedings. The speakers at that conference were largely speculating on how networks might come about; the range of topics covered in this 1979 Conference and the list of vital topics that had to be excluded suggest how much activity has taken place in the intervening decade.

Despite this, much remains to be accomplished. Some participants dubbed the Conference "The Network 500," but I thought about it as the "Camp David of Networking" at which we could begin to lay the framework for a new consensus and strategy for network development as well as enter a new era of library diplomacy which fully recognizes networks, not as emerging, but as actual agencies for library development and planning.

The Conference had four major objectives:

- to identify the major critical issues in cooperative network development
- to provide a forum for discussion of these issues at a three-day conference
- to disseminate findings through published proceedings
- to provide information that would assist U.S.O.E. in its role as a major funder of library and network development

As Principal Investigator for the Conference Project and as Executive Director of the INCOLSA Network which was both a sponsor and subcontractor for the Conference, it is, of course, my hope that these objectives were met and that participants considered their time in Indianapolis well spent. Acknowledgment is due to seven Hoosiers who helped things along: Blanche Woolls (Conference Consultant), Carol Sulanke (Conference Staff), and the following members of our State Planning Committee: Miriam Drake, Bernard Fry, Edward N. Howard, Jean Jose, and Peggy Pfeiffer.

In a three-day Conference time does not permit reflection, and information overload is quickly reached. In the months and years ahead, we hope that the "Network 500" both for the participants and the readers of these proceedings will have helped advance the understanding of the network revolution and will have contributed to U.S. librarianship.

Barbara Evans Markuson
Executive Director and Principal Investigator
Indiana Cooperative Library Services Authority

PART I

The Network Revolution

Revolution and Evolution: Critical Issues in Library Network Development

Barbara Evans Markuson, Executive Director
Indiana Cooperative Library Services
*   Authority (INCOLSA)*
Indianapolis, Indiana

INTRODUCTION

This paper concentrates on a general overview of library network development and does not examine specific topics in detail as do the other theme papers. Perhaps the overriding theme is that, as professionals, librarians have failed to grasp that linking libraries together via telecommunications and computers is not just another good instance of how cooperative librarians are. Rather, that networking provides unparalleled opportunities for a dramatic restructuring of the library as an operational unit and for an astounding array of new information services better designed to meet the needs of an increasingly complex user community. The failure to grasp this essential change in library potential coupled with the failure to grasp the heuristic, entrepreneurial, self-organizing, and evolutionary nature of networks and network technology has caused us to try to address new problems with old, outmoded solutions.

Nine issues have been identified as critical to our ability to cope with the information needs of the year 2000. This is the year that we should focus on in long-range planning since it has, in the past, taken almost two decades to get new programs or new technology distributed throughout the U.S. We should note, however, that even after two decades of federal funding, some libraries do not yet have convenient access to the telephone, surely the minimum entry into any network.

The nine issues are as follows:

- the network as revolution
- understanding networks
- the National Library Network myth
- national planning
- the locus of networking
- access to networks
- standards
- the evolution of networks
- the network nation

I do not expect that many people will agree with what I have to say, but I hope that, at least, it will stimulate discussion and thoughtful analysis of networking.

The word "network" has been used to describe such a broad range of activities that, unless the library field agrees to more rigorous terminology, the present confusion and imprecision will continue. The term "network" has been used to mean: any type of cooperative activity between libraries; formal and informal library consortia; library users having common interests, as in a network of research chemists; information retrieval systems; local on-line systems; all customers using a vendor's system; conceptual systems of the future, as in the evolving national library network; existing systems (such as OCLC) that link libraries through telecommunications with computer-controlled data base access and message switching; and organizations (such as OCLC and SOLINET) that provide the systems just described.

Although a formal dictionary definition of "network" implies a physical connection between the component parts, the above definitions show that, in the library field, the term has been used as a catchall for a broad range of cooperative activities. Some of this misuse apparently stems from the idea that the term "network" is modern or glamorous. Various attempts have been made to promote more precise terminology, but little progress has been made.

In this paper, I have used the term "network" to mean both the organizations and systems that link libraries together via tele-communications with computer-controlled message switching and data-base access, since this is actually the way present networks have evolved. It would, however, be more precise to speak of one as the *network organization* and the hardware and software as the *network system*, but the context will generally reveal which aspect of networking is being discussed. For other types of library cooperation I will use the terms "cooperatives and consortia" since evidence suggests that these efforts stem from totally different conditions and have different goals.

Why this fuss over terminology? When people were able to automate travel, some saw the new invention as a "horseless carriage" thus equating the new creation as a slight change in something old and familiar. But thinking of an automated travel machine as simply a carriage without a horse rather than an "auto-mobile" obscured the tremendous changes that the new machine would bring about because of its inherently different capabilities. Similarly, using the term "network" when we are talking generally about library cooperation, obscures the significant and momentous changes that network technology will bring to the libraries. Use of precise terminology is essential to clear thinking about what is happening, and to our examination of critical issues of the library network as a vital component of a network nation.

ISSUE NO. 1: THE NETWORK REVOLUTION

Social and technical revolutions are more subtle than political revolutions. Thus, many of us live our lives unmindful of the revolution without. Few of us, for example, are yet really *aware* of the enormous change that library and information networks have brought and will bring. Before us are unimagined new linkings of libraries and information sources, of homes to librar-ies, and of users to new and more powerful information media. We are in the midst of a library revolution as a result of computer-based networking and none of us can predict all of the impacts as change begets change in the evolution of network service.

This section will examine the evidence that such a revolution is indeed underway. We need to keep in mind that "a revolution is a relatively sudden set of changes that yield a state of affairs from which a return to the situation just before the revolution is virtually impossible."[1]

Thus, a demonstration that we are in a network revolution rests on the suddenness of change and the irreversible nature of this change. Just nine years ago at a 1970 conference on networking few attendees anticipated the rapidity and nature of network development.[2] In 1971, OCLC began to provide on-line service to a single library with one terminal linked to OCLC's sole computer. Today, OCLC serves nearly 3000 terminals in nearly 2000 libraries, its network system requires a complex of some 30 main-frame and minicomputers, and on June 5, 1979 it will break ground for the first building designed solely for a library network. Paralleling these developments on a smaller scale, the Washington Library Network (WLN) and the Research Libraries Information Network (RLIN) have built significant and sophisticated network systems; the growth of state and multistate networks has been equally rapid.

In any field such swift technical development coupled with the invention of new organizational structures would be noteworthy; in the library field such events are not only dramatically sudden but represent the most widespread change ever to occur within such a short time in the library history of the United States.

However, to be truly revolutionary the network development must also be irreversible. We need, therefore, to identify conditions that would make networks irrelevant or unfeasible and thus reversible. Roughly, we can postulate five types of scenarios: a catastrophic event, an economic crisis, an energy crisis, technological change, and, finally, a major change in libraries themselves. The catastrophic events could be categorized as macro-catastrophies involving the whole society, such as a nuclear disaster, or micro-catastrophies affecting the network system itself. We simply are unable to make any provisions for macro-catastrophies, but we do need to consider whether a catastrophic event to a major library network would destroy networking or merely be a major setback from which recovery would be possible. Prevention of such catastrophies through network design and other measures would make it increasingly difficult to destroy the entire system so that any salvage work could proceed more quickly. (Part of OCLC's desire for a new facility stems from the need for increased security for the central network computer complex.) It is most probable that such catastrophies would be critical setbacks but would not destroy networking—but all networks need to do more work to ensure system integrity.

An economic crisis could destroy networking under at least two conditions. The first would be a macro-economic crisis so severe that library funding was virtually or totally eliminated and, again, most of us have to act as if that will not occur. The second is a crisis setting in motion severe reductions in library budgets. Such a crisis would affect networking to the degree to which libraries could find alternative ways to operate that were less expensive than network services, and to the degree that network budgets are related to library book budgets. It is my contention that, increasingly, this is less likely to occur and that libraries will find that it is more expensive to operate without networks, that networks can foster strong survival mechanisms, and that, in contrast with other cooperatives and consortia that concentrate on external services, severe economic crises might not have the adverse effect on networking that one would first imagine.

We can postulate an energy crisis so severe that libraries would not be given priority for the energy they need. One such instance of this has already occurred forcing OCLC to install a diesel-powered generator as backup during the severe curtailment of electrical power in the winter of 1978. The total energy consumption of the entire network is probably less than the aggregate required to support alternative local automated systems. However, there are simply no data to back this assumption. It could well be that such data need to be gathered to support library demands for equitable energy priorities for networks. This could be a vulnerable area.

Many people suppose that the greatest threat to networking will come from new technologies such as minicomputers with extraordinary memory capabilities, from videodiscs on which whole libraries of information can be stored, and the like. It is undoubtedly true that such technologies would have an impact on certain aspects of networking such as the degree of centralization, but it is difficult to see how they would be competitive with two major network benefits: access to millions and millions of holdings in other libraries and sharing of human labor through input to a common data base. Also, such technological change implies that local libraries will have the resources to apply and adopt the technology, something which has not yet happened on a large scale. Therefore, I conclude that such new technologies will be integrated into network design, will be local extensions of the central networks, and thus will, at least for foreseeable technologies, not reverse networking.

The last condition that could make networks obsolete is a drastic change in the library as an institution. For example, libraries could alter programming so much that network services became irrelevant, or user patterns of information production and access could change so much that libraries themselves would be essentially superfluous links in the information chain. Such events would create changes so radical that they would create a new revolution in the U.S. library system and thus either drastically alter or eliminate the need for networks.

Each of these scenarios needs to be developed by experts and futurists who could elaborate on the probabilities of occurrence. However, at least one expert, Gerard Salton of the Cornell University Computer Center, argues that neither independent library automation, new technology, nor new forms of information recording are likely to provide viable alternatives to networking in the foreseeable future.[3] On balance, none of these scenarios seems so compelling as to lead me to believe that, at least for the next few decades, the trend toward networks is reversible. Notice, however, that I have concentrated on the library network system as a concept rather than on specific network organizations. It is far easier to postulate events that could alter present library network organizations. For example, if the federal government did offer free network services to all libraries and fostered a new organizational structure, it would certainly be difficult for current organizations to survive, since they depend largely on member fees.

I have stressed the network revolution because it is central to any discussion of networks. Only if we recognize the revolution that networks have brought about, and which are affecting almost every part of the library field from hierarchical interlibrary loan structures to cataloging rules and staffing, can we begin to cope with our changing library scene and the reality of networks as a force for change. Only if we come to terms with networking can we effectively marshall our energies to bring about constructive developments, otherwise we will continue to waste enormous resources by perpetuating services and structures for a reality that no longer exists.

On balance, there is much evidence that many of our leaders, planners, and educators have not come to terms with the network as a library revolution. Part of this is due to cultural lag, part to the reluctance to give up familiar habits, and part to fear of the future. Yet it can be easily demonstrated that networks are not an aberration from library tradition but are a development entirely consistent with our long-held goals of universal bibliographic control, rapid and efficient exchange of data, cooperation in support of the research community, and extension of library services to the culturally deprived and information poor peoples and areas. Indeed, it is not too difficult to identify library leaders of the 19th century who probably would espouse networks more readily and understand their potential more completely than do some 20th century leaders. We need more librarians willing and eager to look at the challenging opportunities that revolutions can provide.

ISSUE NO. 2: UNDERSTANDING NETWORKS

To begin to place networks in perspective, we should first give some attention to the U.S. library system. Although we frequently talk about the U.S. health care system, transportation system, and the educational system, even within our own professional circles we don't talk much about the U.S. library system, tending, rather, to focus on some aspect of it, such as large research libraries or the libraries in a single state. Figure 1 shows the major components of this system.

Three features of the U.S. library system are important when we begin to consider network development. First, the numbers give only the merest hint of the size, complexity, richness, and diversity which the system encompasses. Second, the large number of governing bodies reminds us that the salient characteristic of this system is its almost total decentralization and that legal authority and control is largely at the local level. Third, there is almost no hierarchical structure to the system— there is nothing comparable to large national corporations with outlets across the country. As Figure 1 indicates, networks, cooperatives, and consortia comprise the only formal interlibrary components. *It cannot be emphasized too strongly that national plans and schemes that fail to recognize these three characteristics of the U.S. library system are either doomed to failure or will require an unprecedented restructuring of libraries requiring new laws at all levels of government.*

FIGURE 1. The U.S. Library System

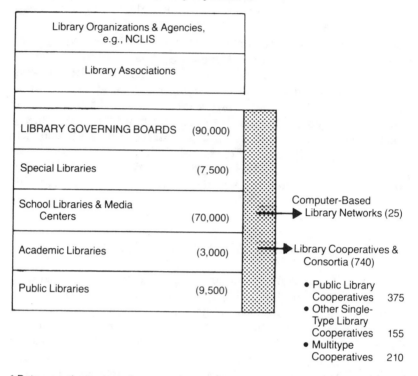

* Data are estimates based on reports in the *U.S. Statistical Abstract* and the Association of State Library Agencies *ASLA Report on Interlibrary Cooperation*, 2d ed. (Chicago, Association of State Library Agencies, 1978).

Library networks developed principally as a mechanism to allow rapid technology transfer in the U.S. library system. The economic costs of computer systems development, the increased operating costs of libraries, and the traditional need of libraries to access data in other libraries lead to the idea of a jointly developed central computer network linking many libraries. The large number of governmental units involved made the creation of a new network organization mandatory. The expense and continuing commitment that computer technology requires made it mandatory that these organizations be formal and legal.

Figure 2 provides a rough model of the U.S. library network system today. The library network organization component is made up of three groups. One group is made up of the organizations concentrating on the centralized computer-based library

Figure 2. The U.S. Library Network System

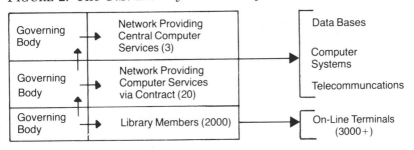

Note: Numbers are Estimates as of May 1979.

network system. There are three such organizations: OCLC, WLN, and the RLIN system run by The Research Libraries Group (RLG). The second group has concentrated principally on making these central networks available to libraries within a state or multistate region. There are roughly 20 such organizations, among them AMIGOS, MINITEX, INCOLSA, and SOLINET. The third component is the libraries that represent both the governors and end users of the networks. There are roughly 2000 libraries now using network systems and perhaps almost as many more that obtain network services indirectly through processing centers, cooperatives, and consortia.

At the 1970 conference on networking, it was predicted that "networks will bring drastic changes to administrative relationships among existing institutions and that new agencies are likely to be created to meet the pressures of networking potential and capabilities."[4] Almost all of the organizations described above have been formed since that 1970 meeting. In addition, the organizations themselves have formed the Council for Computerized Library Networks which is concerned with broad network interests and educational programs related to network issues.

This network organization structure has several features worth noting. First, it was an unplanned structure, evolving as a practical and reasonably efficient way for network services to be provided rapidly to hundreds of libraries in every state and region of the U.S. Second, it allows attention to be paid to local, state, and nationwide developments at the same time through a cooperative structure and role specialization. This role specialization is summarized in Figure 3. Third, it is flexible and largely nonprescriptive, allowing each area of the country to adjust to prevailing political, economic, and library conditions. Fourth,

FIGURE 3. Role Specialization in Network
Development

Network Organizations Providing Computer-Based Systems	Network Organizations Contracting for Computer-Based Network Services
• Financial Planning	• Contracting & Billing for Services
• Capital Acquisition	
• System Design, Development, Test, & Operation	• Installation & Training
	• Consulting & Site Planning
• Program Development	• Monitoring & Feedback
• Output Products	• Interface with Local & State Systems
• System Monitoring	
• System Documentation & Network Staff Training	• Planning
	• User Products
• Research & Development	• User Inquiries

the structure has allowed nationwide participation with the
practical result that the various networks have had access to
different and largely noncompetitive funding sources. Fifth,
because the pool of network users is so large there is economic
support, not only to develop new services, but for some modest
research and development efforts. Figure 4 lists network services
available now, in development, and under exploration. Finally,
perhaps the most notable feature—this development has come
about almost entirely through initiatives at the state and local
level and has been largely self-funded by the participants.

Other conference papers will discuss specific aspects of network organizations and technology. That some 25 functioning
network organizations exist, directly serving over 2000 libraries
from an estimated 3500 on-line terminals, as a result of a self-
organizing and largely self-financed initiative within a single
decade gives some idea of the vitality and strength of the
network movement.

ISSUE NO. 3: THE NATIONAL LIBRARY NETWORK: REALITY OR MYTH?

Despite these developments, a critical issue that we must face
is the almost tacit assumption in many quarters that present
network systems and organizations are ad hoc developments

FIGURE 4. On-line Network Services Now Operational or
Under Development

- Cataloging

- Acquisitions

- Serial Control

- Union Lists of Serials

- Catalog Card & Tape
  Production

- Computer-Output
  Microform Catalogs

- Accessions Lists

- Authority Control

- Distributed Printing of
  Bibliographic Records
  via Terminal Printer

- Management Services*

- Automated Circulation*

- Automated Interlibrary Loan

- Statistics

- Information Retrieval*

- Author, Title, & Subject Access
  to Bibliographic Data Base

* Services Still Largely Under Development

that are perhaps sufficient until the powers that be come to our rescue and design a "National Library Network." It is hard to credit that such a pervasive assumption, based on so little evidence and so contrary to our past and present history, could have gained such universal acceptance. Some day, perhaps, a library historian will be able to trace how the idea of a federally funded and managed National Library Network got started, but despite its origins, the fact that it is an entrenched concept is indisputable.

If one reads the proceedings of the 1970 conference, the contrast between what most participants believed would happen and what did happen is striking. Perhaps we shouldn't be too hard on those folks in 1970 since they were looking to the future. Even so, we are not in good shape if the predictions of our leaders become outmoded in a few short years, let alone the far future. And perhaps you think that with real operating networks now in existence we have begun to come to terms with the complexities of the U.S. library system and with the complexities and realities of building and operating networks. Not so. Entrenched truisms do not die easily. The background paper by Alexander and Shaw in this book, which codifies the resolutions on technology and networking generated at 35 Governor's Conferences held within the past two years, is living testimony that the idea of a National Library Network is going strong.

Here then, are the major themes continually repeated and apparently accepted as truisms at the 1970 conference:

that national planning, leadership and direction are essential
to network development

that large-scale federal funding of library networks is essential to their development

that networks will result from a linkage of local and state
networks and will build upon present state-level cooperatives
and consortia such as the New York NYSILL interlibrary
loan networks and from local academic networks based on
local university computer centers

that some type of national agency, such as NCLIS, Library of
Congress, or a new federal agency, will be required to govern
and manage the development of a national library network.

Here we are in 1979 with a much higher degree of library
network development than even the most optimistic attendee at
the 1970 conference appears to have imagined, yet not one of
these specified *preconditions* for networking has come about.

How could our experts have been so wrong? Partly they failed
to think clearly about the U.S. library system. Thus, there was
insufficient attention to both the decentralization of libraries and
the fact that no national organization or agency has any responsibility whatsoever for local library service. Therefore, although
it is a hard lesson to learn *there was not then and there is not
now* any federal agency seriously developing plans for a National Library Network.

They failed even to consider that centralized networking could
evolve from the "bottom-up" from local initiatives beginning
principally in the academic library community, would create a
cooperative governance and funding strategy, would generally
evolve as nonprofit corporations outside government, would
adopt entrepreneurial funding strategies using grants, business
loans, and fund transfer from member libraries for financing
development, and would be based on the premise that libraries
would pay for network services from budget transfers resulting
from savings from automation of operations. They failed to
consider that networks would not evolve principally from linking
local computer systems but that new systems and a central staff
devoted solely to building networks would develop, and that, as a
result, there would not be the need for a federal agency to "paste"
the hundreds of local networks into a national system.

But to return to the present, here is a sampling of the state
resolutions to be considered at the White House Conference (see
the Alexander/Shaw background paper in this book):

- That NCLIS contract for research for efficient operation of the national . . . network.
- That NCLIS coordinate the formation of an efficient non-profit national library network which LC will coordinate and administer with state libraries coordinating each state's participation.
- That the federal government set standards for network participation.
- That the federal government plan, develop, and implement a nationwide network not infringing upon state networks.
- That there be established a national agency to implement the national network.
- That USOE or the new Department of Education develop channels of communication and facilitate cooperation through legislation.

Various roles suggested for the Library of Congress also include: establish a national computer-based service, take the initiative for the national library network, take responsibility for a national library network, making grants, contracts, etc., and coordinating policy under NCLIS.

Indeed, in the resolutions from 35 states only a handful of resolutions actually recognize existing networks; only a few suggest that networks are not primarily a federal responsibility, and a few resolutions deal with specific services. Two examples of the latter are a library telecommunications rate similar to the library book rate and a resolution calling for an exploration of the feasibility of a national library video network.

If a library Rip Van Winkle fell asleep at the 1970 conference and woke up at the White House Conference during these resolutions, it would be easy for him to conclude that nothing had happened during the intervening nine years.

Why there is such a lack of recognition of the years of work, the millions of dollars expended, and the technical achievements of our existing networks is not easy to understand. When we consider that the compelling feature of the United States library system is its distributed governance and responsibility for library services, and that during the first 200 years no national agency has been given even the slightest authority for local library services, and when we consider all the national moves to deregulation and the inherent fears of government control of information, it is hard to understand why librarians, our supposed guardians of freedom of information, are so eager for government control of library information. It is also difficult to understand why management of computer-based networking is considered beyond the power of the library community unless the federal government steps in. It would be easier to understand if federal government information networks were more sophisticated than nonfederal networks, but this is not apparent and, indeed, there have been some colossal failures in government programs. It is also worth noting that most federal libraries currently participate in networking through existing nonprofit private networks.

We should note also that no well-developed plan for such a national network exists. Thus, both our ideas of what a national library network would be that is different from what we have now and how a federal agency would actually manage a network are characterized by vagueness. What specific attributes of existing networks would be improved by federal management? Would federal management be able to solve technical problems more readily and could services be delivered more efficiently? These questions have yet to be addressed seriously, but I suspect the underlying rationale for all of the interest in federal support of networks is based on the assumption that service would be free and on the assumption that networks are somehow an extension of the bibliographic services provided by organizations such as the Library of Congress. But it is hard to discover a really free federal information program and increasingly federal information programs are on a cost-recovery basis. And networks are rapidly moving into services other than cataloging and bibliographic control.

In summary, a critical issue that we must face is the continual lack of recognition of existing networks, the tendency to consider existing networks as interlopers that have usurped the rightful roles of some unspecified federal agency, and our tacit assumption that a federally managed national library network is in our best interests. Some of us have got to begin to say to the national planners that the Emperor has no clothes.

ISSUE NO. 4: NATIONAL PLANNING

It is difficult to write of national-level network planning without being unduly critical. National planning for networking is or is not a critical issue depending upon one's view. It is perhaps critical if one believes that it is really going on and it is perhaps not critical if one really never believed that it was. It is ironic that agencies and organizations that have to date assumed virtually no responsibility for network implementation claim the principal role as national network planners, while those agencies that have not only to plan, but to implement and operate as well, are seen, in some quarters, as usurpers if they engage in national planning.

As Susan Martin noted some time ago in an editorial in the *Journal of Library Automation,*[5] the list of agencies involved in national network planning is an alphabet soup: LC, CLR, NCLIS, NBS, NSF, NEH, COSLA, and so on. She comments on the difficulty that the average librarian faces in trying to find out what, if anything, is happening. Who is speaking for us and from whence does their authority derive?

Committees, task forces, and studies abound, but the impact has perhaps been so minimal because: 1) the sponsoring agencies are too remote from what is actually happening in networking, 2) the efforts are directed toward ad hoc solutions to isolated problems without prior development of a long-range plan for a national program, 3) too much concern is focused on the political role of institutions and agencies and too little on technical solutions of critical problems, 4) effort is concentrated on present technology and little attention is given to the really significant changes that new technology will bring, and finally, 5) there is not enough attention given to how national-level recommendations and plans will be implemented in the field.

Actually, most federal agencies that do not have a grant program to administer, seem to have limited funds for library network planning. Thus those agencies that should perhaps be in a dominant role, such as LC, USOE, and NCLIS, may actually play an increasingly diminished role as decisionmaking shifts to agencies such as the National Endowment for the Humanities that can influence the shape of things by virtue of the federal funds they have to bestow.

Also engaged in national planning are the networks and their members whose collective actions result in what is actually presently deliverable through networks and what is actually being developed and planned. Thus state library agencies, in their role as granting agencies supporting state and regional network efforts, could play a far greater role in actual national network planning, design, and development than could some federal agencies perceived to be directly engaged in national network planning.

We need, however, to stop and think about why the sudden interest in national planning at all. After all, the library field has developed more or less continuously over the past many decades with virtually no national direction beyond an annual American Library Association meeting, the promulgation of a new catalog code from time to time, and LC's response to pressure for needed new programs. We were able to get a significant amount of federal library funding without benefit of any national planning. Why the sudden desire to put ourselves under the yoke of any self-appointed or mandated national planning group, however well intentioned?

No really clear answers to this question have been advanced by proponents of national level library agencies and planning groups. Presumably improved library funding and services would result and our visability would increase, but one has only to read Hoos[6] on the subject of federal level planning disasters to be somewhat chary of this view. Certainly an alternative approach would be to directly fund networks to plan network activities since they would have to be accountable to their members for results. Thus perhaps an equally compelling argument can be made that, while we need national associations such as ALA, ASIS, SLA, MLA, and so on to provide forums for articulation of network needs from a professional view, and nationally-oriented federal libraries such as LC to play a role in national bibliographic control, we can really dispense with national network planning groups and national library agencies altogether.

ISSUE NO. 5: THE LOCUS OF NETWORKING

There are at least three positions that we can take concerning the locus of networking. The first is that, given the present achievements of networks, largely resulting from initiatives outside federal and state government, we can continue as we are and virtually ignore federal and state plans and current legislative initiatives. The second view is that, given the present dichotomy between state and federal plans on the one hand and network developments on the other, increasing dislocation will occur and millions of federal dollars will be spent each year on efforts and projects that get us nowhere, as far as networking is concerned. The third position is that, despite the inevitable agonies that change brings about, we must work to promote new legislation that brings a fairer share of the federal and state dollar to networks and their members and that brings the locus of networking to more appropriate agencies with network members having a real voice in the use of federal dollars.

A widespread assumption, repeated constantly at the 1970 conference and since promulgated through NCLIS and other agencies, is that states form the building blocks for a national library network. When one seeks rational evidence for this assumption, none is to be found, save the somewhat dubious argument that state library agencies have distributed federal LSCA funds (although they have not been the distributor for other federal library funding) and that states are a recognized political unit. The immediate relationship of these arguments to networking is not obvious.

State library agencies have done a great deal to encourage development of public library systems, local cooperatives, and various hierarchical support systems to promote services such as reference, resource sharing, and document delivery. While these have had an impact, particularly in public libraries, there is little relevance, from a systems viewpoint, between these largely local developments and computer-based library networking. Indeed, the support given by state library agencies for computer networking has been mixed and, on the whole, state library agencies are not leaders in network planning and development.

Indeed, it can even be argued that many of our present state-level cooperatives and consortia have developed largely from national encouragement and, in particular, through the stimulus of federal funding via the Library Services and Construction Act. Although this act is basically addressed to social and political goals such as improved access for the handicapped, improved access for rural areas, and strengthening state library agencies, it has never focused on nationwide planning. As a result, the Act has promoted the establishment of new and uncoordinated cooperative organizations and services within each separate state that, through a hierarchical arrangement, buttress the local public library.

In contrast, the goals of library networks have been more directly focused on the library as an operational unit, with the result that there are a minimum of intervening administrative structures. Network goals such as cooperative use of technology, reduction of the rate of increase of operational costs, facilitating resource sharing via linking libraries into a common system, and building a common resource data base are clearly not couched in social or political terms. The key feature that differentiates computer-based networking from consortia and cooperatives is that *the total network resource is made available equitably and directly to all members.*

Some confusion exists about whether networks will evolve from the "top-down" or from the "bottom-up," and there are proponents of each view. Actually such statements are meaningless unless we define more precisely what we mean by each. Networks cannot evolve from the "bottom-up" if by that we mean that each library designs its own system and somehow, someway, someday, they will all meld together into a nationwide system. If, on the other hand, we mean that present networks can only evolve as local decisions are made to join networks, pay for services, etc., then networks do evolve from collective local decisions. Furthermore, if the local libraries will not use or pay for a network service, then it cannot be foisted on them; again, the local libraries collectively "vote" with their dollars on which network services they will support.

Despite this, central network organizations have evolved which do plan, design, implement, and operate network systems. Thus, the decisions of network staff and Executive Boards affect what services will be available for the local library to "vote" on. Almost all networks have developed governance structures that allow member participation in goal setting and budget allocation, but, inevitably there will be conflict and inevitably decision-making becomes more complex. Thus, networks can also be said to be evolving from the "top-down." Obviously, there is a clear symbiotic relationship between the bottom-up user and the top-down planner and unless communication is good, the network will not prosper.

If, however, by "top-down planning" we mean that national groups are planning or developing networks, then we cannot see evidence that such efforts, to date, have much operational impact. The complexities of designing, developing, monitoring, financing, and operating networks systems are such that, whether we like it or not, it cannot be done by external committees, however well intentioned. Thus it is unlikely that representatives of the 50 states can ever be deeply involved in the central design of nationwide networks, even though they may be represented to some extent through cooperative network planning groups. Neither is it likely that complex nationwide networks can result from planning efforts in the 50 states.

Several legislative proposals are underway which include networking. One feature of these proposals is that computer-based networks are generally lumped in with cooperatives, consortia, and library systems although, as we have shown, these differ significantly from networks. One proposal is that promulgated by the Chief Officers of State Library Agencies (COSLA).[7] This draft *National Library Act*, adopted in April 1979 by COSLA, has been made available for review and comment. As I understand the situation, COSLA has written the Act to cover public libraries and networks (essentially encompassing the old LSCA) and hopes that eventually other additions to the Act will be made to encompass school, special, and academic libraries. The linking of networks with public libraries is a clue that perhaps, despite the specific language describing computer networks, COSLA still sees these networks as essentially outgrowths of the cooperative public library movement.

The draft proposes that:

- Each state would develop a statewide library network plan
- That such plans be coordinated within regional and/or national network planning
- That state library networks are components of the national network and that federal funds be allotted to and distributed by state library agencies to, among other things, develop and maintain bibliographic access, connect individual states into multistate regions where state networks are not feasible.
- That all libraries receiving federal funds must agree to participate in a statewide library network,
- That multistate network funding would be cleared through state library agencies, and
- That federal discretionary grants to multistate networks under specific titles or "set-asides" should be granted by USOE only for specific projects that have been coordinated with the long-range plans of the participating states.

I read this to mean that SOLINET, for example, would have any federal funding it received channeled to it from the ten state library agencies in the states it served. It also seems to mean that RLIN, OCLC, and WLN would follow the same procedure if they served these same ten states. Furthermore, if any of these groups applied for a direct research and development grant, USOE would have to deny the grant unless the work was specifically called for in the long-range plans at the state level. The administrative complexities and red tape involved in funding network development upward from the several states, when multistate and nationwide networking is involved should not be lightly brushed aside.

Regardless of the merits of this specific proposal, state library agencies have at least provided their view of federal funding for networks and their view is that this funding be distributed via the state library agency. Unfortunately, to date the networks have not developed a counter proposal although they have used a number of channels to make their views known to state library agencies.

If there is to be federal funding for computer-based networks, it is critical that we examine carefully how best to do this. Networks are basically operating in an entrepreneurial mode and must fit new developments into existing services in a phased development cycle that may cover several years. Flexibility, forward funding, and risk capital for research and development are essential factors in satisfactory network funding support. Networks are generally agreed that direct funding to each network from a designated federal agency would be a more satisfactory approach, allow more flexibility, actually result in far more coordination of planning and development, and reduce the amount of dollars lost to administrative overhead.

As early as the 1970 conference, Bystrom recommended a careful study of alternatives for network funding and commented that "reliance on the present Federal pattern of block or formula grants or committee approved special grants is not conducive to system growth and operation."[8]

Some federal funding specifically targeted for computer-based network development is a likely future legislative goal. The problem is that computer-based networks are the first major cooperative library systems that transcend state boundaries. Although money is needed to allow libraries in each state to use network services and to participate in network development, it is also needed at the multistate and nationwide network level as well; the latter two needs challenge our old political assumptions and traditions. Doubtless compromises will have to be made in order to achieve any funding at all, let alone funding that advances, rather than hampers, network development and that allows technical network support to evolve at the most efficient political level at a given time in network development. We need also to recognize that while states have not been the building blocks for network development in the technical sense, they may be convenient building blocks for promoting user access to networks.

Since efforts must be made to reach a consensus on the type of federal legislation that sufficiently deals with the revolutionary, evolutionary, and technical nature of library networks, library leaders must develop a legislative proposal that provides funding equitably and efficiently if networks, library members of networks, and users of networks are to benefit from federal library support.

ISSUE NO. 6: ACCESS

A sixth critical issue is the "democratization of networks" a term used by Swank in an excellent paper on networks written several years ago.[9] I have taken this to mean both the problem of serving the literally thousands of small libraries as yet unserved by networks and the problem of eventual direct access to the network by some 200 million potential users.

What will happen if we end up with a dual library system, with the most affluent libraries integrated into networks and the less affluent outside of networks and increasingly isolated? This is a real concern, since inevitably, over time, there will be reduced support for alternative manual sources of information. How would libraries outside networks be affected and what are the dimensions of the problem? Does network participation have the same benefits for these small libraries and, if so, how can they participate?

Swank also drew attention to what he called staggering inequities of access and called for a serious study of this problem. Computer-based networks, coupled with statewide network delivery systems, could help alleviate these inequities, but how would access be supported for these underfunded libraries? Will we continue to rely on outmoded hierarchical systems or will we make a serious attempt to bring networking directly to all libraries, perhaps through a library network services act to provide federal incentives for network services and access designed for libraries serving information-poor areas? In 1970, Hayes[10] reported that it would cost billions of dollars annually to bring all libraries up to ALA standards and, clearly, network access provides an alternative at a far lower cost. An additional benefit is the automation of manual tasks that could relieve the work load in small understaffed libraries.

The extremes of network use need careful study. At the upper range there are perhaps 200 or so libraries that are so large they constitute "mini-networks" and provision of adequate services to them will certainly require sophisticated routines and access support for hundreds of terminals. At the lower range there are virtually thousands of libraries which could, perhaps, be adequately served with one or two on-line terminals. To promote further equitable access to networks, attention needs to be given now, not just for research and development support for the upper range of the library spectrum, but to the lower ranges as well.

ISSUE NO. 7: STANDARDS

The standards that concern computer-based networking are objective, not evaluative or subjective standards. Thus, we are not concerned with standards that restrict the library's autonomy, e.g., by telling the library what to buy, how much to buy, etc., but rather with standards that will facilitate library operation in a network environment.

Support for development of library and information standards and attention to standards in all aspects of the library field, from the educator in the classroom to the practitioner on the job, is critical to library networks. By and large, development of standards has been supported by volunteer effort. Adherence to standards has been casual, in fact, work on standards is frequently offset by the actions of those who, in the classroom and on the job, preach and practice "do-it-yourself" bibliographic control.

Over the past decade, use of computer systems has continually exposed our lack of standards, the lack of specificity in the standards we have, and the casual treatment of standards in libraries throughout the land. Computer-based networking, in which members input to a common data base and in which operational processes are supported for hundreds of libraries, has simply revealed the magnitude of the problem. Needed standards include hardware and software interfacing standards to facilitate linkage of systems, bibliographic standards, operational standards, and procedural and quality standards. Areas as yet virtually unexplored are standards related to acquisition, circulation, user services, and abstracting and indexing.

It is critical that we give attention to better methods for financial support of standards development, documentation, promulgation, review, and training. Although standards are clearly of national concern, no existing library legislation designates any money for standards or even specifically requires adherence to national standards. The background paper in this book, "Standards for Networks and the Identification of Some Missing Links" by Paul Lagueux, provides more substantive treatment of this critical issue.

ISSUE NO. 8: EVOLUTION

In an earlier paper, I drew attention to the key role of networks in the transfer of technology to the library field.[11] I noted that, as a field, we have in the past given little attention to mechanisms for efficient large-scale technology transfer. The level of technology that networks can presently provide has been astounding to many and, in a short time, thousands of library staff members have become well acquainted with on-line service. But others have been disappointed that networks have not made a greater technical breakthrough, for example, that they provide printed catalog cards rather than making the leap to the on-line catalog.

In anthropology there is a formulation known as Romer's Rule which attempts to provide a theory for evolution. Briefly, the law states that organisms evolve, not to adjust to some future condition, *but to be able to survive in their changing present environment.*[12] It is the very change required to cope with an imminent danger that gives the organism a new capability that it lacked before. The new capability then allows the organism to evolve along new and unforseen paths. Although the analogy is imprecise, we can regard networks as following a similar pattern. The first task is to allow libraries to survive in the present environment and to meet immediate dangers. Network support addressed to this immediate task—shared-computer systems, staff, cooperative machine-data bases, user groups, etc.—provide capabilities for future evolution of new services and systems that will allow efficient adaptation to changes in information needs, resources, and technology.

For example, data bases built as a by-product of cataloging

will evolve into on-line catalogs within a very few years. These on-line catalogs could then evolve into specialized access systems such as home TV scanning of library catalogs, perhaps, with first priority installations for physically handicapped or home-bound users. The system could evolve with sophisticated information training packages for library users based on computer-aided instruction and video techniques. We could eventually allow users to build their own "personal catalogs" and files in support of individual research interests and could provide text editing services, such as the Stanford University WILBER system, to assist in eliminating some of the drudgery of writing and research.

A whole range of innovative services for a user-oriented library and information system is suggested by Russell Ackoff in the report on a proposed National Scientific and Technological Communication System[13] and many of these services will be feasible in an evolving library network. We could have a nationwide, on-line library statistical reporting system which provides us not only better management data, but better information as well for those who fund and support library service. We could integrate facsimile transmission systems with information retrieval networks. We could identify materials in the cooperative data base that need to have physical attention so that priorities could be established for state, regional, and national preservation programs. We could deliver on-the-spot bibliographies for researchers and have terminals in classrooms so that instructors could better utilize library resources in their teaching programs. We could build efficient networks to link the user directly with subject experts to improve the depth and quality of reference services.

All of these are potentially viable network services. The implementation of services depends on immediacy of need (the survival mechanism) and funding; but provision of new services will inevitably lead to new capabilities and an evolving, rather than retrogressive, library system.

ISSUE NO. 9: THE NETWORK NATION

The thrust of this paper is that networks are creating a revolution in library service. We are in the dawn of a new era in libraries and, perhaps, most of us can only dimly perceive how networks will evolve. That libraries will eventually be linked, not only to central network data bases, but to users in their class-rooms, offices, and homes is inevitable.

Concerned as we are with libraries, it may have escaped our attention that the U.S. is fast becoming a *network nation* and, indeed, that textbooks and courses on this topic are available. For example, the textbook, *The Network Nation; Human Communication Via Computer*,[14] describes the potential impact of computer networking on organization, social processes, the disadvantaged, political life, domestic relationships, research, education, and lifelong learning. The background paper in this book prepared by Beam and the theme paper by Norwood discuss some of these nonlibrary network developments.

If the network nation will soon be upon us, then it is extraordinarily fortunate that the library field has already achieved a position in the leading edge of networking. It is absolutely critical that we expend our talents, energy, and resources wisely to maintain this lead and to advance even more rapidly. *No other aspect of library development is as important for the next decade.*

Our development of networking is critical if we are to give improved service to users through new technologies. But our leadership in networking is crucial if we are to help ensure that our traditional values of freedom to access information, freedom from censorship, objective preservation of our cultural heritage, and the user's right to privacy, are to be protected as new information regulations and policies emerge for a network society.

We must advance these causes in a network nation; the issues at stake are so vital and so basic a part of the citizen's information rights that we cannot divest ourselves of this responsiblity. We cannot continue to play games as we do at all levels with library network politics while others, for much higher stakes, are playing at the game of information control.

NOTES

1. Charles F. Hockett and Robert Ascher, "The Human Revolution," in Morton H. Fried, ed., *Readings in Anthropology*, 2nd ed. (New York: Thomas Y. Crowell, 1968), p. 324.
2. Joseph Becker, ed., *Proceedings of the Conference on Interlibrary Communications and Information Networks* (Chicago: American Library Association, 1971).

3. Gerard Salton, "Suggestions for Library Network Design," *Journal of Library Automation* 12:39-59 (March, 1979).
4. "Working Group Summary on Network Organization," in Becker, p.215.
5. Susan K. Martin, "Too Much, and Yet Too Little," *Journal of Library Automation* 10:3-4 (March, 1977).
6. Ida R. Hoos, "Methodological Shortcomings in Futures Research," in Jib Fowles, ed., *Handbook of Futures Research* (Westport, Conn.: Greenwood Press, 1978), pp. 53-66.
7. Chief Officers of State Library Agencies, April, 1979, *A COSLA Legislative Proposal* (draft).
8. John Bystrom, "Telecommunication Networks for Libraries and Information Systems: Approaches to Development," in Becker, p. 40.
9. R.C. Swank, "Interlibrary Cooperation, Interlibrary Communcations, and Information Networks—Explanation and Definition," in Becker, pp. 18-26.
10. Phoebe F. Hayes, "Financial Formulas for Library Networks," in Becker, p. 249.
11. Barbara Evans Markuson, "Cooperation and Library Network Development," *College and Research Libraries* 4:125-135 (March, 1979).
12. Hockett and Ascher, "The Human Revolution," p. 326.
13. *Designing a National Scientific and Technological Communication System* (Philadelphia: University of Pennsylvania Press, 1976).
14. Starr Roxanne Hiltz and Murray Turoff, *The Network Nation; Human Communication via Computer* (Reading, Mass.: Addison-Wesley Publishing Company, 1978).

An Historical Perspective on the Concept of Networks: Some Preliminary Considerations

Norman D. Stevens, University Librarian
University of Connecticut Library
Storrs, Connecticut

A CAUTIONARY INTRODUCTION

When the organizers of the Conference on Networks for Networkers asked me to write a paper on the historical aspects of the concept of networks, I felt that it would give me a chance to combine my ten-year active participation in networking with a recently developed interest in library history. I felt that it would not be difficult to write a brief factual history of how the concept of networks developed and to identify the major aspects of that concept. I contemplated being able simply to review and to summarize a handful of significant papers. Then I began to do the necessary research. It initially took me far longer than I had anticipated to assemble what appeared to be relevant material and there was far more of it than I had anticipated. When I finished I found that I had a large mass of undifferentiated material and that it was extremely difficult to separate out the significant from the insignificant. So little had been done previously that there was no way of telling what work had been important and what work had been ignored. I read the material carefully and I tried to organize it, but this led only to somewhat greater confusion since no clear pattern seemed to emerge. I increasingly felt that, since this paper was designed for experienced networkers, to summarize a few papers would provide only a little useful information. I decided to take a somewhat more analytical approach to the subject, which may be premature and which is admittedly both subjective and tentative. This paper, then, is simply a start on what may ultimately become a more polished and less tentative discussion of the subject. At this point I need your reactions and comments to the views that I present. I hope that what I have to say will challenge your thinking and will lead you to discuss with me the ideas presented. In particular I would welcome citations to papers or events that I may have overlooked, or which you feel invalidate or substantiate a particular point that I make. Above all do not accept the remainder of this paper as a definitive history of the network concept. It is certainly not that. At best it is a start.

This paper will contain no definition of the term "network," or "library network." There is an abundant discussion in the literature of definitions, and those articles, such as that by Weinstock,[1] even though they may be somewhat out-of-date, provide an adequate discussion of the semantic history of the term. Most of the definitions of the term "network," as it is presently used in librarianship, are essentially the same. Indeed the definition itself has remained very much the same for the past ten to fifteen years. In any case, we all have our own definition and know what we think is meant by the term. As this paper progresses certain aspects of a definition may emerge but to define the term is not the purpose of this paper. It is not, after all, the definition itself that is important. What is important is the question of how we came to where we are and what the fundamental aspects of the network concept are. Those are the primary questions that this paper will attempt to address.

THE HISTORY OF THE CONCEPT OF
LIBRARY NETWORKS

Pre-History

The concept of library networks emerged in the United States in the mid-1960s but, like most such concepts, it did not emerge suddenly as a new idea. Rather it evolved out of a number of ideas and, as is especially true of library history, out of a number of events. As a starting point, therefore, it is necessary to review briefly those ideas and events.

First the concept of library networks came from a long tradition of cooperation in American librarianship. While there were some earlier fragmented efforts, such a tradition began with Charles Coffin Jewett's ill-fated proposal to use stereotype plates to produce a national union catalog that was presented at the first conference of American librarians in 1853. At any rate since the formation of the American Library Association in 1876, and the early establishment by that Association of cooperative programs, there has been no end of cooperative schemes developed, promoted, and even implemented within American librarianship. That development has been based primarily on two factors. The first is the recognition, that goes back to the early 1900s if not earlier, that no library, not even the largest research library, can be entirely self-sufficient in terms of its collections. For many years there has been an expressed need for libraries to join together to share resources. In addition there has been the even older recognition, which goes back at least to Jewett, that certain of the more complex and professional aspects of librarianship, cataloging is perhaps the best example, involve a high-level intellectual effort that, once it has been accomplished in one library, can be used by several libraries. These cooperative efforts, many of which have involved the development of organizational structures, continue down to the present time. They are an essential aspect of the development of the network concept. In and of themselves, however, those cooperative efforts did not lead to that development.

A second major element in the development of the network concept was the use of automation to handle library routines which began in the late 1930s and early 1940s. In the period prior to 1960 a variety of uses were made of automation in libraries. The initial period of automation had several important characteristics: most applications primarily involved batch processing. With few exceptions most of the activity took place within individual libraries which sought to automate basic routines building from a high level of interest but with limited technical expertise. Much of the activity was promoted, if not carried out, by nonlibrarians who felt that libraries were out-of-date since they did not adopt automation more widely. Finally, there was a good deal of skepticism on the part of many librarians towards the use of computers which was promoted both by the involvement of nonlibrarians who did not seem to understand fully library needs and by the exaggerated claims made for modest programs.

By the early 1960s libraries were in a position to begin to make better use of automation to handle their routines. The developments that started about that time have been marked by: the wider use of on-line systems within individual libraries; the growth of a higher level of skill, expertise, and understanding within libraries; the almost total disappearance of efforts by nonlibrarians to insert themselves in the process; the more effective integration of automated systems into day-to-day operations; and, more recently, by the availability and use of turnkey systems developed by commercial organizations for individual libraries but now increasingly used by groups of libraries. This more effective approach to the use of automation was an essential contribution to the development of the concept of networks.

A third important element in the development of the network concept was the work that took place in the related area of information science. Shera[2] has done an excellent job of summarizing the growth and development of that field with specific reference to events and papers. Early developments in documentation, as the field was originally known, began in the closing decades of the 19th century and continued until the late 1950s. At that time Russian achievements with Sputnik gave a new impetus to the information needs of the scientific community in the United States. That interest, coupled with rapid technological developments, brought about the era of information science in the early 1960s.

From the standpoint of the impact of information science on the development of the concept of networks, it is primarily the general ideas, largely theoretical, of how machines might enable libraries to develop and institute broad cooperative schemes that are of importance. First suggested by Vannevar Bush in his famous article "As We May Think,"[3] that idea was largely promoted for the next 20 years by nonlibrarians, and especially by scientists. Just as individual nonlibrarians saw local libraries as being outmoded because of their reluctance to adopt automation, so, at a national level, the nonlibrary community saw librarianship in general as outmoded in its approach to automation. The work of people such as Kemeny and Licklider[4] best exemplify that attitude. The development of national concern about the lack of adequate scientific information precipitated in part by Sputnik brought about the establishment of a series of national scientific investigatory bodies that produced important reports which, among other things, began to suggest the idea of networks. Those included the Baker, Crawford, Weinberg, SATCOM, and COSATI[5] panels. In addition this development brought about the establishment of a number of specialized science information centers and services that, for some time, were viewed by some people as forming the basis for networking.

Interestingly enough by 1965 librarians had already begun to place those ideas into a more reasonable perspective as they gained experience with automation and confidence in their ability to handle it. A paper by Wilson,[6] that suggests that we were probably further away from the implementation of Bush's ideas than we had thought in 1945, is typical of the level of understanding that had been achieved. In the period since 1965, of course, information science has continued to develop and there continues to be a good deal of theoretical work that contributes to the growth and understanding of the network concept. Fortunately because of the growing sophistication of librarians coupled with practical experience with networks, the ideas of these theoreticians such as Kochen, Lancaster, Licklider, Samuelson, and Salton[7] can be placed in a much better perspective by those who have a better understanding of what library needs are and how those theoretical concepts can be applied to those needs. Nevertheless, it is clear that those ideas and concepts have played an essential role in the development of the network concept.

To those three elements must be added the American tradition of practicality best exemplified in the lack, even to date, of any authoritative national planning organization for librarianship, and in the belief, especially strong in librarianship, that a program must be built from the ground up based on immediate needs rather than on long-range plans developed around general notions of what might be accomplished.

By the mid-1960s all of those elements came together to bring about the formation of the concept of library networks and the actual development of such networks. At that time the primary emphasis was on the broad general concepts of networks. Papers such as that by Meise,[8] which is the first major effort to describe a library network, attempted to present the potentials of technology and the possible applications of technology in strengthening the cooperative interrelationships of libraries. There was also at this initial stage an emphasis on the national aspects of the network concept and, to a somewhat lesser degree, on the organizational characteristics, especially the possible need for a national capping agency.

The Emergence of Library Networks

What ultimately culminated in a decision that must be regarded as the most significant for the actual development of library networks in the United States was the debate over the role of the Library of Congress. The prevailing view over a long period of time, although often challenged unsuccessfully as it was in the Bryant memorandum,[9] has been the Library of Congress's own view that its primary function is to meet the needs of the United States Congress and that its responsibilities to other American libraries are secondary and incidental. That view was clearly dominant in the King report[10] that set the tone for the development of automation at the Library of Congress. More importantly it was dominant in the decisions that were made in the late 1960s about the purpose of the MARC* formats and the potential uses of the MARC tapes generated by the Library of Congress. As the Library of Congress itself viewed it, the most significant result of the 1968 MARC Pilot Project[11] was seen to be the impetus to set standards. It was felt that by developing the formats, setting standards, providing direction to the discussion of such activities as retrospective conversion, and by distributing the MARC data in machine readable form for others to use as they might see fit, the Library of Congress was doing all that it could to fulfill its role. Behind that decision there was also the underlying notion that there were a wide variety of possible uses and applications of the MARC tapes and that, in our practical American way, a wide range of experimentation by a variety of sources would ultimately produce the best results. Perhaps that has in fact been the case. The net result of that decision, however, was that whatever impetus there might have been for the development of a library network beginning at the national level was effectively eliminated. By the late 1960s all of the elements were there that might well have led to such a development organized around the Library of Congress but it was obviously impossible for those involved to see and act upon that at the time.

*MARC (*MA*chine *R*eadable *C*ataloging)—The format for the transmission of machine-readable catalog data developed by the Library of Congress.

It was, thus, the distribution of the MARC tapes with almost no direction as to how they might best be used that has shaped the actual development of the network concept in the past decade. As we all know experimentation was carried out by a number of individual libraries and commercial firms but also by at least two groups of libraries who saw in the availability of the MARC tapes an opportunity to work cooperatively in the application of emerging on-line automated systems to a broad range of library programs. The six New England land-grant university libraries joined together to form NELINET (New England Library Information Network) and the academic libraries in Ohio joined together to form OCLC (Ohio College Library Center). The rest is history.

The more successful application of the MARC tapes with on-line technology by OCLC soon led NELINET to abandon its efforts and to utilize, along with FAUL (Five Associated University Libraries), the OCLC system with the intention of eventually replicating it in their region. An unpublished study by NELINET's Mathews subsequently led to the abandonment of the concept of replication. Soon those initial networks were joined by a host of others throughout the United States generally organized on a regional basis and designed to facilitate contracting with OCLC and use of the OCLC cataloging subsystem.

This stage was clearly marked by the establishment of actual networks, most notably OCLC, and by an emphasis on the type of services that were to be provided. The philosophical concepts of these early network planners were important. They thought, unlike many other participants in the MARC Pilot Project, that the capability of a network to develop and utilize a large-scale bibliographic data-base, while it could be used initially to support cataloging, was an essential element of a program that could be designed to support all of the traditional library functions through a centralized service.

From the success of OCLC and its expansion into a nationwide library service organization there appears to have come a realization that networks were a practical way of offering library services on a cooperative basis. That realization led to the next phase of network development which emphasized organizational matters. That period, which began in the early 1970s and lasted until the mid-1970s, was characterized, on the one hand, by the development of a number of regional library networks around the United States and, on the other hand, by a series of philosophical approaches to the question of networks grounded more in reality than were earlier discussions of those issues in the early 1960s. Thus the NCLIS program[12] itself and a series of related reports, such as *Resources and Bibliographic Support for a Nationwide Library Program*,[13] attempted to deal with these kinds of philosophical and organizational questions. Marking the end of this period was the trend towards greater organizational independence. Initially a number of networks were attached to or affiliated with parent organizations of a more general nature (e.g., SOLINET/SREB) but as those networks became more stable and financially stronger they moved towards independence. OCLC's own shift from a state to a national organization was part of that same development.

From that point developments have moved into what might best be characterized as a political phase with an increasing emphasis on the issues of governance, control, and direction of network activities. This obviously grew out of the earlier phases, especially the emphasis in the preceding phase on organizational questions, and began sometime in the mid-1970s. The elements that in some sense might be said to mark the beginning of this phase include: the transformation of BALLOTS from a program for a single institution to a network; the emergence of the Washington Library Network as an operating and viable network; the establishment of the Research Libraries Group; the formation of the Council for Computerized Library Networks; and finally the establishment by the Library of Congress of the Network Advisory Group/Network Advisory Committee.

It appears that there is now beginning a new phase in which, even as organizational and political issues continue to be addressed and perhaps even resolved, there is an increasing emphasis on the application of new developments in technology to library and library network programs. Recent work by Mathews, McGee, and others in this regard may result in a greater clarification of how various library functions can best be automated and to a better definition of the role of networks in that process.

ASPECTS OF THE NETWORK CONCEPT

Generally speaking, therefore, it seems safe to say that the underlying concept of networks was developed by the mid-1960s and that that concept had become fairly well established by the mid-1970s. Definitions, while they have changed somewhat in wording, seem to have remained relatively stable over that period. Certain issues remain but there has been a remarkably wide acceptance of most of the fundamental aspects of the network concept. In this section of this paper, I will address a number of the aspects of the network concept in an effort to suggest their origins, the extent of their acceptance, and challenges to them. Again it seems necessary to caution the reader that the views advanced are both subjective and tentative. They are open to question and discussion and need clarification. In particular, citations to papers that deal with any of these aspects are most welcome.

Interdependence

One of the most fundamental aspects of the concept of networks is that libraries can no longer be self-sufficient in terms of collections, personnel, or services. Libraries are dependent on one another for the sharing of their basic resources. This understanding goes back well into the early part of this century, grew out of numerous cooperative library programs, and is an almost universally accepted aspect of the network concept. One of the most provocative challenges to the question of interdependence is a paper by Chapin[14] who argues convincingly that, in fact, libraries are to a large degree self-sufficient and that, in any case, elaborate schemes to make the last three to four percent of materials available are ill-founded.

Large-Scale Bibliographic Data Base

Another aspect of the network concept relates to the development and cooperative use of a large-scale bibliographic data base. Of all aspects of the concept this is, in one sense, the oldest for its origins can be traced back to Jewett's 1853 proposal. Certainly it begins in earnest with the sale of catalog cards by the Library of Congress in the early 1900s, the subsequent development of a wide range of printed catalogs, and eventually the production and distribution of the MARC tapes in the late 1960s. In more recent terms the major contemporary network service points, including RLIN, OCLC, and WLN (Washington Library Network), are all based on the availability and use of a large-scale bibliographic data base in machine readable form. This is universally accepted as an essential aspect of the concept of networks. In fact so essential is this element of the concept that in the report of the Library of Congress's Network Advisory Group,[15] the concept of the network was, for the first time, broken down and that report concentrated only on what was described as the library bibliographic component.

Standards and Quality

Closely related to the availability and use of a large-scale bibliographic data base is the question of standards by which that data base can be produced and maintained in a manageable form and at a high level of quality. This aspect of the concept goes back to the development of catalog codes by Cutter, and others, in the 19th century and continues to be a critical element of the network concept. At this time the extent of concern with some aspects of standards and quality, such as authority control, remains high in theory but in an operational sense some networks and some libraries place greater emphasis on other aspects such as local needs and speed.

On-Line Automated Systems

Although far more recent in origin than the above aspects, the use of on-line automated systems is an essential aspect of the concept of networks. Its origin is not only in the obvious availability of such capability but also in the vision shown by people such as Meise and Kilgour[16] who advocated and experimented with the use of those systems for cooperative library applications in the 1960s.

Telecommunications

Closely related to, if not a part of, the use of on-line automated systems on a cooperative basis, is the idea of using telecommunications to link libraries together. Libraries have always been willing to experiment with such devices and numerous examples of such experimentation can be cited. Fundamental to the concept of networks is the notion, which emerged from the ideas of the theoreticians and the practical work of OCLC in the 1960s, that a telecommunication system is necessary as a means of linking libraries to one another and to centralized computing facilities designed to serve a group of libraries. This too is now universally accepted as an essential aspect of the concept.

Loss of Autonomy and Shared Decisionmaking

Although not an aspect of the network concept as it first emerged, through actual experience in the operation of networks it has become clear that libraries must relinquish a certain amount of their autonomy. This aspect of the concept has quickly become accepted as essential. At the same time, there has developed the very strong notion that there must be some system of shared decisionmaking in which each of the libraries making use of network services have, in one way or another, some say in how the network operates. This, to a large degree, comes from the fact that it is the individual libraries that are providing the basic financial support for networks. Often this sharing is, in fact, somewhat limited but it is, nevertheless, essential. The development of an effective method of shared decisionmaking offers one of the greatest challenges there is to effective development of a large-scale, integrated, national library network.

All Library Service

Another aspect of the concept of networks has been the idea that all library functions and all library services can somehow be automated at the network level. This aspect, which is only now being challenged, can be traced fairly directly to the initial planning efforts taken by, among others, NELINET and OCLC when they were contemplating use of the MARC tapes on a cooperative basis. While each began working on a system to use those tapes for cataloging purposes as a starting point, they each saw the eventual development of a total library system on a regional or statewide basis emerging from those tapes. Since so many library functions are directly related to the use of a large-scale bibliographic data base, it is easy to see how this aspect of the concept emerged. The subsequent growth of OCLC into a national organization carried with it, without any reexamination of the basic premises, the notion that what was appropriate in the way of network services for one state was equally appropriate for the nation. In the same fashion the transformation of BALLOTS from a system designed for one library to a system to serve many libraries carried with it the same notions. Much of this aspect remains in the thinking of those responsible for the planning and operation of national systems but this is an aspect that is increasingly open to challenge. The widespread use of turnkey circulation systems, new developments in technology, and the thinking of librarians such as DeGennaro[17] all demonstrate that this is no longer an essential aspect of the network concept. It is increasingly clear that some aspects of automated library services can best be provided at something other than the national level.

Access to All

It is difficult even to suggest the possible origins of the idea that an essential aspect of the network concept is that every individual in the United States should be provided access to all material in every library in the United States, if not in the world. This populist notion, and perhaps that is essentially its origin, emerged quite early in the development of the network concept in the work of people such as Herner and Clapp.[18] It is part of the NCLIS program[19] and is so ingrained there that studies, such as the recent examination of *The Role of the School Library Media Program in Networking*,[20] have been commissioned to make certain that no type of library and no user is omitted from network services. It appears as though, in large measure, this advocacy of universal access is a political device designed to ensure the widest possible support for the network concept and, thus, adequate financial support by governmental units which are sensitive to this populist sense of equality. One of the major complaints about networks, perhaps to some degree well-founded, has been that they are not designed for the small library and the average user. The most provocative discussion of one part of this problem from the standpoint of the user is to be found in Wilson[21] who points out, among other things, the practical fact that even the most sophisticated user cannot make use of all material in all libraries because of limitations in one's own ability to deal with certain languages and/or certain subjects. While this aspect of the concept seems to have been accepted as a fundamental aspect of the network concept, it remains vague and ill-defined. It is an aspect that requires considerable further discussion and clarification.

Integration and Coordination

In the earliest days of network development there was a very strong feeling, especially prevalent among the nonlibrarians at the national level, that networks would emerge from the integration and coordination of existing services. In particular it was suggested, in papers such as that by Aines,[22] that an integration of the emerging specialized scientific and technical information centers and services would form the basis of networking. What in fact has happened is that those scientific and technical information centers and services have become more specialized and remain as independent operations outside the mainstream of library network development. Library network development has instead come about as an independent operation largely relating to new separate operations developed just to provide such services. Despite continued concern about the integration of the information industry and specialized scientific and technical information centers and services with library networks, there is at present little evidence that real possibilities exist in that regard or that much effective work will be accomplished in the near future. More current concern, as evidenced in the work of LC's Network Technical Architecture Group, is clearly with the coordination and integration of the various library network components that have emerged and will continue to develop over the next several years.

One Network for All

Again it is difficult to identify the origins of this aspect of the network concept primarily because it is an aspect that has not been well-defined even though it appears to have been quite widely accepted. Perhaps the notion that a single network can serve all kinds and sizes of libraries in all parts of the United States has at least part of its origin in the view of the Library of Congress as a central focal point for libraries as it emerged from its sale of catalog cards, really the production of cataloging copy, to libraries of all kinds and sizes for so many years. As a counterbalance one must point to the longstanding dichotomy between the use of the Dewey (public and school library) and Library of Congress (academic and research library) classification systems which suggested that there were differences between libraries. The establishment of the American Library Association in 1876 for all libraries probably also contributed to the notion of a similarity in libraries but, of course, the formation of the Special Libraries Association and later the Association of Research Libraries suggested that there were major differences among libraries in this country.

In terms of the actual development of the network concept it was probably the work of the theorists in the 1960s that led to the notion that one network could serve all libraries. In actual fact, of course, the development of networks has shown a somewhat different pattern. Much of the initial practical network development was to serve academic libraries. It has only been in more recent years that there has been increasing participation in networks by public and special libraries and signs that school libraries are at least aware of the prospects and possibilities. At the same time a variety of factors, including dissatisfaction with the lack of authority systems and quality control within OCLC, local or regional support and/or pride, and the idea that there is a distinction between types of libraries, have all combined to lead to the present situation in which there is certainly not just one library network and little immediate prospect that there will be.

Centralization

Closely related to the idea of one network to serve all kinds and sizes of libraries is the idea of centralization of network services. Clearly the idea of a centralized network emerged from the work of the theorists in the 1960s who saw technology as offering that capability. While the decision of the Library of Congress relative to the distribution and use of the MARC tapes led to decentralization, the successful use of those tapes by OCLC soon led towards centralization again. To date the notion has always seemed to be that ultimately technology would provide for one central network system revolving around a single, large-scale bibliographic data base to serve all libraries. To date only WLN, in practical terms, has challenged that view by looking towards a distributed data base and a number of networks throughout the country. The recent Buckland and Basinski study for the Library of Congress [23] also takes the view that the national network is, or should be, a distributed processing system. More recently people such as Mathews [24] and McGee have begun to point out that new technological developments raise serious questions about the need or desirability of centralization, or even of distribution at the level suggested by WLN. Rather those developments suggest the possibility that technology will provide for the effective distribution of the large-scale bibliographic data base back to the local level. This is an aspect of the network concept that is by no means resolved and will undoubtedly undergo considerable change as it is affected by available technology.

Top-up/Bottom-down

The early work of the theorists and the recommendations of the national scientific panels almost universally advocated the development of the network starting at the national level. However, that idea was never accepted as essential to the network concept. Instead both in practice (e.g., OCLC) and in theory (e.g., the NCLIS program statement) the idea has always been accepted that the grassroots approach of building a network from the bottom-up based on libraries' needs and their willingness to support developments was most desirable.

A National Capping Agency

The notion that ultimately there needs to be a national capping agency responsible for the development and coordination of services has always been an accepted aspect of the network concept. There seems to have been at least a philosophical agreement that such an agency is necessary almost from the earliest days of the network concept but there has been little agreement on what agency that should be. This question is closely related to the question of the definition of the role of the Library of Congress. It still appears to be a widely accepted aspect of the network concept with the arguments revolving around the identification of the proper agency and the definition of its scope and responsibilities. In actual fact it is an aspect of the concept that has not yet been fully accepted as the recent developments relating to the National Periodicals Center have shown. The widespread acceptance of the grassroots concept of network development would suggest that the establishment of a national capping agency might come as a last resort after all other portions of the network have been developed. In any case one must wonder, despite some sense that there is a greater movement towards and a greater need for such an agency, whether there is as yet really strong support for this aspect of the concept among the competing network interests and among the libraries of the United States.

Internationalism

From the earliest days of the American Library Association international cooperation has been viewed as important. Since that time there have been continued efforts to promote such cooperation which have culminated in efforts to find a way for the cataloging of material published in a country to be done there in such a way that the basic record can be used on a worldwide basis. Each of the operating networks seems to stress this aspect of the concept and certainly most of the theorists, such as Samuelson,[25] have emphasized the international aspects of networks. In actual fact, of course, we are a long way from achieving any real sense of internationalism in networking. It seems unlikely that this will come about, except to a limited extent with near geographic neighbors, until the issues and understandings are much better resolved within the United States.

Cost and Productivity

American libraries traditionally have been interested in whatever measures would reduce costs and increase productivity. The standardization represented by the adoption of only two classification systems, the use of Library of Congress catalog cards, and other similar ventures is a testimonial to that and indicate the origins of that aspect of the network concept. There is very little in the work of the theorists about the economic aspects of network development. In fact they often seem to regard financial considerations as being unimportant. An analysis of such plans in terms of their economic viability almost always indicates that they are systems that are far beyond an institution's or society's willingness to support. Rather it is those who have worked with the practical aspects of network development, most notably Kilgour,[26] who have from the earliest described as one of the main aspects of networks their ability to be supported by libraries which can come only if they can increase productivity and can decelerate the rate of rise of per unit costs.

Other Aspects

While I have attempted to cover what are generally regarded as the most important aspects of the network concept, it is clear that there are a number of other aspects of the concept that might be considered. Markuson,[27] for example, cites research and development, capital acquisition, and technology transfer as the important aspects of the network concept. In a field as dynamic as this the perspectives on aspects of the concept continue to change and develop and it simply is not possible to cover all of them in detail. Again, however, suggestions as to points that have been omitted would be welcome.

SOME TENTATIVE CONCLUSIONS

It seems, in retrospect, truly amazing that as much has actually been accomplished in the development and implementation of the concept of library networks in a little less than 15 years as has been the case. Certainly we have come a long way from the first tentative description of the network concept by Meise[28] in 1966. Yet, as I have pointed out, certain fundamental aspects of that concept have remained relatively stable over that period of time and are likely to remain so. Other aspects remain open to question and need clarification and clearly need to be addressed in whatever deliberations take place in this conference and in subsequent discussions and debates of the network concept. That kind of discussion is likely to be overshadowed, as it has been in the past, by the actual developments in the operation of networks for it has been, for the most part, those developments that have shaped the concept and not the reverse. Reviewing the history of the development of the network concept and of networks should, however, help us to arrive at a clearer understanding of what it is we are about and what it is we might accomplish in the near future.

NOTES

1. Melvin Weinstock, "Network Concepts in Scientific and Technical Libraries" *Special Libraries* 58:328-34. (1967)
2. Jesse H. Shera and Donald B. Cleveland, "History and Foundation of Information Science," in *Annual Review of Information Science*

and *Technology 1977* (Washington: American Society of Information Science, 1977), pp. 249-75.

3. Vannevar Bush, "As We May Think," *Atlantic Monthly* 175:101-8 (July 1945).

4. John G. Kemeny, "Library of the Future" in his *Man and the Computer* (New York: Scribner's, 1972), pp. 85-98; Joseph C.R. Licklider, *Libraries and the Future* (Cambridge: M.I.T. Press, 1965).

5. U.S. President's Science Advisory Committee, *Improving the Availability of Scientific and Technical Information in the United States* (Washington: Govt. Print. Off., 1958); U.S. Presidential Task Force, *Scientific and Technical Communication in the Government* (Washington: Govt. Print, Off., 1962); U.S. President's Science Advisory Committee, *Science, Government, and Information* (Washington: Govt. Print Off., 1963); National Academy of Sciences. National Academy of Engineering. Committee on Scientific and Technical Communication, *Scientific and Technical Communication: a Pressing National Problem and Recommendations for Its Solution* (Washington: SATCOM, 1969); U.S. Committee on Scientific and Technical Information, *Recommendations for National Document Handling Systems in Science and Technology* (Washington: COSATI, 1965).

6. John H. Wilson, "As We May Have Thought" in Donald V. Black, ed., *Progress in Information Science and Technology* (Washington: American Documentation Institute, 1966).

7. Manfred Kochen, "WISE: a World Information Synthesis and Encyclopedia," *Journal of Documentation* 28:322-42 (1972); Frederick Wilfred Lancaster, *Toward Paperless Information Systems* (New York: Academic Press, 1978); Joseph C.R. Licklider, "A Hypothetical Plan for a Library-Information Network" in Conference on Interlibrary Communications and Information Networks, Airlie House, 1970, *Proceedings* (Chicago: American Library Association, 1971), pp. 310-6; Kjell Samuelson, "Worldwide Information Networks" in Conference on Interlibrary Communications and Information Networks, Airlie House, 1970 (Chicago: American Library Association, 1971), pp. 317-28; Gerard Salton, *Dynamic Information and Library Processing* (Englewood Cliffs, N.J.: Prentice-Hall, 1975).

8. Norman R. Meise, *Conceptual Design of an Automated National Library System* (Metuchen, N.J.: Scarecrow Press, 1969).

9. Douglas W. Bryant, "Library of Congress" [A Memorandum] in U.S. Library of Congress *Annual Report . . . 1962* (Washington: Library of Congress, 1963), p. 89-94.

10. Gilbert King, et al., *Automation and the Library of Congress* (Washington: U.S. Library of Congress, 1963).

11. U.S. Library of Congress, *The MARC Pilot Project* (Washington: U.S. Library of Congress, 1968).

12. National Commission on Libraries and Information Science, *Toward a National Program for Library and Information Services: Goals for Action* (Washington: NCLIS, 1975).
13. National Commission on Libraries and Information Science, *Resources and Bibliographic Support for a Nationwide Library Program* (Washington: NCLIS, 1974).
14. Richard E. Chapin, "Limits of Local Self-Sufficiency," in Conference on Interlibrary Communications and Information Networks, Airlie House, 1970, *Proceedings* (Chicago: American Library Association, 1971), pp. 54-8.
15. U.S. Library of Congress. Network Advisory Group, *Toward a National Library and Information Service Network: the Library Bibliographic Component* (Washington: U.S. Library of Congress, 1977).
16. Frederick G. Kilgour, "Initial System Design for the Ohio College Library Center: a Case History" in University of Illinois. Clinic on Library Applications of Data Processing, 1966, *Proceedings* (Urbana, Ill.: University of Illinois, 1966), pp. 54-78.
17. Richard DeGennaro, "Library Automation: Changing Patterns and New Directions," *Library Journal* 101:175-83 (1976).
18. Saul Herner, "The Place of the Small Medical Library in the National Network," *Journal of Chemical Documentation* 6:171-3 (January 1966); Verner W. Clapp, "Public Libraries and the Network Idea," *Library Journal* 95:121-4 (1970).
19. NCLIS, "Toward a National Program."
20. National Commission on Libraries and Information Science. Task Force on the Role of the School Library Media Program in the National Program, *The Role of the School Library Media Program in Networking* (Washington: NCLIS, 1979).
21. Patrick Wilson, *Public Knowledge, Private Ignorance; Toward a Library and Information Policy* (Westport, Conn.: Greenwood Press, 1977).
22. Andrew A. Aines, "The Promise of National Information Systems," *Library Trends* 16:410-8 (1968).
23. U.S. Library of Congress. Network Development Office, *The Role of the Library of Congress in the Evolving National Network* (Washington: U.S. Library of Congress, 1978).
24. William Mathews, "The Impact of Technology on the Governance of Library Networks," in Thomas J. Galvin and Allen Kent, eds., *The Structure and Governance of Library Networks* (New York: Marcel Dekker, 1979), pp. 121-40.
25. Samuelson, "Worldwide Information Networks."
26. Kilgour, "Initial System Design."
27. Barbara Evans Markuson, "Cooperation and Library Network Development," *College and Research Libraries* 40:125-35 (1979).
28. Miese, "Conceptual Design."

Additional References

Henriette D. Avram, "Bibliographic and Technical Problems in Implementing a National Library Network," *Library Trends* 18:487-502 (1970).

Joseph Becker, "Information Network Prospects in the United States," *Library Trends* 17:306-17 (1969).

Conference on Interlibrary Communications and Information Networks, Airlie House, 1970, *Proceedings* (Chicago: American Library Association, 1971).

J.L. Ebersole, "An Operating Model of a National Information System," *American Documentation* 17:33-40 (1966).

Martin Greenberger and Julius Aronofsky, "Computer and Information Networks," *Science* 182:29-35 (October 5, 1973).

Donald D. Hendricks, "A Report on Library Networks," *Occasional Papers #108* (Urbana, Ill.: University of Illinois, 1973).

Joint Committee on National Library/Information Systems (CONLIS) *Improving Access to Information* (Chicago: American Library Association, 1967).

William T. Knox, "National Information Networks and Special Libraries," *Special Libraries* 57:627-30 (1966).

Lawrence Livingston, "Technology and the Library" in Association of Research Libraries, *Minutes of the 80th Meeting, 1972* (Washington: Association of Research Libraries, 1972), pp. 70-7.

Richard E. Nance, "An Analytical Model of a Library Network," *Journal of the American Society for Information Science* 21:58-66 (1970).

National Academy of Sciences. Computer Science and Engineering Board. Information Systems Panel, *Libraries and Information Technology—a National System Challenge* (Washington: National Academy of Sciences, 1972).

Vladimir Slamecka, "Methods and Research for Design of Information Networks," *Library Trends* 18:551-68 (1970).

C. Walter Stone, "The Library Function Redefined," *Library Trends* 16:181-196 (1967).

Rowena Swanson, *Information System Network* (Washington: U.S. Air Force Office of Aerospace Research, 1966).

System Development Corporation, *Technology and Libraries* (Santa Monica, Calif.: 1967).

Nonlibrary Networks

Karen G. Beam
Ad-Hoc Consultant
Indianapolis, Indiana

Networks are present in all sectors of our society and their proliferation is occurring at a rapid rate. These networks cover a wide variety of subjects and have been designed to fulfill diverse needs. The recent increase in the number of networks may be attributed to technological advancements such as the increased reliability of computers, the availability of inexpensive mini-computers, and the general reduction in communication costs.

Networks may be categorized in a number of ways. In terms of purpose, there are networks developed specifically to meet the internal informational needs of a particular agency or firm; there are networks developed solely for the purpose of marketing the output of the system; and there are others that have been created by government action to provide information for government decisionmaking or to provide information for both the public and private sectors in cases where the profit incentive is lacking to stimulate private development. Other bases for categorization include the subject matter, the input sources, the method of financing, and the format of product and services.

Despite the differences among existing networks, there is a goal they all have in common. "That goal is to provide their users with information not otherwise readily available to them, and to do this as easily, comprehensively and economically as possible."[1] There is not a person in our country today who is not touched in some way by some network. This fact will be illustrated by the network descriptions that follow.

It is impossible in a paper of this length to attempt to provide comprehensive coverage of the many nonlibrary networks. The intent has been, rather, to describe a few networks in order to show the extent to which networking has permeated our society and to show the diversity among such networks. To this end, descriptions are presented below for selected financial industry, real estate industry, information industry, government sponsored, and business management networks.

FINANCIAL INDUSTRY NETWORKS

In November, 1975, E.F. Hutton converted to a high-speed telecommunications system which increased the speed of its communications twelve-fold. The system, COMPASS, utilizes a network of computer terminals and has the capability to send and receive simultaneously. An innovative feature is the integration of COMPASS with the quotations network.

With this system, a Hutton account executive can, from a desk-top unit, communicate with any terminal in the system, receive broadcast messages, directly access Hutton's central data base, and request hardcopy printout of any transmission. The types of information transmitted via the network include market oriented traffic such as orders and executive reports, market news and commentary, interoffice administrative traffic, and computer-originated data such as customer trade confirmations.[2]

Quotron Systems, Inc., Financial Information Service, provides stock market data, news, tickers, and automatic price monitoring on a subscription basis throughout the nation. The central computer center is in New York City and it is linked by direct ticker lines to the stock and commodity exchanges. There are regional computer centers with mass storage capability in six cities that are linked via low-speed and high-speed local lines with multiplexers and data concentrators in 32 cities. Desk-top terminals provide subscribers on-line access to the data sources of their choice. Their own private data bases may be linked in with the total system also.

Quotron began offering financial information services in 1960. Types of information contained in the central data base include quotations, dividends and earnings, earnings forecasts, industry groups, market information, and market statistics. Subscribers may choose from among the following services and formats: on-line access to the data base containing stock market, bond, option, and commodity data; Quotype Service consisting of stock price quotations and statistical data available by a direct connection between administrative teletype loops and the Quotron central computer; Quoteboard Service consisting of boards designed to meet the subscriber's individual specifications for commodity price and statistical data displays; and Quotelist Service which provides last price quotations with requests and responses printed on hardcopy and punched onto paper tape for stocks selected by the subscriber. Quotron's subscribers are not only in the brokerage industry but in banking, insurance, and credit verification industries as well.[3]

REAL ESTATE INDUSTRY NETWORKS

Real Estate Data, Inc., (REDI) has developed computer files containing data on over 30 million parcels of property located in several hundred cities and counties in 32 states. Holdings also include aerial photographs and property identification maps. REDI information and services are available to clients on a fee basis.

There are four basic services provided to the real estate industry. The aerial photography service provides photographs that enable the client to visually evaluate a parcel of land in relation to the development, location, and physical characteristics of the surrounding area. Property identification maps show boundaries, dimensions, and names of streets and roads for a parcel of property and adjacent parcels. On-line data base services include ownership information and Realty Sales Service. Ownership information consists of the owner's name, property address, legal description, assessed valuation and related data. Realty Sales Service provides information on recent real estate transactions for a given area. This information is published annually for each county covered, with periodic updates. REDI clients include realtors, land developers, appraisers, and tax assessors.[4]

Data Communications, Inc., (Da-Com) provides multiple listing distribution services on a fee basis to the real estate industry. The listings are available on-line as well as in books issued weekly. The data are supplied by real estate boards and include information regarding properties listed, sold, or withdrawn from the market.

Realtors who are on-line with Da-Com are able to locate property currently for sale that meets the potential buyer's requirements by specifying the property type or style, price, number of bedrooms, location, and any special features desired. At a later time an inquiry of the system will produce only new listings that meet the requirements and that have been entered into the data base since the previous inquiry. It is also possible, when listing a new property, to check via the computer to find existing prospects. The status of the listings in the data base may be updated within minutes of the actual transaction simply by feeding the information through the terminal in the real estate office.

Additional services include: a loan amortization program that provides relevant loan information and payment schedule for any real estate transaction; home ownership analysis which shows the actual costs and benefits of owning a certain property by calculating down payments, equity buildup, and mortgage amortization; income property analysis which projects return-on-investment over a period of time for a potential buyer; and a business management service which provides general ledger accounting, trust fund records, property management information, and cash-flow projections.[5]

INFORMATION INDUSTRY NETWORKS

Informatics, Inc., Information Services Group, offers comprehensive information handling services to clients in business and government on a contract basis. They claim to be the world's leading independent supplier of software products for a variety of applications. Informatics provides services ranging from data acquisition and preparation through management of data base and document handling systems providing interactive search and retrieval capabilities. In addition to developing data bases and information systems for exclusive use of clients, Informatics offers subscription contracts for on-line access via its telecommunications network to public data bases.

Among the public data bases to which Informatics provides on-line access are the Electric Power Research Institute Research and Development Information System which contains information on projects of the electric utility industry; Highway Safety Literature system which is supported by the National Highway

Traffic Safety Administration of the United States Department of Transportation; Population Information Program data base supported by George Washington University Medical Center; and the Oil and Hazardous Materials Technical Assistance Data System supported by the United States Environmental Protection Agency to provide emergency spill information for more than 1000 hazardous materials.

The United States National Aeronautics and Space Administration's Scientific and Technical Information Office has been operated by Informatics for over ten years. It is among the largest and most technically advanced facilities in the world for processing scientific and technical information, with a data base of over one million documents.[6]

Graphic Scanning Corporation is a special communications company with its own communications network and with computers that process information for clients on a subscription basis. Subscribers are able to transmit messages and data from computer terminals, telex, and TWX terminals. Specialized services that Graphic Scanning has in various stages of development include electronic transfer of funds, money transfer, a facsimile-based electronic mail system and Federal Communications Commission authorization to be involved in international record communications. This facsimile communication system has the capability to transmit illustrations, diagrams, foreign alphabets, and other images.[7]

GOVERNMENT SPONSORED NETWORKS

The Migrant Student Record Transfer System (MSRTS) is an educationally oriented computer network that was established to deliver pertinent academic and health information to schools upon the enrollment of a migrant child. The system functions through the cooperation of the Migrant Branch of the United States Office of Education and the 46 states and Puerto Rico where migrant children attend school. The Arkansas Department of Education operates the system under contract with the Office of Education. Components of the network are the recruiters who visit migrant camps and identify school-age children, the schools in which the children enroll, regional terminals that serve the schools by linking them with the central data base, and the Central Depository in Arkansas.

When a student enters a school system and is identified as a child of a bona fide agricultural or fishing migrant worker, the enrollment is entered in the Central Depository of students' records in Little Rock. This entry activates two responses: critical data about the student are sent via the teleprocessing network to the terminal that serves the school in which the student is enrolled; and a computer-generated printout of cumulative records is mailed to the school on the day after the enrollment is entered. Thus, the time spent in determining the student's instructional entry level is minimized and time spent in instruction/learning may be maximized. When the student withdraws from this school program and moves on to the next location, a summary report is entered into the student's record to update academic and health data.

Information that may be part of a migrant student's record includes types and dates of health screening examinations administered; health screening findings and any subsequent treatment; inoculations needed and those administered; standardized tests administered and the dates and scores; specific educational programs in which the student participated; and accumulated high school credits. In addition to enabling educators to meet more adequately the specific instructional and health needs of individual migrant children, the data base provides information to state and federal program administrators that enhances migrant program planning and management. Data are available to serve as a basis for allocating funds in direct relation to the attendance patterns of the migrant students.

An important concern when managing information such as that contained in the MSRTS is safeguarding the privacy rights of each child. There is a strict policy that the Central Depository releases data to no one other than the school in which the student is enrolled; the school personnel, in turn, handle the information in a confidential manner.[8]

The Union Committee for International Cooperation in Information Retrieval Among Patent Offices (ICIREPAT) was established in 1961 to coordinate the dissemination of technical information among patent offices worldwide. The Union is composed of the national patent offices of 21 countries and an international organization. A Shared Systems Program was developed based on coordinate indexing systems for subject areas covered in scientific publications and United States and foreign patents. These systems make computerized searching possible through cooperating patent offices. There are currently 26 subject areas with indexing systems. Examples of some of these subject areas are lasers and masers, steroid compounds, lubricants, and data-processing systems.

Pertinent foreign and domestic scientific documents such as scientific papers, periodicals, reports, symposia proceedings, and patents are collected. The documents are indexed according to the agreed upon descriptors for each subject area and are entered into the system. The primary users are the patent examiners who perform searches during the process of examining patent applications. In some countries, of which the United States is one, the system is also available to public users, most of which are corporations.[9]

The National Weather Service, part of the United States National Oceanic and Atmospheric Administration, an agency of the United States Department of Commerce, collects, processes, and disseminates meteorological data via high-speed communication networks covering the world. Weather conditions observed on all continents and islands, from ships at sea, and from aircraft in flight are transmitted to the Service.

After computer analysis of the data and preparation of the forecasts, the forecasts are fed back into the network in the form of facsimile transmissions and prognostic charts or as automatic teletypewriter transmissions. The Center is the major source of weather information for airlines, shipping lines, radio and television stations, newspapers, agricultural advisory services, and disaster warning services.[10]

The Chemical Information System (CIS) was established through joint efforts of the National Institutes of Health and the Environmental Protection Agency in the mid-1970s. The CIS consists of a series of numerical and bibliographic data bases together with a number of interactive computer programs that can be used to search for and retrieve information from any of the data bases. Some of the data bases that are part of CIS are mass spectra, carbon-13 NMR spectra, x-ray diffraction data for molecules, and x-ray diffraction patterns. The files are linked by means of Chemical Abstracts Service registry numbers, unique chemical identifiers. There are also several bibliographic files which contain literature citations dealing with mass spectrometry and x-ray crystallography incorporated into the system. In addition to the programs for search and retrieval, there are interactive programs that permit analysis of data.

Each data base component of CIS is initially developed by the

Division of Computer Research and Technology, National Institutes of Health, on their PDP10 computer. When the component is released to the private sector, it is sponsored by a non-United States government organization that pays the disc storage charges. The program component is thereby subject to free market conditions and the necessity of eventually having to generate sufficient revenue via subscription fees to defray the costs of disc storage.

There is worldwide 24-hours per day access to CIS via local telephone lines or satellite links. The system interrogates the user as he or she is interrogating the data base so that the inquiry can be sharpened until the answers are limited to a manageable number. Users have two valuable sources of assistance as they interact with the system. Every program in CIS has a HELP file which can be accessed at any time by a user experiencing difficulty. There is also an extensive manual for each program that describes in detail every aspect of that program.

The success of CIS is dependent upon broad-based cooperation of many countries and of both government and private laboratories and organizations. Attracting substantial numbers of users to the system is essential not only because of financial considerations but because users are also sources of data for the system.[11]

BUSINESS MANAGEMENT NETWORKS

Signode Corporation, Glenville, Illinois, manufactures and distributes strapping systems used for packaging and materials handling by a wide range of industries throughout the world. The Corporation maintains an on-line teleprocessing network with terminals in 35 locations across the United States. Applications of the system are order entry, on-line inquiry and update, customer master file, product inquiry, and administrative message switching. Benefits attributed to use of the network include faster service to customers, shorter billing turn-around time, maintenance of lower stock in inventory, consistent determination of shipping from nearest warehouse to destination, and day-by-day reports to management.[12]

Colonel Sanders Kentucky Fried Chicken has introduced minicomputers in local franchise stores which link the cash drawer function to a computer controlled management information system. During the night the day's data are transmitted to the main computer in the company's central office. The benefits resulting from use of this data network include ease in monitoring effectiveness of advertising or promotions on a daily and weekly basis; automatic store-level inventory of chicken and other raw materials; automatic production of daily operating control reports detailed enough to show what was sold each hour and the sizes and types of items; data for projecting how much chicken and other supplies to order daily, how much to cook each hour, and how to schedule employees; and a hard copy of transactions printed and maintained on a daily basis.[13]

Reynolds & Reynolds supplies approximately 3600 auto dealers across the country with VIM-II on-line electronic data processing systems. The services provided include on-line computerized accounting, payroll makeup, inventory management, car leasing information, and service merchandising of automotive accounts. Terminals in the auto dealerships are connected to the 80 Reynolds computer sites, which have minicomputers with dial-up lines. All reports are printed out at the dealership, eliminating delays due to mail. Because the minicomputers are local, long distance transmission problems and costs are eliminated.

The accounting services provide for daily transactions to be entered into the system via the dealership terminal. Accounting information such as customer account balance, book balance of a used car, and general ledger account balance is available instantaneously 24-hours a day. In addition, management reports such as an inventory listing of new and used cars, list of past-due receivables, and statement of cash in the bank are available upon terminal inquiry.

Other applications pertain to parts, leasing, and service merchandising. An inquiry via the terminal at the parts counter produces the number on hand, the bin location, price, and order status. There is also a master locator so the parts department can search the inventory of other participating dealers in the area. A cost analysis program is available to provide comparative data to aid in customer decisionmaking in regard to auto leasing. The Service Merchandising System enables the service manager to instantaneously obtain information related to a particular vehicle, such as the owner's name and address, the mileage at previous service, and service suggested at last diagnosis.[14]

Airlines are expanding their use of computers and communications networks because of the growth in air traffic and increasing costs of labor, fuel, and equipment. They are relying on their networks to handle efficiently accounting and other traditional electronic data processing (EDP) functions; reservations; departure control activities such as ticketing, check-in, and issuing of boarding passes; cargo control; crew scheduling; catering; maintenance; and updating information for airport flight monitors.[15]

Florafax International, Inc., a wholesale floral supply and distribution company, introduced System XXI, a computer-based management information and communication system, in August 1978. Over 1500 florists have installed terminals in their shops which enables them to send floral orders to other on-line terminals; to order fresh flowers, supplies, and imported items from the distributor for direct shipment to their shops; and to be billed automatically for their orders. Benefits claimed for this network are shorter turn-around time on orders, lower distribution costs, and freeing of local phone lines to receive customer orders.[16]

Holiday Inns, Inc., operates what is said to be the largest computerized reservation system in the hotel industry. The Holidex system has four reservation offices serving 60 principal cities in the United States, Canada and Mexico, and reservation offices in 11 principal cities abroad. The service was recently extended behind the Iron Curtain with the opening of a reservation and sales office in Warsaw, Poland.

Holidex receives reservation requests entered on terminals at each inn, each reservation office, and some major corporations which have high-volume travel requirements. The system immediately confirms reservations or indicates accommodations at alternate Holiday Inn facilities and automatically notifies the appropriate inn of confirmations.[17]

As stated earlier, networks are present in all sectors of our society. Because technology is improving and because persons in industry, business and government require information to be economically and immediately available, there will be an ever-increasing demand for networks throughout society.

NOTES

1. David F. Hersey, "Information Networks: A Look at Future Needs and Improvements," in *Information Systems and Networks*, Elev-

enth Annual Symposium, March 27-29, 1974 (Westport, Conn.: Greenwood Press, 1975), p. 166.

2. Bernard A. Weinstein, "E.F. Hutton First on Wall Street with Total High-Speed Communications System," *Communications News* 13:32-5 (September 1976).
3. Information obtained from descriptive brochures provided by Quotron Systems, Inc., Central Regional Marketing Office, Chicago, Illinois.
4. Anthony T. Kruzas, ed., *Encyclopedia of Information Systems and Services*, 3d. ed. (Detroit: Gale Research Co., 1978), p. 398.
5. *Ibid.*, p. 129.
6. *Ibid.*, pp. 228-9.
7. David G. Santry, "Inside Wall Street: The Speculative Play in Graphic Scanning," *Business Week* (January 16, 1978), p. 92.
8. Arkansas Department of Education, Division of Federal Programs, *The Migrant Student Record Transfer System: An Educational Service for the Mobile American*, (Little Rock: 1979).
9. Kruzas, "Encyclopedia of Information Systems," pp. 700-1.
10. *Ibid.*, pp. 581-2.
11. S.R. Heller, G.W.A. Milne, and R.J. Feldmann, "A Computer-Based Chemical Information System," *Science* 195:253-9 (January 1977).
12. "Data Base and Comm Software Support On-line Network," *Infosystems* 25:110-2 (July 1978).
13. "Data Network Counts the Colonel's Chickens," *Communications News* 15:19 (April 1978).
14. "On-line Data Network Provides Fingertip Info for Auto Dealers," *Communications News* 15:86 (May 1978).
15. Sidney F. Quint, "Software Key as Networks Evolve to Meet Domestic Airlines Needs," *Communications News* 14:73 (September 1977).
16. Boston Security Counsellors, Inc., Memorandum of December, 1978.
17. Moody's Investors Service, Inc., *Industrial Manual* (New York: 1978), vol. 1, p. 894.

PART II

National Policy
and Network Development

National Information Policy

R. Kathleen Molz, Professor
School of Library Service
Columbia University
New York, New York

Over ten years ago, Henry Kissinger, later to become U.S. Secretary of State, made this observation: "There is no such thing, in my view, as a Vietnam policy; there is a series of programs of individual agencies concerned with Vietnam." The distinction is one not merely of semantics. What Kissinger was implying is that the United States did not follow a long-range objective in its policies toward Vietnam but rather that a series of incremental decisions forged at various times and in various parts of the government led the nation into a course of action that may or may not have been consistent with an overarching design. "I have found it next to impossible," Kissinger added, "to convince Frenchmen that there is no such thing as an American foreign policy, and that a series of moves that have produced a certain result may not have been planned to produce that result."[1]

If there is any analogy between foreign and domestic policy, the sense of Kissinger's comment could be applied equally well to one of the nation's key domestic issues: the control of information. To paraphrase Kissinger's remarks: There is no such thing, in my view, as a national information policy; there is, however, a series of programs of individual agencies concerned with information.

My task is to establish coherence in the mass of inchoate and overlapping decisions regarding the accumulation of informa-

63

tion in this country, its dissemination, and its preservation. The task is rendered even more difficult when the highly complex nature of our government is fully realized. The shaping of public policy in this country was initially envisioned by the Founding Fathers as a tripartite responsibility in which the bicameral legislature was to be the dominant performer. Reasoning that the new republic should not be under the authority of princes, they authorized the Congress, the first branch of government, to perform the major step in the policy process—its members were to enact laws. The executive was expected to administer these laws, and the judiciary to interpret them, but neither of these branches of government was to have supremacy over the legislature. As the executive office grew and the federal bureaucracy burgeoned, this original balance of powers became distorted with the result that today literally thousands of government bureaus and offices house a spate of planners and analysts, responsible for highly specialized and discrete policies dealing with energy, transportation, health care, or defense, much of which ends up with statutory authority. Exacerbating the situation has been the concomitant growth of special interest groups which, although outside government, nonetheless shape its policies through powerful and effective lobbies. Political scientist, Peter Woll, characterizes the process of setting contemporary public policy in the United States as fragmented, specialized, and pluralistic.[2] These same attributes also characterize national information policy.

THE INFORMATION ECONOMY

By now it is a truism to speak of the age in which we live as an information age. There exists a labor force employing an ever-increasing body of people who supply ideas and information rather than goods or manufactured products. Ten years ago, Peter Drucker, drawing on the earlier researches of Princeton economist, Fritz Machlup, anticipated the growth of the so-called "knowledge industries." In the mid-1950s these industries accounted for one-quarter of the gross national product; by the mid-1960s, the knowledge sector had grown to one-third; by the late 1970s, it had expanded to one-half of the total gross national product. "Every other dollar," Drucker wrote, "earned and spent in the American economy will be earned by producing and distributing ideas and information, and will be spent on procuring ideas and information."[3] Occupations within this informational workforce include producers and salespersons of information machinery, such as photocopiers and computers; insurance agents; accountants; educators; secretaries; a host of professionals such as physicians, nurses, or lawyers; government-employed bureaucrats who solicit, compile, and report data; and, of course, librarians, library aides, and archivists. This latter group is a relatively small one; according to Marc Uri Porot, author of *The Information Economy*, the salaries of the library group represented less than three percent in the aggregate compensation paid to all information workers during 1967.[4]

The shifts in the economic structure toward greater employment for information workers and processors have also been accompanied by an acceleration of the amount of information being produced and radical changes in its format and distribution. The conjunction of computers with telecommunications circuitry has made it possible to package information into data bases, which can be tapped from any one of many dispersed locations. Whereas bibliographers and librarians of the past confined their efforts to publications in a printed form, their contemporary counterparts are expected to provide access to information stored in many ways, including computer tape, film, videocassette, and others, the very diversification of these formats only adding to the problems of identification, location, and delivery of required or requested information.

At the same time as this information overload exists in the United States, the nation also witnesses extremes of information poverty. Functional illiteracy is not an uncommon phenomenon among the adult population, and all too many children leave the public schools without ever having achieved the basic skills to write or even read a paragraph of sequential sentences, much less to absorb the contents of a novel or essay. Nor is this information poverty necessarily limited to the poor; indeed it is one of the ironies of the information society that even those who are served by an informational *richesse* sometimes find themselves in the position of Coleridge's becalmed mariner who, casting his eyes enviously over the sea, lamented: "Water, water, everywhere/Nor any drop to drink." In this regard, the comments of Congressman Richard Bolling seem pertinent:

Congress is flooded with more information than it can absorb. The daily mail delivers more reports, letters, studies, analyses than any staff, let alone the Member himself, can absorb. The sheer volume makes much of the information unuseable. It is too bulky to store and it is not indexed for retrieval. There are usually no facilities to test its validity.[5]

The information society, in summary then, is one of great contrasts in which the highest in the land as well as the lowest have difficulty in finding what they need to know. Two components of the national information agenda deal specifically with their requirements: information for decisionmakers and policymakers and information for the nation's disadvantaged citizens.

INFORMATION FOR DECISIONMAKERS

Ever since Congress decreed that a decennial census of the country should be taken, the executive branch of the government became charged with the accumulation of statistics, the word being used here in its oldest meaning, i.e., matters dealing with affairs of state.[6] Initially, these data were intended to reveal to policymakers what had happened; the policy requirements of a postindustrial society require, however, data to tell them, not only where we have been but also where we should be going. Thus, today, both the executive branch as well as Congress engage in a wide variety of data-gathering efforts that include the determination of social indicators, computer modeling in the policy process, forecasting, trend setting, and others. With the appointment in 1929 of Herbert Hoover's President's Research Committee on Recent Trends, an advisory group largely composed of academicians, the way was paved to introduce a new participant into the policy process, and today thousands of university professors and specialists in the social and physical sciences, working under contract, conjoin their researches and analyses with those of career civil servants in the executive branch and legislative aides to the Congress.

In the last decade, disappointed with the performance of "the best and the brightest" of presidential advisors, disgruntled with the seamy aspect of the Watergate scandal, and no longer content to let the president take the lead in matters of policy formation, the Congress took a number of steps to increase its base of knowledge and to improve the means by which its members are kept informed. Four in number, these steps were: 1) the 1970 reorganization of the Library of Congress's Legislative

Reference Service, initially founded in 1914, as the Congressional Research Service (CRS); 2) the expansion in 1974 of the functions of the General Accounting Office (GAO) to provide programmatic as well as fiscal auditing for Congress; 3) the establishment in 1972 of an Office of Technology Assessment (OTA); and 4) the formation in 1974 of the Congressional Budget Office (CBO).

Unlike CRS or GAO, which may serve any member's request, the two newest groups, OTA and CBO, are empowered to work only with Congressional committees. OTA, the smallest of the four agencies, is charged with the examination of the total impact of a given technology, evaluating its social, environmental, and cultural impacts to make technology a more effective instrument in achieving social goals. The CBO staff is divided into two primary units, the first dealing with budget, fiscal, and tax analyses, and the second with policy analysis in three principal areas: natural resources and commerce; human resources and community development; and national security and international affairs. A few years ago, the Senate's Commission on the Operation of the Senate afforded a forum for a number of senior political scientists to examine these agencies in light of their effectiveness for policy analysis, and the findings of this panel were published in 1976.[7]

In addition to the formation of new agencies and the alteration of the missions of older ones, members of the Congress in recent years have begun using computer data bases to facilitate their understanding of social and economic problems. Members and their staff now have on-line access to a growing number of data bases, including files indicating the current status of Congressional legislation, and those containing bibliographical citations of selected government documents and periodicals. Other data bases highlight certain significant issues or list national referral center resources. In 1970, the Sentate Committee on Rules and Administration created a Subcommittee on Computer Services, and a similar unit, known as the House Information Systems group, was established by the Committee on House Administration, during the following year.[8]

Whether or not the establishment of new agencies, the redesign of older ones, and greater efficiencies derived from the use of processed data will yield more precision in the policy process is a moot question, but taken together all of these new directions signify a greater realization on the part of Congressional members that information is an important factor in decisionmaking.

Comparable concern over the management of information has also been shown by policymakers in the White House. During President Carter's administration a White House Information Center has been established with access to Congressional data bases, those in the executive agencies, such as the Departments of Commerce and Agriculture, and in the private sector, such as the New York Times Information Bank. A Special Assistant to the President for Information Management has been named, and an Information Services Division has been created within the Executive Office of the President, charged with the provision of automated data-processing services to the president and his staff. In commenting on some of these developments, *Time* correspondent Hugh Sidey observed:

> ...My hunch is, having watched the White House from the Bay of Pigs to the 1978 Camp David Summit on the Middle East, that there is room for vast improvement in furnishing a President a quick, cogent view of what he faces, who he faces, and what the options may be.... Any modern President must, in his domestic policy, be precise, efficient, and quick to respond to changes in the nation. He is and will always be no better at this job than the information he gets.[9]

INFORMATION AND REFERRAL

In contrast to the highly sophisticated approaches taken by policymakers to further their knowledge of issues are the myriad ways by which information about social services programs is being disseminated. Millions of dollars are annually expended on the provision of information and referral (I & R) services designed to reach the poor, the elderly, and other Americans with special needs. Randomly located throughout the United States and funded by a variety of government agencies and departments, including those of Labor; Housing and Urban Development; Health, Education, and Welfare; Agriculture; the Veterans' Administration; and the General Services Administration, these services range from a one-person office with limited files of information or none at all to well-equipped and well-staffed units capable of reaching needy people and properly referring them to social service and welfare agencies. In a report published last year the General Accounting Office presented a somewhat dismal picture of these services:

A coordinated Federal program to deliver I & R efficiently and effectively does not exist. Although many Federal agencies fund I & R providers, the agencies tend to act independently of each other. As a result, many I & R providers receiving Federal funds duplicate their services and compete with each other for clients. In addition, most Federal agencies have failed to prescribe quality standards for I & R providers; as a result, there is no assurance that people are receiving adequate and effective I & R.[10]

Like national policy itself, the policies governing the I & R activity are in themselves highly specialized, fragmented, and pluralistic. The report recommends the establishment of a task force to develop a national policy and plan that would coordinate I & R programs and strive for greater consistency in their administration and management.

THE GOVERNMENT AS PUBLISHER AND SUPPORTER OF LIBRARIES

Other important components of the national information agenda deal with the federal government's role as publisher and as supporter of libraries and employer of librarians. The world's largest publisher is, of course, the Government Printing Office, annually distributing free of charge some 80 to 100 million copies of government publications through Congressional offices and federal agencies, and selling an additional 50 to 60 million copies to the general public, approximately half of this latter number being purchased by business and industry. Through the depository library program government documents are furnished to over 1000 libraries in the United States.[11] Also supported by taxation are thousands of specialized libraries supporting the missions of countless government agencies, of the federal court and penal systems, the various academies training future military and naval personnel, the veterans' hospitals, and many others. Since 1956 federal aid has been distributed to locally supported public libraries, and subsequent enactments dating from 1965 have extended such aid to elementary and secondary school libraries and those of academic institutions. In addition, government funding is making possible the issuance of a series of major data bases having significant implications for bibliographic access and research. These include MARC, the machine-readable cataloging record of the Library of Congress; MEDLINE, which makes the rich resources of the *Index Medicus* and other bibliographic aids available to a worldwide biomedical community; AGRICOLA, the data base of the agricultural literature; JURIS, maintained by the Department of Justice; and others.

EFFECTS OF THE DATA PROCESSING REVOLUTION

None of these data bases would have been possible without the advent of the computer/communications marriage. The interrelationship of these two important technologies seems to be, on the one hand, a valuable societal boon and, on the other, one of the nation's most crippling banes. Although we have come to anticipate and appreciate the benefits of contemporary knowledge technology that can transmit pertinent health-care or legal information quickly and efficiently, we are being made increasingly aware of the dangers inherent in the wired society where information of a personal or even confidential nature can be so easily disclosed. It is no coincidence that amendments to strengthen the Freedom of Information Act were passed in the same year in which the Privacy Act was legislated, for the two laws were intended to operate in tandem. The Freedom of Information Act permits the citizenry access to records of their government and places the burden of proof for the withholding of any requested information on the government itself; the Privacy Act permits individuals to review and challenge records maintained by the government about themselves. The delicate balance of power, however, between too little disclosure and too much has been a subject of great scrutiny by both the administration and Congress, as the hearings and various studies of the last decade attest. In April of this year, President Carter submitted to Congress a legislative package covering the use of medical, research, insurance, credit, and financial records, which was described in the words of the administration as "a comprehensive national policy to protect the privacy of Americans."[12]

Although the privacy issue is a very pressing one, it is by no means the only problem that has popped up from the Pandora's box of the data processing revolution. In the private sector, data processing and its associated costs now amount to an estimated $26 billion annually; approximately four percent of the federal budget, or $15 billion, is the amount estimated for federal governmental expenditures in the data processing field.[13] The ease with which data can be generated, manipulated, and disseminated has resulted in a dramatic escalation in the federal government of paperwork, more terrifying when one considers that almost 95 percent of its records are temporary.[14] In addressing the issue of bureaucratic red tape, the Commission on Federal Paperwork defined the paperwork problem in the following terms: the increase in paperwork reflects the growth of government itself (in 1950, the federal government administered 71 domestic grant programs totaling $2 billion; in 1975 there were over 1000 programs totaling $55 billion); the overlapping nature of government programs; the fragmentation of information and program requirements; vague goals and objectives; the application of technology capable of handling massive amounts of data; and the rising costs not only of data handling equipment but also of the personnel who operate it.[15]

Valuable as the work of the Commission on Federal Paperwork is to our understanding of the dimensions of the information explosion, its contribution is but one of many. Within the last decade, an almost alarming number of national commissions charged with the exploration of information-related issues have been formed. These include the National Commission on Electronic Fund Transfers, the National Commission on New Technological Uses of Copyrighted Works, the Privacy Protection Study Commission, the National Historical Publications and Records Commission, the National Commission on Supplies and Shortages, the National Study Commission on Records and Documents of Federal Officials, the Commission on Postal Service, and the National Commission on Libraries and Information Science. Although each has or had a distinctive function to perform, taken in the aggregate these Commissions are a persuasive reminder that the determination of a national policy regarding information, both as to its provision and to its protection, is a public policy question that is still being debated, one that will, no doubt, be the subject of controversy for some years to come.

THE ROLE OF THE COURTS

Although this paper has concentrated on executive branch and Congressional concerns with the information issues of the

United States, it would be misleading not to note that the federal court system also plays an important part in shaping the course of national information policy. The current dilemma over the prior restraint of *The Progressive* magazine for attempting to print an article dealing with the hydrogen bomb and the recent decision of the Supreme Court in the *F.C.C.* v. *Midwest Video* case, which could result in the curtailment of access by educational and community groups to cable TV channels, are but two examples of the power of the judicial system to determine who reads or sees what and who does not.

WHAT IS INFORMATION?

Nowhere in this paper have I yet defined information; this was a calculated maneuver on my part because the paper is intended to disclose the divergent properties of information itself and the complex characteristics of those who create it, distribute it, make use of it, and govern it. In initially ruling on *The Progressive* case, Judge Robert W. Warren believed that "information" was an article by Howard Morland, which if published would infringe on the national security of this country; to the corporate authors of the Commission on Federal Paperwork, "information" is a valuable national resource that requires, like any natural resource, conservation, recycling, and protection; for Congressman Bolling "information" is the flood of materials that daily lands on his desk; for the users of JURIS, AGRICOLA, or MEDLINE, "information" is the print-out of citations that they will need to examine in the course of their research; according to journalist Sidey, "information" for the president of this country is a profile of the issues, an identification of those who are for and against them, and a listing of alternative courses of action; and for some unidentified little girl, "information" may be the contents of an attractively illustrated picture book purchased for her local public library from federal funds.

Information, then, is a word capable of many meanings and subject to a great diversity of definitions. If, indeed, the word "information" can be interpreted so differently, how can we define the term "information policy?" In its report *National Information Policy*, the Domestic Council Committee on the Right of Privacy wrote:

Although the term "information policy" can have different connotations, the various perspectives which are brought to it are all part of a common family of interdependent and intersecting interests. It is this larger context and the expectation that information policy issues will become more pressing in the future which compel a national information policy. The interrelationships which exist between and among information communications, information technology, information economics, information privacy, information systems, information confidentiality, information science, information networks, and information management have signalled the need for a broader, more comprehensive approach to the problem.[16]

As part of its own resolution of the diffuse aspects of the informational issue, the Committee's report turns inevitably to the locus-of-authority question and calls for the establishment of an Office of Information Policy in the White House. A similar recommendation has been made in the study prepared by Arthur D. Little, Inc., entitled *Into the Information Age*,[17] and even the document prepared for the 1978 President's Program of the American Library Association, "Toward a Conceptual Foundation for a National Information Policy," stressed the need for an appropriate center within the federal government for a national information program.[18] Even if all programs dealing with information and communications were combined and the aggregate were to be elevated to cabinet-level status and we were to have a Secretary of the Information/Communications Department, would we really have resolved the problem of determining a national information policy? The disputes over energy conservation and consumption have not gone away with the creation of a Department of Energy, and concerns about rail or air transport in this country have not disappeared with the formation of a Department of Transportation, to cite the two newest cabinet offices.

Although the locus-of-authority question should not be denigrated nor would any of us have any real objections to the appointment of a high-level presidential advisor, I am somewhat skeptical as to its effect. It has become a commonplace in our society to say that information is power, in some ways investing information with the attributes of energy itself. Facts and data become then so many gallons of gas to fuel the engine, and let the vehicle run. But information isn't like gasoline or oil from which it is derived; it is not a natural resource the supply of which may be eventually depleted. Information is an intellectual resource generated by people who in many cases have very legitimate proprietary rights in its distribution and dissemination. The Founding Fathers recognized those rights in the granting of copyrights and patents to protect not a natural resource but rather an intellectual property that could grow through the uses of other intellectual properties. To the findings of latter-day economists who have suddenly discovered that information is linked with economic power, I can only suggest that they ponder the implications of this excerpt from a letter written by Thomas Jefferson to James Madison in 1821: "Books constitute capital. A library book lasts as a house, for hundreds of years. It is not, then, an article of mere consumption but fairly of capital, and often in the case of professional men, setting out in life it is their only capital." [19]

INFORMATION AS BOTH CONTENT AND PROCESS

For over two centuries this nation was able to accept the thesis that the acquisition and storage of informational content and its absorption by the citizenry was not unlike a capital investment in the educational and intellectual wealth of the United States; what makes our present discontinuous with our past is the advent of information not as content but as process, to use a distinction that Joseph Becker has recently made.[20] To take but one example, Judge Warren would, in all probability, not have ruled to restrain *The Progressive*, a small journal with relatively few subscribers, were it not that he feared that the processing of Morland's article through the international news media would circularize its content around the world. Is it the content of the article which is so dangerous, or the dissemination of that content? It is important to remember that Thomas Paine's revolutionary tract *Common Sense* was first issued as a pamphlet; today its publication might warrant a multi-media event. Even as late as this century when Einstein originally set forth his extraordinary theories he did so in the pages of a highly specialized journal read by only a handful of scientists; in our present age of high-speed circuitry and satellite communication, Morland's disclosures would be instantly and internationally known. It is information as process, not content, that really lies at the heart of *The Progressive* case.

In shaping a national information policy we are going to have to deal with information both as content as well as process, and our dilemma will in part be to find the proper balance between the two. As a nation, we have lived, sometimes uneasily, with opposites: we have proclaimed individual liberty, which stresses separatism, divergency, and idiosyncracy, while at the same time declaring that all men are equal;[21] we posit equality as a philosophical good yet allow differentials in income and buying power to be used in ways that make the framework of our economy much at variance with the egalitarian structure of our public policy (economist Arthur Okun perceives the latter distinction as one between efficiency and equality; he calls it "the big tradeoff");[22] we protect under our Constitution the concept that reward for intellection should be made and yet promote the idea that information is a public good to which anyone can have free access. Our society is one which respects the economics of the competitive marketplace, yet proclaims itself essentially democratic and communal. The question is begged: can national information policy escape the dichotomies inherent in many of our other national policies?

I am not overly sanguine as to the outcome. A member of the House of Representatives, who is serving on the subcommittee to revise the Communications Act of 1934, described our wired society in these terms:

> The unspoken fact is, in today's society, that information is power, and the terms of access to information determine who has influence and who reaps benefits in our society. Think of that for a moment. We are talking about economic power, about social and intellectual standing and about political participation. All are fundamentally affected by the availability of knowledge, which depends upon information which is rooted in technology.[23]

Think of that for a moment, and then reflect on the traditional division of the reins of power in this country. Distrustful of government, yet acknowledging the necessity for its existence, the Founding Fathers created a fairly effective system of checks and balances. The national government was divided into three parts, affording Congress responsibility to oversee the presidency, and acceding the role of the judiciary in reviewing them both. For many years, a kind of dual sovereignity existed, which allocated distinctive functions both to the states and to the nation. Local government was more or less a creature of the states, which with their longstanding antipathy to cities hardly

ever afforded any major metropolis the status of serving as a
state capital. Though long neglected, the county, currently enriched in size by the population increases in suburban areas, now
emerges as a substantive participant in the policy process, a
factor rendered more significant at a time when future projections indicate that suburban representation in Congress will
increase while that from rural areas and center cities will decline. Each of these layers or parts has had its distinctive
prerogatives and each has shown in the past dissatisfaction if
those prerogatives were threatened or usurped. Each of these
parts has also had its own unique informational sources. Originally such sources were quite simple things like libraries.
Credited with founding in Philadelphia the first subscription
library in the nation, Benjamin Franklin saw nothing unusual
or strange in sending back to the United States from France a
selection of books to aid the nascent state library in Harrisburg.
After all, a journey to the State Capital from Philadelphia was a
long trek for an 18th century Pennsylvania legislator. But at that
time, information was content, not process, and the Harrisburg-
based lawmaker needed information at his fingertips, not at
some distant location like Philadelphia or far-away Boston or
New York. Although the telecommunications revolution radically changes our long-held concepts about local library self-
sufficiency by demonstrating that information from one site can
be made easily available in another, it cannot quite yet erase
centuries-old traditions of information gathering for distinctive
and discrete clienteles.

In its own way, the Harrisburg example serves as but a
microcosm of the macrocosmic recognition that the United
States, contrary to much widely-held contemporary belief, has
long recognized that the control of information was indeed
linked to economic power, social and intellectual standing, and
political participation. The interrelationships between intellectual and economic and social wealth can be readily demonstrated from the days when Jefferson assembled his handsome
library at his Virginia country estate to the continuing benefac-
tions of the Astor family to the research collections of The New
York Public Library.

The discontinuity of our present society with its past is not
linked to the recognition that information can lend power, but
rather that the power of information can now be so easily shared.
At the international level, the implications of this latter concept

are a little frightening (hence the national security issue), and at the national, regional, state, local, and institutional level, the concept, if not frightening, is at least somewhat disconcerting. If information is power, may there not be some reluctance to share that power wisely and without divisiveness? As a nation we have not been without our own Maginot lines; there have been traditional rivalries between our two principal political parties, between Senate and House, between Congress and the presidency, between nation and state, and between state and locality. Networking and the wiring of our society may indeed eradicate these rivalries and enable the nation to govern itself in its third century with greater cohesion and less separatism, but such radical change not only in the nature of our governance but also in its tradition will not come about easily, despite the technology. Our inheritance of so complex a division of powers attests to innate fears of a loss of autonomy and to a long history of individual parts jealously guarding their own place in the governmental and legislative sun. Even the evidence of recent Congressional hearings dealing with the Library of Congress leads me to believe that at least some members of Congress have not accepted the fact that the rich resources of "their" library are to be made so widely available; the often uneasy balance with which the Library of Congress has strived, often nobly, to perform its twin missions of service to the Congress and to the nation is but one demonstration that society has not fully accepted the notion that information is process as well as content.

In the pluralistic, specialized, fragmented world in which we live, we will not doubt thrash out the nucleus of some national informational policies, but the task will not be easy nor the outcome unaffected by compromise between competing groups in the public and private sectors, at various levels of government, and among a whole host of client groups with many diverse interests and requirements. The visibility given to the issues inherent in determining a national information policy through study, commission reports, Congressional hearings and testimony, and executive branch scrutiny, is all to the good, but the distinctive character of all of these activities prefigures in the end the shaping of not one policy but probably a good many. This paper began with a quotation from an address by Henry Kissinger; it will close with another selection from it: "I am pessimistic about the ability of modern bureaucratic society to manage a world which is quite discontinuous with its previous experience, and especially to do so with generosity and vision. I am not saying it's technically impossible, but the challenges are so much greater."

NOTES

1. Henry Kissinger, "Bureaucracy and Policy," *The Washington Post* (September 17, 1973), p. A24.
2. Peter Woll, *Public Policy* (Cambridge, Mass.: Winthrop Publishers, 1974), pp. 14-20.
3. Peter F. Drucker, *The Age of Discontinuity* (New York and Evanston: Harper & Row, 1969), p. 263. See also Fritz Machlup, *The Production and Distribution of Knowledge in the United* (Princeton, N.J.: Princeton University Press, 1962).
4. Marc Uri Porot, *The Information Economy: Definition and Measurement* (Washington, D.C.: Govt. Print. Off. 1977), pp. 106-11.
5. Richard Bolling, "The Management of Congress," *Public Administration Review* 35:492 (September-October 1975).
6. For an historic review of the role of the federal government in the provision of national statistics, see Philip M. Hauser, "Social Accounting," in Paul F. Lazarsfeld, et al., *The Uses of Sociology* (New York: Basic Books, Inc., 1967), pp. 839-75.
7. U.S. Congress. Senate. Commission on the Operation of the Senate, *Congressional Support Agencies: A Compilation of Papers.* At head of title: 94th Cong., 2nd Sess. Committee Print. (Washington, D.C.: Govt. Print. Off., 1976).
8. See Robert Lee Chartrand, "Information Science in the Legislative Process," in *Annual Review of Information Science and Technology* (Washington, D.C.: American Society for Information Science, 1976), Vol. 11, pp. 299-344; U.S. Congress. Senate. Committee on Rules and Administration. Subcommittee on Computer Services. *Information Support for the U.S. Senate: A Survey of Computerized CRS Resources and Services*; At head of title: 95th Cong., 1st Sess. Committee Print (Washington, D.C.: Govt. Print. Off., 1977); and "Congress in the Information Age," *Bulletin of the American Society for Information Science* 1:8-24 (April 1975).
9. Hugh Sidey, "Information in the Presidency: A Journalist's View," *Bulletin of the American Society for Information Science* 5:10 (December 1978).
10. The contents of this particular issue of the *Bulletin* were devoted to "The Presidency in the Information Age," pp. 13-26, *passim.*
11. Bernard Fry, *Government Publications: Their Role in the National Program for Library and Information Services* (Washington, D.C.: Govt. Print. Off., 1979), pp. 51-2.

12. Martin Tolchin, "Carter Maps Policy to Protect Privacy," *The New York Times* (April 13, 1979), p. 1. For a critical assessment of the complexities of administering these two statutes and a description of their shortcomings, see also U.S. Commission on Federal Paperwork, *Confidentiality and Privacy* (Washington, D.C.: Govt. Print. Off., 1977).

13. U.S. Commission on Federal Paperwork, *Information Resources Management*, p. 3.

14. U.S. General Services Administration, National Archives and Records Service, Office of Federal Records Centers, *Disposition of Federal Records* (Washington, D.C.: Govt. Print. Off., 1978), p. 4.

15. U.S. Commission on Federal Paperwork, *Information Resources Management*, p. 3.

16. U.S. Domestic Council Committee on the Right of Privacy, *National Information Policy* (Washington, D.C.: Govt. Print. Off., 1976), p. xii.

17. Arthur D. Little, Inc., *Into the Information Age: A Perspective for Federal Action on Information* (Chicago, Ill.: American Library Association, 1978), p. 91.

18. David Kaser, et al., "Toward a Conceptual Foundation for a National Information Policy," *Wilson Library Bulletin* 52:548 (March 1978).

19. Letter of Thomas Jefferson to James Madison, Sept. 16, 1821. Cited in *The Works of Thomas Jefferson*, Paul Leicester Ford, ed., (New York and London: G.P. Putnam Sons, 1905), v. XII, p. 210.

20. Joseph Becker, "U.S. Information Policy," *Bulletin of the American Society for Information Science* 4:14-18 (August 1978).

21. For an excellent analysis of the interplay between liberty and equality in American life, see J.R. Pole, *The Pursuit of Equality in American History* (Berkeley, Calif.: University of California Press, 1978).

22. Arthur M. Okun, *Equality and Efficiency: The Big Tradeoff* (Washington, D.C.: The Brookings Institution, 1975).

23. Timothy E. Wirth, cited in David Burnham, "Nation Facing Crucial Decisions Over Policies on Communications," *The New York Times* (July 8, 1977), p. A10.

Evolution, Libraries, and National Information Policy*

Don R. Swanson, Professor
Graduate Library School
University of Chicago
Chicago, Illinois

This paper covers somewhat more than its title suggests; it is really about cancer, guessing, evolution, accidents, mutation, Hamlet, willful machines, death, taxes, bankruptcy, bloody hands, croquet, hedgehogs, flamingos, zombies, red herrings, Proposition 13, Hagar the Horrible, poker, the irrelevance of libraries, and the prevention of national information policy.**†

An earlier paper, "Libraries and the Growth of Knowledge,"[1] provides background for this paper. Certain of the earlier ideas, particularly those concerned with the process of evolutionary change, will be further explored here. The background paper begins with a problem—the problem of how libraries can best facilitate the growth of knowledge. It is important to distinguish the growth of knowledge from the growth of literature. While

*This paper is based on talks presented by the author at the 40th Annual Conference of the University of Chicago Graduate Library School, May 18, 1979, and at the conference on Networks for Networkers, Indianapolis, May 31, 1979; it is to be published in the *Library Quarterly*, v.50 (1), January, 1980.

**Any resemblance to the opening lines of Kurt Vonnegut's address to the Association of College and Research Libraries 1978 National Conference (Boston, Nov. 9) is partly coincidental.

†It may be noted in passing that this paper is likely to turn up in all future data-base searches, no matter what key words are chosen as search terms.

growth in the quantity of literature poses problems on its own, the two questions are not identical. Knowledge may take a great leap with only a small jump in the amount of literature, while in some disciplines the quantity of publication grows like cancer with little or no increment in knowledge. Such literature growth indeed may inhibit the growth of knowledge.[2] So it is of special importance to try to understand the process by which knowledge grows. That question is very large in scope, for it encompasses much of the philosophy of knowledge, or epistemology. Without pretending to do justice to such topics, I shall briefly extend certain arguments offered in the background paper to the effect that a Popperian approach to the philosophy of science and to epistemology may be of particular relevance to librarianship.

INDUCTION, GUESSWORK, AND EPISTEMOLOGY

According to conventional wisdom, we learn about the world, and scientific knowledge advances by a process of induction. That is, through repeated experiences we extrapolate or induce somehow what we are likely to experience in the future. Or, science begins with observations, then from observations we produce a theory through the process of induction. Rejecting such conventional wisdom, Karl Popper claims that there is no such thing as induction by repetition, and that the process of acquiring new knowledge does not begin with observations. Rather, it begins with a problem and a conjectural solution or theory. Literally, we jump to conclusions first, then try out our conclusions, reject them if they don't work, and then jump anew. That is, we guess, then test our guesses. So we learn through an endless spiral of conjectures and refutations.[3] All theories and all knowledge are forever conjectural. The best knowledge consists of conjectures that have survived the severest tests, and withstood the most searching criticism.

Let me suggest an experiment that might illuminate the contrast between the competing theories of guessing and inducing. Recite to someone the names of the decimal digits, slowly, in the following order: eight, five, four, nine, one, seven. Pause at any point, such as here, and ask your victim to figure out the order—that is, to theorize about the rule you are following, and try to name the remaining digits. You might hint that librarians are likely to be better prepared than mathematicians to answer the question. The sequence continues: six, three, two, zero. Allow at least a few minutes of serious thought before disclosing the answer, for the point now is to try to ascertain what one really does in trying to solve such a puzzle. Conventionally, we might say that something like induction takes place—that one accumulates experience with early numbers in the sequence and, through perceiving a repetitive pattern, extrapolates to the answer in some manner. If Popper is right, however, we proceed by guessing, and try out each guess to see if it fits the sequence. I'll leave it to you to judge which is the more satisfying explanation—after you've tried the experiment.

The digits above were named in alphabetic order. Now it would seem to me that one would have to think of looking for the alphabetic arrangement *before* one could possibly notice it. That is, theory, or guesswork, must *precede* any meaningful observation, as Popper suggests. There is nothing worth noticing until you have a theory. Students often approach research by gathering a mountain of data, and then contemplating it, hoping a thesis will emerge phoenixlike from the ashes. Their idea is mistaken—it is backwards. They will see nothing until they have decided what to look for. One must start with a guess or theory, then collect data in the light of such guess to see what it reveals. Guessing and testing can be described in several other ways—for example, in terms of "trial-and-error,"* conjectures and refutations, or as I shall argue in a moment, variation and selection. These ideas provide a foundation not only for explaining how scientific knowledge grows, but for a more general epistemology, or theory of how we learn about the world.

THE PROCESS OF CHANGE IN LIBRARIES

The problem of how libraries might best facilitate the growth of knowledge was the first and most basic problem explored in the background paper, but a second class of problems received equal attention—problems of how libraries and information services change and improve. My thesis is that evolutionary mechanisms are central to the solution of both types of problems. That is, libraries improve by a process similar to the way

---

*Throughout, I shall take "trial-and-error" to mean "trial, and error-elimination"—that is, trial followed by the elimination of erroneous or unsuccessful trials.

knowledge grows—through trial-and-error. It is the second problem, the process of change, that I wish to explore further in the light of that thesis.

Biological Evolution

Before proceeding with my argument, I shall try to clarify my use of the term "evolution." The often-used sense of unfolding or gradual change, as contrasted with revolutionary change, is either vacuous or misleading. I shall base my definition of evolution on the idea of trial-and-error or, equivalently, variation and selection. Darwinian, or biological, evolution may be taken as our basic model or prototype.

There are three components of a biological evolutionary process: variation, natural selection, and transmission of traits to succeeding generations. Through the accumulation of accidental genetic mutations, a population of living organisms will carry a high degree of diversity in its genetic material. As the organisms reproduce, this diversity becomes manifest in high variability of traits among the organisms. Some of these traits are relevant to survival and reproduction. Most mutations are harmful, and so the mutant gene is eliminated either because the organism carrying it does not survive long enough to reproduce, or because that organism or its progeny are sterile. But on rare occasions, chance confers some kind of advantage on the organism, an advantage which enables it to leave more progeny than its competitors, and which advantage is transmitted to those progeny. This "improved" variant of the parent organism then tends to become dominant and serves as a new point of departure for further variation and selection. So it was that certain living organisms lurched forward through the generations in a haphazard, aimless fashion, but somehow achieved ever higher degrees of organization and complexity, and arrived, for better or worse, at an astonishing collection of molecules that became aware of its own existence and chose to call itself "man"—and at a more advanced evolutionary stage—"person." The idea that a chain of a million accidental mutations, a vast trial-and-error process, without goal, plan, or design, can lead to such a piece of work as man is captivating. The suggestive power of the idea of variation and selection is not limited to biological evolution, and my next purpose is to explore some of its broader implications.

EVOLUTIONARY MECHANISMS IN THE ACTIVITIES AND INSTITUTIONS OF MANKIND

What particulary commands one's interest in the idea of trial-and-error, or variation and selection, is the possibility for understanding something about the behavior of large, complex systems—in particular, systems whose components are, or can be, free to pursue their own aims and interests. We may think of such systems as having distributed autonomy, or perhaps as systems with willful components. Such a description implies at the outset that we are not concerned with machines as the components of our systems, if only because any machine that started to behave willfully would no longer be considered a machine. The components of interest here are people, groups of people, or institutions. Now in Darwinian evolution, it is the living organism itself that is selected to survive or to die. To go beyond the purely biological idea, we shall have to imagine instead that variation and selection act upon certain activities or products of people. Popper indeed saw variation and selection as operating on our ideas or theories—our conjectures. That is, conjectures can be seen as analogous to mutations or variations. Such conjectures are then put to the test, either systematically as in the case of scientific investigation, or willy-nilly in everyday experience. Theories or guesses that clash with reality—that are mistaken—are then eliminated, or modified, in a process very much like natural selection. The surviving theories are those that best solve the problems that they are meant to solve. This Popperian philosophy of knowledge is appropriately called an evolutionary epistemology.[4]

The idea of variation and selection can be still further extended to embrace social, economic, and cultural activities of people interacting with one another, an arena toward which both Popper and Hayek, among others, have directed many well-constructed arguments.[5,6,7] Biological evolution has drastic error correction methods; faulty living organisms die. The central questions in extending evolution to other systems are these: How is error eliminated? How can we create correctable systems? What are the conditions that foster variation and selection?

I should like particularly to consider the business and economic activities of mankind in the context of the foregoing questions. If there is freedom to innovate, to invent and offer new products and services, to try out new ventures, then conditions are hospitable to variability. Selective pressures will emerge if customers are free to choose to buy or not, and if the service or product depends for its life on having customers. Services or products not perceived by the customers as necessary or desirable, for the price offered, will die. Or they will die if competitors offer the same thing or better for a lower price. Price and competition therefore constitute a means of insuring that goods and services on the market are limited to those that are perceived as valuable. The rest are eliminated in a process analogous to natural selection. Variation and selection are thought of here as pertaining to business ventures, where ventures may refer either to specific products or services, or to the institution (corporation, partnership, or proprietorship) that does the venturing.

Do the forces of selectivity really operate, or are business ventures run by a privileged few—an established elite? If the latter is the case, the elite at least are not few in number; there are some 14 million corporations, partnerships, or proprietorships in the United States. There is good evidence moreover that competition and selection operate fiercely. There are, for example, about 8-10,000 business failures per year—that is, bankruptcies, receiverships, etc. But such litigated failures may be only the tip of the selection iceberg. About 400,000 new corporations are formed each year, yet the total number of corporations doing business (around 2 million) grows at the rate of only 60,000 or so per year.[8] What happens to the other 340,000 is not altogether clear, but it is at least plausible to assume that a very large number represents ventures that are unsuccessful and just fade away—losers in the evolutionary game.* The "invisible hand of competition" seems to be quite bloody.

In sum, I have identified four areas in which evolutionary mechanisms seem to have remarkable explanatory power: 1) biological evolution; 2) science—method of refutations; 3) epistemology—or theory of knowledge; 4) social/economic activities—entrepreneurship and competition.

*Two authors from the Small Business Administration quote roughly similar figures (without citing a source), in the context of suggesting that business failure rate is very high. They are, however, similarly equivocal as to the meaning of the quoted figures: "Each year in the United States, some 500,000 new business starts are made—and 400,000 disappearances recorded. Not all the disappearances can be called failures. Some owners sell out to acquire larger interests and others simply tire of the trials of running a business."[9]

Some further comments on the relationship between the first and fourth areas may forestall any erroneous notion that I am arguing on behalf of the justifiably discredited 19th century idea of Social Darwinism. First, I see biological evolution and entrepreneurial evolution as two independent expressions of the more general idea of variation and selection. Each of these two must stand on its own merits; there is no justification for claiming, for example, that entrepreneurial evolution follows logically from, and so has the force of, some natural law of biological evolution. Second, entrepreneurial evolution refers to the selection and survival of institutions, or their products and services, but not to the people who either own or run them. Third, successful traits in a social/economic system are transmitted by imitation, not by genetic inheritance. Finally, the fact that the "fittest" institutions necessarily survive entails no value judgment about "fitness" other than what may be implied by survival itself. The value of any specific institution is to be judged on its own merits; such institutions can be eliminated or modified by deliberate human action. The result becomes a part of the spontaneous social order to which the evolutionary process gives rise. There are no "laws of evolution" to which man is subject; the argument for preserving evolutionary mechanisms in society is no more than an argument on behalf of a correctable society—one in which we can learn from our mistakes and take corrective action on a piecemeal basis.[10]

LARGE-SCALE SYSTEMS PLANNING AS AN ALTERNATIVE TO EVOLUTION

Evolutionary, or trial-and-error, mechanisms are slow, blundering, and inefficient. One can be impressed with the fact that it took a billion years to produce humans, that people have been pursuing truth for several thousand years without capturing it, that nothing we know is secure, and that more new business ventures fail than succeed. As a philosophy of how a complex system should be changed or improved, evolution, in short, leaves something to be desired. Given any choice in the matter, would we really wish to rely on so haphazard a process? Why not simply design systems correctly in the first place—that is, by-pass all errors in the trial-and-error process? If, for example, our system embraces all of the economic, production, and distribution activities of society, then the alternative to evolutionary change presumably would be for someone sufficiently wise, and well-informed, to decide in advance who is to produce how much of what services or goods, and what prices are to be charged. It remains only to give unlimited authority to a benevolent leader to enforce such decisions, to achieve then an optimally designed society. It is impressive that schemes of this kind have never proved workable.

Among the many difficulties with such proposals, three seem particulary worth noting in order to sharpen the contrast with evolutionary, pluralistic systems.

First, the sheer number of variables in the allocation problem (that is, the problem of allocating resources to producers) is enormous—certainly in the millions. It is necessary, moreover, continually to take account of changing demand for millions of individual products and services and feed this information to some point of centralized decisionmaking in order to permit corrective action. That is, one must substitute explicit calculations on a vast scale (a scale much greater than any that has ever been demonstrated to be feasible) to carry out what, in a pluralistic system, would be accomplished by the self-regulative mechanism of the market. Attempts to do away with market mechanisms never work; shortages become pandemic. Squeezed tightly enough by controls, markets turn black. A totally controlled economy is no doubt unobjectionable if applied to a commune of a few hundred people, but on the scale of western society today it seems quixotic, to say the least. It could be considered an idea whose time has gone, were it not for the many politicians whose faith that controls can somehow be made to work is apparently eternal.

The second difficulty arises from the necessary surrender of autonomy to some central authority. With such loss of local autonomy, the opportunity to respond resourcefully to locally perceived problems is also lost. It is difficult to see any role for innovation in such a monolithic system, and accordingly difficult to envision how progress or improvement can take place. Such a system would seem to require an impossible centralization of knowledge, creativity, inventiveness, and resourcefulness, in addition to authority. The need to centralize authority ultimately raises serious questions about whether the political structure is correctable by peaceful means, which questions bring us to the next difficulty.

Third, the whole idea seems to count heavily on the benevolence and incorruptibility of those who wield absolute power, an assumption not known for an impressive track record. A pluralistic and evolving system, because it does not require so authoritarian a political structure, can proceed on the opposite and safer assumption—namely, that power corrupts, so it is necessary to throw the rascals out peacefully every so often and install new ones.

EVOLUTIONARY APPROACH TO LIBRARY SYSTEMS

The idea of trial-and-error evolutionary mechanisms has proved to be powerful; it has come to occupy a central position in both the philosophy of science and the philosophy of social thought. My aim now is to examine how such an idea might have some bearing on how we should perceive and think about a particular system—one that encompasses all libraries and information services in the country. So loose an aggregate is perhaps not a system in the usual sense of the word. Yet we do so consider it in addressing problems of national information policy, universal bibliographic control, networks, or resource sharing, among other things. If we were to think of such a system in monolithic terms, as though it were a clock, a computer, or perhaps a factory, but in any event a system serving a single-minded goal, and set about the job of planning and designing it, we would almost surely encounter serious difficulties. Libraries serve autonomous institutions that have their own aims and goals. But in such a monolithic system as described above individual goals are subordinated to an overall goal; the many thousands of individual units must, in effect, surrender their autonomy. It is hardly thinkable that one could with any certainty attain some specific overall goal if the components of the system were both inclined and free to go their own way. We would find ourselves, as Alice did, in a croquet game in which the soldiers-as-wickets and hedgehogs-as-balls wandered about unpredictably, and the flamingos-as-mallets behaved a good deal more like flamingos than like mallets. Systems planning in these circumstances is a whole new croquet game—largely an exercise in futility. It is not to be thought of as applied science or engineering, perhaps it is a social science. I believe that Patrick Wilson's argument that there are no theories in social science that permit prediction and control[11] is not unrelated to my point. That is, it is futile to try to impose overall goals, or to draw exact blueprints, for systems whose components are people and institutions in pursuit of their own goals and interests. Though no one is seriously proposing to turn all libraries and information services in the country into a gigantic piece of clockwork, there are some who seem to believe that this would be a good idea if only we knew how to carry it out, and they reason therefore that at least we should try. All of my arguments here are directed against such a notion. In contrast to clockwork, systems that are left alone to evolve are neither designed nor managed—they have no goals other than those of their autonomous units. There is no surrender of local autonomy. My assertion that evolutionary systems are to be preferred does not rest on analogy to biological systems, to society at large, or to croquet. I propose that a solid argument can be developed by examining the consequences of failure.

Successful trial-and-error mechanisms in a large, pluralistic system operate at the level of the small, numerous individual components within the system; only a single component is eliminated with each failure. By contrast, a very large, monolithic or clockwork system, if it fails, dies on a very large scale. If all units are part of an overall plan and design, with a single overarching goal, then the whole works goes down if the design is unsound, or if unexpected technological change points the way to a wholly new design. Ultimately, all systems (and all theories) must be put to the test, and might fail. The larger and more complex the system, the more calamitous the failure. *So the trick is to design complex systems such that only small units die rather than the whole system whenever a failure occurs;* and one should assume that failures of some kind are frequent and inevitable. But that implies giving individual units the freedom to both try and die, and so, in effect, abandons the idea of an overall goal or plan, in favor of allowing such units to pursue their own interests.

If information services are free to proceed on a trial-and-error basis, one does not have to count on "user studies" to ascertain what is needed. In general, users are singularly unimaginative in expressing a need for information services not yet invented. In an evolving system, the need for an innovative service is revealed when that service succeeds in attracting customers and in prevailing over its competitors. Cuadra[12] reports having found no need for on-line data bases when he conducted a user survey just prior to offering SDC's ORBIT! One innovative idea is worth far more than a thousand thoughtless opinions. In a track meet, one man able to jump seven feet is considerably more valuable than seven who can jump one foot.*

Under certain conditions, a new system or service that fails is not necessarily eliminated. If it doesn't depend on customers for its sustenance, then the fact that it has failed may go unnoticed. The system may continue as a zombie, dead but propped up by subsidies as though it were alive and well. One suspects that certain library and information services fall into this category. In general, any system insulated from the forces of competition and the market may be particularly vulnerable to undetected failure.

For large, complex systems with distributed autonomy, we should attempt to create conditions that foster small-scale, trial-and-error type improvements at the level of individual components—that is, evolutionary mechanisms. Henriette Avram, in a recent article on networks makes a point that I agree with: "Individuals involved with complex systems work in that wonderful gray world where ideas can be proven to be neither right nor wrong until tried, and then there is high praise for success and high price for failure. There is no well defined map to follow that will guarantee arrival at the destination, but one thing is for sure—we are on our way!"[13] (I would add, however, that there isn't even any destination.)

I propose then a philosophy of large-scale systems planning in which the systems analyst focusses not on the system itself, but on the environment in which it functions. Conditions favorable to evolution should be created—freedom and incentive to innovate and strong mechanisms for eliminating failures or errors. Goals in general should originate in the autonomous units, and are not to be imposed from above on a systemwide basis. This is not to rule out certain types of positive constructive action that indirectly serve overall goals. One can and should look for specific areas wherein pursuit of self-interest advances the common good. This principle was well understood by Dik Browne's comic strip character, *Hagar the Horrible*. Hagar and his crew of Vikings were setting out to sea. From the prow of their boat, Hagar announces: "On this trip everybody is going to have a job. But first—is there anybody who can't swim?" Lucky Eddie

---

*The latter approach, applied to a research team, is sometimes called the Delphi method.

raises his hand. "Good!," Hagar says, "you're in charge of leaks."

There are other means whereby purely voluntary transactions with self-serving motives can advance systemwide goals. One important type of mechanism to achieve that end is a centralized service voluntarily used by individual units on a contractual or subscription basis. It provides incentive for common procedures, and for standardization without imposing Procrustean constraints. Any sacrifice of autonomy is minimal. Both the Library of Congress MARC Distribution Service and OCLC are excellent examples of such a philosophy. By making available a centralized service, a spontaneous order or structure among those who voluntarily subscribe to the service is allowed to develop without overall goals.

In arguing the necessity of error-elimination, I have implied that regulative mechanisms of price and competition in a free market are the only means of bringing this about. In any event, no other methods have been demonstrably successful. Of especial importance is the fact that the market mechanism preserves local autonomy, for all transactions in a free market are voluntary, and so are carried out only if each party to the transaction sees it as being to its own advantage.

FEE VS. FREE SERVICES

There are of course types of library services not supportable by the market, but clearly of great social value. I do not equate quality and marketability in any rigid sense. Scholars in many areas, including the public at large, need expensive library collections that they cannot pay for as individuals. The tradition of "free" (that is, tax-supported or institutionally supported) library service is deeply a part of the American scene, and, in my opinion, should be protected and nourished. But I believe it is seriously mistaken to insist on some ad hoc principle that free libraries must never offer extra services supported by user fees.

What exactly is the argument against charging for extra information services? The argument that some people would then be unable to afford such services is I believe a red herring. If it is agreed by the body politic that public interest is served by providing certain types of service to those who can't afford to pay a fee, then, instead of public subsidy of any specific service itself, one can charge user fees for a variety of services, but give grants to certain users—grants that can then be applied to purchase any of the competing services. Choices of whom to subsidize in this way, or what projects to subsidize, are political choices in the public sector, or policy choices in any event that are outside the prerogatives of librarians. This approach preserves the regulative mechanism of the market, allows greater individual freedom by the recipients of aid in choosing information services, and still can permit as high a level of support for socially desirable activities unsupportable by the market as can any method of providing public services directly. Admittedly it may in some cases be more efficient to make a subsidized service available to all than to identify and administer aid to appropriate recipients. For certain services, such advantages in efficiency may outweigh the competing advantage of a market mechanism.

The polarization of arguments and feelings on the fee vs. free issue has tended to befog the obvious advantages of a dual system. A basic level of free service supplemented by extra services for a price has a particular strength that I think has not been widely noted. The two types of service can in some sense compete with one another, and find a natural equilibrium governed by the relative level of financial support from their respective sources. It is nevertheless the fee-based services that are likely to lead the way toward improvements from which all services ultimately benefit. This especially tends to be so for services stimulated by incentives, and subject to the forces of competition, in the private sector. On-line data base services are a prime example about which I shall say more in a moment. Within the library community itself, leadership in automation has been seized by a fee-based service—OCLC. Whatever its shortcomings, its customers voted with their dollars not only to sustain it, but to keep it expanding at an astonishing rate.

All mechanical systems operate with feedback and control devices, that is, with regulative mechanisms such as speed governors. An engine without a governor is prone to accelerate to self-destructive speeds; such a runaway engine can of course be stopped by completely shutting down the source of fuel. In effect something like that took place last year in California, with the Jarvis-Gann amendment—Proposition 13. Because regulative mechanisms were absent, fed up taxpayers could only turn off the main flow of funds to what they saw as runaway government services. A better balance between fee-based library services and free services might have led to more resilience in the face of shifts in the level of public support. Fee-based services might also give librarians better visibility over what services are really wanted or needed. Without such visibility the temptation to expand social and community programs with dubious connection to librarianship may be difficult to resist. The top priority recommendation of the Illinois White House conference is remarkable. "Library services should be provided to the unserved, underserved, and *unmotivated*."[14] Now those who are unmotivated, and in some cases illiterate, and who have some legitimate claim on public resources, may perceive other needs as having a higher priority than library services; for librarians to ask reluctant taxpayers for money to provide low-priority services to unwilling recipients may be seen as self-serving—however well intentioned.

In sum, I have offered four arguments in support of fee-based services to supplement free services within the public and not-for-profit sectors of the library field.

- Users of library services will benefit from having a wider range of choices. The more who choose to pay for extra services, the cheaper such services will tend to become for everyone.
- The support derived from user fees will cushion the impact of shifts in the level of public (or institutional) support.
- The choices made by users willing to pay for services will provide librarians with a vitally needed form of visibility or feedback indicating which services are most valued and which are inefficient or useless. Evolutionary selection can operate. Librarians will have a better method for knowing whether a service is dead or alive.
- User-fees will create conditions more hospitable to competition from the private sector, and so enhance both innovation and selective pressures. If this competition results in the death of certain services in either sector, then so be it; evolutionary mechanisms will have operated to the general benefit.

Peter Watson in a good overview of the issues in fee-based services has laid a heavy burden on librarians who oppose fees. They will have to show, he says, that fees are "ethically wrong, politically unwise, educationally unsound, and economically inefficient."[15]

ON-LINE INFORMATION SERVICES

The contemporary phenomenon of on-line information services searchable for a price is remarkable in many respects. I don't think that anyone nowadays is likely to argue against whatever claims are advanced as to the extraordinary potential importance of these services to the scientist and the scholar, and so to the growth of knowledge. Even so there is evidence that the circumstances responsible for this development may not be fully appreciated. I have been arguing that mechanisms of trial and error-elimination are crucial to the successful operation of certain kinds of complex systems. I suggest that this argument may be relevant to the rapid development of on-line services.

The relationship of these newer services to traditional library services can be seen from several perspectives. On-line services are in one sense an extension and enhancement of the bibliographic service that the research library has traditionally provided. Most on-line searches are in fact presently mediated by librarians.

However, such ties of dependency are becoming tenuous, and a different perspective may be more illuminating, or at least more provocative. A scientist or social scientist whose primary use of recorded knowledge is based on journal and report literature can now have in his office a bibliographic capability almost equivalent for his purposes to that of a large research library. The investment required is not out of reach of many individuals— $1000-$2000 or so for a computer terminal, perhaps a week of time learning the index structure and search command language for four or five key data bases relevant to the researcher's own specialty, and funds to cover costs per search. The degree of capability is no doubt higher in some specialties than others, and does not extend appreciably to the monograph literature, but my point is that coverage in some areas and some circumstances is as effective as that offered by a large library. Moreover the researcher is not totally dependent on a library even for the primary journal literature itself. Several data-base producers offer a mail-order service for copies of most journal articles or documents covered by the data base. Such services will take a great leap forward during 1979 if Lockheed carries out its stated intention[16] to supply a similar service for all (90 or so) DIALOG data bases. Of course all this is done for a price; its cost-effectiveness depends on how the user of the service values his time, and on the alternatives available. Even for those who have a large research library immediately at hand, it may in some situations now be more convenient and economical to bypass the library and use a commercial service on a pay-as-you-search basis. Moreover, such situations are expanding. In effect, then, some of the most important and most rapid improvements of library services have taken place outside of libraries, and, indeed, may eventually tend to diminish the relevance of libraries for at least some types of research. What can we learn from this state of affairs? Unforeseeable technological change is and always will be of central importance, but it is not the only factor. New technology is just as available to libraries as to other institutions, and need not in itself give rise to information services that bypass libraries. But it is clear that entrepreneurs in the private sector are much quicker to perceive and exploit the potential of new technology—and so tend to lead the way.

The fact that this rapid and extraordinary progress has taken place outside of libraries, independently of national planning, and even independently of large multi-institution coordination is not accidental. The services have developed in precisely the context that would be expected to foster progress and improvement in large, complex systems with distributed autonomy—a context that offers strong incentives to innovate, and which exacts a high price—annihilation by competitors—for failure. It is therefore a context especially hospitable to the evolutionary mechanisms of variation and selection.

PROPOSED CONSTRAINTS ON NATIONAL POLICY

Difficult problems and issues related to the interaction between the public and private sectors in the provision of information services have been of growing concern for several decades. Volume 13 of the *Annual Review of Information Science and Technology* includes, for the first time in that series, a chapter devoted to the literature of such issues. The authors particularly stress the "need for a clearer demarcation in the roles and responsibilities of the two sectors."[17] The arguments that I have offered in this paper can be seen as having certain implications with respect to such a demarcation. In particular, I propose that any national policy for library and information services be subject to certain specific constraints. That constraints are

necessary seems clear on the basis of certain published statements on national information goals, some aspects of which I
have commented upon in the Appendix of the background
paper.[18]

The cornerstone of national information policy should be to do
as little damage as possible. That is, national policy and programs should not interfere with the basic conditions within the
private sector that foster development of improved information
services. Such conditions are essentially twofold:

- the freedom and the incentive for individuals and institutions to assume risk and to take the initiative in developing
  and offering innovative information services.
- the presence of intense competition to insure that, through
  the mechanism of price, inefficient or non-useful services
  will be driven out.

It follows from the above that, insofar as the federal government establishes, operates, or subsidizes information services
that could feasibly be supplied by the private sector, and, provided vigorous competition within the private sector could arise,
such government services should recover costs from their users
at a level that would not preclude competition from the private
sector.

It is understood that social benefit may result from offering an
adequate and appropriate level of information services to economically disadvantaged users who may be unable to afford user
fees, including scholars working in many areas requiring extensive and expensive library materials. Rather than subsidize
what may be marginally useful or even unwanted information
services, it is preferable to subsidize users directly, by means that
might include grants as well as other mechanisms, so that the
recipients may then exercise choice in using information services
that they prefer.

Nothing in these constraints is intended to limit the extent of
federal, state, and local aid to libraries, to networks, and information services, or the degree to which disadvantaged individuals are assisted. It is the mechanism of assistance that is of
primary concern, a mechanism that will maximally preserve the
automatic, self-regulative evolutionary processes of variation
and selection that have demonstrably been effective in improving information services to the scientist, the scholar, and to the
public.

One hears much nowadays, particularly from the National Commission on Libraries and Information Science (NCLIS), about the "evolving national system." NCLIS claims to propose an evolutionary system, while at the same time proposes that it be "implemented" and "managed." These latter ideas are incompatible with evolution. One perhaps can have a little of either; but the more of one, the less of the other. To the extent that a system is designed, implemented, or managed, it's freedom to evolve is diminished. National planning can be directed toward the preservation of evolutionary mechanisms, but, insofar as it is, the result is in principle quite different from what is usually meant by a "national system."

It does not follow from my arguments that each library will or should choose to go its own way and disregard other libraries. Insofar as it is mutually advantageous for libraries to take collective action of some kind, cooperative arrangements can be expected to evolve. Mancur Olson has offered general arguments about the logic of collective action from which one might speculatively infer that small-scale cooperative networks of libraries are more likely to be formed than very large ones.[19] Hundreds of such networks have indeed formed. The conditions that Olson considers perhaps do not include, however, the circumstance in which the cohesion of a group depends on utilizing and contributing to a centralized service—a circumstance that accounts for the largest and most important networks, including OCLC. This question, admittedly, deserves closer study than I have been able to give it.

In the Appendix of the background paper,[20] I argued in effect that the NCLIS-ALA goal of "equal opportunity of access to information" is unintelligible. That does not mean, however, that it is innocuous; obviously there are people who claim to understand what it means and who will try to apply it. It poses therefore a direct threat to evolutionary mechanisms, and so to improvements, in library and information services. The nature of this threat should be widely understood, for its scope is not limited to libraries.

The notion of equality is complex and elusive. Equality before the law, and political equality, are not problematic in our consideration of evolutionary mechanisms. To speak of "equal opportunity," however, raises problems of serious proportions and differences of opinion; one can argue, for example, that the unequal distribution of wealth and income creates substantial inequities of opportunity. Or, the argument can be turned around. If everyone starts out with the same opportunity, great differences in economic outcome will result simply because people differ greatly in ability, inventiveness, resourcefulness, and productivity—even putting aside some rather important questions of pure luck. The pursuit of equality in American history, a story of many facets, is told by J.R. Pole in a scholarly monograph.[21] It is interesting to note that he gives little attention to the issue of what adverse effects on entrepreneurial trial-and-error mechanisms such a pursuit may have. Clearly a levelling of wealth and income would do away with all of the usual incentives to undertake ventures that entail new products and services, or to engage in risky, exploratory behavior in trying to discover the most suitable niche in the economic eco-system for ones' own special abilities and interests. *In short, the successful pursuit of equality of economic condition or outcome can bring entrepreneurial evolution to a stop.* We can all agree no doubt that it is unfair for someone to cheat in a poker game—and that everyone is to be treated equally under the rules of fair play—but there are many nowadays who seem to believe that it is equally unfair if someone wins. If winnings are automatically redistributed it becomes unclear as to who would then be willing to play the game. Evolution breeds both winners and losers; the only certain route to equality of condition is to arrange it so that we are all losers.

NOTES

1. Don R. Swanson, "Libraries and the Growth of Knowledge," *Library Quarterly* 49:1, 3-25 (1979).
2. Ibid., p. 15.
3. Karl R. Popper, *Conjectures and Refutations: The Growth of Scientific Knowledge* (New York: Harper Torchbooks, 1968). See Chapter 1.
4. Karl R. Popper, *Objective Knowledge—An Evolutionary Approach* (Oxford: Clarendon Press, 1975).
5. Karl R. Popper, *The Open Society and Its Enemies*, vols. 1 and 2 (New York: Harper Torchbooks, 1963).
6. Friedrich A. Hayek, *The Constitution of Liberty* (Chicago: University of Chicago Press, 1960).
7. Friedrich A. Hayek, *Law, Legislation, and Liberty*, vol. 1, Rules and Order (Chicago: University of Chicago Press, 1973).
8. U.S. Department of Commerce, Bureau of the Census. *Statistical Abstract of the United States*, 1978, p. 561, 581.

9. Pat L. Burr and Richard J. Heckman, "Why So Many Small Businesses Flop—and Some Succeed," *Across the Board* 16:2, 46-48 (Feb. 1979).
10. Popper, "The Open Society and Its Enemies," vol. 1, p. 162.
11. Patrick Wilson, Paper presented May 18 at the 40th Annual Conference of the Graduate Library School, University of Chicago.*
12. Carlos Cuadra, Paper presented May 19 at the 40th Annual Conference of the Graduate Library School, University of Chicago.*
13. Henriette D. Avram, "Toward a Nationwide Library Network," *Journal of Library Automation,* 11:4 (December 1978), p. 287.
14. Illinois White House Conference on Libraries and Information Science. Newsletter, February, 1979.
15. Peter Watson, "The Dilemma of Fees for Service: Issues and Action for Librarians," in *The ALA Yearbook 1978.* (Chicago: American Library Association, 1979), p. xxi
16. *Chronolog,* December 1978, vol. 6, p. 1.
17. Douglas E. Berninger and Burton W. Adkinson, "Interaction between the Public and Private Sectors in National Information Programs," in *Annual Review of Information Science and Technology,* vol. 13, Martha E. Williams, ed., 1978, pp. 3-36.
18. Swanson, "Libraries and the Growth of Knowledge," p. 20.
19. Mancur Olson, *The Logic of Collective Action: Public Goods and the Theory of Groups.* Harvard Economic Studies, vol. cxxiv (Cambridge, Mass.: Harvard University Press, 1971).
20. Swanson, "Libraries and the Growth of Knowledge," p. 22.
21. Jack Richon Pole, *The Pursuit of Equality in American History* (Berkeley, Calif.: University of California Press, 1978).

*To be published: Library Quarterly 50(1), January, 1980.

Coordinating
National Library Programs

Robert Wedgeworth, Executive Director
American Library Association
Chicago, Illinois

When the White House Conference on Libraries and Information Services opens on November 15 of this year, there is a major topic that is not likely to be given full discussion. This is an insider topic, one not likely to be uppermost in the minds of the largely lay delegation that will convene.

Notwithstanding, the fears and apprehensions of the library and information service community, the lay delegates are likely to bring a perspective and potential source of support to programs that sorely need it. Yet lurking just beneath the surface of discussions of new programs and unmet information needs will be the principal question of implementation.

Perhaps the ability to reorganize, revitalize and coordinate the recommended national library programs may well be the most significant problem facing the U.S. library and information service community today.

Our apparent inability to mount effective national plans and strategies to attack the preservation and conservation difficulties or to address the funding crises are not due to a failure of will as the courage of librarians has not been found wanting in their individual institutions. It is not due to a lack of creativity as the whole field is alive with new and ingenious ways to accomplish our chosen work. New network interconnections, new outreach services and new applications of ideas and technology are announced each month.

It is my contention that our difficulties lie in our lack of appreciation of the complexities of national coordination in a society where decisionmaking is not centered entirely within the government. I do not propose here to provide answers to these difficulties, but what I hope to do is to provoke what will be a continuing discussion of some basic concepts that need to be understood before we can determine an effective model for national coordination of U.S. library programs that we agree to implement.

In brief, the three concepts I wish to discuss are: 1) governance, or "who's in charge?"; 2) service, or "what do I get?"; and, 3) finance, or "who pays?" Rather than engage in a theoretical discussion of these yet undefined concepts, I would like to illustrate the problem by using two developments of 1978 as vehicles for analysis. First, the revision of the *Anglo-American Cataloging Rules*, and second, the proposal for a National Periodicals Center.

AACR2

The first discussion of a revision of the *Anglo-American Cataloging Rules*; which was published initially in 1967, occurred in March 1974, when representatives from the U.S., Canada and United Kingdom met at ALA Headquarters in Chicago to establish a Joint Steering Committee for this purpose. The objectives as announced were quite simple, the most basic of which was to reconcile the North American and the British text; but, of course, they also intended to move ahead by incorporating all changes which had occurred since 1967 to both editions, and to include all work that was in process.

Funds were obtained from the Council on Library Resources, Inc. to carry out the work, and the ALA Resources and Technical Services Division Cataloging Code Revision Committee undertook the job of coordinating U.S. participation. The record is quite clear that every party who had a legitimate interest in the revision of the *Anglo-American Cataloging Rules* (AACR2) was contacted; that the Committee met publicly twelve times, six times during ALA Annual or Midwinter Meetings; and that in the course of their work they recorded 894 separate decisions that were then fed into the deliberations of the Joint Steering Committee.

The real doubts about endorsing AACR2 surfaced just prior to ALA Annual Conference, when a letter from the Research Libraries Group formally requested a delay in considering the revision. At that point the letter was too late to be considered in detail, and the ALA with some discussion agreed on the text, whereupon the Library of Congress agreed to adopt the revised Rules effective 1 January 1980. The text was scheduled to be delivered to ALA by the editors in early 1978. When it was finally delivered in June of 1978, there was considerable controversy developing over a new code, at a time when management was being very cost-conscious.

During the 1978 ALA Annual Conference, the issue came to a head, leading to a proposal to organize a general meeting in August 1978 to bring together all organizations with an interest in the Rules revision to discuss these matters. In the meantime, the Association for Research Libraries voted to recommend a one-year delay by the Library of Congress.

The general meeting was held on August 3, 1978, at ALA Headquarters in Chicago. And it became clear that the revision of AACR was not the real issue, but that the proposed revision had brought to a head concern over the confluence of at least three developments: the revision of AACR2, the closing of the Library of Congress catalog, and the complexities of adopting new catalog forms such as on-line catalogs and computer-produced microfiche catalogs.

It is quite interesting to note that the National Library of Medicine, during the course of the August 3 meeting and the earlier controversy, could literally sit around smiling, since they were the only major research library to adopt the 1967 Rules in their entirety, and they were well aware that the revision of the 1967 Rules would have no great impact on those institutions which had not followed the Library of Congress in its superimposition policy, which meant that certain rules were not adopted from the original edition.

The purpose of going through this brief summary of events leading to the publication of the Second Edition of the *Anglo-American Cataloging Rules* in November 1978 is to suggest that two of the three concepts I have introduced here are applicable. It is interesting to note that 25 years ago the American Library Association and the Library of Congress might have decided the question of revising the Cataloging Rules, undertaken the work, announced the results to the library community, and gained its acceptance. The major difference between that time and today is that today the number and influence of organizations interested in this activity have grown enormously.

Twenty-five years ago, there was no National Commission on Libraries and Information Science, nor was there an OCLC Inc., or a Biomedical Communications Network. Specialized library associations for law, medicine and special libraries were, of course, active, but were also less vocal in terms of the technical concerns represented by the revision of the Rules. Moreover, the majority of the library directors leading the request to delay implementation of the revised rules were not in their present position in 1967. But the major difference today is not the increase in the number and the influence of organizations with interest in the revision of the Rules, but the fact that any significant combination of these organizations can effectively stall a national library program. This, indeed, is a significant governance issue, because the issue is not just *what* organization or which combination of organizations can make such decisions, but, indeed, *who* can make such decisions and have them be credible to the broader library community.

Although service was not an issue, there was considerable interest in finance, for the managers who became involved in the controversy over the revision of the Rules were concerned about how superimposition, notwithstanding extensive changes in the Rules, could be forced on any group without its agreement. It did not make a difference to the managers that they had had adequate opportunity to address these issues during the process of the revision; the fact was that assessing costs became the rallying point for opposition, the question being who was going to pay for the allegedly extensive changes resulting from the revision of the Rules?

The resolution was that the ad hoc meeting called at ALA Headquarters cleared the air, relieved the pressure by having the Library of Congress agree to a one-year delay in implementation of the new Rules, and it also resulted in ALA agreeing to establish a monitoring and communications mechanism to guide the implementation of AACR2 and future revision plans. It raised the visibility of the issue to a national level, and obtained clear agreement on the approach, hence, credibility with the broader library community.

One lesson that the technical experts involved in the revision of the Rules might learn is that the politics of change may be every bit as important as the substance of change. In this case what was at stake was the ability to implement the changes in Rules, once the changes had been agreed upon.

The August 3 meeting can be viewed as a symbolic occasion for no new data was presented and no substantive challenges to AACR2 emerged in the discussion. The fact that the Library of Congress agreed to a one-year delay in implementing the revised code at the request of the group assembled represented a symbolic victory.

NATIONAL PERIODICALS CENTER

The second development in 1978 which is of interest is the proposal for a national periodicals center to be administered by a national library agency. Briefly, in 1977 the National Commission on Libraries and Information Science proposed the creation of a National Periodicals Center in order to improve access to the nation's journal literature collections. The proposal recommended that the Library of Congress assume the responsibility for developing, managing and operating the Center. The Library of Congress in turn asked that the Council on Library Resources, Inc., prepare a technical development plan which could be used to prepare for establishing such a facility.

The Technical Development Plan was released in late 1978. The NCLIS assumptions involved in this plan were that there would be a National Periodicals System consisting of three tiers: the bottom tier being local, state and regional capabilities to provide access to journal literature; the middle tier being the National Periodicals Center for periodical literature in moderate demand, and it was estimated that a collection of 36,000 titles could satisfy 90% of the demand for journal literature; and the top tier being a referral system to the many specialized collections of journal literature around the nation which would be accessed via some mechanism to be administered by the Library of Congress.

From the very beginning there appeared to be a general consensus in favor of the National Periodicals Center, with the primary benefits seen to be a reduction in collection maintenance costs, and an improvement in the efficiency of the interlibrary loan system. However, when the Technical Plan was introduced last fall, controversy was ignited by the little gem buried on page

136 of the Technical Development Plan, proposing that there be a national library board or a national library agency to administer the Center and other national programs projected, including a communications system.

Immediately, questions arose. Who would appoint the members of such a national library board? What authority would the National Library Agency have over existing agencies at the federal, state and local level? Would it divert funding from other library programs, specifically from the Library Services and Construction Act, and from the Higher Education Act?

It is interesting to note here that there was some confusion over which organizations were the sponsors of this proposal. Was it the Council on Library Resources, Inc., which had brought together a number of foundations to provide support for the development of national bibliographic plans? Was it the Association for Research Libraries, was it the Center for Research Libraries, or was it the National Commission? And where, indeed, did the American Library Association figure into those plans?

Since the late 1978 controversy, the library community has moved to resolve this controversy by using a familiar mechanism—another ad hoc meeting. This meeting convened in mid-March, reviewed the plans, and provided a consensus of support for a National Periodicals Center, but set aside the proposal for a National Library Agency. The major concepts involved in this particular development are governance, service and finance.

Here, too, it was obvious that no clear mechanism had been identified for addressing the question of a National Periodicals Center, for coming to precise conclusions, and for developing plans for implementation. Significant elements of the library community important for the implementation of a plan were left out of the early deliberations, specifically, the American Library Association and the state library agencies. The institution with the most extensive periodicals access system operating in this country, the National Library of Medicine, was not prominently included in the plans to develop the Center or the National Periodicals System. These statements are not to be taken as indictments of the proposal, but as further evidence of our lack of a governance structure that allows us to take in questions of national significance, analyze them, research them, and reach appropriate conclusions involving all of the interested parties.

As far as service is concerned, there still remain many unchallenged assumptions. The first regards cost reductions. Our experience with state and regional resource sharing would suggest that greater efficiencies generate greater demand, hence, larger expenditures. Yet in the proposal, we are generally faced with an assumption that the development of a National Periodicals Center will reduce the amount of money spent on gaining access to periodical literature.

We are also facing the unchallenged assumption that a central lending library operation similar to the British Lending Library improves efficiency. Yet, we can only say in response to this, as an economist might say, other things being equal. For 1) we are assuming low cost, fast delivery systems—the U.S. mail? 2) a low inventory, staff intensive heavily duplicated collection; 3) a simple transaction system—the Copyright Clearance Center? 4) no copyright problems; and 5) abundant, inexpensive labor. While none of these are determinative factors, they are quite influential in being able to reach the objectives of improving efficiency through a centralized operation. We can be sure that at some level there will need to be a National Periodicals Center, but the scope of parameters of the services that will be offered by a National Periodicals Center might very well result from a careful assessment of what can be provided through systems already operating on state and regional bases as well as the resources available locally, with the National Periodicals Center backing up those systems and providing additional services.

In general, we can say that increased access to the nation's periodical literature will come as much through increased computer-based access mechanisms, as through increased stores of journal literature.

But finance is still the most elusive question. Some assert that the climate is not right for federal financing of a National Periodicals Center. Yet we all realize that at some point there will have to be such a Center. Can the concept be implemented without heavy subsidies, and what is the price of federal financing? I would assert that we must find a better means to address these questions and to move them toward concrete implementation than our present reliance on the ad hoc meeting to discuss any significant proposal that comes along.

When the White House Conference is over and the field is heir to its recommendations some organized method for pursuing implementation programs will need to develop.

While the ad hoc meetings to revolve crises address the limitations of authority and influence of organizations, they lack continuity of involvement, emotional overtones distort the issues under discussion, and they are doubtful in terms of their long range effectiveness. We need to recognize that the major actors on the American library organization stage have multiplied; that while a statutory solution to the problem of governance may not be acceptable to the library community in the form of a National Library Agency created by the Congress, we cannot ignore that we have a problem with governance when we reject such a solution.

In my opinion, the library community lacks the strength to control appointments to a statutory body, and perhaps a voluntary governance mechanism is an obvious next step. We need to give greater scrutiny to services as distinct from needs, moving away from what I like to call the unanalyzed abstraction, such as giving equal access to periodical literature, to recognize that there can be no operational entity until the concepts are defined in operational terms.

Shared expectations can lead to effective compromises on reality. The different organizations involved in the development of national library services have different interests, but until we can come to share those interests and develop optimal solutions, we will not be able to develop effective programs based on the realities of library life.

Finally, we must learn to use organizational response mechanisms effectively. Negotiation, compromise and trade-offs should not be considered in negative terms alone. These are effective ways of resolving differences and given the many different responsible agencies in the library field in America, we must learn to use them.

Given the richness and diversity of library and information service programs in the U.S., any governance mechanism we adopt must recognize that our world has become much more complex over the past two decades. The interdependence of government agencies, private for-profit and private not-for-profit organizations are a distinct advantage we enjoy: commercial support, innovative capital-intensive programs and service. Government agencies develop and sustain costly services that are needed but are needed but are not necessarily viable commercially. Nonprofit organizations provide leadership and continuity oriented toward professional goals.

Once the White House Conference has provided guidance from our user publics, those who comprise the enduring support for information service programs must move quickly to agree upon a governance structure that encourages the discussion of national library problems.

Increasingly, such discussions will take place in international arenas like IFLA, FID, ICA and UNESCO. Who will speak for the U.S. in these arenas?

We must move to answer that and other governance questions before the issues have left us in favor of less judicious solutions.

PART III

Network Technology and Standards

Network Technology Today*

Hank Epstein, President
Information Transform Industries
Costa Mesa, California

INTRODUCTION

In order to describe the current state of on-line library network technology, it will be necessary to describe the physical and functional aspects of these networks: the network services and products provided, the form of terminals and network communications utilized, the factors affecting network growth, and an overview of network cost factors for each type of network. Centralized and distributed network architecture, current network limitations, and future trends in networking are then described in terms of the same physical and functional aspects.

What Is an On-line Network?

Figure 1 provides a first look at the *functional* attributes of a network. The key to all network services is the network file; the network service must provide a useful file for the members to share. The network members must be conveniently able to locate the records they require. After locating the appropriate records in a network file, the users of the service generally perform one of three types of activities: 1) copy the records, i.e., search services; 2) copy and modify for localized use, i.e., cataloging or other

*Portions of this paper are based on the author's article "The Networking of Networks: An Overview of U.S. Networks" which appeared in the June 1979 issue of the Bulletin of the American Society of Information Science.

111

Figure 1. What Is a Network?

(in functional terms)
    —function
    —example
    —end products

Generally, a network vendor (or consortium) has an on-line file

which many users from different libraries wish to search in order to find a particular item

and:
a. *copy (unchanged) for local use*
        i.e., Search Services—
        The end products are abstracts and citations to journal articles

b. *copy, modify as needed, or add a new item, and replace in the file*
        i.e., Cataloging Services—
        The end products are catalog cards, computer tapes, and a shared file (for cataloging and ILL), and
        Book Ordering Services—
        The end products are purchase orders sent on-line to the book dealer

c. *keep a record of their own activity*
        i.e., Circulation Services—
        The end products are up-to-the moment files showing the circulation status of library material, and periodic reports and notices (Turnkey system)

customized services; or 3) update a file to keep track of local activity, i.e., circulation or serials check-in services (See Figure 1).

Search Service Networks

The search service networks provide multiple data bases or files to search; major search services are illustrated (See Figure 2). The multiple data-base vendors tend to be commercial (Lockheed, System Development Corporation (SDC), Bibliographic Retrieval Services (BRS) and provide access to over 30 million unique bibliographic records for over 4000 users. The vendors generally obtain the data bases from data base suppliers (mostly the abstracting and indexing [A&I] services) on a fixed and/or royalty cost basis.

The users generally search one file at a time (unless the files and their indexes have been combined by the search service vendor) and print the results of the search on their local terminal printer during the search process (for a moderate amount of output) or the vendor's high speed printer (for extensive output). This printed output is then mailed to the user. The user price is determined by the particular file selected and the amount of searching (the time connected to the search service computer).

FIGURE 2. Search Services and Value Added Networks (VANs)

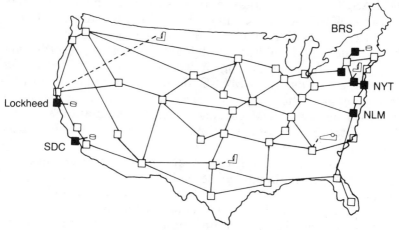

VAN: TYMNET, TELENET

SEARCH SERVICES: LOCKHEED, SDC, BRS

Users: 4000 libraries, companies, agencies

Files: 150–200 (30 million records)

Access: VAN, dial-up, dedicated line

Terminals: Hardcopy, CRT (not OCLC)

Search services do not provide the ability for users to modify the records in the files, nor to modify the output. That is not the nature of the service. Recently some pilot experiments have been implemented to capture the search results in machine readable form, from approved data bases, during the on-line session for further processing and later display.

Occasionally a data base supplier provides the exclusive searching to their own files (New York Times [NYT], National Library of Medicine [NLM]) and becomes in effect a single, data-base search service.

Customized Service Networks

Customized service networks provide bibliographic files for users to search, modify individual records for their local use, and obtain a variety of printed and machine readable products showing their localized data. The individual records in the network files are most often obtained from the network users themselves or from MARC tapes from the Library of Congress (LC).

The most widely known customized service networks are the "cataloging" networks (OCLC, RLIN-BALLOTS, WLN, UTLAS). OCLC, the largest of these services, supports over 1600 libraries with files approaching five million records (See Figure 3). OCLC users add 3000 new shared cataloging records and 40,000 additional holdings statements to existing records each day. Each of the cataloging networks supply users with magnetic tape records (in the MARC format) containing the library's local changes. These tapes are used to generate supplementary products such as COM catalogs, files for circulation systems, union catalogs and, at some time in the future, local data bases for on-line catalogs.

Circulation systems form the next type of customized network (See Figure 4). Although most on-line circulation systems are "stand-alone" (all of the circulation hardware including the main computer and the files is located within the library) several users have formed an automated interlibrary loan (ILL) network by interconnecting their computers on a dial-up basis and processing ILL requests. These ILL requests are transmitted from the terminal at the borrowing library, through its own computer and files, to the computer and into the files of the lending library. There are also many network examples of multiple libraries

FIGURE 3. Cataloging: OCLC Network

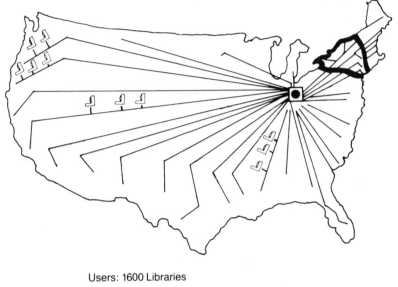

Users: 1600 Libraries

Terminals: 2000 on Dedicated Lines

Daily Activity: 40,000 existing records customized

3000 new records added

Searching (4.5 million records)

Interlibrary Loan Location (45 million holdings)

New Interlibrary Loan Subsystem

sharing a single stand-alone system, where the central computer and files are located in one of the member libraries, and the terminals are located in all libraries that are members of the network.

Circulation files tend to be as large as the number of titles and volumes held in a library, once the records have been converted to machine-readable form. File sizes of 10,000 titles and 100,000 volumes with a circulation of one million items per year is not uncommon for a circulation system. Large libraries with multimillion volume collections tend to keep circulation records for only a portion of their collection, generally the highly circulated materials. There are a few notable exceptions where the entire collection of a large library has been converted and is circulated through the automated system. A few circulation systems oper-

FIGURE 4. Circulation: Stand-Alone and Networks

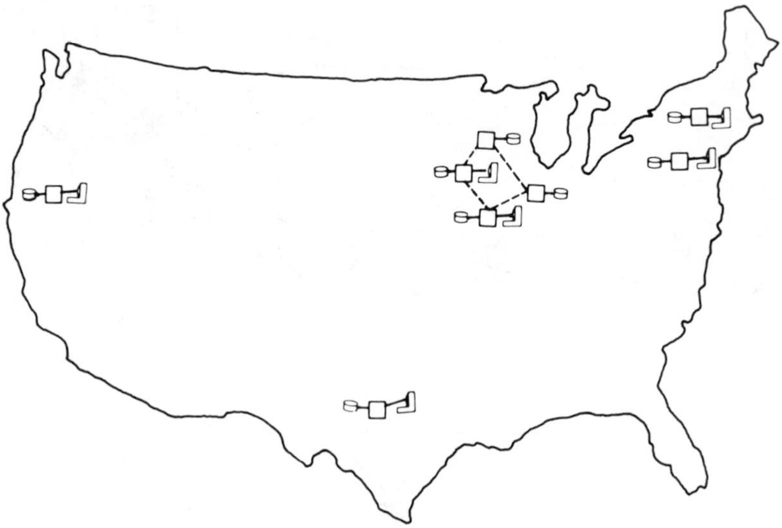

Installations: 200 (approx.)

Systems: 6 vendors, in-house

Interlibrary Loan: by dial-up

Circulation: 200,000 to 1 million each installation

Files: Books, copies, patrons

Unmet Need: Cost effective communications for ILL

ate on shared large computers as one of several simultaneous library and nonlibrary applications. Most of the circulation systems, however, are stand-alone and operate on a mini-computer.

At least one circulation vendor does have a centralized and partially distributed circulation network. With this network the circulation and patron files are stored centrally, and the day's transactions are collected on a minicomputer or a portable recorder and transmitted to the central computer regularly.

ILL Network (From a Cataloging File)

The newest ILL network is the pilot ILL subsystem at OCLC. The OCLC catalog file contains over 4.5 million records and 45 million holdings statements, representing an average of ten copies of each of the 4.5 million titles. These holdings statements, which are a by-product of the cataloging process, form the largest location file available on a network today. Its value as an ILL location tool has already changed the method and style of ILL processing in U.S. libraries, even prior to the pilot ILL subsystem.

Retrospective Conversion Network

Customized service networks also support on-line retrospective conversion network activities. All of the cataloging networks provide this service, allowing a user to search a file, modify a record if found or key in a new record, and obtain the custom record on magnetic tape.

Network Growth Factors

Five major factors that affect the growth of networks are illustrated (See Figure 5). The response to these factors for the search, cataloging, and circulation networks is also shown.

Network Cost Factors

The cost factors for networks are enumerated (See Figure 6); the user price formula and economy of scale considerations, and exceptions, are also shown in the Figure.

Network Synergy

One of the most interesting and profound activities in networking is the continual arrival of new products and services that affect networks. In many cases the new service is the product of two previously unrelated or incompatible services. For example, as a pilot test the 1.2 million record resource file of a COM vendor was combined with an on-line stand-alone circulation system to form a stand-alone conversion service. Using the standard circulation mini-computer (with some additional terminals and disc storage) a large public library obtained an 85 percent hit rate for 250,000 titles from this file. As a result of this joint venture the two vendors are now installing an on-line network

FIGURE 5. Why Have Networks Developed and Continued to Grow?

Five Factors
1. Main advantage of service
2. Vendors primary contribution to service
3. Alternatives to network service
4. Vendors investment in network service
5. Users investment in network service

A. *Search Services—*
1. Others have generated the files (A&I)
2. Vendor has arranged files to find relevant items
3. Alternatives: printed files, single indexes
4. Software, hardware, files (license and storage)
5. Terminal, $/hour searching, training

B. *Cataloging Services—*
1. Others have generated majority of records
2. Vendor has made it "easy" to modify or add records
3. Copy reference cataloging, do original cataloging, type cards
4. Software, hardware, network communications
5. File contributions, terminals, $/transaction, training

C. *Circulation Services—*
1. Record keeping is highly automated
2. Vendor has made it "simple" to update the file
3. Write out, photocopy, file, search manually
4. Software, hardware (until purchase), maintenance
5. $'s for hardware, file conversion, $'s for maintenance

Bottom Line Questions
1. Is the network service worth the price?
      (value of the file is a critical component)
2. Is the network unit price less than the cost of providing the service
      locally? (the answer changes over time)

FIGURE 6. Cost of Networks

A. *Fixed Costs* (75-95% of total costs)
   1. Data Collection
   2. Data conversion
   3. Data storage
   4. File processing—operations
   5. Hardware
   6. Facilities
   7. Development

B. *Variable Costs—User Generated* (5-25% of total costs)
   1. Searching
   2. Processing
   3. Terminal and printer output
   4. Operations

C. *User Price* (Costs to User)
   1. Total Cost = Fixed + Variable Costs

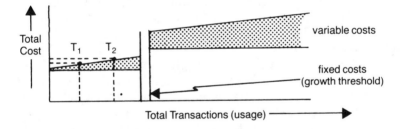

   2. User Price = $\dfrac{\text{Total Cost (+ profit)}}{\text{Total User Transactions*}}$

   3. *"Economy of Scale"*—The unit cost will decrease with an increase
      in transactions.**
           Exceptions: system expansion beyond threshold,
                —new technology and network architecture are
                     functions of time,
                —local availability of useful resource files
                     (also a function of time)

*(search hours, titles cataloged, etc.)
**T_2 = twice the transaction load of T_1.
   The cost of T_2 is slightly more than the cost of T_1.
   The unit cost of T_2 transactions is much less than for T_1 transactions.

service where a library rents the terminals, performs the retrospective conversion, returns the terminals, and receives the magnetic tapes and/or discs. This type of synergy is appearing more frequently in U.S. networks. Other examples will be described in later sections.

Service Center Networks

This type of network is an organization rather than an on-line network, and does not now provide automated services directly. Service center networks are the people side of the networks in the sense of training, consulting, installation, and planning for a large group of libraries. Currently the automated services are provided through the cataloging or search service vendors, with the service centers acting as brokers. The service center networks are organizationally separate from the on-line network vendors and often represent the member libraries in network matters. Many of these networks will become on-line service providers within the next five years. Service center networks generally represent a geographic area: New England (NELINET), Southern (SOLINET), Southwest (AMIGOS), and others. Some service center networks support one type of library, such as federal or law.

Several service center networks have begun planning and development activities for a variety of on-line and batch network services including: the merging of member library tapes to form regional services such as a union catalog; conversion of catalog tapes to circulation files; the loading of the cataloging, circulation and conversion tapes from member libraries into a regional on-line catalog with subject searching; local and regaional authority files; interlibrary loan and reference searching.

Generation of Files

The proliferation of machine-readable records representing library holdings and bibliographic data has overcome one of the major roadblocks to the implementation of automation and on-line network services—the cost of generating a file large enough to offer some reasonable level of service. (For instance, a file of the last six months of cataloging has limited reference and patron value, while a file of the last five years of cataloging activity is a much more useful resource.)

Files are beginning to beget other files. One new and innovative service being offered by a retrospective conversion vendor is to take a tape copy of a circulation file (which generally contains very brief bibliographic records with detailed holdings, locations and copy data), convert this to a file of full bibliographic records from a resource file, and produce a COM catalog. (Normally users of automated cataloging services have taken their full cataloging records and stripped them down to brief circulation records.) Libraries without automated cataloging systems or a machine-readable file have generally keyed in brief circulation records to the circulation system; through this new conversion service, they now have the ability to obtain full bibliographic records in machine-readable form (from their brief bibliographic records) for local use.

THE TECHNOLOGY OF NETWORKS

These same networks can now be described by the form of *network technology* utilized by the network. All of the services described above (except the stand-alone circulation systems) are "centralized" networks; that is, there is a central computer plus central files which are accessed by all terminals on the network (See Figure 7A). The search services, customized services (including cataloging and ILL networks), and service centers deal with centralized networks.

Distributed Networks

Another form of network is the "distributed" network where the computers (hosts) and their associated files are distributed throughout the network. Although there have been several designs for distributed systems (where the network transactions are routed from the local terminal to the local host, then to the proper host for the service requested, processed by the new host and the response returned to the original host, files and terminal), the only example of a distributed network system now in operation is the interlibrary loan network described above which interconnects on-line (stand-alone) circulation systems (See Figure 7B). Each of the circulation hosts, while independently processing circulation transactions, will also process a network interlibrary loan transaction on request from another host and

FIGURE 7. Architecture of Networks

A. Centralized Network

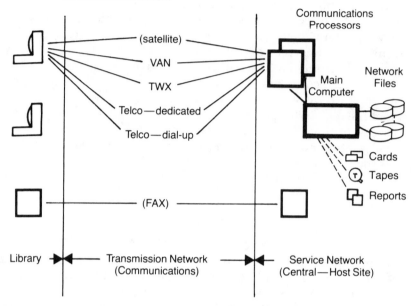

B. Distributed Network—Stand-alone Based

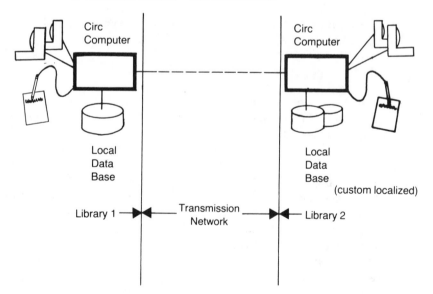

FIGURE 7. *Continued*

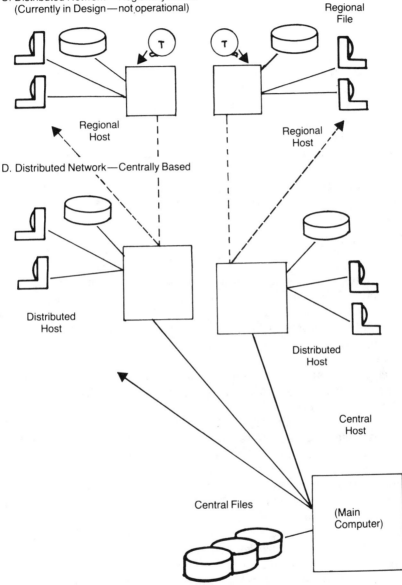

C. Distributed Network—Regionally Based
(Currently in Design—not operational)

Regional
File

Regional
Host

Regional
Host

D. Distributed Network—Centrally Based

Distributed
Host

Distributed
Host

Central
Host

Central Files

(Main
Computer)

return to its original stand-alone workload. Many of the current stand-alone systems will eventually be linked together to form networks. Different types of network architecture are portrayed in Figure 7.

COMMUNICATION NETWORKS

Communication networks consist of the hardware and software necessary to transmit messages from the user's terminal to the host computer. The hardware consists of the lines, modems, communications computers and the users' terminals. Several types of communication services and networks are available, from those offering services to the user who needs one terminal to access a host for a few minutes per month, to those for a user who has 25 terminals on-line for 12 hours per day.

Value Added Networks

The most widely used communications networks are the commercial Value Added Networks (VANs). The VANs (See Figure 2) lease a large number of inter-city telephone lines from the telephone companies, and place small message switching computers at various nodes. In each city served by a VAN there is communications equipment capable of receiving dozens to hundreds of simultaneous calls from terminals. There are also network hosts (computers offering various services) including the network vendors (providing search services and cataloging services) which pay the VAN to connect to the VAN network. A library user at a dial-up terminal in one of the VAN cities served can dial a local telephone number of the VAN equipment and indicate which of the various service hosts (search service, cataloging service and others) is to be connected to the terminal for the current terminal session. From then on, the message switching computers will route all messages from that terminal to the selected host and from the selected host back to the terminal. Since a message transaction takes a small fraction of a second to transmit, many terminals can share the same line, in much the same way that many autos can share the same highway lane.

In this way the VAN makes heavier use of the line than a single user paying for a long distance call. The VANs charge the network host, who in turn bills the user, for the amount of time connected and the number of messages and characters transmitted. Since there is no charge component for geographic distance, the user 3000 miles from a service host and a user 150 miles from the same host pay the same cost for the same service. There is a great cost advantage to the distant user, since the savings between a long distance call and the VAN charge is larger with distance.

Most service networks that are hosts on a VAN network also have dial-up capability independent of the VAN which allows the user to dial the host computer directly. This is advantageous for users located nearby the host and users with special telephone service such as WATS. Terminals that have dial-up capability can be used either for direct dial or by accessing the VAN network.

Dedicated Line Networks

Heavy users of terminal services may lease a permanent (24 hour per day) dedicated line from their terminal directly to a host. The cost is dependent on line speed and distance of the line, and can become quite expensive if the line is long and can only be used by one terminal.

Service networks that require heavy use of lines generally lease telephone lines from the host computer to the terminals. In the case of the cataloging networks the "intelligent" terminals have the ability to distinguish between messages meant for other terminals on the line and messages directed to the particular terminal. This allows many terminals to share a dedicated line in a manner similar to a telephone party line. The OCLC network (See Figure 3) has 2000 terminals with approximately 25 terminals on each line, reducing the per terminal share of the line cost by a factor of 25, equalizing the cost among all the terminals on the line. The additional use of these lines, and some extensions to these lines, for interfaces to other hosts, other networks, and other terminals would provide a great amount of additional service for a relatively small increment cost.

NETWORKING OF NETWORKS

There is a growing need to provide an on-line interface between existing networks and between stand-alone systems and networks. The services or records available on one network are required on another network. The current network limitations in this area are shown (See Figure 8), along with the current solution required to overcome the limitation.

The National Network Goals

A connection between two cataloging networks would make the records of each network available to the users and files of the other network. This is currently being planned as part of the national network development activity.

In developing a national network, the technical problems to be overcome include the noncompatible terminals, records, communications lines, line protocols, search languages, commands, search responses, output screen formats and interactive dialog between the user and the terminal. The results, however, will be well worth the development effort. Users on their existing termi-

Figure 8. Current Network Limitations

Limitations	Today's Solution	Impact of Solution
A. Terminals not compatible between networks	Use multiple terminals	$2000 to $4000 each
B. Communication lines not compatible —Dedicated lines not shared between networks —VAN lines not efficient —Dial-up lines very expensive	Use different or redundant transmission services	Pay redundant line costs —Higher costs —Slower response time
C. Network user language not compatible	Learn all required languages	Human limits to memory Multiple training costs
D. Files and records not compatible	Convert to tape Mail to user Reconvert to new file —Circulation files —COM —Union catalog —On-line catalog	Added development cost Time delay for information transfer

nals and lines could search, extract, review and modify records from the other network, and add the revised record to their own files.

Interfaces

The interface between a dedicated line network such as the cataloging networks and the search service computers (See Figure 9) would provide the cataloging users with a much less expensive interface to the search services. In addition to the charge paid for searching a data base, users currently must pay a communication cost either in the form of a charge from the telephone company for a telephone call to the search service computer or, most often, to the search service for the use of one of the VANs (See Figure 7A). This communications cost would be replaced by the (presumably lower) cost charged by the cataloging network for the communication service. The three cataloging networks and at least one of the circulation vendors are planning

FIGURE 9. Interfaces: Networking of Networks

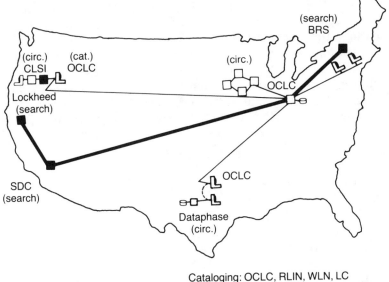

Cataloging: OCLC, RLIN, WLN, LC

Circulation: CLSI, Dataphase, Gaylord, LCS

Search Services: Lockheed, SDC, BRS

interfaces to the search services. This interface should be implemented by 1985 for most of the networks.

The interface between a circulation system and a cataloging or ILL network (See Figure 9) would provide the circulation system with the ability to copy bibliographic records from a cataloging file and place these records in the circulation file, and to request interlibrary loan material. The ILL user at a terminal could review the circulation status of all copies of a title from a circulation file and request an interlibrary loan or place a hold on an item. At present there are two different circulation systems that can search a cataloging network's files, extract, modify and convert the record into the circulation format, and place the custom record in the circulation file; all of this activity occurs on-line in a matter of a few seconds (beyond the time necessary for the user to key in any bibliographic variances).

NEW TRENDS IN NETWORKING

There are many new trends in networking; due to space limitations it is only possible to mention a few.

1. There will be a continual array of new service and product offerings. For example, OCLC is planning the installation of a Remote Communications Processor (RCP) to reduce the communications line costs of the network (See Figure 10). As a result of this development, it will then be possible to add a user owned computer called a "foreign host" to the OCLC RCP and provide additional user developed regional services to the libraries within the region. Some of the additional regional services being considered by the SUNY/OCLC network are shown below.

Potential SUNY Host Applications (Regional Services)

SUNY/OCLC—NYSILL Interface
NYSILL ILL Request Transmission
SUNY/OCLC Electronic Mail
Interface with Search Services
On-line Circulation Interface
Tape Processing of OCLC Tapes
Interface to Other Networks
On-line Training Modules
   a. CAI
   b. Audio-Digital

FIGURE 10. OCLC Plans and Development

Line Concentration and Foreign Host

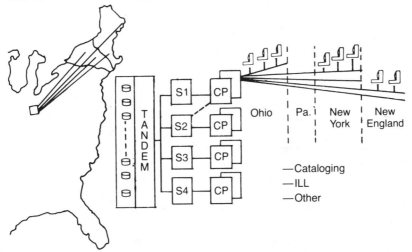

a—Current Line Configuration, Applications, and Message Switching

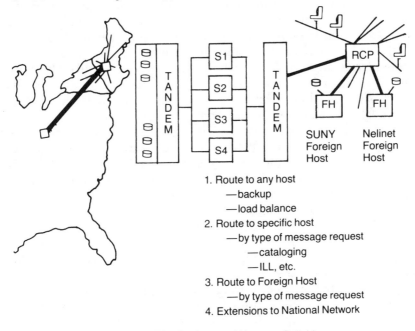

1. Route to any host
   —backup
   —load balance
2. Route to specific host
   —by type of message request
      —cataloging
      —ILL, etc.
3. Route to Foreign Host
   —by type of message request
4. Extensions to National Network

b—Future Line Configuration, Applications, and Message Switching

Text Editing, Word Processing, Publishing
Special Reports
Electronic Conferencing

2. Many of these offerings will have significant impact on the services offered by libraries, and the form of these services. The impact of patron touch terminals and on-line catalogs are two examples.

3. Vendors of a particular service, such as circulation or cataloging, will expand their services to other areas with high overlap of services between vendors of different services. For example, "circulation" vendors now offer ILL networking, on-line cataloging and retrospective conversion. "Cataloging" networks now offer ILL and retrospective conversion, and are planning to offer various forms of circulation services.

4. Vendors of different services are building interfaces between their services, sometimes creating new services. Most of the examples described in this paper have been developed within the last 12 to 18 months.

5. Interfaces of stand-alone systems into "sub-networks," which in turn will become larger networks and eventually part of the "national network," will continue throughout the 1980s.

6. On-line networks are considering offering services normally considered stand-alone, such as circulation, serials check-in, local on-line catalogs and regional ILL. These services would be part of a distributed network with local or regional files, yet be connected to the central host computer and files.

7. Planning of network services among users will improve as more clearly defined and technically reasonable requirements, schedules, and priorities are generated and documented. Several service centers and individual states are developing long-range plans with associated budgets to provide some of the services, products and interfaces described.

8. As technology continues to improve in power and decrease in cost, there will be additional activities supported at the regional and local library levels. These activities will in effect be transferred from the centralized cataloging services to the regionally distributed network service centers (See Figure 11), and eventually to the local libraries (See Figure 12). This is a somewhat unique example of points 1 through 7 above.

9. The "national data base" will not be a single data base but rather a highly distributed and hierarchical network of data

FIGURE 11. Regional Data Bases

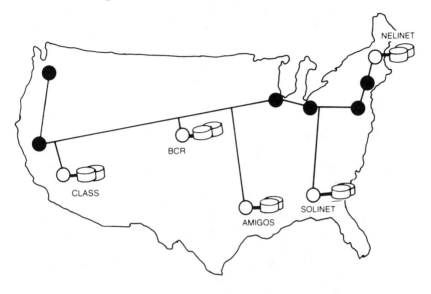

FIGURE 12. Local Library Data Bases

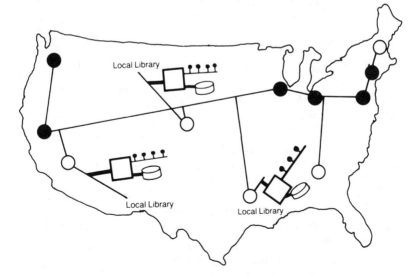

bases (See Figure 13). Detailed data of local interest, such as circulation data, will be maintained at the local library; data sufficient to satisfy the local patron, such as searching the on-line catalog, will also be maintained locally. Regional data bases will maintain a summary of local library data sufficient to provide regional services such as interlibrary loan.

UNMET NEEDS

Message Protocols

The greatest unmet need in library networking is the lack of implemented network standards for network message traffic. Successful implementation of the library network line and message protocols would provide the ability of any network to communicate with any other network. The ability for any terminal to access any host or data base through the local terminal connection, request any of a number of different services, and receive the results of the service on the local terminal and in the local file is one of the major goals of the national network (See Figure 14). The service requested could be any service offered on the network. Some of the preliminary design work to develop the protocols has been completed through committees of network developers and coordinated by LC. What remains is to complete the detailed design, and implement the network protocols on a variety of hosts including cataloging, circulation, ILL and any other type of host that wishes to offer on-line services to libraries.

Access to Multiple Data Bases

In all current operational networks the user must learn the search language and search strategy of any service to be utilized. To use four systems requires training in all four systems plus the ability to remember the rules, languages, and other facets without applying the transactions to the wrong system. Reference searchers are familiar with this problem area since some reference searchers are frequently called upon to search six to eight networks, each somewhat different.

With some form of augmented user interface, a trained OCLC user wishing to use Lockheed, or a trained National Library of Medicine (NLM) user wishing to search a circulation file, would be able to express the request in the original language, perhaps respond to some additional questions presented as part of the new interface and wait for the results.

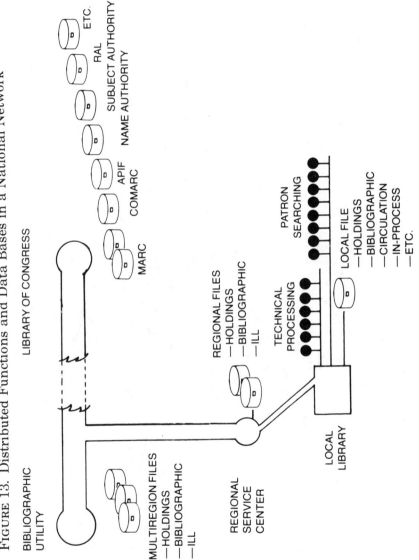

Figure 13. Distributed Functions and Data Bases in a National Network

BIBLIOGRAPHIC
UTILITY

LIBRARY OF CONGRESS

MARC
COMARC
APIF
NAME AUTHORITY
SUBJECT AUTHORITY
RAL
ETC.

MULTIREGION FILES
—HOLDINGS
—BIBLIOGRAPHIC
—ILL

REGIONAL
SERVICE
CENTER

REGIONAL FILES
—HOLDINGS
—BIBLIOGRAPHIC
—ILL

TECHNICAL
PROCESSING

PATRON
SEARCHING

LOCAL
LIBRARY

LOCAL FILE
—HOLDINGS
—BIBLIOGRAPHIC
—CIRCULATION
—IN-PROCESS
—ETC.

FIGURE 14. The National Network: All Networks are Created
Equal

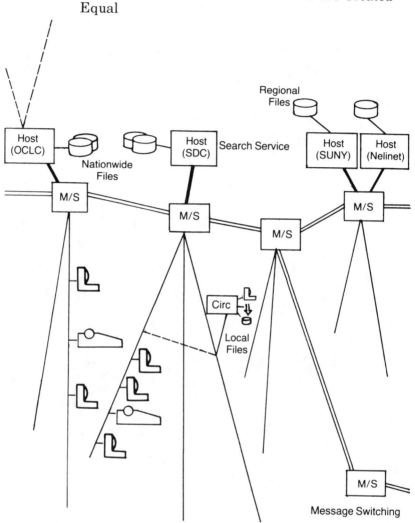

Unmet Needs: Line Protocol (term. & host)

Message Protocol (term. & host)

M/S and Communications Network

(Search Language & Commands)

Formats and Conversion

Natural Language Interface

Current research in the area of augmented user interface is exploring many different aspects and approaches of solving this problem. One approach is to develop a natural language interface where the computer attempts to understand the use of "plain" English including disciplinary jargon, conversational ellipsis, and incomplete sentences.

Another research approach is to present the user with a menu to fill out and, based on the results of one menu, choose the next menu until enough information is available to select the appropriate data base, provide the selected host with the proper search terms, act in an interactive mode (or let the user participate in the interactive responses) and display the results. One experimental system on a minicomputer at the Massachusetts Institute of Technology (MIT) can interface with several different VANs, search service hosts, and individual data bases by dialing up and logging on to the VAN and the host, and select the proper data base. Another less complex system at an abstracting and indexing (A&I) service can interface with a single VAN and one search service, including log-on and selection of a single data base (from those data base suppliers that permit the receipt of machine-readable output), perform the search, collect all the search results and log off the system. The system then presents the search results to the user for review. The user will eventually be able to select and reject records (from the set of previously recorded records) and format the final results for display or printing.

It is entirely possible that a combination of approaches will evolve as the most practical and effective improvement in the interface to multiple data base network services.

CONCLUSION

On-line networks are vital to the successful operation of libraries. As more services involving the transfer and exchange of information about library material become available, on-line networks will become an integral part of the library environment. The technology is changing very rapidly; new innovative services will continue to be introduced and in turn be offered as new services directly to the library patron or indirectly on behalf of the patron. During the 1980s many of the services will eventually be available in the patron's home.

The Future of Computer Technology in Library Networking

James K. Barrentine
Director of Technical Planning
OCLC, Inc.
Columbus, Ohio

INTRODUCTION

The future of computer technology cannot be clearly understood unless the present state of the art is understood. I would like to describe the way things are now, how and why they became that way, and how I think they will affect future library networks.

For those of us who make a business of forecasting where technology is going, there are really only two techniques available. One thing that can be done is to extrapolate from the current technology and say, "if someone can build a widget that goes 100 miles an hour today, there is no reason why in three years someone cannot build a widget that will go 120 miles an hour." For example, I can remember when the speeds at the Indianapolis 500 were well within the 120 mile an hour range. At the time that was happening, which was probably in the late 1950s, people could have predicted that by 1980 those cars would be going somewhere in the neighborhood of 200 miles an hour. There was no reason that the cars could not be going that fast.

However, this particular technique is not so great for coping with an entirely new technology. Someone in 1939, flying in a

DC3, could not predict that by 1959 he would be flying in a 707 because piston engine aircraft would not have predicted jets. This is where the second technique is used, which is to investigate the on-going research in university research labs and industry research labs. The basic rule of thumb is: *if someone has not got something working on a lab bench today, it will not be seen in commercial service for at least five years.* Of course there have been exceptions, but the exceptions have been notorious crash programs. For example, the U.S. Space Program was a case where lab bench technology went into production much faster than five years (probably more like five months in some of the cases). For the sorts of things that we are talking about, however, five years is a reasonable time frame.

These techniques can be used to predict any sort of technology. However, in using these techniques one will be wrong approximately 90 percent of the time. Why will the predictions be wrong? One of the things that can happen is that the particular technology that is being considered can be overtaken by an entirely new technology. Something may come along while the development of technology "X" is on-going that completely outstrips it and takes its place. That was essentially the case of piston engine aircraft. Probably there were people at the time the piston-engined DC6's were flying who were predicting more advanced piston engine aircraft. Then suddenly Boeing built a 707; after that no one was interested in building bigger piston engine aircraft and so it was never done. This was a case of a newborn technology taking over another technology.

Often the predictions fail because the need for the technology does not exist anymore. Whatever the technology was supposed to solve has gone away. Specific examples of this case are difficult to find, but we can speculate on the fact that in the horse-and-buggy days someone was probably inventing an elaborate way to make buggy whips because he thought that people were going to need millions of buggy whips per year. Suddenly there were no more buggies. Therefore, the need for making buggy whips was not there anymore and the technology was abandoned.

Another reason for the failure of predictions is that the technology is often not commercially feasible, which is another way of saying that someone misunderstood the market. Here it is; we have developed it; now no one will buy it; so it just withers and dies.

The final reason for the failure of predictions is the economic considerations of the technology. The current energy crisis would be a good example. If someone had been working on something since 1970 that consumed a lot of energy, it would not be feasible, no matter how wonderful it was, simply because the thing that it consumed (electricity) had become so expensive.

I shall now describe some multiple successes in the past (and some notable failures to go along with them) that probably were predicted by people using these same sorts of techniques. One thing that has been very accurately predicted since the start of the computer industry is advances in disc drive technology. Since about 1965 storage capacity and the speeds of disc drives have been predicted extremely accurately—almost down to the month that things were going to be announced. The other area of computer technology that has been very accurately predicted is the increasing speeds of the central processing unit (CPU).

In describing the failures, I will not pick examples from the computer industry because the majority of people have never heard of them. I'll pick some failures that are well known. In the early 1960s everyone was going to have a picture phone. How many people now have picture phones? That was a case of misreading of the market by AT&T. Once moving sidewalks were going to be everywhere. Moving sidewalks are in operation, but only in very isolated areas (e.g., a few airports).

COMPUTER TECHNOLOGY

The world of computer technology as it relates to library networking may be divided into several areas: the computer system itself, the delivery mechanism that is necessary to get that computer power to the end-user, and the device (which is commonly called a terminal) for interfacing with the user. Then there is a whole conglomerate of material called software (the programs that make all that hardware work together).

The basic computer system consists of three parts: a processor or a central processing unit (hence the abbreviation CPU), a memory for the processor, and input and output capabilities.

Processors

The current computer processors are much the same type of processor that was designed some 25 years ago. The commercial processors that are bought today are really of the same architecture as the ones designed in 1950. Current processors are much faster and smaller and cheaper, but they are really the same; and they are what are generally called "traditional" computers.

I certainly expect to see speed advances in the processors of the future, either by multiplications of the processors themselves to make them faster, or by modifications that seem to make the processors faster (i.e., electronic tricks that are done in computer architectures that make the processors look like they are going faster). The processor gets more work done in per unit time; therefore, it appears to go faster whether it actually does or not. One thing that has occurred and will certainly continue to occur is a drastic improvement in reliability.

The original computers, of course, were vacuum tubes—and vacuum tubes do not last very long. Technology has now gone from vacuum tubes to solid state devices (transistors), to integrated circuits, and from medium-scale integration to large-scale integration, to very large-scale integration. About six weeks ago, when I was at Bell Labs, I saw what Bell Labs claims to be the first micro-computer ever built. All components of the computer—the processor, the input/output capability, and the memory itself—were on a single chip (it was about the size of the end of a finger and contained about 3,000 words of memory on each little chip). Bell intends to put these micro-computers in telephones so that the custom calling features that are now available (for example, the phone "remembers" eight numbers, a person pushes one key of their telephone, and the telephone dials the number for them) will soon be handled in the individual telephones. The telephone will be able to do all sorts of other things for people too, such as control input into fire alarm and burglar alarm systems in homes. When the system is activated, the telephone will automatically call the fire department or the police department. People will never know that the micro-computer is there.

We in the computing field have seen and will continue to see cost reductions in processors. Microprocessors, especially, are now incredibly cheap and are getting cheaper by the month. I can remember the first microprocessors used in the OCLC Model 100 terminals; these cost $126 each when we first started buying them as spares; they are less than a dollar each now. The general trend in microprocessor price reductions has basically ꞓen as follows: within one year after a microprocessor comes out, the price will be reduced to a quarter to half of that at which it was originally listed. Over the years we in the computing industry have seen computers use less energy, and this is becoming more and more important. Current computers consume only about 1/10 of the energy of those of a few years ago.

So much for traditional processors. I will now consider some novel processors, those that are not the same as the ones that people have been building recently. Such processors are not commonplace, and certainly are not, to my knowledge, in use in the library networking community. These novel processors are generally used in very specialized applications.

One such novel processor, the *associative processor*, has been around for a long time. Basically, the associative processor differs from traditional processors in the following aspects: a traditional processor retrieves things from its memory (no matter where that memory may be, within itself, on a disc, or whatever) by addressing a specific location (e.g., requesting record number 1738 or requesting a piece of memory at location 1738). Essentially, associative processors request the piece of memory that has the name "Jones" in it, or the pieces of memory that have the names "Jones." Thus the associative processors associate the key "Jones" with what is actually in the memory itself, hence the name associative processors.

Associative processors are generally used today for processing vast amounts of information that can be held within the computer at one time. They are currently used to process data such as weather information transmitted back from satellites. Some of the weather information is processed so that an entire map of the United States is fed into one of these machines at one time, and all the particular weather patterns are predicted for a 24-hour period.

Some computers are built specifically for string manipulation or for handling strings of characters. The computers that are used in the library networking business, although they handle strings of characters, were built to handle numbers—to add, to subtract, to multiply, and to divide numbers. The characters have been made to become numbers, essentially to "fake out" the computers. In that way, the computers "think" that they are handling numbers.

Some people have built computers specifically for handling characters. Obviously, if these character-handling computers came into wide use, they would have a great impact on those of us who process information rather than numbers. However, such computers are in very short supply and I don't see many people doing much work in the area of developing character-handling computers. Thus, we who process information are piggy-backing on those who handle numbers, and the people who handle numbers are the ones who currently control the direction in which computer technology is going.

Storage Systems

I shall now turn from processors to storage systems—one of the most critical areas in computer technology. The whole reason for having computers is to manipulate information. Before information can be manipulated, it must be in machine readable form, and it has to be stored somewhere before it can manipulated. The first storage system that I will describe will be the computer memory itself. The computer memory is where the computer's programs reside and where the computer holds small amounts of data for processing. The largest computer systems have no more than about 16 million characters of this storage, which is not very large. The more common computers now have approximately 4 to 8 million characters of actual computer memory. This memory might consist of what is called core memory (the old-fashioned kind), or it might consist of semiconductor memory (the kind that is currently being used and which is much faster than core memory).

Another type of memory that is found in computer systems is disc drives, the current way of storing large amounts of data on computers. Disc drives, available in a variety of forms, are movable electromechanical devices that store anywhere from 5 million characters up to about 600 million characters. Disc drives with 600 million characters of storage cost about $30,000 each. Probably within the next few years disc drives will be made that hold up to about a billion characters per drive—the obtainable maximum. It is a maximum because of a physical limitation inherent in disc drive technology itself, and is related to the size of atomic particles. Since there is not much that can be done about atomic particles in this world, further advances beyond the billion character stage are not going to come; something else will have to be devised before storage devices can be bigger than that.

What new types of storage devices might there be? One device that has been around for awhile is usually known by the term *mass storage device*. (The IBM model number for it is 3850, but other companies also make them.) To put things in perspective, the current disc drives that OCLC uses hold from about 250 million to about 300 million characters. This means that it takes four of these disc drives to hold a billion characters. The mass storage device holds about 500 billion characters, or the equivalent of 2000 disc drives (as we know them today).

How does this electromechanical device work? The data are stored on small cylinders, about as big around as half the size of a beer can, and the cylinders are stored in honeycombs on a vertical plane. When the device wants to read one of the cylinders, an arm goes down and pulls the cylinder out of the honeycomb and carries it to a read/write station. The arm drops the little cylinder into the reading device, which unwinds a piece of magnetic tape that is inside of the cylinder, and reads it. The device actually reads the tape by transferring the data onto a standard disc drive, and the computer thinks that it is talking to a standard disc drive.

Since there are already hundreds and hundreds of computers that talk to standard disc drives, mass storage devices have been designed so that these cylinders hang on the backs of the disc drive. When the computer requests something from the disc that really is not there, the mass storage device will get it and put it on that disc. The computer will then be able to read the information. Considering that the actual storage capacity of the mass storage system is 472 billion characters, and considering how many characters are on a printed page and how many pages there are in the average book, it is obvious that we could store quite a lot of real information (and not just bibliographic information) in these devices. These mass storage systems have been around for awhile, however, but not many people are using them. I don't know of any of the library networking agencies that use them.

One reason that the mass storage systems are not used is that they are very expensive. Another reason these devices are not used more is that it takes a long time to get the information from the little cell out to the user; sometimes as long as two minutes. A physical limitation is also present because it is an electromechanical device which can only move so fast without tearing itself into pieces.

The solution would be for someone to develop computer software that has the capability to predict what the user is going to want, based upon his past performance, before he actually asks for it. Such predictions are fairly simple if one is talking about a person sitting and reading a book, because if he is on page ten now, presumably in a few minutes he is going to be on page 11, and after awhile he will be on page 20. Therefore, a system could be designed that would preread the information and have the data ready for the reader so that he would never be aware that it took two minutes. However, with typical information retrieval systems or with bibliographic systems like OCLC, there is no predictive mechanism available, and information can only be retrieved the moment the user asks for it; a two minute response time is not acceptable to most people. If someone could design a predictive algorithm that could be implemented on computers, it would drastically increase the amount of on-line storage that is available today. Hopefully someone will come up with such algorithms.

There are two other storage technologies that are of interest. From a technological standpoint, *bubble memory* is an interesting device, designed to fill the gap between the disc drives and the very high speed, very expensive computer memory itself. While computer memory is a great deal faster for retrieval than a disc drive, it is also much more expensive; therefore, the people at Bell Labs developed bubble memory. Bubble memory, which is faster than disc drive and cheaper than computer memory, is a medium-sized storage device. Laboratory models contain perhaps a quarter of a million characters and are fairly expensive. Perhaps within a year's time bubble memory will be available in commerical quantities and could be incorporated into all sorts of devices. I believe bubble memory will drastically increase the power of the computer terminal sitting on the user's desk, because that is the likely place to put storage of that size. A quarter of a million characters of storage is more memory, by a factor of two, than OCLC had in its first computer. Therefore, if a person has that much storage sitting on a desk in a terminal, many things can be accomplished. Some of them I will describe shortly.

Another storage technology still in the experimental stages today, that will, I think, have a drastic impact on the future of library networking is the *videodisc*. It is understandable that some people are interested in the videodisc primarily for its video capabilities, but the thing that interests me about the videodisc is its data storage capabilities. A videodisc is an optical device currently used for storing optical images. One can get about 54,000 frames on each side of a videodisc.

However, devices are already available that are capable of recording and playing back digital information that can be stored on a videodisc. In commercial quantities, a videodisc playback unit would cost somewhere around $3000. However, the problem is with recording data on the videodisc. Discs are made like records; they are pressed (produced) in one technology and played back (with a laser) using another technology. As with phonorecords, a stamping out process is involved which can produce 1000 discs; one single custom-made disc would be too expensive. If one could take all the bibliographic records of OCLC, videodiscs could be produced to hold all the OCLC records (and it wouldn't take very many). The records are now nonvolatile; in other words, they are permanent records that will be there forever.

Playback equipment would be inexpensive. Small stand-alone systems costing about $3000, could provide access to what is currently on disc drives costing one and one-quarter million dollars. It would be possible to change the information by changing records, just as is done on a phonograph.

The big problem to be solved in videodisc technology is the errors which would result in the flicker on the screen. When videodisc is used for a human optical recording device (our eyes), this flicker is not serious since the human eye can compensate for it. A computer cannot easily make such compensations. Computers also "see" errors on standard type discs, but over the years error recovery algorithms have been developed that essentially solve these problems; the algorithms fix the errors in the data that occur in transmission or storage. The same algorithms will not work for videodiscs. Better error correcting schemes have to be developed before videodiscs can be commercially used for computers in anything other than experimental operations.

COMMUNICATIONS SYSTEMS

Communications systems deliver information to the user of the computer system. The traditional way of delivering information between a computer and a distant user is over facilities provided by the telephone company. These facilities consist of circuits which carry electrical signals, and devices called modems which convert computer data into these electrical signals. The circuits may be leased on a full-time basis or they may be paid for on a "dial-up" or "as-used" basis. Once the telephone company, or in some cases a private vendor, has provided the user with these two types of facilities, the user is on his own as to their utilization.

Probably 99 percent of the communication to computer terminals is currently being done this way. Why aren't people developing more sophisticated ways? Well, some people are, but the fact remains that the people who transmit data over communication lines are essentially a bother to AT&T. Data service accounts for less than 4 percent of the total AT&T revenues; more than 96 percent of AT&T revenues come from the standard voice telephone service. As AT&T says, "Where are you going to spend your development efforts, on 4 percent of the business or on 96 percent of the business?" The problem with this approach is that it is self-serving. If AT&T continues to spend 96 percent of its development efforts on the 96 percent revenue producing voice service, the 4 percent will never become greater than 4 percent.

The common method used by AT&T for providing this circuit service is cable. A copper cable is strung along the telephone pole or laid under the ground. Another method, not uncommon, is microwave transmission; in fact, most of the cross-country transmission is currently provided by microwave.

In the future, the cable and microwave systems will have higher and higher capabilities over the same facilities. This higher capability allows the phone company to decrease its rates. This is the reason long distance phone calls today don't cost as much as they used to cost years ago. Since AT&T can handle more telephone calls (or more data) with a given facility than was previously possible (without any additional investment), they can charge less for each individual call.

The telephone company has an incredible investment in physical plants in this country, and this investment is one of their problems. By its own admission, AT&T is very slow to take advantage of new technology. Taking advantage of that new technology would make obsolete a considerable amount of present equipment. For years the telephone company wrote off its physical plant equipment on a 30 year depreciation schedule. Since nothing lasts for 30 years in this country, AT&T's problem is that it is carrying 25-year-old equipment on the books as still being worth something. If AT&T suddenly wrote off all of that equipment, its year-end statements would not look so good. Recently, AT&T has begun amortizing its equipment over more reasonable time frames, such as seven years.

AT&T is now using fiber optics, which will have the impact of further reduction of communication costs. Fiber optics uses a cable made of glass fibers over which data are transmitted as light and not as electricity. Fiber optics is now cheaper to lay than cable; thus, AT&T has now made the decision to lay no more cable in major metropolitan areas.

A project, which you may have seen on some AT&T television commercials, was recently carried out in Chicago. When four 900-pair copper cables are put together, a hole is left in the middle; AT&T ran the small fiber optics cable (about as big around as a little finger) down between the big cables. In this field experiment, AT&T linemen attempted to splice the fiber optics cable in the middle of winter, while sitting in a man-hole that was half full of water (which, sometimes, their linemen have to do). AT&T determined that linemen could handle fiber optics and thus made the decision that from now on in major metropolitan areas no more copper cable will be laid—it will all be fiber optics.

While the transmission capabilities of fiber optics are literally staggering, it is still not economically feasible for the telephone company to start using fiber optics for cross-country transmissions. It is my opinion that in the future it will become economically feasible, and that we will see fiber optics replacing cables in all aspects of the telephone company's system, even down to the lines that actually come into a private home. In fact, the AT&T labs already have fiber optic cables that are suitable for running into a home. The telephone company could then sell transmission facilities on these fiber optics cables to anyone else who wants them.

It is now common practice that when someone orders a new telephone to be put into a house, the telephone company doesn't run just one pair of lines into the house. In some places, two or even four lines may be run since it is cheaper to go ahead and put them in at the beginning rather than having to go back and add the lines later (in case the customer should later decide that additional phone lines are needed). Even the smallest fiber optics cable offers more throughput than four lines.

Imagine the phone company selling services to cable television companies. This opens up the possibility of nationwide cable television companies. The cable television companies would not have to string their own cables because the phone company has already done it for them. All kinds of delivery systems could be provided directly to the home because this incredible capability for providing them has already been furnished for everyone by the telephone company.

Value-Added Systems

The U.S. is currently served by two value-added systems, Tymnet and Telenet. Both systems operate in essentially the same manner; they have their own communications circuits, which are in turn leased from AT&T or one of the other carriers. Both systems provide the user with a communication service, i.e., between a computer somewhere and a number of terminals somewhere else. Both systems provide this communication without the user having any investment in physical facilities or having to pay a set monthly usage charge, other than a very nominal one, if the service is not used. If OCLC suddenly stopped providing cataloging service, the bill from AT&T would continue to arrive for the dedicated telephone lines and that is currently about $300,000 a month. AT&T expects to get paid whether we use the facility or not. The OCLC system is now operable 87 hours per week, but there are a lot more hours in the week than 87. What happens to that communication facility when we at OCLC are not using it? Nothing—it just lays there and we (and the user) pay for it.

Value-added networks do not operate in that way. No one owns anything full-time, everyone shares everything all the time. For example, on a wire running from Indianapolis to Columbus, there might be a transmission going to OCLC at one minute, the next minute there might be a transmission going to Battelle, and the next minute there might be a transmission going to Ohio State University. All of the transmitters will be using the same value-added network. AT&T has proposed that they themselves get into the value-added network business with something called Advanced Communication System (ACS). If AT&T is allowed to get into the value-added network business, it will be quite a few years before they do it. In order for AT&T to offer service, it must be tariffed by the Federal Communications Commission (FCC), and that requires a long time, especially for something as major and as complicated as ACS. It is my opinion that ultimately AT&T will get approval, but I suspect that it will be six or seven years before they are actually offering their ACS service.

One of the possibilities in the value-added network area is something that I call LCS, Library Communication System. There is no reason why we couldn't have a specialized value-added network for library service providers and library service users. Tymnet and Telenet did not start as value-added networks. For example, one of them began by providing computer services to one set of computers. It later became feasible for them to sell communication service.

Suppose there was an organization formed that operated a value-added network just for the OCLC's, the Research Libraries Information Networks (RLIN's), the SOLINET's, the NELINET's, and whatever. This organization would then provide a nationwide communications network. Just the circuits that OCLC alone has would form the basis for a nationwide library communications network, and would considerably reduce the market entry barriers for anyone who wanted to provide library services requiring telecommunications. Right now each new group has to develop its own telecommunications network or has to contract with Telenet or Tymnet, which make the proposed library service more expensive. Suppose the library communications system existed; as people developed some new network application that someone wanted to sell or wanted to buy—the delivery mechanism would already be there for it.

Satellites

Satellites, according to Bell Labs, are one of those things that technology is going to by-pass. Satellites for interactive two-way communications will probably never happen. This is because satellites, while fine for broadcasting, have and will continue to have serious problems, such as delay, for interactive systems. AT&T believes that fiber optics will overtake satellites for intercontinental transmissions (New York to Los Angeles or New York to London). Broadcast technology is becoming less expensive. For example, a Japanese company is selling a satellite receiver antenna for $260. This antenna will allow anyone to pick up any television program in this country, because television programs are all broadcast by satellite.

The economics is not so encouraging for two-way communications. Currently a major problem to overcome before entering two-way satellite communications is the ground station equipment. The cost of building a ground station that can both transmit and receive is presently about $120,000. Receive-only ground stations are considerably cheaper, but are naturally not worth much for two-way communications. Receive-only ground stations are fine, however, for broadcast, which is why local television stations use them. Within the next five years, I predict that two-way satellite ground stations will be in the $30,000 price range. This would still be more than most libraries could afford, though. Perhaps OCLC can own one to communicate with the Library of Congress (LC) or with RLIN, and maybe that will happen. For most communication, the use of satellites is not practical.

TERMINALS

Terminals are used to communicate with the other services that have been discussed above. I suppose the word "terminal" came from the fact that those who named them were on the end (terminal) of the communication system. The first terminals were modified IBM electric typewriters and made paper copy. In the late 1960s these devices were replaced by cathode ray tube (CRT) terminals, which had televisionlike screens.

Why did the typewriter terminals get replaced? There were two simple reasons: 1) reliability—the typewriters, mechanical devices, could not be driven at the speeds that computers wanted to run them and still last very long; typewriters were high maintenance items; 2) speed itself—no matter how good and reliable the mechanism was, and no matter how fast it was driven, a physical limit existed at which the type element on a Selectric typewriter could move. So the computer technology people developed the cathode ray tube terminals.

Cathode ray tube terminals are taken as the standard of two-way interactive on-line systems today because, except in a very rare number of cases, no hard copy units of the traditional typewriter version can even approach the speeds that can be obtained with video units. The OCLC terminals operate at 240 characters per second. The fastest hard copy unit that I know about operates at 180 characters per second.

The computer terminal consists of a screen that usually measures 12 to 15 inches on the diagonal, and a keyboard, for entering data, that looks more or less like a typewriter keyboard. The keyboards are fine for people who are accustomed to using a terminal, but keyboards are not so fine for the vast majority of people in this country. The vast majority of people in this country, and probably the vast majority of the patrons in libraries, would have some difficulty in handling a keyboard terminal. In order to verify that fact, just look at the self-operated cash dispensing machines designed for banks. These machines don't look anything like a typewriter or terminal keyboard. They are specialized devices designed just to be able to dispense cash or provide banking transactions to the majority of people in the world.

Before terminals are put out for everyone to use for on-line catalog access, a special terminal would have to be developed. This special terminal cannot be a general purpose keyboard-type terminal. Although this would be less of a problem for academic libraries, because, increasingly everyone in academic institutions is now required to take a computer course and is already accustomed to working with conventional terminals. However, patrons of small public libraries may be intimidated by these terminals and may not be willing to use them. We need a specially designed terminal that "walks" the user through its own operation and does not require a command language. The special terminal will ask the patron a series of questions (e.g., "What do you want to do?"), and will give the patron several choices. The patron will touch, probably on a touch-sensitive screen, the actual choice that he or she wants to make. The terminal will then indicate that the patron actually did make a choice. This process would then continue through a series of such iterations.

Viewdata

Since another paper in this book describes Viewdata, I shall just add some personal observations. I have seen the Viewdata system operate both in the United Kingdom and in this country. OCLC and other groups have people who are looking into this particular technology for the delivery of information. In essence, all that has been done is that a standard home television has been made into a cheap computer terminal. This may not seem like such a great accomplishment, since people could have bought a computer terminal and had exactly the same thing. In England the Viewdata system is almost free. About 80 percent of the people in England rent television sets; if a Viewdata device were standard in all television sets, people would pay for it whether they wanted it or not. Because the people already have it, they are going to use information services that can be accessed with that particular device.

In this country television sets are made by a variety of manufacturers including a number of companies in foreign countries. Because the television manufacturers could not be expected to incorporate Viewdata systems into televisions, a more feasible solution in the U.S. would be to buy a little box that sits on top of the television and hooks onto the same place as the antenna. The little box would have a small keyboard on it.

After reading some information on Viewdata (which was no more than their public relations material), one of our OCLC engineers went to a local electronics store, bought the electronic parts in single unit quantities, and built a prototype at OCLC just to see what could be done with a Viewdata system. The unit cost $350 to build, which means that someone (such as Radio Shack or Texas Instruments) could probably produce it for less than $100 in quantity. The small cost would allow many persons to buy these devices and hook them to their televisions. Since systems like Viewdata use standard telephone communications, they require no additional wiring into the house. Anyone who has a telephone can access the services they want. If the service is not priced as "value-added" ("pay as you go" basis or "if I don't use it I don't pay"), but rather is a standard cost whether you use it or not, a lot of people are going to access a lot of systems a little. When this is added up countrywide, you have a massive number of people wanting information in their hands. Either the libraries and the library network organizations are going to be capable of providing that information, or someone else is going to come along and do it. In the future, people will not go to libraries for the same reasons that they now go to libraries. Instead they will go to the television set sitting in their living room and get information delivered directly to their home.

SOFTWARE

Now I come to the bad part of all of this technology. As we have seen, there is a lot of hardware around, but, a lot of high-priced people are required to write programs to run on this hardware. Unfortunately, these people get more expensive while the hardware gets less expensive; and the people seem to get more expensive faster than the hardware gets less expensive. It is clear that software development will be necessary to link any sort of networking system, whether it be for libraries or anybody else. It is clearly the biggest, most expensive part of the whole operation. It is also the part in which the least effort is being spent. There is not even good software to link computers built by the same manufacturers. Even if we in the library networking business bought all new hardware that was all made by one company, the networking software that would link it together would still not be there.

None of the library networks operate on any of the same hardware today anyway. OCLC has three different types of computers operating in the same machine room. RLIN has something different from OCLC, and WLN has something different from both. Each of the circulation control vendors uses something still different from all three networks. In a recent issue of *Datamation*, there is a letter by the man who is in charge of software development for British Leyland. He is essentially writing to the United States saying, "Surely some of you folks in the great United States have already developed all this software to hook all these wonderful computers together." The man got a sad response, "No, there isn't any such thing." It is clearly the area where we are going to have to spend the most effort, and it is going to be the most expensive.

THE FUTURE

I will finish by responding to the question, "What do I think the national network (or whatever you want to call it) is going to look like, based on the kinds of things that I've told you?" My concept of the national network is a bit different from the others being proposed. My concept is that the national network (the feasible one) is, in fact, a communications facility. It is, in fact, this library communications system that I talked about. In ten years libraries will be able to buy from a variety of vendors (some of which will be commercial operations) turnkey minicomputer-based systems. Some of those systems may be all on one single terminal. That system will come preprogrammed, ready to interface into this national network.

The national network will provide a communications facility between any one of those terminals that is connected to it and any supplier of information that is also connected with it. It will be that piece of equipment, which is located on the library's own premises, that essentially runs the operation. It is going to be that piece of equipment that will enable the library to use the cataloging services of OCLC and the acquisitions services of RLIN. As far as the library is concerned, every service is being provided by that one box sitting right there in the library. I do not mean that each user is going to have to have their own development staff. Since development staff will be the most expensive part of this operation, users will not want this staff. Rather, the system will come with all software developed by the vendor. The library will be able to operate the equipment in much the same way as they operate any other piece of equipment. This type of system will allow ultimate flexibility for the library to buy services without requiring large software development staffs and expenditures.

I believe that such a national network will slowly evolve over the next ten to fifteen years, and will be firmly in place by the end of the 20th century.

The Emerging Telecommunications Environment

Frank W. Norwood, Executive Director
Joint Council on Educational
*   Telecommunications*
Washington, D.C.

INTRODUCTION

Almost ten years ago, at the last national conference on library networking in which I participated, I began my small contribution with a reference to Dan Cordtz's article in the April, 1970 issue of *Fortune*.[1] The article was called, "The Coming Shake-Up in Telecommunications."[2] The shake-up did come, but the tremors now under our feet are no less, and indeed may be greater, than those Dan Cordtz wrote about. Some of these changes may have direct effects upon networking for libraries; all of them will affect the context in which library networking develops. Mindful of the Chinese proverb which says, "It is very difficult to make predictions ... particularly in regard to the future," this paper will not attempt to focus exclusively upon the new media, technology, and communications policy as they touch directly upon networking among libraries and information resources—although where such close coupling can be identified its implications will be explored. Rather, the purpose of this paper is to attempt to map the broad outlines of the probable communications landscape of the next decade, as its title attempts to suggest.

There was a considerable temptation to borrow again from Mr. Cordtz, since his title is still apt, but that temptation was overwhelmed by a still stronger urge to do my stealing closer to home and write a small variation on my friend Bill Donnelly's phrase, "the emerging video environment." I'm not the first, and probably not the last to steal Bill's words. A few weeks ago I was in the audience for an investment seminar organized by Merrill Lynch, Pierce, Fenner and Smith in which Bill, who is Vice President and Group Supervisor of New Electronic Media for Young and Rubicam, was among the distinguished participants. In that seminar on "The Emerging Video Environment," Bill and the other panelists were on the floor of Madison Square Garden. Some 150 of us in the audience were in Madison Square Garden stands. But we were only a small part of the total seminar audience. Others were in Honolulu, Hawaii, in Anchorage, Alaska, and in some 18 other cities from coast to coast. The conference was transmitted on two domestic satellites and delivered in various locations by closed circuit, by Multipoint Distribution Service, by pay television and by two-way cable . . . an ample demonstration that the video and telecommunications environment has already begun to emerge.

BORN AGAIN CABLE TV

Cable television, often called "CATV" from its origins as "community antenna television," was declared by the Sloan Commission to be the "television of abundance."[3] But cable's advocates saw its "blue sky" future quickly darken with the storm clouds of rising interest rates and diminishing interest by big city dwellers in the improved reception of local stations plus a few "distant signals," imported from neighboring cities.

Cable operators wanting to increase their saturation of existing markets and to persuade more householders to hook up to the cable which passed their doors, evidenced increased interest in new, nonbroadcast services. In Manhattan, and then in the New York suburbs, the home games of the New York Knicks and New York Rangers were televised exclusively on the cable. Time-Life's subsidiary, Home Box Office, Inc. (HBO), offered a schedule of uncut, uninterrupted movies, sports and TV specials via a pay channel for which subscribers interested in HBO's fare willingly paid an additional monthly fee. It was HBO which had the imagination and the courage to multiply its potential market by leasing time on two channels of RCA's Satcom I satellite and offering HBO service to any cable system prepared to invest in the cost of a satellite receive-only earth station.

In the past three years, the marriage of satellite and cable has surpassed all expectation. With the prospect of new revenues from HBO's pay TV service as initial motivation, cable operators quickly responded to the challenge and invested in satellite earth stations. When the Federal Communications Commission (FCC) amended its rules to permit the use of smaller 4.5 meter dishes, and costs dropped from approximately $90,000 to something under $20,000, the "space rush" was on.

Once an earth station is installed, the investment to receive additional channels is minimal, and so soon Madison Square Garden's sports events were added (thus the origination of the Merrill Lynch seminar from the Garden floor), religious programming from the Christian Broadcasting Network, PTL ("Praise the Lord" or "People that Love"), and the Trinity Broadcasting Network, and a variety of other pay and non-pay services. From Atlanta, sportsman, broadcaster, and entrepreneur, Ted Turner turned his local WTCG-TV into a "super station" whose programs are seen on cable systems from Honolulu to Maine. In addition to telecasts of the games of the Atlanta Falcons, Braves and Hawks, WTCG-Super Seventeen's new schedule will add two and one-half hours per day of commercial-free "educational children's programming," and a five-night-a-week strip of prestige series such as "The Ascent of Man," "America" and "Elizabeth R."[4]

Additional program variety results from the development of new cable-satellite services quite unlike conventional commercial or public television. The Cable-Satellite Public Affairs Network (C-SPAN) is a nonprofit organization supported by some of the major cable system operators. C-SPAN's initial offering is gavel-to-gavel coverage of the U.S. House of Representatives. Another public service venture has been announced by the Public Service Satellite Consortium (PSSC): its National Satellite Network (NSN). PSSC is a consortium of more than 100 organizations and institutions (including the American Library Association, the Colorado State Library and OCLC). NSN is not a permanent interconnection of a number of fixed points, but a flexible ad hocracy, assembled on order by PSSC to meet specific communication needs. NSN's new Hospital Interconnection uses satellite and cable to bring a schedule of patient education and professional development programs to health care institutions across the country.[5]

The Appalachian Educational Satellite Project (AESP) had its beginnings in 1974 on the National Aeronautics and Space Administration's experimental ATS-6 satellite. Starting in September of this year, AESP will initiate the Community Service Network (CSN), a 35-hour-per-week schedule of daily educational and instructional programs.[6] Major program categories will be developed by the CSN and will be based upon continuing cable and community inputs with actual program content being jointly determined by participating organizations and CSN staff.

Not all the new cable services will be television, conventional, or novel. Alphanumeric text services are also beginning to appear, but these will be discussed below.

VIDEO RECORDINGS: CASSETTES AND/OR DISCS

Some time before 1979 is over, there will be more than one million home videocassette players in use.[7] That magnitude is sufficient to attract the eager attention of the major film studios. Thus Paramount Pictures and United Artists join 20th Century Fox and Allied Artists in offering Hollywood films to home viewers in the new one-half inch videotape cassette formats. At a recent International Tape Association (now called, simply, "ITA") conference, 20th Century Fox Telecommunications president, Steve Roberts, predicted that home video will eventually be a billion dollar industry, although he cautioned that the video-cassette's present "double standard" with the "Beta" and "VHS" formats sharing the market could give way to a sea of complexity if new cassette formats are introduced.

The much-heralded and long-awaited videodisc (or at least one version thereof) became a present reality at Christmas time when MCA and Magnavox introduced the "Magnavision" player and an initial offering of "DiscoVision" releases in Atlanta. The market test proved a sensational sellout, with those who bought the player for $695 being offered as much as $2000 by those who missed the opportunity to be "the first kid on the block," and many who could not buy the player stocking up on DiscoVision discs for future use.[8]

The ultimate fate of the videodisc is a bit risky to predict. The emergence of first consumer models does not guarantee ultimate success, as the fate of the late Peter Goldmark's Electronic Video Recording (EVR) and the Telefunken-Decca videodisc system (known as Teldec or TeD) attest. One major question is whether there will be a proliferation of incompatible videodisc systems launched by competitive interests. While the Phillips-MCA system will soon be given another "test flight" in the Seattle-Tacoma market, with more to follow, a number of other disc systems are in the wings. RCA, Thompson-CSF, Victor Corporation of Japan and Matsushita each have different systems (different from Phillips-MCA's and different from each other) in the laboratory and/or on the way to the marketplace. Consumer hesitancy and confusion in the face of a multiplicity of disc systems could have a critical negative effect on the acceptance of the videodisc as a home entertainment device.

Steve Robert's predictions are based upon the reasonable but speculative assumptions that the cost of videodisc players and programs can be kept to half the equivalent costs of their cassette counterparts. That being the case, Roberts sees a healthy market for home video split evenly between the two media, and a total penetration of 50 percent of the U.S. TV households by 1990. In round numbers, that would be 20 million disc players and 20 million cassette machines.

MDS—NONBROADCAST TELEVISION—AND ITFS

To most television viewers, the initials "MDS" and "ITFS" are meaningless, but these over-the-air TV services may represent a resource the exploitation of which is just beginning.

ITFS is the Instructional Television Fixed Service. First established by the Federal Communications Commission in 1963, ITFS is a low-power TV system designed for use by school systems, universities, hospitals and others to enable them to transmit as many as four simultaneous programs at microwave frequencies to specially-equipped receivers which "down-convert" the signals to conventional TV channels. While ITFS is an over-the-air system, it is not *broadcasting* since the signals are not intended for, nor can they be received by, the general public.[9]

The Multipoint Distribution Service (MDS) is in most respects technically similar to ITFS, except that while 28 ITFS channels are available for use, the spectrum allocation for MDS provides room for only one—or at most—two such channels. By regulation, MDS operators are common carriers, prohibited from offering their own programs or services, but open to all users on a first-come-first-served basis.

ITFS, during the past 15 years, has had a modest success in a variety of contexts. In elementary and secondary education, ITFS has been used primarily to distribute school programming, its multichannel capability providing both greater flexibility than conventional television broadcasting and the opportunity to repeat classroom programs to match the variability of school schedules.

In higher education, ITFS has been a boon to extension education, bringing undergraduate, graduate, and refresher courses to engineers and other professionals at the locations where they work. Thus, working engineers in the San Francisco Bay area may participate in classes for an advanced degree by going to the corporate conference room rather than losing half a day in commuting to the Stanford University campus. In medical education, ITFS can link the medical school with the teaching hospitals or, as in Cleveland, make possible a network of hospitals sharing patient education, professional development programs and, in some cases, teleconferencing among health-care leaders and administrators.

As with cable, the principal uses to date have been for video, but new uses are emerging and both MDS and ITFS may well find a place in library networking and in extending information services to the ultimate users.

NEW SATELLITE SERVICES

At present, there are three domestic communications satellite systems in the United States.[10] Technically, their similarities are greater than their differences: each operates in the rather crowded 4-6 GHz portion of the spectrum with limited satellite power, and consequently, needs to locate earth stations (particularly send-receive stations) in relatively isolated areas where interference will present no problem. Each satellite carries 12 (in the case of the Western Union satellites) or 24 (RCA's Satcom satellites and Comsat General's Comstars) transponders. A transponder is a device which receives relatively weak signals from a transmitting earth station, amplifies them and retransmits them back to earth at another frequency. Under typical circumstances, a single transponder can carry one full-color TV signal, or, through subdivision of its capacity can provide 600 two-way voice circuits or an even greater number of teletypewriter or data channels.

Both the Western Union and RCA satellites are used for a wide variety of services. Comsat General, a subsidiary of the Communications Satellite Corporation, leases its satellites on an exclusive basis to the American Telephone and Telegraph Co. (AT&T) and GTE (formerly General Telephone and Electronics), the nation's second largest phone company. Under FCC restrictions, which are due to be lifted soon, AT&T and GTE may employ the Comstar satellites only for long-distance toll message service.

Now, a new satellite system and new satellite services appear on the horizon. Called Satellite Business Systems (SBS), the enterprise is a joint venture of Comsat General, International Business Machines and Aetna Life and Casualty. SBS projects a target date of 1981 for the inauguration of a new satellite system intended to meet the communications needs of those business giants which make up the *Fortune* 500. Because the SBS satellites (one to be in use, a second to operate as an in-orbit spare) will operate in the less crowded 11 and 14 GHz bands and with more power than present domestic satellites, earth stations can be located directly on users' premises. The SBS system will be digital, providing voice, data, and imaging (i.e., facsimile and still picture video). According to SBS's C. T. Rush, they will offer such innovative services as "private networks" rather than "circuits," dynamic allocation of capacity based upon demand "and the potential for entirely new applications."[11]

It is anticipated that the SBS system may be cost-effective in some large organizations solely on the basis of daytime voice traffic, and that the same satellite capacity can be reallocated in off-peak hours for other applications: the transmission of micro-images, teleconferencing, and document delivery. With a data capacity of 43 Mbps in each of ten transponders and the ability to broadcast on a point-to-points basis, SBS believes users will find new opportunities for such tasks as load leveling and resource sharing.

Those in the nonprofit sector of the economy who find the SBS scenario attractive should be warned that they are not the target of SBS's marketing plans. SBS proposes to lease end-to-end service to its users, rather than transponder time as does Western Union and RCA. Although users may buy and own their own earth stations, the fact that the SBS system will operate in an all-digital mode contributes to the cost of the earth station, estimated by E.F. Hutton to be approximately $345,000.[12]

The announced plans of Satellite Business Systems have been followed by other proposals to serve the users of data communications. Xerox, in November, 1978, declared its intention to join the common carrier ranks with an end-to-end digital transmission service for document distribution, data communications and teleconferencing.[13] To be called "XTEN," for Xerox Telecommunications Network, the service could be available as early as 1981. Unlike SBS, Xerox will not build its own satellites, but plans to lease capacity from existing carriers. Further, XTEN will not attempt to locate satellite earth stations at user premises, but will develop a new class of "end loops" at microwave frequencies in the band 10.5 to 10.68 GHz spectrum presently allocated for mobile radio use. Messages would flow from user premises at up to 256 Kbps via microwave link to a central "city node" which would relay the message via microwave for intracity or via satellite for intercity traffic.

Xerox has not revealed proposed tariff rates, but has said that a key feature of XTEN would be low entry and operating costs. The system, according to Xerox, "will be able to accommodate a significant segment of intra- and inter-company data communications requirements at costs affordable even by small customers."

Back on earth, AT&T is proposing a terrestrial system to be called its Advanced Communications Service (ACS), also addressed to such user problems as incompatibility, underutilization of separate user-developed networks, the difficulties of modifying existing networks, the expense of monitoring and managing multiple networks, and the problem of high opportunity costs for new users and new services. AT&T has, however, run into considerable opposition from other carriers, computer suppliers, and those offering terminals and services. Other complications have arisen as evidenced by Mother Bell's admission that the development of software for ACS will be more difficult than previously anticipated.[14]

NEW MEDIA AND APPLICATIONS

In Columbus, Ohio, cable television is more than a purveyor of local and distant television stations and the new rash of TV signals relayed by satellite. Multiple-systems-operator Warner Cable has a $10 million bet riding on the most sophisticated cable communications operation in the world. Called "Qube," for no better reason than that Warner executives liked the sound of the word, the 30-channel system is equally divided among conventional television (four local stations and five imported signals), community programs and "premium" or pay channels with a variety of new and classic movies, arts, sports and educational fare. In addition, there are Qube's interactive services. Each subscriber is equipped with a calculatorlike selector; in addition to using it to tune the proper channel, the viewer can push one of the five "response buttons" to participate in local game shows, vote on referenda, respond to quiz questions or order merchandise (the controlling computer with its stored lists of subscribers and their addresses knows where to send the merchandise).[15]

Almost since its earliest days, cable TV has been used to deliver alphanumeric information as well as conventional television. Early cable operators employed unused channels to transmit information about upcoming programs, community events and/or real estate and other local services available, by means of hand-lettered or typewritten cards placed on a slowly rotating drum scanned by a low-cost industrial television camera. As the technology became available, character generators with typewriterlike keyboards provided all-electronic displays. Now such information displays are taking their place as a significant auxiliary service to conventional cable services. Weather, comparative shopping information, news bulletins, and other data are offered by many cable systems and provide an information component which complements cable's traditional entertainment role.

No present service is more sophisticated than that offered in New York by Reuters. The Reuter Monitor services allow subscribing businesses to retrieve financial, market and related information at high speed for display on a conventional TV set.[16] The system uses minicomputers with disc storage to cycle the entire data base every five seconds, using a full TV channel bandwidth of 4.2 MHz, six Mbps in digital form. The user, by selecting the appropriate group number and page, "grabs" the desired row of data which is buffered and displayed on his television screen. General Market Information, Options, Financial News, New York Securities Exchange (NYSE) and Amex quotes, Money Markets, and a range of services concerning commodities are available.

The Reuters service is an example of a growing family of videotext systems which are now beginning to emerge from the laboratory. In the United Kingdom, both the BBC and the Independent Broadcasting Authority have developed systems which transmit such information during the vertical interval which comes between each transmitted TV frame. Such an approach is under test now in the United States via a commercial TV station in Salt Lake City and over a Philadelphia MDS operation.

Such systems are essentially limited in two ways. The short interval between TV frames permits a relatively limited number of "pages" of text, the actual number being a function of the number of vertical interval lines used and the "call-up" time between repetitions of the same page. Too, since these are essentially broadcast devices (whether transmitted by conventional stations, MDS or cable), their one-way nature limits the user to making a selection from the available materials.

Somewhat more sophisticated is the approach taken by the British Post Office in a system once called "Viewdata," but now redubbed "Prestel." Here, the viewer can interact with the data base because the connection is made by telephone line to his television set and Prestel control unit. Since the pages are not cycled but called up on command, there is no theoretical limit to the size of the data base. After a pilot trial which began in 1976, the British Post Office initiated a market trial in June, 1978 with some 1000 users drawn from the domestic and business sectors in London, Birmingham, and Norwich. The central data bank now contains some 60,000 pages of information. Since the Prestel system is interactive, the user can employ the keypad control to make limited entries into the system. For example, users can order theater tickets or merchandise and even, by selecting among numbered alternatives, construct a message which may be deposited in the electronic "mailbox" of another subscriber.

The videodisc—at least in some of its possible manifestations—is also a potentially powerful medium for alphanumeric information. White it is often noted that a videodisc of a 30-minute television program contains 54,000 individual frames, two facts must be kept in mind. *Any* recorded video medium uses 54,000 frames for a half-hour program (30 minutes x 60 seconds x 30 frames/second) so there is no magic exclusive to the disc. The second fact to remember is that television resolution is distinctly limited, so that recording a page of printed text or even a typewritten page on each television frame is not feasible.

Nonetheless, the videodisc does offer important advantages, particularly in those versions which use one revolution to store each frame and in which reproduction is not dependent upon hard contact between player and disc. Having one frame for each 360° rotation means that positioning the playback head in a stationary mode can constantly refresh the same picture. If there is no hard contact between disc and player, a single frame can be maintained and constantly replayed without wear. While the MCA laser-based system offers these features, the consumer version first marketed in Atlanta does not. The MCA Magnavision player operates in two modes: 1800 rpm with 360° per frame and a playing time of 30 minutes per side, and a variable speed mode which sacrifices the single frame per rotation for a longer playing time of 60 minutes. The frame access options on the Magnavision player are:

- "Slow Motion" which permits a frame-by-frame progression in either direction
  a. "Reverse/Forward" permitting a predetermined slow speed in the selected direction
  b. "Variable Slider" which allows control of the rate of presentation
- "Play: Reverse/Forward"
- "Fast Forward"
- "Audio: Channel 1, Channel 2"
- "Search: Reverse/Forward"
- "Index"

The last three controls require a word of explanation. The audio selection permits the choice of either of two audio tracks (or the use of both for stereo). Educational applications might include bilingual presentations, questions-and-explanations and the like. The "search" function sends the mechanism backward or forward to stop at a preselected frame. "Index" displays the otherwise invisible frame number in the upper left hand corner of the picture.[18]

While the Maganavox subsidiary of the Dutch giant, Phillips, manufactures the consumer model, its partner MCA has, since

1976, been at work on its own player, more complex, more expensive and designed for the industrial-educational market. The CIA, various medical groups, and the military are among the potential clients with which MCA has been working. Col. James Lane of Ft. Belvoir says, "... we can combine the storage capabilities of the book with the interactive ability of the computer disc and the dynamics of the motion picture ... and we can wrap it all up in a single videodisc." Lane anticipates that a single two-sided disc, playing 30 minutes per side, could carry a 45 hour course of study combining 51 minutes of full motion television plus 16,200 frames of text.[19] McGraw-Hill has also been at work in a similar context, developing a pilot model in senior high school and college-level biology courses in which the disc's 30 minute side contains approximately 26½ minutes of sound motion picture sequences selected from 4 McGraw-Hill films and a special 2½ minute introductory sequence. Of the remaining minute on the disc, about 40 seconds are used for start-up instructions. With all but 20 seconds of the disc's running time accounted for, the remaining 600 frames are devoted to text materials, the equivalent of a fair-sized text book.[20]

What seems apparent is that the new technologies are blurring longstanding distinctions which have separated print from nonprint media. The rapid development of the home computer may—or may not—foreshadow another communications device's entry into the parlor and office. The home computer may always be the expensive plaything of a relatively small band of enthusiasts, but even if this should prove to be the case, other developments already suggested by current happenings in the evolution of cable television may expand computer utility. The introduction of teletext and an announcement in the May 19, 1979 issue of the *New York Times* that Mattel and Jerrold Electronics have combined forces to test market "Playcable," which will permit cable subscribers (for an additional $10 per month) to interact with a central computer to play Major League Baseball and Electric Company Math, leave open the possibility that the computer will enter the home in a different guise.[21]

TELECOMMUNICATIONS POLICIES AND REGULATION

As in no recent time, the arena of communications policy is crowded with new players and new ideas on the future of communications. One of the important new players is the National Telecommunications and Information Administration (NTIA). Established within the Department of Commerce, it is headed by former FCC Chief Counsel, Henry Geller, who holds the rank of Assistant Secretary. NTIA is the successor to the former White House Office of Telecommunications Policy (OTP) and also incorporates Commerce's Office of Telecommunications which functioned as a technical support agency for OTP.

NTIA's work encompasses four major program elements: Policy Analysis and Development (including the task of developing options for broadcasting and cable television deregulation), Telecommunications Applications, Federal Systems and Spectrum Management, and Telecommunications Sciences (e.g., "Develop user-oriented standards for Federal data communications systems").[22] Among NTIA's Telecommunications Applications concerns is the improvement of communications services to rural areas. NTIA is one of the agencies involved in implementing the White House's Rural Development Initiatives, outlined in a White House publication of February, 1979.[23] So far, three specific regulatory changes have been proposed by NTIA, acting as spokesperson for the Administration. In FCC Broadcast Docket 78-253, NTIA has proposed that low-power television transmitters, such as those now used in rural areas to repeat the signals of conventional broadcast stations, might be licensed as low-power broadcast stations. NTIA also proposes that the FCC deregulate the licensing of receive-only satellite earth stations. (Low-power television stations combined with programming distributed by satellite could result in greater viewer choice, not only in rural America, but in urban areas as well. The Spanish International Network, which has affiliates in cities with large Latino populations, would like to extend its service to other areas by such a combination.) Finally, NTIA is urging the FCC to exempt small town telephone companies from present regulations which prohibit telephone companies from offering cable television service.

Another aspect of the White House Rural Development Initiatives is HEW's Telecommunications Demonstration Program, which supports a variety of innovative applications of technology, including six which have application to rural areas. One is a University of Denver Graduate School of Librarianship project which uses telefax, slow-scan television and telephone to provide information services for the public and continuing education for librarians in five rural communities.[24]

NTIA's concern with deregulation and improved market place competition is not unique. Since the landmark FCC actions discussed by Cordtz—the Carter-fone decision which opened the telephone system to "foreign attachments," and the FCC's approval of the Microwave Communications, Inc. (MCI) application for authority to establish itself as a "special service common carrier" for intercity data traffic—the trend has grown rapidly. Even the American Telephone and Telegraph Company, the biggest company on earth, appears to accept this "trend of the times." In past Congresses, a Bell-supported "Consumer Communications Reform Act" had been introduced, designed to protect the economies of scale and efficiencies possible with a single, monolithic telephone system—AT&T's. Now, with a new chairman, Charles Brown, Bell is turning to aggressive marketing and the development of user-oriented services, such as ACS, described above.

Best and most dramatic evidence is found in the three bills in Congress to rewrite the Communications Act of 1934. Two versions are in the Senate: S. 611, introduced by Senate Communications Subcommittee chairperson, Ernest F. Hollings (D-SC); and S. 622, offered by Senators Goldwater (R-AZ) and Schmitt (R-NM). The current House rewrite bill is a new version of that introduced last session by Lionel Van Deerlin (D-CA), chairperson of the House Subcommittee on Communications.

The Van Deerlin bill is by far the most comprehensive, being, as its sponsor calls it, "a basement-to-attic" revision of domestic communications regulation. A thorough examination of each provision would require a paper of its own, but among the highlights are its proposals to levy a "spectrum use fee" from all who occupy frequencies including nonbroadcast services as well as broadcasters; substantial deregulation of radio immediately, with deregulation of TV to follow; deregulation of cable, leaving to the Department of Justice the question of cross-ownership between cable and broadcasting; and replacement of the Federal Communications Commission by a new Communications Regulatory Commission. In addition, the present Department of Commerce National Telecommunications and Information Administration would be replaced by an independent agency to be called the National Telecommunications Agency.

In the common carrier field, the Van Deerlin bill authorizes regulation of interstate and foreign telecommunications only when "market place forces fail to protect the public interest," and notes that "competition shall be relied upon to the maximum extent possible to determine the variety, quality and cost of telecommunications services and facilities."[25] The bill would deregulate all but the "dominant carrier," i.e., the Bell System, in providing intercity services. Basic telephone voice service at the local level would be the regulatory province of each state, but each local carrier would have to provide interconnection for any interexchange carrier (Bell, MCI, SP Communications or any other entrant in the field).[26] AT&T would not be required to divest itself of its manufacturing subsidiary, Western Electric, (as called for in a previous version of the Van Deerlin bill) but Western Electric would have to make its products available to all potential buyers. Further, the 1956 consent decree by which Bell agreed to abstain from such services as data processing and cable television would be set aside. On the local level, local phone companies could offer cable TV services, and cable operators could, if they wished, enter the telephone market. Local telephone companies could provide traditional CATV services (i.e., the retransmission of broadcast signals), "electronic mass media" services (such as pay TV and electronic newspapers), or remote meter reading and fire and burglar alarms. But, if they offer program services ("electronic mass media"), they must insure that others can offer the same services at equivalent rates.

On the international scene, the Communications Satellite Corporation (Comsat) is also designated a "dominant carrier," but would be permitted to offer service directly to the public (Comsat is presently a "carriers' carrier") through an arm's length subsidiary.

Networkers, present and potential, will note that the Van Deerlin bill would have the effect of immediately deregulating shared use and resale. A "carrier" is defined as any legal person who "provides any interexchange telecommunications service, intraexchange telecommunications service, or international transmission. Such term does not include the shared use of telecommunications services and facilities on a nonprofit basis."

The two Senate bills are far less comprehensive, concentrating primarily upon common carrier services. As does Congressman Van Deerlin's bill, they place renewed emphasis on market mechanisms for responding to public needs, and look to regulation to operate where market forces are not sufficient.[27] The Hollings bill is designed to give the FCC more options in regulating telecommunications services beyond the "regulated" vs. the "unregulated" bimodal system now in use. Companies which provide nothing but equipment, information services, or software would remain completely unregulated by the FCC, as is now the case. "Category I" telecommunications carriers are those which provide a service for which the market is largely competitive. These carriers would only be obliged to submit to the FCC such information as may be necessary for the Commission to monitor the market. The FCC could change a Category I carrier to Category II when evidence indicates that it so dominates the market that essential services are not subject to effective competition.

In the Hollings bill, as in the Van Deerlin bill in the House, the effect of the 1956 consent decree would be substantially set aside, the "boundary" between communications and data processing no longer being the determinant. AT&T would be allowed to enter any market it might wish, including unregulated information services—but to do so it would have to set up a "fully separated" subsidiary.

The Goldwater-Schmitt bill also requires the FCC to "classify common carriers according to the degree of regulation necessary" and to review such classification every two years. Neither measure would require AT&T to divest itself of Western Electric.

The two Senate bills do differ in the international communications sphere. S. 611, the Hollings bill, would establish a nonprofit International Telecommunications Management Corporation, owned collectively by the U.S. international carriers, to coordinate planning and management and to negotiate with foreign entities. S. 622, the Goldwater bill, would leave responsibility with the FCC.

All three bills provide some sort of user fee for spectrum use, but they vary widely in scope, purpose, and amount. The Goldwater bill, consistent with its sponsor's reluctance to support a spectrum fee for more than the cost of communications regulation, would raise the fewest dollars. The Hollings bill would raise some $80 million to go to the government's general revenues. The Van Deerlin measure in the House, with higher fees to be phased in over a ten-year period, is estimated to generate about $150 million. Unlike the previous House bill, these monies would not be earmarked for the Communications Regulatory Commission, public broadcasting or loans to minority communicators, but would go to the Treasury.[28]

INTERNATIONAL ISSUES

In September, 1979 the International Telecommunications Union, a United Nations agency whose roots go back 100 years to the beginnings of international telegraphy, will convene the first General World Administrative Radio Conference (GWARC) in 20 years. While World Administrative Radio Conferences are held regularly to deal with specific issues (Space Communications in 1971, Broadcast Satellites in 1977, and others), a GWARC has the broadest of mandates and is free to consider frequency allocations across the entire usable spectrum for any and all services.

While a good bit of rhetoric about a possible face-to-face confrontation between the developed and developing worlds has been generated in this country and abroad, most of the issues of greatest interest to the United States are not likely to divide the "haves" from the "have nots." One notable exception is the High Frequencies; the U.S. and others want additional allocations for international shortwave radio broadcasting and are proposing to share some of the spectrum now assigned to the fixed service.[29]

The so-called North-South division, which separates the industrialized nations, capitalist *and* socialist, from the less developed countries, as the East-West split formerly divided the world, is nonetheless real. Articulate spokespeople for the developing world are calling for a "New World Information Order" to parallel a "New World Economic Order" in which the poor countries would receive what they characterize as a fairer share of the planet's resources . . . including its intellectual resources.[30]

International discussions abound with ringing phrases from which it is hard to take exception. But when we try to convert these to pragmatic definitions, agreement is difficult and conflict is almost inevitable. The United States' dedication to the Free Flow of Information in one context gives opposition to any attempts to block information, inbound or outbound, at national borders; but our equally strong concerns with the Right of Privacy and with the property rights which are protected by national and international copyright agreements sets some limits to the freedom of free flow.

Much of the Third World is also concerned about perceived threats to its "cultural integrity." Particularly, many complain about the "Americanization" of the entire world by our export of popular television series at prices which mean that a developing (or a developed) nation can have a full color adventure or comedy series for less than the cost of a locally produced black-and-white series. (The same economic factors are at work when American public television imports British products and often somewhat similar cries are heard here.) While television has been one of the most obvious topics of concern, books, magazines, and data bases also enter the discussion.

"Transborder data flow" is another current term in the discussion of international problems regarding telecommunications. In Sweden, the government collects an increasing amount of personal data on Swedish citizens. Swedish law requires that such data be stored and processed within the country, lest they be used in ways contrary to Swedish law. Canadians express concern at the growing body of information on Canadian citizens stored in U.S. computers over which Canadian authorities have no control. Fear is even expressed on the possibilities of countries, or even ship-borne computers in international waters, that will become "data havens" outside the law.

IMPLICATIONS

Networkers, librarians, all who are engaged in the communications business and, in fact, citizens in general, need to be mindful of the rapidly changing telecommunications environment in which we all find ourselves. Cries that "the Information Age is coming" may divert our attention from the degree to which it has already arrived. William Donnelly's "Emerging Video Environment," with multiple channels of cable television, videocassettes and videodiscs, and the possibility of new broadcast networks, already exists in some parts of the United States. While video is still regarded largely as an entertainment medium, other applications are emerging, and the network-based dispersed bibliographic control center may have to deal with video forms as well as books and documents, media which may lend themselves to electronic transfer in ways similar to the means by which information about them is exchanged between libraries.

But, as video increasingly includes still as well as moving pictures, and alphanumeric as well as pictorial applications, and as the potential for home facsimile is realized, networkers may find as yet unrealized opportunities to "talk" not only to each other but to the ultimate users of information in their offices and homes.

In the regulatory sphere, many forces are at work. While the general trend seems to be in the direction of easier entry into the communications field, and the hope of lower communications prices through open competition is raised, networkers will need to study such developments closely to decide which of the many options under consideration are most desirable from the viewpoint of the library community—and then to mount those informational and political activities likely to assure that events take the desired course.

To that end, networkers and other members of the library and information community would do well to seek out their colleagues and natural allies, to discuss and define their mutual interests and common goals, and to take such concerted action as can be mustered. The stakes are high, and the high rollers of communications are already in the game. If librarians, educators, and others in the public sector are to be among the winners, they will have to do more than to trust Lady Luck.

NOTES

1. Frank W. Norwood, "Telecommunications Programs Affecting Network Development," in Joseph Becker, ed., *Interlibrary Communications and Information Networks* (Chicago: American Library Association, 1971), pp. 59-68.
2. Dan Cordtz, "The Coming Shake-Up in Telecommunications," *Fortune* (April 1970), p. 69.
3. Sloan Commission on Cable Communications, *On the Cable* (New York: McGraw-Hill, 1971).
4. "WTCG Polishes Superstation Image by Cutting Commercials, Adding Programs," *Home Video Report* (May 10, 1979), p. 6.
5. "Satellite Will Link Hospitals to Deliver Health Education to Patients," press release dated May 1 (1979), Public Service Satellite Consortium, 4040 Sorrento Valley Boulevard, San Diego, California 92121.
6. "Community Service Network Fact Sheet," dated April 11 (1979), Community Service Network, 1666 Connecticut Avenue, N.W., Washington, D.C. 20036.
7. "ITS 9th Annual Seminar: A Home Videodisc & Programming Update," *Videoplay Report* (April 16, 1979), p. 1.
8. "The First Videodisc Catalogue: Something for Everyone," *Videoplay Report* (January 8, 1979), p. 2.
9. Bernarr Cooper, ed., *ITFS Instructional Television Fixed Service (2500 megahertz), What It Is . . . How to Plan* (Washington: National Education Association, 1967).

10. Frank W. Norwood, "Communications Satellite Services in the United States," in Melvin J. Voigt and Gerhard J. Hanneman, eds., *Progress in Communication Sciences*, Vol. 1 (Norwood, N.J.: Ablex Publishing Corp.), pp. 167-89.
11. Morris Edwards, "Innovative Services Pave Way for the Info Age of the 80's," *Communications News* (April 1979), p. 44.
12. Thomas J. Crotty, "Satellite Business Systems," *E. F. Hutton Research Review* (August 9, 1978).
13. Edwards, "Innovative Services."
14. "ACS Filing Snagged by Software Program," *Communications News* (April 1979), p. 1.
15. "Two-way Cable Poised for Major Test in Columbus," *Broadcasting* (November 21, 1977), p. 42.
16. "Reuter Monitor (Financial)," and "Reuter Monitor (Grains/Oilseeds)," n.d., Reuters, 2 Wall Street, New York, NY 10005.
17. "Viewdata," Post Office Telecommunications, British Post Office (June, 1977); Gary D. Rosch, "New Data and Information System Set for Commercial Market Trial," *Telephony* (March 20, 1978).
18. "Magnavox/MCA Here at Last: The 'Ken & Norman Show' Begins," *Videoplay Report* (December 25, 1978), p. 4.
19. "Videodisc Update: Instruction and Training," *Videoplay Report* (July 10, 1978), pp. 3-4.
20. "Videodisc Update: McGraw-Hill's 'The Development of Living Things,'" *Videoplay Report* (July 24, 1978), pp. 2-3.
21. "Cable-TV System to Enable Viewers to Play Games," *New York Times* (May 19, 1978), p. 48.
22. *An Overview: National Telecommunications and Information Administration* (Washington: Department of Commerce, n.d.).
23. *White House Rural Development Initiatives* (Washington: Office of Management and Budget, n.d.).
24. *Awards Announcement* (Washington: Department of Health, Education and Welfare, n.d.).
25. H.R. 3333, 96th Congress, 1st Session.
26. *Telecommunications Report* (April 2, 1979), pp. 1-10.
27. *Telecommunications Report* (March 19, 1979), pp. 1-10.
28. *Broadcasting* (April 9, 1979) displays the features of each bill relating to radio-television in a chart on pp. 32-33.
29. Frank W. Norwood, "U.S. Set to Tackle World Broadcasters at WARC," *BM/E—Broadcast Management/Engineering* (March 1979), pp. 55-60.
30. M. Mustapha Masmoudi, *The New World Information Order* (Paris: International Commission for the Study of Communications Problems, 1978).
31. George Kroloff and Scott Cohen, "The New World Information Order: A Report to the Committee on Foreign Relations of the U.S. Senate" (Washington), pp. 36-8.

Standards for Networks and the Identification of Some Missing Links

Paul B. Lagueux
Information Systems Specialist
Council on Library Resources, Inc.
Washington, D.C.

During the course of preparing this paper, it occurred to me that the meaning of the word "standard" can be somewhat elusive. Among the many variations listed in *Webster's Dictionary*, the following illustrates the sense or feel for what is meant or can be included for our purposes:

- Something established by authority, custom, or general consent as a model or example
- Something set up or established by authority as a rule for the measure of quantity, weight, extent, value, or quality.

The intransitive form of the verb would appear to corroborate the above inasmuch as "to standardize" is defined solely in context of bringing into conformity or comparing with a standard.

There are three important points to consider. First, a body such as a central authority must decree or an organizational base must consent to standards for their effective implementation. Second, the intended scope of a standard must be explicit as should be its targeted audience. Finally, and perhaps most important, the bases for the generation, implementation, and maintenance of standards are for the most part economic in

174

nature. This last point is particularly compelling since the development and implementation of standards are costly processes. Therefore, standards that are developed for the sake of standards alone and that will serve no useful purpose should be discouraged. Conversely, the early development and implementation of standards that are necessary will result in long-term benefits and greater economies though there may be some costs associated with the conversion process.

Very early forms of standardization were value oriented, i.e., based upon the relative worth or significance of an item. On the basis of an agreed upon value, goods, products, and services were exchanged or bartered. Obviously, some fared better than others. Today, as Hill and Walkowicz[1] have pointed out, standards play an extremely significant role in our daily lives and yet we are unmindful of their impact on one hand and take standards for granted on the other hand. One need only casually look about the room and find standards applied to the height of desk tops, electrical receptacles and sockets, telephone jacks; or look about the street and take notice of the standards applied to signal lights at street intersections, various specifications for automobile and truck component parts, and others. Indeed, one of the early formal standards organizations in the United States that embodied the three principal points was the Standards Committee of Automotive Engineers which was established in 1910, several years earlier than Ford developed assembly line, mass production techniques. Whether spurred by Leland's success with the application of interchangeable parts, the plethora of fledgling manufacturers, or a combination of these and other factors, the economic advantages of standard wheels and tires among other standard component parts pioneered the way for other industrial applications in this country. Meanwhile, as a bad example that illustrates negative economic impact, railroads that dominated land transportation in Europe continued to struggle with the problem of varying track gauges because of the lack of standardization. In fact, this obstacle still continues to hamper railroad transportation in some parts of Europe.

At this point it would be well to discuss, albeit briefly, two primary types of standards, namely, *de facto* and *de jure*. As impled, *de facto* standards generally have come about through custom or practice without any official sanction, although official approval may have been granted at the local level for use internally or by agreement with external representatives for use among similar interests. Often times, *de facto* standards that prevade throughout a sector of a community or across an application will be sanctioned by a formal body and thus become a *de jure* standard.

In the field of information transfer, the first formal body to organize and implement standards began in the year 1865 with the birth of the International Telegraph Union. Historically, as technology progressed, new frameworks for the development of standards came into being. For example, the Underwriters Laboratories was established in 1894, the National Bureau of Standards in 1901, American National Standards Institute in 1918, the Electronic Industries Association in 1924, International Organization for Standardization in 1926, American National Standards Committee (ANSC) Z39 in 1939, International Telegraph and Telephone Consultative Committee (CCITT) in 1957, International Federation for Information Processing (IFIP) in 1960, and ANSC X3 and ANSC X4 in 1961. Clearly then, the organizational framework for the development of standards, including those that relate to information processing, has not come about in recent years. These and many other organizations are clearly identified, including their relationship and scope of activities.[2] Who are these organizations and what are their roles?

The International Standards Organization (ISO) was established to promote the development of standards in order to facilitate the international exchange of goods and services as well as to develop mutual cooperation in certain areas of activity. ISO's principal work consists of facilitating the coordination and unification of national standards and, hopefully, establishing international standards. It is a nongovernmental organization comprised of more than 80 member bodies. Only the national institute that best represents the standardization activities for each country can be an ISO member. Although ISO standards have no legal force, Avram has pointed out that more than half of its members are governmental agencies or bodies incorporated by law.[3] ISO accomplishes its work through the establishment of Technical Committees in specified program areas that are analogous to our own American National Standards Committees. For example, ISO TC46 is the counterpart to Z39—Library Work and Documentation, and TC97 is the counterpart to X3—Computers, and TC95 is the counterpart to X4—Office Equipment.

The American National Standards Insitute (ANSI) is the nationally recognized clearinghouse and coordinating agency for the voluntary development and implementation of standards in the United States. As such, it is also the official member body of the ISO. ANSI is a private nonprofit federation representing approximately 200 organizations. Although ANSI does not develop standards *per se*, it does provide the framework for identifying standards requirements as well as managing and coordinating the voluntary development, approval, adoption, and publication of standards. Since the development of standards is voluntary in nature, the process requires that organizations reach consensus for approval of the proposed standards. There are three methods recognized by ANSI as evidence of consensus prior to its approval of a proposed standard—these are the Accredited Organization Method, the American National Standards Committee Method, and the Canvass Method.

The Accredited Organization Method permits the organization involved in standards work to seek accreditation from ANSI. The criterion requires that the procedures implemented in the development of standards be comparable to those of the American National Standards Committee Method in reaching consensus. Standards developed under this method are then transmitted to ANSI and processed in the same fashion as those developed by the Committee Method.

The Standards Committee Method requires that a Standards Committee be established and operate under the provisos of ANSI. Once established, the Committee has a continuing responsibility to operate within a specific scope of interest. A Committee will review standards developed by others or, as necessary, develop its own standards by any of several methods. Usually, the preparation of standards is carried on by subcommittees, but this is not always necessarily so. Generally, proposed standards are forwarded to an ANSI standards management board via its secretariat. The secretariat is the organization authorized by ANSI to assume the responsibilities as defined in ANSI procedures.[4] In reaching consensus, designated representatives of member organizations are polled in order to demonstrate the commitment to consensus. Provided that consensus is reached, the secretariat will then forward the results of the formal ballot along with the proposed standard for approval.

The Canvass Method may be used by any responsible organization desiring to introduce a proposed standard in an area of its concern. The organization is then responsible for preparing a list of organizations that it intends to canvass or poll that are known to have concerns or competence about the subject proposed for a standard. In general, sponsors are responsible for preparing the ballot and other pertinent materials and insuring that each organization or individual on the canvass list responds within a six month time limit that is established for this method. Following this, the sponsoring organization then fowards to ANSI all pertinent documentation including the proposed standard, the canvass list, comments received and any responses developed to these comments by the sponsoring organization. Further processing by ANSI is the same as that developed by the American National Standards Committee Method in the approval process.

American National Standards Committee Z39 (ANSC Z39), Library and Information Sciences and Related Publishing Practices, is organized under procedures of ANSI to identify new standards and review, modify, reaffirm or terminate existing ANSC Z39 standards. ANSC Z39 also participates in the development of related international standards such as those prepared by ISO. Its stated scope of interest is in the development of standards relevant to information systems, products and services as they relate to libraries, information services and publishing.[5] Membership in ANSC Z39 is open to any association, organization or company having concern in matters falling within the scope of Z39. Subcommittees carry out charges established by the ANSC Z39 for the development of draft standards as well as the review of existing standards for update determination.

Elected officers of Z39 consist of a chairperson, a vice-chairperson, and six councilors who in turn advise the Executive Council. The councilors represent three major areas or interets, namely: libraries, information services, and publishers. The executive director and a representative of the secretariat are also members *ex officio* of the Executive Council. As stated in the draft bylaws, the executive director is responsible for the administration of the programs and activities of ANSC Z39. The executive director is directly responsible to the chairperson of ANSC Z39 for day-to-day operations and to the Z39 secretariat as well. Member organizations respond to letter ballots by responding with a yes vote, a no vote with an accompanying reason, or abstention when the proposed standard lies outside the interest of the member organization. The Council of National Library and Information Associations is the secretariat and is responsible to ANSI for the general administration of Z39.

American National Standards Committee X3 (ANSC X3), Computers and Information Processing, is concerned with standardization in the areas of computers and information processing and peripheral equipment, devices and media related thereto. The Computer and Business Equipment Manufacturers Association (CBEMA) is both the secretariat and the sponsor of ANSC X3. As secretariat, it is responsible to ANSI for carrying out the responsibilities; as sponsor, it has assumed the responsibility of the development and publication of its standards. ANSC X3 has three standing committees which are the International Advisory Committee, a Standards Planning and Requirements Committee, and a Standards Steering Committee (SSC).

The SSC is responsible for coordinating the activities of all its technical committees. The SSC is organized into three groups that are concerned with hardware, software, and systems. Various technical committees are responsible for the development of draft standards dealing with such problems as optical character recognition; physical and coding characteristics of magnetic tape and magnetic disc; standard languages such as BASIC, PL/1, FORTRAN and others; flowcharting techniques and design; character sets and codes; digital data communications; and others.

The American National Standards Committee X4 (ANSC X4), Office Machines and Supplies, is concerned with functional characteristics of office machines plus accessories, but excluding data processing media such as punched paper tape and punched cards. ANSC X4 has established four technical committees that deal with paper forms and layout, electrical characteristics and safety of office machines, credit identification cards and word processing systems. There are also two task groups. They concern themselves with keyboard arrangements. CBEMA is the designated secretariat for ANSC X3 also.

The Federal Information Processing Standards Coordinating and Advisory Committee (FIPSCAC) was established by the Secretary of Commerce to advise the Secretary on matters concerned with federal, automatic data processing (ADP) standards. FIPSCAC also serves as a vehicle for coordinating the work of the Federal Information Processing Standards (FIPS) Task Groups. FIPSCAC reports to the Associate Director for ADP Standards, Institute for Computer Science and Technology,

National Bureau of Standards. The Institute develops FIPS and is responsible for managing the standards program for ADP equipment in the Executive Branch of the federal government.

In developing standards, the institute works with special interest communities by establishing task groups composed of knowledgeable personnel to work on matters relating to the development, adoption, and implementation of ADP standards. Recommendations emanating from the task groups are forwarded to the National Bureau of Standards via FIPSCAC for adoption. Their work deals with many of the problems of concern to the organizations identified above, such as programming language standards, optical character recognition, computer performance, computer systems security, data telecommunications standards, and others. Through participating members, the National Bureau of Standards (NBS) also provides representation to various other standards organizations such as ANSI and ISO.

This is a terribly long prelude—but essential in making the point that standards are deemed necessary and serve a useful purpose. Many organizations and individuals are indeed working on problems held in common and, although it may appear there may be significant overlap and duplication of effort, this is not always necessarily the case. Almost by definition, the standards process is extremely time-consuming since it generally requires consensus. With respect to standards as they relate to networking issues, it would seem that we are at the crossroads of the decisionmaking process, i.e., whether to link the bibliographic utilities as we know them today. If we are to take the National Commission's National Program for Library and Information Services seriously, then we should also consider the state and regional networks, the information industry and others, by taking them into consideration when discussing standards.

Networks would seem to break down into two classifications. First is a user services network whereby users are linked with the providers of products and services. In the general sense, these are the data files that are processed by the computer and intended to service user needs which may require further processing. This form of a network could involve the collection or grouping of users who are organized in order to enhance their cataloging, processing, and reference capabilities.

The other standards concerns are related to the transmission network for communications facilities. This network is concerned with the delivery of the message and, more specifically, the message processors and the transmission of messages that takes place between host computer systems that are connected to the communications network. Stated differently, this is the linkage that allows for the exchange of information between processors, if one views the host computer as the processor, at a terminal node of the network.

The network data bases that are of concern at this time contain the following information. They have citations that are used for a variety of functions which include acquisitions, cataloging, research and reference services, interlibrary loan, and collection management. Location information is also available from the networks, and some networks accommodate interlibrary loan transactions. However, there are no documents (i.e., storage of the text of documents) in any of the networks under consideration, so this paper will not address the contents of documents. This, then, would appear to be the gist of our concerns and the type of information that we are trying to share.

In regards to where we are in the standards arena at this point, we have made great progress with bibliographic citations. We have gone a long way toward standardization in machine-readable formats, namely MARC,[6] and we are getting closer and closer to a standard cataloging code for libraries with the advent of Anglo-American Cataloging Rules 2 (AACR 2).[7] It is important to note that considerable progress has also been made in the work on a bibliographic description which will provide a standard way of describing an item regardless of the form of material.

With respect to the computer systems, nothing has been done about standardizing the software procedures that have been developed or the equipment that has been selected. Thus, the likelihood of undertaking such a task is extremely remote. It would be too costly to justify redoing these procedures. Furthermore, identical systems are not likely to occur in the United States because the managers are free to design their own internal formats and processing procedures as well as free to develop various products and services in response to users' needs.[8] However, if we want to share resources, a method of communicating bibliographic data between disparate systems must be implemented. By standardizing the structure, content designators and data content of the records to be transmitted, compatibility can be achieved; the MARC format is one way of doing this.

Equipment is not standard either. The standards that are

needed to exchange and share information from one computer processor to another are lacking, although a number of standard protocols for linking computers *per se* exists, e.g., character-oriented ANS X3.28, bit-oriented ISO High Level Data Link Procedures (HDLC) and, more recently, the CCITT X.25 as an interface between data terminals and host computers in a packet switched network environment.[9] However, until the NCLIS/NBS Task Force on Computer Network Protocol developed an application level protocol for use in the bibliographic network environment, there was no means for determining what kind of a message was being sent. The proposed computer to computer protocol has been designed to allow application tasks at one host to converse with application tasks on another host regardless of the differences in computer or computer systems.

This protocol relies on other standard protocols identified above for supplying a reliable communications subnetwork.[10] Again, however, there exist differences in command and query languages between the systems. Unfortunately, this would mean that the burden would be on the user, i.e., the user would be required to learn each system on the network in order to have access to a particular host.

In order to alleviate this problem and make the procedures transparent for the users, Long developed a normalized or standard query, response and error control protocol for the data potion of the message.[11] However, neither of these have been tested, although a general requirements document for a message delivery system has been published.[12] The document identifies the scope of technical network activities, system development methodology and the technical work that must be undertaken to realize bidirectional computer links between bibliographic utilities.

It would seem appropriate to discuss how to critique standards and what this process involves. Before acquiring expertise and becoming a critic of standards, some significant problems should be noted. There are some who believe that national standards are not the answer because the new technology will provide extended uses beyond the system's capacity.[13] Others indicate that not enough attention is being given to standards in the information related fields.[14] Unquestionably, getting standards into widespread use is a major stumbling block. Also it is important to realize that standards are never the optimum because they will not satisfy all users and all uses.

One of the criteria for judging a standard is knowledge of other related standards that exist both nationally and internationally. Another criteria is assurance that the standard will satisfy a need that is shared in common by multiple users without limiting their capabilities. In addition, the proposed standard should accommodate the current state of the art and should not be based solely on past capacities. Finally, we must be willing to accept standards developed elsewhere, such as other ANSI and ISO standards, that meet our requirements. Conversely, we must be willing to make our standards known and available so that they may be used by others.

In conclusion, this paper has not addressed certain proposed standards that are currently in developmental progress. These are well known to the community and the fact that they are not addressed in this paper makes them no less significant. Specifically, there is a marked need for a standard library identification number, a standard address number (formerly a standard account number), a standard for summary and detailed serial holdings statements, and library patron and item identification codes.

NOTES

1. Marjorie F. Hill and Josephine L. Walkowicz, *The World of EDP Standards*, 2nd Ed. (Washington: National Bureau of Standards, 1976).
2. Marjorie F. Hill, "Federal Information Processing Standards Index," *Federal Information Processing Standards Publication 12-2* (December 1, 1974); ISO Information Centre, *Information Transfer: Handbook on International Standards Governing Information Transfer* (ISO Standards Handbook 1) (Geneva, Switzerland: International Organization for Standardization, 1977); American National Standards Institute, *American National Standards Insitute Procedures for Management and Coordination of American National Standards* (New York: ANSI, 1974).
3. Henriette D. Avram from an oral presentation entitled, "International Standardization Activities," given at the ANSC Z39 Annual Business Meeting, May 9, 1979, Washington, D.C.
4. *American National Standards Institute Procedures . . .*
5. *Bylaws of the American National Standards Committee Z39: Library and Information Sciences, and Related Publishing Practices* (Washington: ANSC Z39, 1979) in draft.

6. Henriette D. Avram, *MARC, It's History and Implications* (Washington: Library of Congress, 1975); Council of National Library Associations, *American National Standard for Bibliographic Information Interchange on Magnetic Tape* (New York: American National Standards Insitute, 1970).

7. American Library Association et al., *Anglo-American Cataloguing Rules*, 2nd ed. (Chicago: American Library Association, 1978).

8. Lawrence G. Livingston, "Bibliographic Standards and the Evolving National Library Network," in Herbert Poole, ed. *Academic Libraries by the Year 2000: Essays Honoring Jerrold Orne* (New York: R. R. Bowker, 1977); Lawrence F. Buckland and William F. Basinski, *The Role of the Library of Congress in the Evolving National Network* (Washington: Library of Congress, 1978).

9. Ira W. Cotton, *Computer Science & Technology: Computer Network Interconnection: Problems and Prospects* (Washington: National Bureau of Standards, 1977).

10. National Commission on Libraries and Information Science, *A Computer Network Protocol for Library and Information Science Applications* (Washington: NCLIS, 1977).

11. Philip L. Long, *Study of Message Text Formats: Bibliographic Search Queries*. Network Planning Paper, no. 5. (Washington: Library of Congress, 1979).

12. Network Technical Architecture Group, *Message Delivery System for the National Library and Information Service Network: General Requirements*, ed. by David C. Hartmann (Washington: Library of Congress, 1978).

13. Calvin N. Mooers, "Rigors of a Pioneer in Information Science," *Bulletin of the American Society for Information Science* 5:16 (February 1979).

14. American National Standards Committee Z39, *Recommended Future Directions* (Washington: National Commission on Libraries and Information Science, 1977).

PART IV

Network Governance and Funding

The Diversity Among Legal Structures of Library Networks

Huntington Carlile, Attorney at Law
Carlile Patchen Murphy & Allison
Columbus, Ohio

I. INTRODUCTION

This paper represents an overview of the structure and governance of library networks. It looks specifically at the diverse legal organizational structures of networks, and the various ends to be served by networks, and a comparison of the various means towards those ends. The author has directly studied the authority source and governance structure of about one-half dozen library networks in the United States, and has incorporated a less extensive review of about the same number again of others culled from position papers and academic journals relating to that subject.

This paper is organized as follows: Part II sets forth and evaluates purposes and goals to be served by any library network governance, which will be the guiding principles of analysis in the subsequent parts of the paper. Part III will review in the abstract the various types of legal network structures. Part IV reviews a number of existing library networks and their legal organization and governances. Finally, Part V attempts to synthesize and summarize conclusions drawn from the review.

II. PURPOSES AND GOALS OF LIBRARY NETWORK GOVERNANCE AND ORGANIZATION

Economic and Political Context

Although at first blush the following may seem a simplistic syllogism, a network governance and organization should ideally serve the purposes and goals of its library network. Those purposes and goals generally will vary as widely as the ingenuity and perception of human beings allow. The ideal library network organization and governance will meet the aspirations of the network organizers but must, at the same time, be able to cope successfully with problems which all libraries are facing.

Although it may be presumptuous for an attorney to so simplify the problem, which I am sure has as many facets as a watermelon has seeds, I would like to suggest that there are basically two general, fundamental problems facing libraries today. First, there is the economic plight of libraries and their parent institutions. Everyone is familiar with Proposition 13 in California, the move to put a constitutional or at least legislative lid on federal spending, the failure of school levies across the country, and the general tightening of credit and available money. This calls into immediate question the prospective availability of state and federal grants and funding. As long as the stock and other investment markets remain stagnant, there is also a question as to the continuing availability of private foundation funding.[1]

The problem is not unique to libraries and library networks, but is shared by all governmental and private enterprise in the United States today. What is unique to the library and library network world is the current political and jurisdictional circumstances in which libraries and library networks must fend for themselves. Unique to libraries and library networks is the fact that they have historically eschewed parochial, political self-assertiveness for a more altruistic spirit of cooperation. However, it is ironic that, because of this very spirit in the past, its continuation in a meaningful sense has become more difficult.

From sharing and cooperation have sprung, in the last 50 years in the United States, numerous and various amalgamations of libraries on the local, municipal, state, regional and national levels, all of which have taken many different forms and all of which have their own ends and means of achieving those ends. Inevitably some of these amalgamations brush against others.

New or evolving library networks must meet the threshold issue of cooperation with appropriate assertiveness. Only then will they be able to work efficiently and productively to achieve their goals, avoid unnecessary duplication and reach optimal results.

At the other end of this spectrum of diversity is the current initiative for central planning for a National Library Network. Spirited by such groups as the National Commission on Libraries and Information Science, the Network Advisory Committee of the Library of Congress, and the Council on Library Resources, Inc., this current movement points up in its most dramatic form the dilemma of library networking in this country. That dilemma is based in the political and jurisdictional diversity of extant networks in all their multiple forms and facets, and in the tension created by the attempt to forge unity and centrality out of multiplicity and decentralization.[2]

This tension has created a fear of possible loss of local autonomy, a reluctance to take part in a reciprocal arrangement, and questions regarding mutual benefits and reciprocal burdens. No one likes to be dependent on anybody else, nor to have others dependent on them. This is all exacerbated by physical, geographical, legal and administrative barriers, but reduces really to the age old question of "turf."[3]

Another unique aspect of the current condition of libraries and library networks in the United States is the failure of the private for-profit sector to rise to the occasion and fill the demands of information and resource sharing in this area. Although there are, of course, exceptions to this, both in the information data base and in computer systems fields, it might be said that the failure of the private sector is really matched only by the failure of the federal government to play a substantial part in the information sharing revolution spearheaded by libraries in this country. This failure occurs in spite of new technological developments exploited in other areas by private interests and in spite of much rhetoric and talk at the federal level.[4]

The other side of this coin is the inescapable fact that what success there has been in information resource sharing has come from the grass roots level up. It is the municipal, local, state, and regional libraries and library networks which have spearheaded this effort. OCLC is a good example, for although it has become a national computerized library resource, it started only ten years ago as the Ohio College Library Center. Both BALLOTS (Bibliographic Automation of Large Library Operations Systems) and WLN (Washington Library Network) are likewise examples of innovative and developing networking. In Part IV of this paper we will address the rich variety and number of such library networks.

The most immediate and pressing factor in the minds of most funding authorities of libraries with regard to the sharing of library resources in a network form is the possible saving of money, rather than other factors such as sharing of resources for utilitarian purposes.[5] Such governing institutions may be reluctant to provide funds at the outset when the return on such investment and monetary savings may seem far removed, both in time and in potential. However, a library network of any appreciable size which generates a one percent savings per year for its library members would generate enough money to pay for itself; greater savings could be passed on as real savings to the libraries.[6]

The lesson to be learned here is that the network should be efficiently structured so as to benefit its members enough to make it worth their membership and to support the network. In other words, the network should be able to provide its members services and resources they could not otherwise get, at a cost which they could not otherwise afford, while paying for itself.[7]

To accomplish this end in the current political and jurisdictional context, it is essential for the library network to foster and coordinate cooperative channeling of current and new resources to their members in order to assure maximum utility of these resources among its members and other libraries of other networks.

This approach was followed by the Western Interstate Commission for Higher Education (WICHE). WICHE, recognizing already existing networks such as BCR (Bibliographic Center for Research) and AMIGOS (AMIGOS Bibliographic Council) in the Southwest, decided that its activities should be programmed under an existing organization rather than creating a new organization (as expected by its sponsor, Council on Library Resources, Inc.). WICHE's approach was chosen to generate cooperation rather than competition, including a flexible and practical ability to mesh with existing organizations and networks.[8] This was also recognized by the Pennsylvania planners who agreed that existing activities and groups such as PALINET/ULC (Pennsylvania Area Library Network/Union Library Catalog) and PRLC (Pittsburgh Regional Library Center) should be cooperatively meshed with any statewide activity and not engaged in competitive activity.[9]

The converse of this is that a library network should realize its own limitations, and should avoid reinventing the wheel. This was recognized by the founders of MIDLNET (Midwest Region Library Network), including COWL (Council of Wisconsin Libraries, Inc.), when they perceived that individual states cannot always provide and support the necessary data base for a meaningful sharing of information.[10]

In most states today, success, at a bare minimum, requires the ability to politically coordinate with the state's library agency. Today, under statutory revision and upgrading of resources, state library agencies tend to be more active and stronger than in the past in the coordination of state library resources, continuing education and other uses of information. In addition, the state library lends all of its prestige and clout to any cooperation with other regional and national activities.

In sum, the library network must be able to perform various contractual, consultation, or membership roles under various state and federal laws and with various local, regional, state, and federal committees and library groups.[11]

Specific Characteristics of the Ideal Network

Having generally reviewed the context in which library networks must operate, let us now look more specifically at the characteristics and qualities needed to successfully navigate these deep and turgid waters. Assuming that proper foundations and tools are provided, intelligent and qualified management can build on these foundations and use these tools successfully. However, it is the laying of the foundations and the forging of the tools which is the threshold and paramount concern.

There are basically three aspects of library networks which achieve this threshold importance. They are: 1) the legal structure of the organization, 2) the membership or constituency of the organization, and 3) the governance of the organization.

The legal structure of the organization is simply the formal, organic ordering of the activity pursuant to the law from which it derives its existence and authority to act (See Part III below).

The membership or constituency of the network provides the market, financial support, the needs to be served and the interests to which to render account.

The governance of the organization is the structure and administration of the power relationships among the various organizational stakeholders (members or constituents) within the shared activity or network. This must be opposed to the management, which is the operational process by which resources are obtained and used to accomplish the organizational objectives set by the governance.[12] Governance is based both on the governing documents and experience of the people working within those documents.[13] In essence, governance powers include the basic and essential definition and continuity of purpose and existence of the corporation.

These three factors will, in all instances, define and limit the scope of activity and the success in carrying out that activity. With this in mind, I would like to provide a list of the characteristics and qualities that any network should have reflected in its legal structure, membership and constituency, and governance:

- Balanced representation of diverse constituency in the governance, either directly or indirectly.
- Communication from the constituency to governance, and accountability from governance to constituency, regarding the needs and resources of the constituency and the network.
- Flexibility to assure participation in or with various other governmental or private entities and programs, both today and as they change over time, and eligibility for funding both on a general cooperative project basis and on a specific institutional basis.
- Authority and power to execute the purposes of the network.
- Authority and power to enforce membership in accordance with the purposes of the network.
- Ability to foster interdependent interaction and mutual trust.
- Ability to coordinate cooperative planning of shared resources, both those in existence and those to be developed in the future, by contract with third parties, cooperation among members and internal development.
- Ability to balance centrality of control and direction with the diverse needs of the constituency, avoiding overbroad distribution of power while rendering the governance responsive to the constituency.

- Provision of status, prestige, and support for the standards and programs of the network.
- Ease of implementation and operation.
- Continuity of internal control and direction.
- Assurance of financial stability.
- Provision of an interface with the private sector, and federal and state governments.
- Ability to generate correct and intelligent decisions quickly and under pressure.
- Ability to avoid political obstacles to performance.
- Ability to make realistic evaluations of the purposes, intents, and abilities of both its constituency and third parties.
- Ability to communicate with and direct management.
- Self-criticism and evaluation regarding performance and its furtherance of the public purpose of the network.
- Ability to act on behalf of, protect and shield the membership.
- Ability to set procedures and guidelines for action by constituents and by management.
- Ability to act as a vehicle for capitalization or funding.
- Ability to provide a united face on behalf of the network to third parties who deal with the network legally, fiscally, and contractually.[14]

III. GENERAL REVIEW OF THE VARIOUS TYPES OF LEGAL NETWORK ORGANIZATIONAL STRUCTURES

A review of the various types of institutions that can comprise a network's membership or constituency is outside the scope of this paper. A review of the various types of governances available to networks is partly a function of the legal structure and partly a function of the ingenuity of the founders of a given network. In this part of the paper, we will look at the legal structures available in the abstract, and in the next part of this paper we will review directly the governance and organizational structures of a number of extant library networks.

In this immediately following review, we will adopt the categorization of library network types used by Charles Stevens in his article entitled "Governance of Library Networks." These are governmental, quasi-governmental, and membership/legal charter type organizations.[15]

Governmental Networks

Governmental library networks are created directly pursuant to statutory mandate by federal, state, or local legislative bodies to act as state agencies of their respective government. For example, note such federal library networks as those maintained by the Atomic Energy Commission, the National Library of Medicine, the State Department, the Department of Defense, the Department of Interior, and the Interagency Federal Library Commission.[16]

On the state level, governmental library networks usually take one of two forms. The most familiar is the state library, which today is taking on a greater leadership role in many states under new legislative mandates to plan and implement new library services, funnel funding, and provide authority and example leadership.[17] The other type of state library network is that type organized as part of a State Board of Higher Education. This was initiated in 1932 by the Oregon State Board of Higher Education, and has been duplicated in such areas as the New England Board of Higher Education and the Minnesota Higher Education Coordinating Board.[18] Finally, there are local and subregional library networks in many states organized along county and multicounty political subdivision levels.

Of the three types of library networks, the pure governmental type is probably the least flexible and the most difficult for which to provide continuity and direction. They are government owned and controlled and thus are, to a large extent, subject to the accidents of history and political origin of the governing institution. They generally serve "the interest of the general public," at least in theory, although in practice they often are more subject to special interests, and tread the troubled path of political and jurisdictional conflict.[19] As noted earlier, any governmental network on a level below the federal may not be able to provide or support a data base of a size necessary for the operation of a full library network.

It is often the case that the libraries outside the jurisdiction of a state or local network cannot participate in their activities. This was true, for example, in Pennsylvania in 1976.[20]

The growth potential for governmental library networks is an open question. However, any library network today must be structured and governed in such a way as to allow it to work closely with, and accommodate, the various types of governmental library networks that will continue in existence and continue to play a central role in librarianship in this country.

Quasi-Governmental Library Networks

Several different types of quasi-governmental structures are available for library networks. One is the authority, such as the New York Port Authority, which is an independent entity created by special statute, sustained for its users' fees, and given specified powers and discretion including regulatory and advisory functions relating to its area of expertise.[21]

A second is an interstate compact, which can either be a general, broad mandate to cooperate among numerous state parties, or a narrowly defined specialized compact between contiguous states only. Often such compacts generate autonomous programs which are subject only to bylaw approval or discontinuance control by the compact. Finally, there is also the federal interstate compact for federal funding and participation, and the more unusual multistate corporations.[22]

In general, although such entities provide governmental status, prestige and legislative mandate, they are difficult and time-consuming to create and implement, and are fairly inflexible and subject to the same political and jurisdictional problems to which the purely governmental institution is subject. However, the quasi-governmental network would be slightly more flexible than the purely governmental, where it is a contract between several governments rather than an agency of only one.[23]

Any sort of interstate agreement, whether designated a compact or an authority, requires the consent of Congress pursuant to Article I, Section 10, Clause 3 of the U.S. Constitution. Since such consent is not equivalent to a treaty or statute, it is not appealable to the Supreme Court under 28 U.S.C. §1257(1). However, Congress need not always consent to such compacts in advance nor by express detailed action, but may both adopt or approve submitted proceedings after the fact, or do so by general implicit approval.[24] Of course, the contracting parties must go forward in compliance with any Congressional conditions attached.[25]

Subject to the consent of Congress, the contracting states may agree upon anything within the broad scope of their sovereign power specifically reserved to them, unless otherwise preempted by the Constitution, pursuant to the 10th Amendment. This includes education.

Such compacts are similar to but more involved than typical contracts, since they attempt to cover formally and seriously all possible stipulations affecting the conduct of the parties.[26] Although the states (and not their citizens) are parties, the citizens are all bound by the compact.[27]

Once entered into, no party state may unilaterally nullify or even interpret the compact.[28] The meaning of such compacts is a question of federal law involving all aspects of federalism and interstate commerce, and is subject to participation by all parties.[29] The Supreme Court has final jurisdiction over conflicts arising out of the operation of such compacts, and litigation may be brought by the parties or by private litigants.[30]

Examples of expressly coordinated legislation exist between states which do not require congressional approval. This would include operation of railroads in some instances.[31] Query: What about a library network utility? It is also possible for the various states and the federal government to compact subject to Congressional consent, although this has generally been reserved for situations in which the federal government cedes to a state under its eminent domain power.[32]

There are also ways to coordinate corporations among various states. Thus, corporations may be incorporated under interstate compacts.[33] Corporations may also be incorporated in two or more states pursuant to appropriate coordinated legislation without the consent of Congress.[34] Finally, corporations may be simultaneously chartered as new and separate corporations in the several states.[35]

More esoteric means of accomplishing this sort of coordinated activity include the consolidation of existing corporations of several states by coordinating legislation, or the reincorporation of corporations under several states' laws, pursuant to the corporate statute of such states.[36] In fact, some states require actual incorporation, rather than merely qualification, in order for the corporation to acquire property rights, do business, have the right to sue or enforce contracts, or even exist in the state.[37] Such multistate corporate activity involves inherent ambiguity. The corporation acts distinctly and separately within each state under its laws, and is separately subject to the interpretation and enforcement of all of the laws of the states involved.[38] It is unclear whether such a corporation is one corporation or several corporations, and such corporations may have multistate citizenship.[39]

Interstate cooperatives or compacts are not used very much in the Midwest. MIDLNET followed the model of such compact although it did so in corporate form.[40] However, examples in the Western states include the Western Regional Education Compact, its subordinate Western Interstate Commission for Higher Education, its subordinate Western Interstate Library Coordinating Organization, and the California Library Authority of Systems and Services (CLASS). In all, 25 states have adopted an interstate library compact.[41]

In the Western states such interstate compacts often act as program agents for each member state to facilitate fund transfers among the state agencies involved. This solves such problems as those encountered when libraries attempt to interact with such states as California and New Mexico, which at least one time refused to pay money in advance to not-for-profit corporations. Such organizations thus serve as receptacles for funds, on behalf of their institutions, which would otherwise not be available.[42]

Federal corporations are also created under the implicit constitutional power of the federal government to take all necessary and proper means to carry out its functions. Such corporations must be means to an express federal end set forth in Article I of the Constitution.[43] For example, 31 U.S.C. §846 sets forth the various wholly owned federal corporations including the Inter-American Educational Foundation, Inc.[44] Wholly owned federal corporations are agencies of the federal government.[45] There are also partial federal corporations. Any federal corporation has its status and power determined under the rules of federalism and under its charter, and is both a separate entity and an agency of the government.[46]

Nonprofit Membership Corporation

That peculiar entity which is a nonstock, nonprofit membership corporation is recognized and provided for by the statutes of most states. Most Midwestern states have similar statutes. We will look later at Ohio's nonprofit corporation statute.[47] The following is a list of the advantages of the corporate form:

- Relative ease of creation.
- Existence of a separate legal entity.
- The availability of central management.

- Continuity of life or existence.
- Limited liability (for a nonstock corporation, there is not even the usual liability to the extent of shares owned).
- Favorable tax structure. All corporations enjoy lower tax rates than individuals to encourage accumulation of capital. Corporations (as well as community chests, funds or foundations) may enjoy complete income tax exemption, under federal taxation pursuant to §501(c)(3) of the Internal Revenue Code, if they are organizations:

> organized and operated exclusively for religious, charitable, scientific, testing for public safety or literary, or educational purposes . . . no part of the earnings of which inures to the benefit of any private shareholder or individual, no substantial part of the activities is carrying on propaganda, or otherwise attempting to influence legislation, (except as otherwise provided in subsection [h]) and which does not participate in, or intervene in (including the publishing or distributing of statements) any political campaign on behalf of any candidate for public office.

Note carefully the limitations on legislative lobbying, which can be done only subject to very restrictive and complicated regulations. The sale, use, franchise, and income tax laws of the several states are very different, however, both among themselves and compared to federal income tax law.

- Flexibility and malleability with regard to defining the organizational form of the entity; the detail and scope of its purpose, powers and membership; its organization and governance, whether loosely or tightly held, and however distributed among management, the governing board and members.
- Subject to states' statutes on qualification or reincorporation, corporations can operate as separate, independent entities in any state.
- More subtle advantages include corporate accountability to members, corporate power over members, peer pressure among members, and the self-interest of the corporation and members.[48]

Let us review briefly the Ohio nonprofit corporation law, Ohio Revised Code §1702.01 *et seq.*

Section 1702.01(C) defines the nonprofit corporation as "a

corporation which is not formed for the pecuniary gain or profit of and whose net earnings or any part thereof is not distributable to, its members, trustees, officers or other private persons."

Section 1702.01(D) defines a charitable corporation as "a corporation organized and operated exclusively for religious, charitable, scientific testing, testing for public safety, literary or educational purposes . . ." among other purposes.

Section 1702.01(G) defines an incorporator as "a person who signed the original Articles of Incorporation."

Section 1702.01(H) defines a member as "one having membership rights and privileges in a corporation in accordance with its Articles or Regulations; voting member means a member possessing voting rights . . ."

Section 1702.01(K) defines the trustees as "the persons vested with the authority to conduct the affairs of the corporation irrespective of the name by which they are designated."

Section 1702.03 states that a "corporation may be formed for any purpose or purposes for which natural persons lawfully may associate themselves . . ."

Section 1702.04(A) provides that "any citizen, singly or jointly with others, and without regard to residence, domicile or state of incorporation, may form a corporation by signing and filing with the Secretary of State Articles of Incorporation," which shall set forth the name, the place of the principal office, and the purposes of the corporation; identify the three natural persons who are the initial trustees; and which also may, but need not, set forth membership qualification and classification; relationship to any other national associations, societies, foundations or corporations; definition of the exercise of authority by the corporation among the incorporators, trustees, officers and members; definition of the voting or the property right of the members of the corporation.

Section 1702.10 provides that either the incorporators or the members may adopt a Code of Regulations.

Section 1702.11 provides for a much more detailed definition of the membership structure and voting rights, the mechanics of its operation, the meetings of the trustees and the members, the designation of officers, and so forth, in said Code.

Section 1702.12 authorizes a nonprofit corporation to sue and be sued; to take property of any description by gift, devise or bequest; to make donations for the public welfare, charity or in furtherance of any of its other purposes; to indemnify the trustees, officers, employees or agents of the corporation under certain terms and conditions; to purchase insurance for such purposes; to contract, lease, form or acquire control of other corporations; to participate in associations or other enterprises; to borrow money, sell notes and grant security; to become a member of another corporation; to conduct its affairs in the state and elsewhere and do all other things permitted by law within its purposes, including investment in the shares of other corporations.

Generally, the Ohio Code allows total control on the part of the incorporators or members in defining the above matters, but provides statutory terms and conditions when such are not expressly provided for.

Unincorporated Associations and Cooperatives

Such entities are generally nothing more than collections of persons joined together in a loose and more or less informal manner for a common purpose. Under the common law, they have no separate legal identity or status, and have no legal powers or abilities. Because of this, lacking statutory language to the contrary, associations have none of the advantages of the corporation as described above. Picture them as similar to the 13 original states acting under the original Articles of Confederation prior to the passage of the United States Constitution.[49]

Such entities can be for-profit, in which case the members are generally thought of as partners for other legal purposes; or nonprofit, in which case they are not thought of as partners.[50] Such organizations generally operate pursuant to bylaws, constitutions or articles which govern the rules of discipline, doctrine, internal policy and interpretation. However, these have no more effect than any contract between parties and, therefore, the parties must assent to them to be bound, which assent is presumed upon joining.[51] Membership in such an organization is a privilege and there is no right to membership enforceable by the courts. On the other hand, members must assent to become such.[52]

Under the common law, property owned by such organizations is owned by the members as tenants in common.[53] Also, members of such organizations and of their boards are personally liable for contracts thereof since they are conceived as agents acting on behalf of an incapacitated principal.[54]

However, many states have by statute granted more substance to the unincorporated association entity. For example, under Ohio statutes such associations may contract, sue or be sued on behalf of their members or on their own behalf. The association's assets are subject to all judgments, executions, and other processes against the association, but only as against the association as an entity.[55] Such associations are often called cooperatives or consortia in the library sphere. These arrangements are particularly useful on a local basis or for a small number of libraries. See, for example, the Joint University Libraries founded in 1936 between Vanderbilt University, George Peabody College, and Scarrott College in Tennessee. Another example are the Claremont Colleges in Claremont, California.[56]

IV. COMPARATIVE SURVEY OF THE GOVERNANCE AND LEGAL STRUCTURES OF SEVERAL LIBRARY NETWORKS

AMIGOS Bibliographic Council

Starting out as a program of the InterUniversity Council in Texas, AMIGOS Bibliographic Council, Inc. was incorporated in 1979 under the nonprofit statutes of Texas, and has since received a 501(c)(3) tax exemption status from the Internal Revenue Service. Its purposes run from the particular provision of the services of OCLC to the more general promotion of cooperative activity among its members, development of potential of such members by research and development, and participation in the development and operation of a national library network. Library agencies having current membership contracts and being current in fee payments are voting members of AMIGOS, and are "primarily . . . nonprofit library agencies." Services may also be provided to nonmembers. Fees are set by the Board of Trustees.

The Board of Trustees ranges between six and twelve members, and all are elected by the membership. When complete, nine of these must be represented as voting members of AMIGOS and three must be active in the private sector. The executive director is an ex officio nonvoting member. The Board has all corporate authority and control of the corporate affairs of AMIGOS, although such peripheral powers not specifically delegated thereto are reserved for the members. The Board has the responsibility for hiring and firing network staff, for establishing committees, for delegating authority to contract, and for approval of programs, policies and budgets. The Board of Trustees' officers include the chair, vice-chair, secretary and treasurer. The corporation may indemnify the officers and trustees.

The articles expressly provide for an executive director to handle day-to-day business of the corporation. The corporation is authorized to participate in other corporations in furtherance of its purpose.

CLASS

The California Library Authority of Systems and Services (CLASS) is an intrastate joint powers agreement created by statute in California and acting as a coordinating agent for various state agencies of higher education, political subdivisions and school districts. It is governed by a Board of Governors which sets all policy for the system not in conflict with the statute. One of the purposes that it serves is to allow California, and any other states with which California libraries may participate, to fund the activities in advance since many Western states (including California at one time) could not pay nonprofit corporations in advance.

The Illinois Regional Library Council

The Council is an independent, nonprofit corporation governed by a 15 member Board of Directors, each representing one of the multitypes of library units making up the charter membership, of which there are 89 charter member libraries. These include school districts, colleges, universities, public libraries, public library systems, and special libraries in both profit and nonprofit institutions. There are also Directors-at-Large representing the community and library user. The statement of objectives of the corporation is a deliberately flexible one, both in its bylaws and in later statements by its ad hoc committee.

This not-for-profit corporation was created to provide leadership for Illinois libraries by the 1965 Network of Public Library Systems Act, even though the Illinois State Library had already played an important and useful role prior to that time in providing the integrated systems desired. The state library program known as the Illinois Library and Information Network

(ILLINET) is directly constituted by the 18 public library systems of Illinois, their public library members, nonpublic library affiliates, reference and research centers and the special resource centers of Illinois. The Regional Council in 1976 had not yet been integrated with ILLINET.[57]

INCOLSA

The Indiana Cooperative Library Services Authority (INCOLSA) is a creature of the 1967 Library Services Authority Act of Indiana. It was enacted to "encourage the development and improvement of all types of library service and to promote the efficient use of finances, personnel, materials and properties." The Act specifically provides for joint agreements between any jurisdictional or governmental entity having library services into a library services authority equivalent to a municipal corporation, having all the powers, privileges, and authority generally exercised by a public agency of Indiana (other than tax levying). The Act provides for the Board of Directors for such authorities to be made up of representatives of the constituent governing authorities under the joint powers agreement. The Board of Directors is empowered to draft the bylaws of the entity. However, the day-to-day management of the authority is handled by an executive director reporting to an executive committee subject to approval by the Board of Directors on specified matters. Membership fees on behalf of each member of the governing authority must be collected by taxes levied by that member.

Although the act seems to contemplate the possibility of more than one authority, in fact only one state-wide authority has been created, INCOLSA, in 1974. Its membership includes 131 library governing units representing over 146 school, public, special and academic libraries. It is governed cooperatively by a 131 member Board of Directors and a 7 member executive committee.

MIDLNET

The Midwest Regional Library Network (MIDLNET) is a not-for-profit corporation organized and existing under the laws of Illinois. The bylaws and articles create flexible powers and purposes to assure future eligibility for interstate, federal corporate compacts, and eligibility for state and federal funding. Members are from a number of states in the Midwest. Board members come from 20 libraries with a budget over $750,000 per year, each of whom is considered a major resource center (such as a state library, a statewide library system or network). MIDLNET also has a number of general members who do not vote. These libraries have budgets between a quarter and three-quarters of a million dollars per year.

Major policy is determined by the executive committee, made up of officers of the Board of Directors and the executive director. This system was devised in order to assure a threshold, minimum provision of services and resources for the large resource libraries considered to be a necessary backbone for any network.[58]

MINITEX

The Minnesota Interlibrary Telecommunications Exchange (MINITEX) is a statutorily created program funded by foundation and federal library funds. It is made available to various public, community, and regional libraries pursuant to contract with the State Department of Education and with the Office of Public Libraries and Interlibrary Cooperation. Libraries from other states are also granted access through reciprocal, contractual agreements.

MINITEX is but one of 30 programs (20 state and 10 federal) of the Minnesota Higher Education Coordinating Board, a state agency formed in 1965 pursuant to statute. The Board is appointed by the governor with the consent of the senate. The Board generally plans and coordinates postsecondary education activities for the state of Minnesota. It has an executive director and also is advised by the Higher Education Advisory Council, made up of heads of the universities of the state.

NELINET

The New England Library Information Network (NELINET) began as a program of the New England Board of Higher Education. Governed by an executive committee and an executive director, it was once very similar to MINITEX. Just this year, however, in order to carry out its objectives with more independence and flexibility, NELINET was spun-off from the

New England Board of Higher Education and has been incorporated as a not-for-profit, tax-exempt corporation.

OCLC

The Ohio College Library Center (OCLC) has always been an Ohio nonprofit corporation exempt under the federal income tax laws. Until 1977, OCLC's membership was limited to the Ohio libraries participating in its system. These members elected the Board of Trustees and retained the power to amend its Articles and Code of Regulations.

In 1977, pursuant to the flexible, open-ended nature of the Ohio not-for-profit corporate statute, OCLC radically changed its organizational and governance status, becoming OCLC, Inc. Membership was granted to all participating libraries nationwide. The Board of Trustees was expanded from nine to fifteen (six of whom are elected by a Users' Council), made up of representatives of the various networks with whom OCLC contracts. This Council also must ratify any changes in the corporation's organic code or articles. The full Board of Trustees acting as trustee members elect the remaining eight trustees, with the executive director acting as an ex officio trustee. The Board has the sole power to initiate amendments to the code and articles. Finally, the actual library members elect delegates to the Users' Council. Thus, there has been a diffusion of membership assuring a means of communication and representation for all members, while there is still retained a centrality of control and governance.

OHIONET

OHIONET was formed simultaneously with the expansion of OCLC membership in 1977. It too is an Ohio not-for-profit corporation, tax-exempt under the federal income tax laws. Its members are Ohio libraries participating in the OCLC system. They retain the right to amend the code and articles of the corporation and also elect its trustees.

SUNY

The State University of New York (SUNY) is a full state university system governed by 16 trustees and administered by a chancellor and other officers. The SUNY library network is operated as a program or office denominated as Library Services. This office is part of the Educational Services branch of the university system under a vice-chancellor. Library Services is administered by an executive director.

Although it has no organic governance power, the SUNY/ OCLC Advisory Committee (SONAC) does provide advisory and planning expertise for New York users of the OCLC system. SONAC has nine representatives, three from each of three classes of participants including public higher education libraries, independent higher education libraries and other libraries. From these nine representatives are elected the delegates to the OCLC Users' Council.

WICHE

The Western Interstate Commission for Higher Education (WICHE) acts pursuant to the Western Regional Education Compact, an interstate compact among several Western states. WICHE operates WILCO, the Western Interstate Library Coordinating Organization, which is a consulting and study organization attempting to coordinate library cooperation among the independent libraries in the West as well as among such other networks as BCR and AMIGOS.

It is governed by an Executive Board of Directors which develops plans and programs for approval by a steering committee. The Board is made up of representatives of the multitype library members, internal staff members, and visitors who serve on a rotating basis.[59]

V. CONCLUSION

One of the foci of this paper is to delineate the ideal library network and governance structure. We have looked at what a library organizational structure should accomplish. We have analyzed the various types of legal structures available, and have made the point that the governance structure, membership, and constituency can usually be defined to the specifications of the founders by the organic statute, charter or contract. We have also seen that there are as many types of library network organizations and governance structures in existence as the pluralistic and diverse legal background would allow.

We have set forth 22 characteristics or qualities that a library governance, organizational structure, and constituency should provide. Perhaps a mathematical analysis of the relative comparative performance of various combinations of these three factors of governance, structure and constituency, with regard to performance and fulfillment of the 22 criteria, is possible. However, I do not think that this is the case. Rather, it seems to me that the conclusion that might be drawn from the study is that the ideal mix of constituency, governance, and organizational structure depends on factual questions which change from year to year and from place to place.

Certainly in much of the country, especially the Midwest and the East, the most common form of library network is either a nonprofit corporation or a state agency or program under a state agency. AMIGOS and NELINET may reflect a trend towards spinning off state agencies into nonprofit corporations for this purpose. On the other hand, MINITEX and MIDLNET (operating as a state agency and a not-for-profit corporation respectively) actually bear many of the features of interstate compacts on an informal contractual basis rather than on a formal constitutional basis.

The formal interstate compact approach has been used in the Western states, as WICHE demonstrates. The CLASS system in California is a sort of intrastate compact or joint powers agreement between various local and state governmental agencies or political subdivisions. A similar approach was first seen in Indiana.

There seems to be no general conclusion that can be drawn from these facts other than that any person or persons attempting to set up a library network ought to carefully review its constituency, its ends, its resources, the persons with whom it will cooperate or coordinate activities, the sources of its funds and limitations on obtaining them, tax impacts of its activities among the various states or with the federal government, and what already existing statutory tools or resources are available. For example, one may be able to determine what a state's plans for libraries are by checking with the federal Office of Education. States are required to submit plans to that office under the federal Library Services and Construction Act.

The ultimate conclusion is that no simple solution exists. If a substantial number of academic, nonacademic, public, and private libraries or library institutions are interested in establishing, improving, or otherwise modifying a network, this in itself will provide the necessary prestige. Appropriate public purpose and general political clout will allow the participants, with advice perhaps from consultants, to formulate just about any kind of structure and governance desired. Happy networking!

NOTES

1. Charles T. Meadows, "A Plan for Library Cooperation in Pennsylvania," ERIC No. ED 136757 (July 6, 1976): p. 10; Arthur D. Little, Inc., "A New Governance Structure for OCLC: Principles and Recommendations," (November 1977): pp. 3, 23.
2. Arthur D. Little, Inc., "A New Governance Structure for OCLC," p. 4.
3. "Networks and Cooperation: The Jurisdictional Debate," *Library Journal* 99: 3174 (December 15, 1974).
4. Arthur D. Little, Inc., "A New Governance Structure for OCLC," p. 4.
5. "Networks and Cooperation," p. 3174.
6. "Initiating the Design and Development of a Western Interstate Bibliographic Network, 3d Quarterly Report," ERIC No. ED 136813 (May 31, 1976).
7. Arthur D. Little, Inc., "A New Governance Structure for OCLC," p. 24.
8. "Initiating the Design and Development of a Western Interstate Network," pp. 7, 8.
9. Meadows, "A Plan for Library Cooperation in Pennsylvania," p. 10.
10. Barbara Markuson, "The Midwest Regional Library Network (MIDLNET): A Progress Report to the Library Community," ERIC No. ED 112873 (June 1975): p. 9.
11. National Commission of Libraries and Information Science," *Annual Report to the President and Congress, 5th Annual Report,* ERIC No. ED 140799.
12. Arthur D. Little, Inc., "A New Governance Structure for OCLC," p. 73.
13. Charles H. Stevens, "Governance of Library Networks," *Library Trends* (Fall 1977): p. 221.
14. "Initiating the Design and Development of a Western Interstate Network," pp. 35, 36; Barbara Markuson, "The Midwest Regional Library Network," p. 19; Charles T. Meadows, "A Plan for Library Cooperation . . . ," p. 42; Arthur D. Little, Inc., "A New Governance Structure for OCLC," pp. 3, 4, 9, 10, 18, 73, 79, 86, 87; Charles H. Stevens, "Governance of Library Networks," pp. 220, 221.
15. Charles H. Stevens, "Governance of Library Networks," p. 224.

16. *Ibid.*
17. Barbara Markuson, "MIDLNET: Progress Report," p. 15.
18. Charles H. Stevens, "Governance of Library Networks," p. 223.
19. Arthur D. Little, Inc., "A New Governance Structure for OCLC," p. 5.
20. Charles T. Meadows, "A Plan for Library Cooperation in Pennsylvania," p. 28.
21. "Initiating the Design and Development of a Western Interstate Network," p. 29.
22. *Ibid.*, p. 29, 30; 72 Am. Jur. 2d States 35; 134 A.L.R. 1411.
23. Harry S. Martin, "Coordination by Compact: A Legal Basis for Interstate Library Cooperation," *Library Trends* 24: 191, 213 (October 1975).
24. *Wharton v. Wise*, 153 U.S. 155, 14 S.Ct. 735 (1894).
25. *Petty v. Tennessee-Missouri Bridge Commission*, 359 U.S. 275, 79 S.Ct. 785 (1959).
26. *Virginia v. Tennessee*, 148 U.S. 503, 13 S.Ct. 728 (1883).
27. *Hinderlinder v. LaPlata River and Creek Dutch Co.*, 304 U.S. 92, 58 S.Ct. 83 (1938).
28. *West Virginia ex rel Dyer v. Sims*, 345 U.S. 22, 71 S.Ct. 557 (1950).
29. *Petty v. Bridge Commission, supra.*
30. *Nebraska v. LaPlata, supra.*
31. *St. Louis & San Francisco Railroad Co. v. James*, 161 U.S. 545, 15 S. Ct. 621 (1895).
32. *James v. Dravo Contracting Co.*, 302 U.S. 134, 58 S.Ct. 208 (1937).
33. *Delaware River Joint Tollbridge Commission v. Colburn*, 310 U.S. 419, 60 S.Ct. 1039 (1940); 36 Am. Jur. 2d. Foreign Corporations §104.
34. *St. Louis & San Francisco Railroad Co., supra.*
35. *Boston & Massachusetts Railroad Co. v. Hurd*, 108 F. 116 (1st Cir., cert. den. 184 U.S. 700, 22 S.Ct. 939 (1902).
36. 36 Am. Jur. 2d Foreign Corporation §§392,378.
37. 36 Am. Jur. 2d Foreign Corporation § 376.
38. 36 Am. Jur. 2d Foreign Corporation §105.
39. 36 Am. Jur. 2d Foreign Corporation §§ 108,110.
40. Barbara Markuson, "MIDLNET: Progress Report," p. 20.
41. Charles H. Stevens, "Governance of Library Networks," pp. 229-231.
42. "Initiating the Design and Development of a Western Interstate Network", p. 30.
43. 36 Am. Jur. 2d Foreign Corporation §112.
44. 31 U.S.C. §846.
45. 31 U.S.C. §852.
46. 36 Am. Jur. 2d Foreign Corporation §§ 113,115.
47. Barbara Markuson, "MIDLNET: Progress Report,"p. 20.
48. Charles H. Stevens, "Governance of Library Networks," p. 235.
49. 6 Am. Jur. 2d Associations and Clubs §1.
50. 6 Am. Jur. 2d Associations and Clubs §2 *Scanlon v. Duffield*, 103 F.2d 572 (6th Cir., 1939).

51. 6 Am. Jur. 2d Associations and Clubs §5.
52. 6 Am. Jur. 2d Associations and Clubs §18.
53. 6 Am. Jur. 2d Associations and Clubs §18.
54. 6 Am. Jur. 2d Associations and Clubs §§ 45, 46.
55. Ohio Revised Code §1745 *et seq.*
56. Charles H. Stevens, "Governance of Library Networks," p. 223.
57. F. A. Hamilton, "Principles of Programs of a Metropolitan Multi-Type Library Cooperative," *Special Libraries* 67 (January 1976).
58. Barbara Markuson, "MIDLNET: Progress Report."
59. "Initiating the Design and Development of a Western Interstate Network."

The Economics of Library Networks

Miriam A. Drake
Assistant Director for Administrative
Services
Purdue University Libraries/Audio-Visual
Center
West Lafayette, Indiana

INTRODUCTION

This paper attempts to describe the economics of libraries and networks, traditional funding sources for local libraries, cooperative networks, fee versus free network services, and the critical issues of funding. Given the paucity of data and a highly charged political environment, this is a large assignment.

However, the real topics of this paper are economics, choices, rain dances, and outcomes. The economist's approach to libraries and funding creates a problem which was articulated by Cheryl Casper, an economist at Kent State University. Dr. Casper observed that noneconomists expect economists to give them answers, while economists can only provide choices.

In order to make choices there must be a framework that relates funding to desired outcomes. The funding of library networks involves choices, but library networks are not ends or outcomes in themselves. Library networks are a means of achieving desired outcomes in the provision of library and information services. Where do the rain dances fit in this discussion? "Rainmaker Theory Number One" is offered as a word of caution. The

211

theory is, "The rainmaker gets so involved with the dance that he sometimes forgets that he has to make rain."[1]

The data presented in this paper provide an economic framework within which funding choices may be considered. The economics of libraries and networks is reviewed and possible solutions to funding problems are discussed. Since these solutions involve politics as well as economics, the rainmaking theory should be kept in mind.

CURRENT FUNDING

Current comprehensive data on the amounts and sources of funds for libraries are impossible to obtain. The most recent data for public, school, college and university library funding were gathered by the Library General Information Survey (LIBGIS) in 1974. This survey excluded special libraries and federal libraries.

The 1974 LIBGIS expenditure data were not consistent for each library type. For example, public library data include expenditures for the operation and maintenance of physical plant while school and higher education survey data do not. Excluding capital and the cost of operating physical facilities, total expenditures in 1974 for the three groups of libraries was just over $3 billion (See Table 1). The largest amount, 39 percent, was spent for school library media centers. Public libraries accounted for 30 percent of the total while expenditures for college and university libraries were 31 percent of the total.[2]

More comprehensive and recent data are available on the employment of librarians. In 1976, the Bureau of Labor Statistics

TABLE 1. Library Expenditures—1974
(*millions of dollars*)

• PUBLIC LIBRARIES	$ 911
• COLLEGE AND UNIVERSITY LIBRARIES	960
• PUBLIC SCHOOL LIBRARY MEDIA CENTERS	1182
• TOTAL	$3053

TABLE 2. Employment of Librarians and Library Technicians and Assistants—1976

	LIBRARIANS	LIBRARY TECHNICIANS AND ASSISTANTS
NUMBER EMPLOYED	128,000	143,000
% EMPLOYED BY LIBRARY TYPE		
SCHOOL	44	16
ACADEMIC	20	36
PUBLIC	23	36
SPECIAL	13	12
	100%	100%

SOURCE: U.S. BUREAU OF LABOR STATISTICS, OCCUPATIONAL OUTLOOK HANDBOOK 1978-79 EDITION, WASHINGTON, D.C., 1978.

estimated that there were approximately 120,000 professional librarians and 143,000 library technicians and assistants employed in the U.S.[3] The distribution of employees among the various types of libraries is shown in Table 2.

These estimates plus more recent data on public library funding and college and university funding [4,5] would indicate current spending for libraries, excluding federal libraries, to be roughly $6 billion. Approximately $3.5 billion is spent by libraries in educational institutions and $500 million is the estimated expenditure for special libraries. Public libraries spend approximately $2 billion.

It should be noted that although consumers buy library services indirectly through tax and tuition payments, they buy other forms of education, information, and recreation services directly. For example, in 1974 it has been estimated that consumers spent about $22 billion for legal gambling and $5 billion for illegal gambling.[6] In 1977, consumers spent $4 billion for admissions to motion picture theaters, $2 billion for spectator sports and $4 billion for books and maps.[7]

Since the major portion of library expenditures are made from tax dollars, it is useful to examine the sources of these dollars. NCLIS has estimated that tax support for public libraries is distributed at 82 percent local, 13 percent state and 5 percent federal.[8] Similar data for other types of libraries are not readily available.

The fiscal year 1979 federal appropriation for libraries included $180 million for school libraries, $67 million for LSCA, $10 million for college libraries and $6 million for research libraries.[9] President Carter's 1980 budget proposal indicates cutbacks or elimination of these programs.

FUTURE FUNDING FOR LIBRARIES

The prospect of increased funds for libraries in the future is not bright. Current economic and political trends indicate that funds available for libraries are likely to decline absolutely by the mid to late 1980s. Projections in the growth and aging of the U.S. population, school enrollments, tax revenues and expenditures for education and a more conservative view of government are among the more critical factors which will affect funding for libraries. The forecasts presented are not wish lists or absolute predictions but are projections of events which are likely to occur if nothing intervenes to reverse current trends.

Population Trends

The U.S. population is projected to increase to about 260 million by the year 2000 (See Figure 1). The rate of growth in the 1980s and 1990s will be substantially below the growth rates of earlier years. This lower rate of population growth is due in large part to the lower number of births.

In the 1960s over 4 million births per year were recorded. This number has declined to about 3.3 million for the late 1970s, and projections on the number of births to the year 2000 are shown in Figure 2. A lower number of births accompanied by increased longevity will result in the so called "graying of America." The median age of the U.S. population in 1975 was 28.8 years, and the median age is projected to increase gradually to 35.5 years in 2000 (See Figure 3).

The percentage of the population in the 5-17 year age group will decline from 23.6 in 1975 to 19.7 in 2000 while the percentage of people 65 years or older will increase from 10.5 in 1975 to 12.2 in 2000 (See Figure 4).

FIGURE 1

ESTIMATED AND PROJECTED
UNITED STATES POPULATION
1950-2025

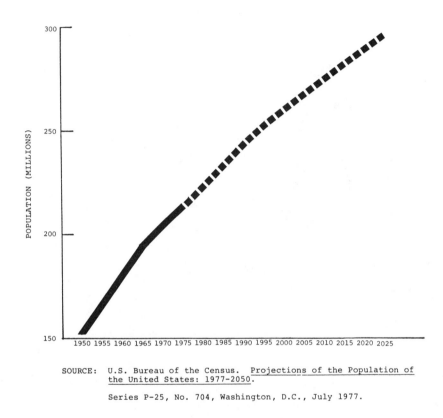

SOURCE: U.S. Bureau of the Census.   Projections of the Population of
the United States: 1977-2050.

Series P-25, No. 704, Washington, D.C., July 1977.

The impact on school and higher education enrollments is reflected in the data which follows. School enrollment in grades K-12 was 51.3 million in 1970. By 1986 this enrollment will drop to 45.2 million (See Figures 5 and 6).

Enrollment in four-year institutions of higher education is projected to peak at 7.4 million in 1980 and to decline to 6.9 million by 1986. Given the projected age distribution this enrollment will continue to decline into the 1990s.

The Economy

The availability of funds for libraries and library networks will depend, in part, on the state of the economy. Current

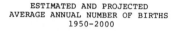

FIGURE 2

ESTIMATED AND PROJECTED
AVERAGE ANNUAL NUMBER OF BIRTHS
1950-2000

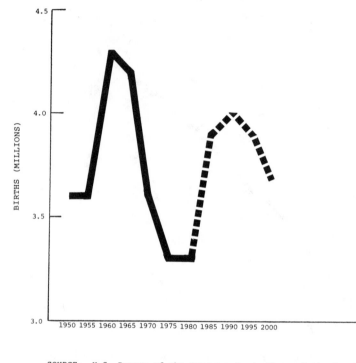

SOURCE: U.S. Bureau of the Census. Projections of the Population of
the United States: 1977-2050.

Series P-25, No. 704, Washington, D.C., July 1977.

economic forecasting has produced a myriad of projections and outlooks. Because old rules have been broken and patterns disrupted, it is possible to produce a forecast to justify any position.

The forecasts presented here are those of the Bureau of Labor Statistics and are based on the following assumptions: 1) slow declines in inflation and unemployment, 2) lower tax rates and moderate levels of government expenditure, and 3) a lower rate of expansion in the labor force. The annual rate of growth in the Gross National Product is projected to decline from 4.3 percent in the 1977-80 period to 3.2 percent in 1985-90.[10] Inflation is pro-

FIGURE 3

ESTIMATED AND PROJECTED
MEDIAN AGE OF U.S. POPULATION
1950-2000

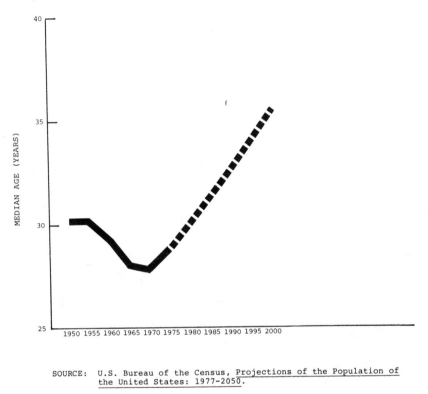

SOURCE: U.S. Bureau of the Census, Projections of the Population of
the United States: 1977-2050.

Series P-25, No. 704, Washington, D.C., July 1977.

jected to decline from an average rate of 6.7 percent during 1977-80 to 5.2 percent for the decade 1980-90. Given continuing double digit inflation, increases in energy prices, and the failure of the President's wage/price guideline program, the inflation projection is unrealistic.

Government (federal, state, and local) purchases are projected to decline from 20.2 percent of GNP in 1979 to 15.5 percent in 1990. This projection seems more realistic in terms of trends at all levels of government to cut spending. The so called "tax revolt" that resulted in the passage of Proposition 13 is not confined to California. The current national campaign to con-

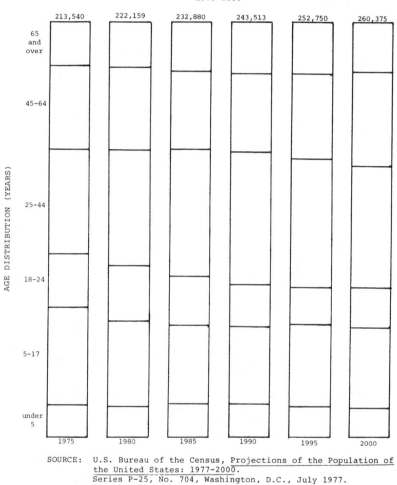

FIGURE 4

ESTIMATED AND PROJECTED
AGE DISTRIBUTION OF THE U.S. POPULATION
1975-2000

SOURCE: U.S. Bureau of the Census, Projections of the Population of
the United States: 1977-2000.
Series P-25, No. 704, Washington, D.C., July 1977.

vene a constitutional convention to amend the U.S. Constitution
to prohibit deficit spending is a key indicator that the public is
unhappy with current taxing and spending levels. This indication is further corroborated by the passage of a variety of
referenda in 1978 for limiting taxes or spending on local and
state levels. Referenda to limit taxes appeared on ballots in nine
states. In six states these measures succeeded. Measures to limit
state spending were voted upon favorably by the voters in six
other states.[11]

FIGURE 5

ESTIMATED AND PROJECTED
SCHOOL ENROLLMENT K-12
FALL 1970-1985

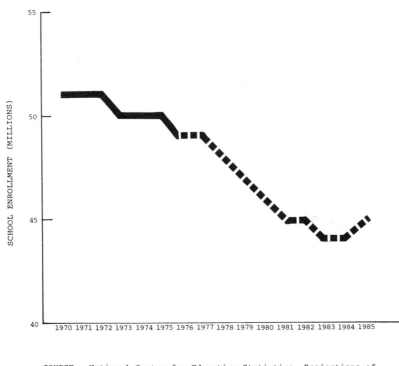

SOURCE: National Center for Education Statistics, <u>Projections of
Education Statistics to 1986-87</u>, Washington, D.C., 1978.

The impact of taxing and spending limitations as well as declining school enrollments is reflected in two projections of education expenditures. In 1973, educational purchases represented 42.3 percent of all state and local government expenditures. By 1990 it is expected that educational purchases will decline to 34.1 percent of all state and local government purchases.[12] Saunders of the Bureau of Labor Statistics indicates ". . . growth of education purchases is expected to slow markedly to an average rate of 2.2 percent annually between 1977 and 1980 and to undergo an absolute decline of -0.7 percent annually for the entire decade of the 1980's."[13] The National Center for Educational Statistics, in its projection of educational and general expenditures by institutions of higher education, indicates

FIGURE 6

ESTIMATED AND PROJECTED
ENROLLMENT IN 4 YEAR INSTITUTIONS OF
HIGHER EDUCATION
FALL 1970-1985

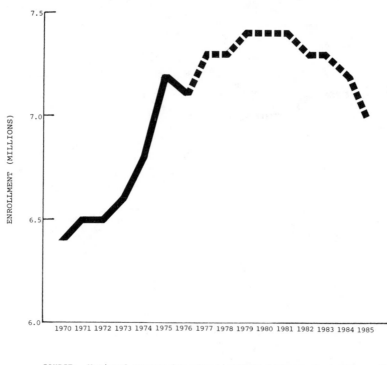

SOURCE: National Center for Educational Statistics, Projections of
Education Statistics to 1986-87, Washington, D.C., 1978.

that these expenditures will peak in 1984 at $33.3 billion in 1976-77 dollars and decline thereafter (See Figure 7).

Sufficient data are not available to forecast or project library expenditures in the years ahead; however, there are clear indications that there will be fewer dollars available by the mid-1980s. Tax cuts at state and local levels, accompanied by fewer school age people, could dramatically affect public school and state supported college and university library spending. With fewer dollars available, continuous inflation and an aging population, a different set of priorities may emerge for government spending at all levels.

Some librarians and educators have indicated that expanded

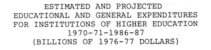

FIGURE 7

ESTIMATED AND PROJECTED
EDUCATIONAL AND GENERAL EXPENDITURES
FOR INSTITUTIONS OF HIGHER EDUCATION
1970-71-1986-87
(BILLIONS OF 1976-77 DOLLARS)

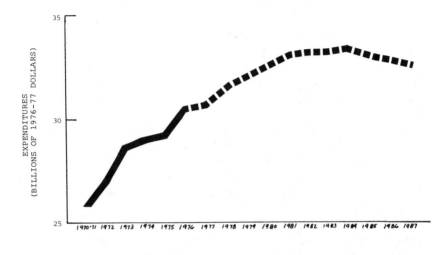

SOURCE: National Center for Educational Statistics, Projections of
Education Statistics to 1986-87, Washington, D.C., 1978.

programs of adult education and increased leisure time will help
to keep library budgets at current levels. At present, it appears
doubtful that these developments will occur with sufficient rapidity to compensate for expected losses in the 1980s.

ECONOMICS OF LIBRARIES

If libraries are to remain viable service organizations, changes
in input/output relationships will be necessary. Libraries are
becoming increasingly expensive and are declining in cost effectiveness at a time when taxpayer demands for greater efficiency
are increasing. The cost effectiveness criterion means that output must increase or improve with relatively constant levels of
funding or remain constant at reduced levels of funding.

The library economy consists of approximately 100,000 units,
most of which are too small to operate efficiently or effectively.
There is some indication that large libraries, using manual

methods, experience substantial inefficiencies in both housekeeping and user information finding.

The costs of library operations have accelerated rapidly in recent years resulting in higher costs per unit of output and lower labor productivity. The prices of library inputs, that is, books, journals, and labor, have increased more rapidly than prices generally. An estimate of a library price index for academic libraries indicates that prices paid by libraries for inputs are consistently higher than prices paid by institutions of higher education or firms generally as reflected in the wholesale price index (See Figure 8). The library price index was constructed to give only an indication of prices paid by academic libraries. The budget distribution assumptions used in construction of the index were 15 percent books, 15 percent periodicals, 55 percent labor and 15 percent for supplies and expenses, fringe benefits, and equipment. The index is somewhat deceptive because it focuses on the items in the academic library budget and excludes the cost of building depreciation and maintenance and the cost of utilities.

Building and utilities costs are significant items in the public library budget and will continue to increase rapidly due to energy costs. The 1974 LIBGIS survey indicated that building related expenditures were 9.4 percent of total public library expenditures.[14] For public libraries in the state of Indiana operating expenditures for items other than books, magazines, and staff were 27.8 percent of total operating expenditures in 1974 and 43.6 percent in 1977. This increase reflects higher maintenance staff salaries and the higher cost of utilities. Circulation per registered borrower in Indiana increased roughly 5 percent between 1974 and 1977 while the operating expenditures per registered borrower increased 57 percent in the same period.[15]

Labor Costs

A review of budgets for all types of libraries shows that libraries are becoming increasingly labor intensive. The wages and salaries portion of the Big Ten university library budgets increased from 58 percent in 1966-67 to 62 percent in 1976-77.[16] This trend is likely to continue because of continuing inflation; however, it is unlikely that these increases will be matched by increases in labor productivity. Libraries are not unique in this situation because most service industries are experiencing simi-

FIGURE 8

PRICE INDICES 1973-1978
1976 = 100

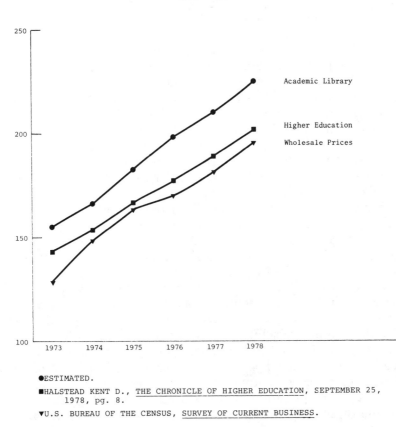

●ESTIMATED.

■HALSTEAD KENT D., THE CHRONICLE OF HIGHER EDUCATION, SEPTEMBER 25, 1978, pg. 8.

▼U.S. BUREAU OF THE CENSUS, SURVEY OF CURRENT BUSINESS.

lar difficulties. The lack of increase in library labor productivity results from the increasing costs of maintaining growing collections and the inability or unwillingness to purchase labor saving devices. In general, libraries are technologically underdeveloped and starved for capital.

The cost of labor saving devices and processes is declining while the costs of labor and collection maintenance are increasing. The primary tools for saving labor in libraries will be computers, telecommunications, and better management. It has been estimated that in the next decade the costs of computer logic will decline 25 percent per year and that communication costs will decline 10 percent per year.[17] Telefacsimile and electronic mail systems are now cost competitive with other forms of message and document delivery systems. The use of digital data transmission, optical fibers, and packet switching networks will reduce costs more in the future.[18]

Adapting these technological developments to library operations will require significant changes in library budgeting, management, and understanding of technological innovation. The major problems will be to find the needed capital and convince library funders that capital investment is essential. Currently, the amount of capital investment per library worker is miniscule, probably less than $300. The average capitalization for a factory worker has been estimated at $25,000.[19]

Libraries typically have high fixed costs which must be paid regardless of output level or book use. If output level increases and costs remain constant, the unit cost declines until some capacity level is reached. This level may be reached when a major expansion of space and staff is necessitated by growth in the collections and the increased labor required to maintain collections. The space and staff expansions are independent of material use and output level.

"The literature indicates that two-thirds of the total budget of libraries or information centers goes into input and a third into output."[20] Additional book acquisitions and increasing collection sizes drive input cost higher every year. Library materials are part of the fixed input cost because they are purchased with the idea that they should be available for use. With constant or decreasing levels of output and rapidly increasing costs, the fixed input cost per unit of output increases rapidly over time.

While these costs are rising, consumers are demanding more responsive service at a lower cost from tax supported institutions. Academic libraries are caught in a double bind because teaching faculty remain insistent that the libraries buy more and more.

The increasing pressure for cost effective library operations will place academic librarians in an impossible position. In some instances, libraries will need to be more problem and consumer oriented, while in other cases the solution will lie in providing appropriate facilities so that the user may be self-sufficient in locating bibliographic information and finding needed books and documents.

In order to improve the relationships between input and output, libraries will have to utilize computers and faster and cheaper means of telecommunications. The costs of processing library materials and collection and catalog maintenance will have to be reduced to supply resources for more responsive public service or for increasing the productivity of the library user.

The adoption and implementation of these technologies necessitate a change in the library budget which will produce more capital for labor-saving equipment and processes. It will be essential for university administrators and faculty, public library boards and school boards to increase their understanding of library economics and the financial or other pay-offs resulting from investment in labor-saving technology. The process of reallocating resources for the integration of technology will be difficult. Library funders are reluctant to cut back materials purchasing or user services in order to generate the needed capital. It is unlikely, given the economic forecasts discussed earlier, that this capital will be available from increased public funding.

Since most libraries are too small to take advantage of economics of scale and too poor to fund technological development by themselves, they will have to pool resources for technological development. This pooling already has taken place through networks.

ECONOMICS OF NETWORKS

The primary sources of revenue for library networks are fees for service paid by libraries from their operating budgets. These revenues are enhanced by federal funds, state funds, and private foundation grants in different proportions for each network. The amounts of funding derived from the various souces are not readily available. The National Center for Educational Statistics is in the process of surveying library networks and cooperatives. When these data become available it should be possible to determine the revenues and expenditures of networks as well as the sources of revenue. Details of grant funds available are reviewed in Robinson's background paper in these proceedings.

In some of the state and regional networks a surcharge is added to shared cataloging cost to pay for local network services. Some states contribute LSCA funds to network operating budgets. In the state of Indiana, network operating expenses are subsidized by a direct appropriation of the state legislature. This appropriation does not provide research and development funds but is sufficient, at this time, to cover administration, orientation, training, terminal maintenance and telecommunications.

For the individual library the benefits of participation in computer-based library networking are related to reductions in unit cost which result from economies of scale. Economists define economies of scale as ". . . the reduction in unit cost that comes from increasing output. They result from more advanced technology, more specialization of labor and sometimes from the ability to purchase large quantities of input at discount prices."[21] As a result of economies of scale the long run average costs of production fall. The application of technological economies can improve the efficiency of inputs and quality of outputs.

Shared cataloging provides an excellent example of technological economies of scale which result in lower unit costs and, in some instances, improvements in quality. Large libraries which do not participate in shared cataloging systems experience increasing cost per unit of cataloging output because greater amounts of higher priced labor are needed to perform cataloging functions. The input/output relationships for libraries using shared cataloging depend on the portion of titles found in the data base or the "hit rate." The higher the hit rate, the lower the unit cost (See Figure 9). The details of the cost calculations are presented at the end of this paper.

Participation in shared cataloging also changes the relationship of labor and capital input. Capital, in the form of terminals and shared computer processing, replaces labor in the cataloging function. While expenditures for capital increase (in one year if equipment is expensed, or over several years if equipment is amortized), the amount of labor needed to produce the output is reduced.

Cataloging becomes a shared resource both in terms of labor and material. The benefit of an individual cataloger's skill and specialization are shared by many libraries instead of accruing only to one library. The cost of card production for all libraries is reduced in a shared cataloging system.

The library user benefit derived from shared cataloging is not quantifiable but real. The materials arrive on the shelf faster and are not hidden away from users in the cataloging department for months and months. Hewitt, in his study of the impact of OCLC, found that the strongest impact of OCLC ". . . was on the speed with which books are cataloged and ready for use." Estimates from 28 libraries indicated a mean reduction in catalog time of 2.8 months.[22]

In addition to obtaining material faster, the user benefits from access to the data base. Blood, in his article on the use of OCLC

FIGURE 9

SHARED AND MANUAL CATALOGING
COST PER TITLE FOR
50,000 TITLES

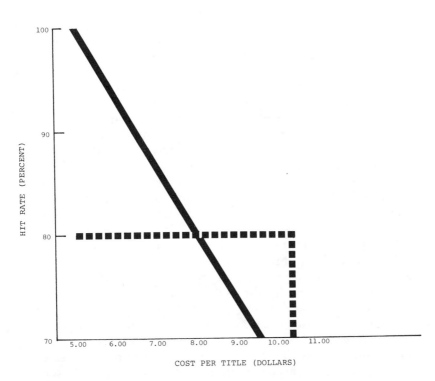

COST PER TITLE (DOLLARS)

in reference service, indicates that library users benefit from
both the scope and access points provided. He cites six features
of the OCLC system which improve reference service: 1) reduction of cataloging and filing backlogs, 2) bibliographic access
during the interim between cataloging, receipt and filing of the
cards, 3) access to items not normally cataloged by libraries,
such as federal government publications and technical reports,
4) better title access, 5) bibliographic access to monographs in
series, and 6) expedited searches for works cited inaccurately.[23]
Users of the RLIN and WLN systems also have access by subject
heading.

The addition of the interlibrary loan subsystem to OCLC's
services should result in faster delivery of material to users who
need to borrow material from other libraries. As librarians gain
experience in the use of this system unit costs of processing
interlibrary loans should be reduced. File size can be reduced and

files may be eliminated. The amount of keyboarding required by the OCLC system is minimal compared to TWX or other paper systems.

Systems, such as OCLC, RLIN, and WLN, in addition to providing valuable services to libraries and users, perform the needed functions of capital formation and research and development. Few libraries have sufficient capital to design and implement large computer-based systems. By purchasing these services from networks, libraries are pooling their capital and providing the financial base needed to provide basic and enhanced services. Large or small libraries which use MARC tapes in their own cataloging system are spending more per unit of cataloging output because they lack access to the larger data base with its high volume of contributed records. In 1977/78 OCLC members contributed over 500,000 records to the data base compared with 227,000 records from the Library of Congress. Academic libraries were the largest contributors with 444,000 records.[24]

Traditional sources of capital for organizations in the private and quasi-public not-for-profit sectors of the economy are retained earnings or issuance of debt securities against future earnings. These organizations do not operate in the same manner as an individual library which must function with fixed revenue. Appropriate pricing and investment policies permit not-for-profit institutions to accrue capital for research, development, and investment in equipment through retention of excess revenue or building of corporate equity. Institutions also can turn to the market place for investment funds. In order to acquire these funds, however, the firm must have collateral in the form of real property or equipment and sufficient future revenue to cover debt service and repayment. The capital obtained through resource pooling and borrowing funds in the market place builds a financial base for research and development as well as acquisition of large-scale equipment needed to provide service to many libraries.

THE ECONOMIST'S VIEW

As indicated earlier, the taxpayers are funding most library services and most library networks. The question of who is paying has been answered. If library networks are essential to effective and efficient operations for the individual library and if libraries are to continue to serve the public and provide social benefit, who should pay? And how should the payment be assessed? Economists warn that there's no free lunch, no free love,[25] and no free libraries. There are choices in the allocation of societal or individual resources, but each choice involves giving up a purchase or activity to acquire a desired item or implement a new program. The decision to use or spend limited resources is made in the context of opportunity cost.

Since most libraries and library services are funded with tax dollars it seems appropriate to ask if these dollars are being used in a manner which reflects the public's choice or preference. There is evidence from California that library services are not as important as fire and police protection and other public services. A public opinion poll conducted for the American Library Association indicated that the heaviest library users, 9 percent of the sample, were 18-34 years of age, college educated and living in the eastern United States. Regarding additional funds for local libraries, 50 percent did not favor increasing taxes to cover costs and 51 percent favored the library charging the people who use it.[26] One of the social functions performed by libraries is a form of income redistribution. The wealthy through higher taxes subsidize library services for the poor. The ALA Gallup opinion poll indicates that this redistribution is not taking place.

These data reflect, in part, the trend to individuals desiring greater amounts of discretionary income to spend for goods and services they wish to purchase. The trend to lower taxes and the taxpayer revolts discussed earlier reinforce the idea that the public is getting more government services than it wants and it is willing to give up some public services for greater freedom of choice in the marketplace. As with every social trend there is a countertrend, which is that people have developed an attitide that it is morally wrong to make a profit from health care, religion, or education. While there seems to be no moral problem with contracting garbage collection or street cleaning to private industry, the idea of contracting educational or library services away from the public sector is not to be considered.

The expenditure of public funds and the allocation of taxpayer money to various public services is basically a political problem; however, there are some concepts in economics that are useful to provide a framework for the policy issues. The first concept is public goods which should not be confused with what librarians, politicians, physicians, and clergymen think is good for the public. Pure public goods are consumed by society as a whole.

There is no way to sell portions of these goods and no way to prevent citizens from consuming them. The usual examples of public or social goods are national defense, police protection, spraying to kill insects, and reduction in air pollution. Citizens benefit from these programs whether they want them or not.

Private goods do not benefit society as a whole. They can be divided into pieces and sold in the marketplace. The benefit from private goods accrues solely to the individual consuming them.

The consumption of public goods by individuals may benefit society as a whole even though they have not been consumed directly by society. Samuelson points out, "The benefits from a social good unlike those from a purely private good, are seen to involve external consumption effects on more than one individual."[27] The external consumption effects are among a group of conditions called externalities. These externalities may result in a positive benefit for society in the case of education or disbenefits in occurrences of air or water pollution or airport noise.

Library services can be characterized as a public good or a private good. Casper characterizes library service as a semipublic good. Her rationale is, "At the heart of most library services is information. Information is never consumed in the traditional sense; it is 'used' but never 'used up' . . . once a piece of information comes into existence it can be used repeatedly without eliminating its possible availability to other users."[28] In other words the supply of information is never exhausted or depleted. The process of using information may yield a benefit to the entire society or it may profit only the user.

Recreational reading is less likely to yield a social benefit and is more nearly a pure private good. Marilyn Gell points out that while people have information needs they do not use the public library to satisfy those needs. Most adults use the public library to satisfy recreational needs.[29]

The rationale for government provision of public library service is based on the public goods arguments stated above and the idea that it is more efficient for government to provide this service. The potential revenue generated by transaction fees on individual loans, materials use and other services would not be adequate to cover the cost of collecting fees; therefore, taxpayer support may result in a net saving for the taxpayer.

Examples of semi-public goods which are partially subsidized and partially paid for directly by consumers include the U.S. Postal Service, public transportation, and hospitals. When the government established the Post Office it did so not only to provide mail delivery, but also to ensure a communications system for the nation.[30] Public transit systems are financed by government to conserve energy and provide relatively cheap transportation for the poor. Hospitals are financed by a combination of public and private funds including insurance payments from private carriers as well as government payments through Medicare, Medicaid, Veterans Administration, welfare, and public health programs.

There are both emotional and rational arguments advanced on both sides of the fee versus free service in libraries. Opponents of fees argue that imposition of fees will deny access to information, especially to the poor. The fact that the poor generally do not use libraries does not enter into their thinking because as Gell indicates, "Librarians have always defined their mission in heroic terms and proclaimed it with an almost religious fervor . . ."[31] This mission is to educate and provide information for all people regardless of ability to pay. Another argument advanced by opponents to user fees is that freedom of information, essential to the well-being of the republic, will cease if information is not provided for free.

The proponents of user fees argue that only a portion of the public actually use libraries and that users should pay for the service. Library service can be withheld from those who do not pay; therefore, it does not meet the indivisibility criterion of a pure public good. An additional argument for the imposition of user fees is that people value services or goods for which they pay directly. By placing library service in the arena of the marketplace, a more efficient and effective allocation of economic resources will result because people will not buy services which are not needed or wanted.

The middle ground in this controversy recognizes that libraries provide both private goods and social services. Open and unimpeded access to information is important. The freedom to know and to learn is essential in a democratic society. Taxpayer subsidy of purely private goods, however, is no longer affordable. Clearly there is a need for compromise which includes subsidy or taxpayer support for libraries so that basic information can be provided to all segments of society and user fees for services which are tailored to individual needs and result in private benefit.

The precedents for this approach are the use of rental collections in public libraries and the use of fees for special services such as bibliographic data base searching. In other areas of the economy, users' fees for service are imposed in a variety of ways. The interstate highway system is financed by gasoline taxes through the Highway Trust Fund. Recently, some Highway Trust Fund money was released to subsidize public transit projects. The air traffic control system and airport construction and operation are financed through ticket taxes, fuel taxes, and landing fees.

The U.S. and international air carriers finance a network type reservation system from revenues. The purposes of this system are to facilitate passenger reservations for all airlines and to allow one airline to book a seat on another airline. While the public convenience is served by this network, it is not subsidized by the government.

ECONOMIC ISSUES

One of the key issues of this conference is whether library networks should be funded by government directly. Markuson has hypothesized that "... networks provide three critical services: research and development, capital acquisition and technology transfer mechanisms."[32] The main sources of revenue for these activities have been allocations from libraries' budgets. The services provided by networks to date have been consumed by library users indirectly. The networks have provided services to libraries to enable them to provide more efficient service just as the airlines reservations systems enable air carriers to book and over-book airline flights more efficiently. At present, the library user does not access network services directly except for bibliographic searching. This situation may change dramatically in the future. The networks could be the agencies through which bibliographic information, fact retrieval, and text retrieval are provided directly to users in their homes and offices. Networks also may function as providers of telecommunications for users and libraries.

Presently, networks are performing an important economic function, the diffusion of technology. In addition "... library networks can be viewed as market perfecting institutions" which promote more effective linkages between supply and demand.[33] On the supply side, networks have changed the production function by substituting capital for labor and have provided the means for greater labor specialization. On the demand side, networks are providing the means for aggregating demand, resource sharing, and satisfying a higher portion of consumer demand at a faster rate.

The question of who should pay for networks services has been answered in part by the present system of library payments for service. The issue of who *should* pay for research and development and technology transfer beyond the level being currently provided is not clear. The choices will be addressed later in this paper.

CURRENT ECONOMIC PROBLEMS

The current economic problems of libraries are lack of capital, institutional barriers to innovation, and competitive pressure from more technologically advanced and responsive systems.

Lack of capital is likely to be an increasingly difficult problem to solve especially in academic and public libraries. The annual budget process encourages spending all funds in one year for materials, salaries and expenses, and impedes accumulation of funds for future capital needs. The prevailing philosophy at all levels of government has been "use it or lose it." With the amount of available dollars decreasing, the pressure to spend for immediate needs will be greater. In universities, the tendency has been to try to satisfy the expanding appetites of faculty for more and more books at the expense of efficiency in library housekeeping and adoption of technological innovation. Many librarians are in an impossible position being damned if they do and damned if they don't.

Additional institutional barriers to innovation are lack of understanding of cost/effectiveness relationships and input/output relationships. In industrial situations capital investment, research and development, and innovation are evaluated on the basis of return on investment. A project likely to increase the firm's return on investment or labor productivity will be pursued. Funders of libraries are not sensitive to problems of labor productivity, of maximizing social return on investment, or of operating in a cost effective fashion. As in other not-for-profit situations such as hospitals, museums and government agencies, the name of the game is an increasing budget rather then cost effectiveness or efficient allocation of resources.

As indicated earlier, without increases in output or implementation of labor-saving systems, library costs on a per unit basis can only rise over time. The shared cataloging system is an example of how the trend of per unit catalog costs can be reversed through the substitution of capital for labor and sharing of resources.

Consumer demand presents another economic problem for libraries. As the composition of the population changes, the demand for library service may change. Libraries are not in a position to react quickly to these changes or to plan future services based on projected population and school enrollment data.

Technology will have a major impact on the public library of the future whether the library plans for technology or not. Telecommunications and microelectronic technology may make public libraries obsolete for information functions, leaving the remaining functions of repository and recreational reading. A variety of data, information, and text will be retrievable with the home or office microcomputer or television set with telecommunications capability. Academic libraries will be similarly affected. At present it is not unusual to find faculty members at large research insitiutions paying information brokers and freelance librarians to retrieve and deliver appropriate documents and information. A faculty member at my university said, "I'm sure the library could help me, but I don't have the time to use it." The value of time for the faculty member who is engaged in teaching, research, and writing is too great to be spent in the library trying to find needed information. The same time value situation applies to the business person who needs relevant information quickly. Given the value of time it is cheaper to hire an information specialist. Faculty members whose work loads are light or others who do not have demands on their time can afford the luxury of time consuming activities, such as browsing and searching files.

Librarians in special libraries in many industrial corporations have had to familiarize themselves with concepts of investment, return on investment, and value of time. Management requires some statement of pay-off from library or information services as a justification for the library's budget. Return on investment (ROI) and contribution to profit provide the special librarian with a measurement. Academic, public, and school librarians do not have such convenient meter sticks. These libraries along with hospitals, museums, and religious organizations must use other measurements which are less precise. "It is not the objective of these organizations to widen the spread between outputs and inputs. In general, their objective is to render as much service as is possible with a given amount of resources, or to use as few resources as possible to render a given amount of service."[34] In this context it is difficult to demonstrate that more dollars will result in better performance or provide more or better social service.

In competing for resources in academic institutions, school systems or companies, libraries are hindered because they are part of the overhead. One of the goals of management in any organization is to minimize overhead or indirect   costs. The recent activities of Sears Roebuck in suing the U.S. Government and refusing to accept $20 million of government business are reflections of the concerns of management to reduce overhead costs. Activities that increase overhead costs include libraries as well as personnel administration and accounting.

Managers in all types of organizations are looking increasingly at opportunity costs and asking which activities will produce the biggest pay-offs in financial or social returns. Situations which involve a fixed budget with no means of raising revenue necessitate: 1) the evaluation of alternatives and 2) effective choices in terms of achieving organizational goals. This competition places a particularly heavy burden on libraries to create a set of output measures against which management can assess input and investment.

Technology transfer is a major problem for libraries. Hardware items cannot be bought from the shelf, plugged in and made to bring instant solutions to libraries. While the number of turnkey systems are increasing they are not without problems. Some systems are designed for small libraries while others are limited in the tasks they can perform; still other systems do not provide appropriate interfaces with existing systems.

Knowing that microcomputers, minicomputers, storage devices, and telecommunications systems have the potential to improve library service is merely the first step. These devices require software tailored to library tasks. Often the hardware or existing software must be modified to accommodate the peculiarities of an individual library. Staff must be prepared and trained to use these systems. Large amounts of capital are required to acquire and adapt systems. The leadership of an academic institution or a public library board must have vision in terms of transferring technology to libraries and fostering continuing innovation in library work.

If forecasts of government expenditures prove to be correct and the private sector continues to grow in the information field, libraries will be in a less than favorable competitive position. Libraries do not have a monopoly in the provision of information. Although the library may provide information at no direct cost to the user, the user incurs cost in using the library. An old saying is "what is cheap is expensive."

If libraries are to be key factors in the information delivery system of the future, they will have to reallocate resources to generate capital not only for equipment and software but also for development work. In addition, libraries will have little choice but to institute fees for special services. A study by Forecasting International Ltd. concluded that librarians and users could accept user fees for greater efficiency or new products and services.[35] Many of these faster systems and new products could be produced by library networks. As explained earlier, library networks carry out the capital formation function by aggregating revenues from many libraries. Some networks also have the option of going to the market place for funds which will be repaid from future revenues. By using these mechanisms library networks can produce more bang for the buck.

CHOICES AND SOLUTIONS

At the outset I indicated that the economist's role here is to present choices. These choices relate to the allocation of economic resources, both private and public.

The individual library's choices are constrained by the rules of the parent institution or governing body. If there were no constraints, or only minor limits, libraries could consider reallocating present and future funding to generate capital. This reallocation necessitates a careful look at the value of current services to library clientele, use of library labor and the manner in which processing and housekeeping are being accomplished. Are there services being offered which are obsolete and little used? Could they be eliminated? Do processing routines involve redundant effort? Are tasks being duplicated? These questions and similar issues need to be explored by each library within its own institutional setting.

Another option for the library is the imposition of users' fees for special services on a full cost recovery basis. Basic services could continue to be subsidized while expedited, or better quality services are paid for directly by the people who use them. Some of the revenue could be used to pay for network services.

The easiest answer to the network funding question yields a solution which is most difficult to implement—let the government do it, either with LSCA funds or a new program. Many network activities have been financed with LSCA funds, why not continue? There are two reasons why LSCA as presently constituted is not a reliable source of funding for networks: first, networks must compete with their own members for funds and, second, allocation of LSCA funds to networks denies funds to other special programs, such as special services to the handicapped and the elderly. As the population ages, the demand for these special services will grow. Competition for LSCA funds in the present environment means either that individual libraries, networks or other programs are denied funding or small amounts are distributed over many programs with little impact.

Another option for networks is to seek state funding. INCOLSA sought and received state funding in 1978. The state legislature in Indiana recognized that certain activities are most logically carried out on a statewide basis; however, the appropriation is designated for operating costs and includes no funds for research and development. INCOLSA, like other networks, will be looking to membership fees and other sources for development funding in the near future. State legislators usually are relatively conservative when it comes to funding programs which affect only one relatively well-off segment of the population. In Indiana we were fortunate that the legislature recognized the need to improve library services and that library users statewide would benefit from INCOLSA's activity. It is important to note that INCOLSA's appropriation represents state subsidy to individual libraries.

The National Commission on Libraries and Information Science (NCLIS) in its 1978 document *Goals for Action* states that: 1) libraries and information services must cooperate, 2) local communities should maintain basic services, 3) adequate special services should be provided to special constituencies and 4) a new federal agency is required to implement and coordinate a national program. Specifically, NCLIS said, "Implementation of the National Program will require new administrative and operational functions. It will require a Federal agency where policies with respect to library and information service activities will be transformed into action."[36]

Given the developments of the last ten years in deregulation and other federal activities, the idea of a new federal agency appears not to be a feasible choice. The U.S. Congress has passed or is in the process of considering deregulation for the transportation industry and the telecommunications industry. As a result of an act of Congress the Civil Aeronautics Board is scheduled to go out of business in the 1980s. "The Interstate Commerce Commission whose surface transportation industries shelled out $11 billion for compliance in 1976, is moving steadily to relax regulations in the huge trucking industry."[37] Currently, the Congress is considering a major revision to the Communications Act. The trend clearly is to deregulate, move away from unnecessary involvement by government, and return some activities to the marketplace.

The NCLIS document setting forth the goals for the National Program stated that the responsibility of the proposed federal agency would not be authoritarian or regulatory; therefore, the CAB, ICC and FCC analogies do not apply. The model discussed among librarians is the Corporation for Public Broadcasting.

On the surface the Corporation for Public Broadcasting provides an appealing choice. The legislation that established the Corporation intended to provide taxpayer funds for noncommercial broadcasting to enhance the cultural and educational uses of television with a minimum of government interference. In practice, the Corporation for Public Broadcasting has not been free of government interference and, according to the Carnegie Commission on the Future of Public Broadcasting, the enterprise has been seriously underfunded.

Files of the White House Office of Telecommunications Policy for the years 1969-74, obtained under the Freedom of Information Act, clearly show that the Nixon administration had no intention of allowing the Corporation to function without government interference. These files, as disclosed in the *New York Times*, indicated that the Nixon administration attempted, and to some degree succeeded, to gain control of the governing board and to break up the network by channeling funds directly to the stations. Clay Whitehead, Director of the Office of Telecommunications Policy, in a speech to public broadcasters in 1971 said, "An institution receiving federal support had no business dealing in news and public affairs." In addition, the *Times* article indicated that consideration was being given to a revision in the tax law which would prohibit private foundations from giving money to support news and public commentary."[38]

Two assumptions about government have been challenged in recent years. The first assumption is that government can do some jobs more efficiently because it does not have to make a profit. The recent history of AMTRAK and CONRAIL are clear evidence that government operations do not lead automatically to efficient and better service. Tullock, an advocate of transferring government activities to the private sector, ". . . likes to cite what he calls the Bureaucratic Rule of Two: 'The removal of an activity from the private to the public sector will double its unit cost of production.'"[39]

The second assumption is that bureaucrats and politicians always act in the public interest. A daily reading of your local newspaper should shatter that assumption.

Given this background it is naive to assume that a federal agency would not impose some rules and regulations, and that politicians fearful of losing power would not be authoritative or regulatory. Librarians have vociferously defended their rights to make unpopular works available to any person who wants to read them. Librarians have placed their jobs and reputations on the line so that libraries could be free from censorship and library users could have open access to information. A federal library bureau or agency operating in a resurgence of the McCarthy or Nixon eras could seriously jeopardize those freedoms. As responsible librarians we need to question the "federal solution" and ask if it is worth the price we may have to pay.

If a federal bureau or agency is not the ideal solution, is there any way to gain federal funds for networks without federal control? The answer is "no," but there may be ways to fund networks with less federal control than would be involved in a federal agency.

One possibility is to allocate research and development money to networks through the U.S. Office of Education for a limited program or for specific grants. The arguments in favor of this approach are that libraries and networks constitute an "infant" industry in terms of the use of technology and the USOE is experienced in funding network programs; therefore, a new agency would not be needed. The airline industry was initially funded through federal subsidy. As the industry grew and was able to generate sufficient revenue to survive on its own, the subsidy decreased. Satellite development also was funded initially by the government. A federal program limited to research and development for networks could provide some of the capital needed to adapt technology to library and network operations.

Another possibility for funding would involve limited federal funding with matching state grants to be given directly to networks. Federal money could also be used in conjunction with private foundation funds for challenge grants.

As indicated earlier in the Bureau of Labor Statistics forecast on the economy, effective tax rates on personal incomes on the state and federal levels are expected to decline. These declining tax rates will yield real growth in disposable personal incomes. The result of these changes will mean less spending by governments and more spending by consumers directly for wanted goods and services.

Tax monies available for publicly supported libraries are likely to decline. Many libraries will have no choice but to impose user fees to obtain revenue from consumers' disposable personal incomes. In an era of declining government spending, it is unlikely that massive spending and subsidies for libraries will materialize.

In the quest for funding we should remember the rain dance and not lose sight of why we are seeking the funding. Armstrong has stated, "The rain dance has something for everyone. The dancer gets paid."[40] Librarians and their constituents can watch a good dance. The journals can print items and articles about the dance. Conferences about the dance can be held and librarians can get to be good dancers. The dance allows us to foist the funding problem on to the Congress, the President, or the gods.

While the prospects for funding in this paper justify the labelling of economics, "the dismal science," the future for libraries and librarianship never has been brighter or more exciting. The products of technology and organizational innovation have given us the tools to shape a future in which our "heroic mission" can be transformed into realistic and realizable goals.

CATALOGING COST CALCULATIONS

Assumptions:

- In manual cataloging systems, 80% of titles are cataloged with copy provided by NUC, CIP, etc.

- The cost of copy cataloging is $8.00 per title.
- The cost of original cataloging is $20.00 per title.
- The cost of cataloging on a shared catalog system for titles found in the data base is $5.00 per title.
- Unit cost for manual cataloging =

$$UC = \frac{\text{Copy cat titles (8.00) + original titles (20.00)}}{\text{total titles}}$$

- Unit cost for shared cataloging =

$$UC = \frac{\text{titles found (5.00) + original titles (20.00)}}{\text{total titles}}$$

Manual Cataloging:

The unit cost of manual cataloging 50,000 titles =

$$UC = \frac{40,000 \ (8.00) + 10,000 \ (20.00)}{50,000}$$

$$UC = \$10.40$$

Shared Cataloging:

For 50,000 titles at various hit rates shared cataloging unit costs are:

Hit Rate (percent)	Titles Found	Titles Originally Cataloged	Unit Cost
70	35000	15000	9.50
75	37500	12500	8.75
80	40000	10000	8.00
85	42500	7500	7.25
90	45000	5000	6.50
95	47500	2500	5.75
100	50000	0	5.00

NOTES

1. J. Scott Armstrong, *Long Range Forecasting: From Crystal Ball to Computer* (New York: Wiley, 1978), p. 15.
2. *The Bowker Annual of Library and Book Trade Information*, 23rd ed. (New York: Bowker, 1978).
3. U.S. Bureau of Labor Statistics, *Occupational Outlook Handbook 1978-1979 Edition* (Washington, D.C.: U.S. Bureau of Labor Statistics, 1978).

4. American Library Association, *A Perspective on Libraries* (Chicago: ALA, 1979).
5. National Center for Educational Statistics, *Preliminary Report on the Survey of College and University Libraries Fall 1976* (Washington: NCES, 1977).
6. U.S. Bureau of the Census, *Statistical Abstract of the United States 1978*, 99th ed. (Washington: U.S. Bureau of the Census, 1978).
7. *Survey of Current Business* (July 1978), p. 37.
8. National Commission on Libraries and Information Science, *Public Libraries: Who Should Pay the Bills?* (Washington: NCLIS, 1978).
9. *ALA Washington Newsletter* 31 (January 29, 1979).
10. Norman C. Saunders, "The U.S. Economy to 1990: Two Projections for Growth," *Monthly Labor Review* 101: 36-46 (December 1978).
11. Adam Clymer, "Tax Revolt: An Idea Whose Time Has Come?" *New York Times National Economic Survey* (January 7, 1979), p. 12.
12. Arthur Andreassen, "Changing Patterns of Demand: BLS Projections to 1990," *Monthly Labor Review* 101:47-55 (December 1978).
13. Saunders, "U.S. Economy to 1990."
14. *Bowker Annual.*
15. Indiana State Library, *Statistics of Indiana Libraries* (Indianapolis: Indiana State Library, 1976, 1977).
16. M.S. Drake, "Management Control in Academic Libraries," *New Horizons for Academic Libraries: ACRL 1978 National Conference* (Chicago: American Library Association, 1978).
17. J. Christopher Burns, "The Evolution of Office Information Systems," *Datamation* 23:60-4 (April 1977).
18. James Martin, *Future Developments in Telecommunications*, 2nd ed. (Englewood Cliffs, N.J.: Prentice-Hall, 1977).
19. *Business Week* (June 30, 1975), p. 53.
20. Gordon Wills and Christine Oldman, "An Examination of Cost/Benefit Approaches to the Evaluation of Library and Information Services," in F.W. Lancaster and C.W. Cleverdon, eds. *Evaluation and Scientific Management of Libraries and Information Centres* (Leyden: Noordkoff, 1977), p. 174.
21. Paul W. Barkley, *Economics: The Way We Choose* (New York: Harcourt Brace, 1977), p. 325.
22. Joe A. Hewitt, "The Impact of OCLC: The Good and the Bad as Recorded by Researcher Joe A. Hewitt in our Epic Journey to Every Charter Library of the On-Line System," *American Libraries* 7:268-75 (May 1976).
23. Richard W. Blood, "Impact of OCLC on Reference Service," *Journal of Academic Librarianship* 3:68-73 (1977).
24. Frederick Kilgour, OCLC Inc.
25. Richard B. McKenzie and Gordon Tullock, *The New World of Economics* (Homewood, Ill: Irwin, 1975): pp. 49-65.
26. American Library Association, *A Perspective on Libraries.*

27. Paul A Samuelson, *Economics*, 8th ed. (New York: McGraw-Hill, 1970).
28. Cheryl A. Casper, "Subsidies for Library Services," in *Encyclopedia of Library and Information Science* (New York: Dekker, to be published).
29. Marilyn Gell, "User Fees II: The Library Response," *Library Journal* 104:170-73 (January 15, 1979).
30. Robert N. Anthony and Regina E. Herzlinger. *Management Control in Nonprofit Organizations* (Homewood, Ill.: Irwin, 1975), pp. 10-11.
31. Gell, "User Fees II."
32. Barbara E. Markuson, "Cooperation and Library Network Development," *College and Research Libraries* 40:125-35 (March 1979).
33. M.A. Drake and H.A. Olsen, "The Economics of Library Innovation," *Library Trends* 28: 89-105 (Summer, 1979).
34. Anthony and Herzlinger, "Management Control."
35. Audrey Clayton and E. Bishop, "Potential Effects of Fee-for-Service and Automation Upon Library Staff and Library Users," in *Information Management in the 80's; Proceedings of the ASIS Annual Meeting 14* (October 1977).
36. National Commission on Libraries and Information Science, *Toward a National Program for Library and Information Services: Goals for Action: An Overview* (Washington: NCLIS, 1978).
37. Ernest Holsendolph, "Deregulation: Panacea of Pandora's Box?" *New York Times Magazine* (January 7, 1979).
38. *New York Times* (February 24, 1979), pp. 1, 9.
39. Tom Alexander, "Why Bureaucracy Keeps Growing," *Fortune* (May 7, 1979), pp. 164-76.
40. J. Scott Armstrong, *Long Range Forecasting*, p. 329.

Funding for Library Networks: Types and Sources of Available Funds

Barbara Robinson
Metropolitan Washington Library Council
Washington, D.C.

INTRODUCTION

At present, libraries are participating in a wide variety of automated and manual resource sharing networks. These networks provide two or more libraries, or library-related organizations, with the mechanism to exchange library data, materials, or services in support of their shared objectives.[1] "Networking as a formalization of our friend interlibrary cooperation is a must and a fact of life,"[2] according to one librarian, and it is fair to say that networks are widely viewed as the exciting and inevitable next step in library development. Participating libraries are joining networks because they:

- promote interlibrary cooperation—information exchange, planning
- improve bibliographic access—cataloging, processing, delivery
- offer continuing education and training
- provide reference assistance—manual or machine-assisted
- produce cooperative tools—union lists, catalogs, directories
- organize cooperative acquisitions

New networks are appearing all the time during this period of change. Many of them are formal, with bylaws and governing boards, and a good many of them provide some type of automated service. Since formal networks are relatively recent additions to the library scene, not much data have been collected that provide a complete picture of what these and the more informal and/or manual cooperatives look like. (Under the broad definition of a network used in this paper, cooperatives and networks are virtually synonymous. The term "network," however, is often used to connote a formal organization and an automated environment, while the term "cooperative," in another context, might be used to describe the more informal organization and/or manual environment.) For example, we do not know what the total purchasing power of networks is or how much, in total, their respective members spend to participate in networks.[3] Indeed we cannot determine these figures even for the automated networks. Ruth Patrick, based on her recent survey of 56 state library agencies, estimated that in FY 1976, $39.8 million was spent from all funding sources on multitype library cooperation and networking activities.[4]

Since there are a bewildering number of networks which perform a wide variety of services, it is useful to provide a categorization by their distinguishing characteristics:

- membership composition, i.e., the number, type, size, and geographic location of each network's member libraries
- topology of the network, i.e., star, hierarchical, distributed, or totally decentralized
- range and orientation of services, i.e., single or multiple services provided; manual or automated, technical services (in support of library operations) or public services
- targeted end users (librarians or other such as the general public, college students, researchers, business people, government officials, etc.)
- type and mix of funding (e.g., internally generated or external)

It would be surprising if any two networks were exactly matched according to all of these characteristics. The particular mixture of characteristics in any given network, however, may make it eligible to compete for certain outside funds, entitle it to apply for certain funds, or reduce its chances of receiving outside funds.

This paper will describe the types and sources of funding for library networks that are currently available and discuss the types of activities that are likely to be funded in the future.

TYPES OF FUNDS NEEDED BY NETWORKS

Networks have a variety of costs to cover that require funds in differing amounts and at different times in their growth. Funding requirements usually fall into the following categories:

- design—systems analyses and feasibility studies to determine the most appropriate configuration for network organization and services
- implementation—the cost of starting up
- operation—annual costs of staff, overhead, hardware
- expansion of service including:
    demonstration projects
    software development
    production of cooperative tools (e.g., union lists)
    training costs
    upgrading the quality of the network by acquiring new
        hardware, software, hiring more skilled management

Ideally, every network should be based on a grand design which is implemented, made operational, and then expanded over time to accommodate the changing demands of member libraries and the new opportunities offered by advances in the field. Of course, a good number of networks have simply evolved. Either way, funds for the design and implementation of a network have often come as seed money from outside sources. Once a network is up and running, the day-to-day operating costs are usually covered by the network itself through internally generated funds which will be described briefly below. As the network matures, it might expand its complement of services and upgrade the quality of its hardware, software, or management to keep pace with advances in the field. It appears that some outside funds have been available for service expansion, particularly demonstration projects that serve as a prototype for adoption in other network settings.

In addition to funds needed for these four stages, financial support is needed to conduct research on optimal network design.

One route is to develop a simulation model as Professor Allen Kent is doing at the University of Pittsburgh. Another is to study networks which lie outside the library environment and learn from these other network experiences. The research perspective should be broad enough to attract study by a range of experts. In addition to librarians and information scientists, network design should capitalize on engineering, systems analysis, computer science, operations research, economics, sociology and psychology, to name a few. This type of research is being conducted by some of the network staff, as well as by library science educators such as Professor Kent, and by researchers in such organizations as the Mitre Corporation. Research money then should be distributed in the future to networks, academic researchers, and private research organizations.

TYPES OF FUNDS CURRENTLY
AVAILABLE TO NETWORKS

As mentioned briefly above, there are two channels for network funding: 1) funds that are internally generated (membership dues, fees-for-service, and support from a parent organization), and 2) funds which come from outside sources (federal, state and/or local, and foundation grants). Given the paucity of outside funds available to libraries in general, one suspects that a good percentage of networks either generate their own funds internally or operate under constant uncertainty by going from grant to grant. For example, most of the networks belonging to the Council for Computerized Library Networks charge their member libraries an annual membership fee (the amount varies from network to network) and also charge for services performed such as brokering for systems such as OCLC, Lockheed, SDC and BRS.[5] Glyn Evans, the Director of the SUNY network, summed up the financial situation as follows:

> We have had primarily to exist on our own resources which may not be such a bad thing. It gives us flexibility and responsibility. Not operating on soft money forces us to make hard decisions. It means that we have to work to insure that the libraries which join us will find it sufficiently cost beneficial to reallocate some of their resources to the network. In 1975 the SUNY network became self supporting. We promised to hold our service fees constant for two years. Indeed we have been able to extend that promise by three additional years.[6]

Some networks do receive support from their parent organizations. For example, in the private sector, the Bell Library System is supported by AT&T. In the federal sector, there are some very well established networks, the most notable being the National Library of Medicine's Regional Medical Library Program (funded under the Medical Library Assistance Act of 1965 which funds 11 already existing medical libraries that provide service on a regional basis).

CURRENT SOURCES OF OUTSIDE FUNDS FOR NETWORKERS

Unfortunately, the discussion that follows is hardly sanguine. Outside sources of funds for libraries, in general, and for networks, in particular, are scanty. The bitter irony is that just as libraries are readying themselves to embrace the technology developed in the 1960s, public funding at every level appears to be drying up. In addition, private foundation money to libraries has never been very plentiful, with approximately one percent spent on libraries and library activities in 1977.[7] In recent years, however, a few foundations have supported the design, implementation, and expansion of several networks and the "national network." Not long ago, Lee Burchinal of the National Science Foundation painted a gloomy picture in his remarks made at the Pittsburgh Conference on the On-line Revolution in Libraries:

> With increased costs, greater automated and associated capital operations, new sources of revenue will be necessary to sustain the more costly, but far more effective services users are becoming accustomed to having. Increased public funding to meet these costs is not likely. More likely, users will be required to pay at least part of the costs of more sophisticated services in the future.[8]

The outside funds currently available to networks come from three major sources: federal, other governmental (state and local), and foundations. At this time, there has not been any financial assistance to the networks from the private sector apart from group discounts for high volume use of telecommunications. Perhaps this situation will change in the future as the hardware producers begin to see networks as agents for aggregating the market and introducing innovation. Let us look at some of the sources of funds in each of the three categories.

FEDERAL FUNDS: CATEGORICAL GRANTS TO LIBRARIES

There are two types of categorical federal funds: formula grants earmarked for certain types of libraries and required by law to go to those libraries, and discretionary grants which are awarded on a competitive basis.

Formula Grants

Federal funds have been available to public libraries and libraries in educational institutions—elementary, secondary and academic—since the 1950s. The principal legislation that provides categorical federal funds to libraries has come as a result of the following acts: the Library Services and Construction Act (LSCA), the Higher Education Act (HEA), and the Elementary and Secondary Education Act (ESEA). LSCA and ESEA are administered at the state level and distributed on a formula basis (the ingredients of the formula are not the same for each act) by the states, while HEA is administered as a mixture of categorical and discretionary grants. Since ESEA Title IV-B, the School Library Resources and Instructional Equipment Program, is for the acquisition of materials and equipment rather than interlibrary cooperation, it will be excluded from the following discussion. HEA Titles A, B, and C will be discussed in the next section on federal discretionary grants.

LSCA Title III, Interlibrary Cooperation.   LSCA grew out of the old Library Services Act and expanded what had been a program for establishing libraries in rural areas into a broader program of funding for public libraries across the country. In 1966, LSCA was expanded to include unrestricted funding "for establishing and operating local, regional, state or interstate cooperative networks of libraries."[10] Initially, the states were required to match federal funds. In 1970, however, the matching funds requirement was dropped.

Title III is millions of dollars short of the funding level requested by the library community ($20 million in FY 1978, 1979, and 1980). In 1979, $5 million was appropriated for interlibrary cooperation, and only after a last minute effort was the appropriation increased from $3.3 million. Now in the President's FY 1980 budget, once again it appears at the $3.3 million level. Title III is administered by the state library agencies on a state formula grant basis. In FY 1979 the 50 states, the District of

Columbia and Puerto Rico received a basic allotment of $40,000. Other outlying areas received $10,000. The balance is distributed on the basis of the total resident population as of July 1, 1976. Amounts in FY 1979 ranged from $45,366 (Alaska) to $323,055 (California). Given the meager funds allocated, it would be impractical to apportion the funds equally among all networks or interlibrary cooperatives in a given state.

Title III has had a major impact on interlibrary cooperation in this country and has apparently stimulated some related legislation in at least two states.[11] According to Joe Shubert, then State Librarian of Ohio and now State Librarian of New York:

> The LSCA program placed new and major responsibility on the state agencies . . . this is particularly true of Title III, which brought state library agencies into a new relationship with university, school and special libraries as well as with the major public libraries. LSCA assisted programs, shaped network development and caused major changes in interlibrary sharing and communications.[12]

The strength of Title III is its flexibility. Funds may be spent as needed by the recipient, whether for design, implementation, operations, service expansion, or research. The disadvantages of Title III are that funds are uncertain and scanty. This is particularly unfortunate at this time of network evolution. In addition, while Title III permits funds to be spent on a multistate basis, funds tend to be spent often on intrastate cooperative efforts. Networks that are multistate in scope feel that they are receiving short shrift and predict that as more networks become regional, there will be more pressure on state librarians to fund regional efforts. For example, Title III funds have been spent jointly for a number of years by three state library agencies of the District of Columbia, Maryland, and Virginia in support of the Metropolitan Washington Library Council, a tri-state, multitype library cooperative.

LSCA-Title I. Like Title III, Title I is very broad in scope. Unlike Title III, however, Title I requires matching state funds. Enacted in 1956 as part of an expanded Library Services Act, the intent of Title I was to secure interlibrary cooperation and generally to extend library services to ". . . groups of citizens who may be out of the mainstream of public library services and thus underserved." Mentioned specifically in the Act are the physically handicapped, the disadvantaged, and the institutionalized.

In addition, the Act calls for "strengthening metropolitan public libraries which serve as national or regional resource centers."

The 95th Congress amended the Act, mandating a special share for urban libraries when funding of Title I exceeds $60 million. This year the Title I appropriation has just topped the required level ($62.5 million) and as a result the urban libraries are eligible to receive as much as 50 percent of the $2.5 million. Unfortunately, the President's 1980 budget would lower the funding to its 1978 level of $56.9 million. Unless the Congress revises the figures, urban libraries would not receive an extra allotment next year.

Yet another purpose of Title I is "for extending public library services to geographical areas and groups of persons without such services and improving such services in such areas and for such groups as may have inadequate public library services." Consequently, Title I has been used for interlibrary cooperation over the years.

The assumption was that the new Title III would provide funding for interlibrary cooperation and Title I could concentrate on its other missions. Given the interest in and growth of networks, however, it is not at all surprising that state library agencies have needed to use Title I to supplement the scanty Title III support for networks. It appears, for example, that in FY 1976 almost $3 million of Title I money (a sum nearly equal to the Title III appropriations that year) was used for Title III-like goals.[13] The extent of this trend will be clarified once the U.S. Office of Education-sponsored study of LSCA Title I is completed later this year.[14]

Discretionary Grants

In addition to the formula grants listed above, libraries have been able to turn to Title II, Part B, of the Higher Education Act of 1965 for very modest discretionary grants. These grants are awarded by the U.S. Office of Education Office of Libraries and Learning Resources. Proposals may be submitted by individuals and institutions on issues relating to libraries. Grants are awarded on a competitive basis by USOE project officers who work with a panel of outside readers. HEA Title II-B actually is two-pronged. It provides grants for research and demonstration and also grants for training. It is an unusual program because it is intended to serve the needs of the library community rather than the mission orientation of the federal agency through which it is administered.

HEA Title II-B, Research and Demonstration. Over the years, funds from the Research and Demonstration Section of HEA II-B have been used to support a number of notable projects, including a number of network projects. OCLC has received Title II-B funding for design, implementation, service enhancement, and research on and off over the last ten years. BALLOTS, the Washington Library Network (WLN), the New England Library Network (NELINET), and the Cooperative College Library Center in Atlanta have all had projects funded in past years. The HEA Title II-B (Research and Demonstration) is nearly as flexible and broad in scope as LSCA III. Its program categories match the network funding needs quite closely. They are: Planning and Development, Functional Development, Technology, Institutional Cooperation, and Education and Training. Operational funding is really the only funding area which is not included.

Unfortunately, this program has been in constant danger of becoming extinct. It has been zero-funded in the President's budget in past years and is again left out of the 1980 budget. Since 1975, it has received roughly $1 million per year, an embarrassingly small amount of funding compared to its $3.4 million funding level 10 years ago.

HEA Title II-B, Training. This program provides library grants for training institutes as well as for fellowships and traineeships to individuals in such areas as Library Services, Resources, Administration, Technology, and Education. Like its sister program described above, funding has declined dramatically in recent years from a peak of nearly $8.2 million in 1969 to $2 million in 1978/79. It too is zero-funded in the President's current budget.

Networks and cooperatives, along with library schools and state and local governmental agencies, have received funds for training institutes. The objective of funding these institutes is to upgrade the skills of participating librarians. At this time, when the profession is undergoing such change, librarians, and particularly those librarians who work in network offices or who use network services, need intensive training in working in a network environment. One hopes that HEA Title II-B Training will continue to be funded. Networks badly need the opportunity to educate their customers and their own staffs.

HEA Title II-C and HEA Title II-A.   There are two additional sections of HEA-II worth mentioning briefly in the network context. Title II-C, Strengthening Research Libraries Resources and Title II-A, College Library Resources.

In 1978, 20 research libraries for the first time received $5 million under Title II-C, in recognition of their contribution to scholarship and research by maintaining and strengthening their collections and making their resources available to "individual researchers and scholars and to other libraries whose users have need for such research materials." The need for special support to these libraries is embodied in the Title II-C legislation. It is far below the $15 million the library community requested, and appears only at a level of $6 million in the President's 1980 budget.

HEA Title II-A provided just under $10 million to academic institutions and certain eligible library agencies in FY 1979. Funds are to be used for the purchase of materials and to a limited extent for grants for acquisitions (up to $5000); supplemental grants for particularly needy institutions are authorized. The third category of grant—special purpose—best applies to academic networks and cooperatives. It allows for matching grants to support special activities such as those involving consortia, cooperatives and combinations of public and private institutions. Funds for special purpose grants, however, only become available when HEA Title II-A has provided all eligible institutions with basic grants. If you multiply $5000 by roughly 2500 eligible institutions, $12.5 million is needed before the special-purpose grants can be funded. The prospects of achieving this level of funding look bleak; at this moment the President's budget proposes zero-funding for Title II-A for next year.

Federal Funds: Library-Related Programs[15]

In addition to the earmarked funds for libraries listed above, there are a few established sources of funds for libraries and networks in at least two federal agencies: the National Endowment for the Humanities and the National Science Foundation. In addition, there are a number of other pockets of federal money which are listed in *Federal Programs for Libraries*, a directory recently prepared by the USOE.[16] While the directory lists nine federal library programs and 72 federal library-related programs, only a handful appear to pertain to networks, and then probably only if the proposer can make a persuasive case for why his or her proposal is not being funded by the Office of Education.

The National Endowment for the Humanities (NEH). NEH was created in 1965 as an independent grant-making agency to support research, education, and public activity in the humanities. The Division of Research Grants and the Division of Public Programs have been the principal funders of library and network programs over the last few years. NEH provides one year planning grants as well as implementation grants that cover up to a three year period. NEH also has a philosophy of stimulating funding from other sources. Therefore, in addition to providing outright grants, it also has a pool of matching grant money which is used to stimulate grantees to seek gifts and matching grant money from other sources. For every dollar raised by an outside source, a dollar of NEH money is available. The gifts and matching program usually come into play for projects of over $100,000. The outright grants also require a match-in-kind or in cash. The percentage required varies with the program.

The Research Collections Program is the primary program in the Division of Research Grants which supports some of the network functions described in the beginning of this paper. This program has $3 million of annual grant money to award outright (requiring a 40 percent match for projects that the institution could be expected to support, and a 20 percent match on a new project). The Division has also been able to tap some of the pool money to be used for stimulating gifts and matching grants. Some of the design and implementation costs of BALLOTS and the University of Chicago's Library Data Management System, has been underwritten by this program, and it will shortly be providing some matching grant money to OCLC. The commitment to fund network activities is being expressed in a variety of ways. Last year, a prototype project was funded to link the New York Public Library's system to the Library of Congress so that NYPL's computer could directly query LC's computer for needed MARC records. LC could then transmit the MARC data back to NYPL.

A second funded project has involved distributed cataloging. Northwestern University, together with a consortium of libraries, is sending bibliographic tapes of holdings in its Africaniana collection to the Library of Congress. LC validates the records on the tapes, and upgrades them to MARC records which then appear on the MARC tapes.

The most notable grant for FY 1979-81 goes to the Council on Library Resources for $1.8 million ($300,000 per year outright for three years and $900,000 matching). The Council will be working to develop links among OCLC, WLN and the recent Research Libraries Information Network. This effort constitutes a first step in bringing together already existing pieces of a network which is referred to as "the emerging national network" by some. The Council will be using these funds for the Bibliographic Services Development Program, which is described under the Foundation section later in this paper.

Overall, the program has some of the same flexibility of LSCA Title III and HEA Title II-B, Research and Demonstration. Funds have been used for feasibility studies, start up, expansion (e.g., demonstration projects, software and upgrading) and research. It does not provide support for the development of new tools, which are under the domain of the Research Materials Program (which mainly funds bibliographies), or training.

In the past the Division of Public Programs has funded library programs as part of its mission. As of this year, however, the Public Library Program is now a separate program under the Division, with a grant budget of $1.6 million. According to recent guidelines, it provides funds "to strengthen library programs that stimulate and respond to public interest in the humanities; to enhance the ability of library staff to plan and implement these programs; and to increase the public's awareness and use of a library's existing humanities resources." It requires a 20 percent in-kind or cash match on all projects funded outright.

One of the 15 projects awarded so far (there are four rounds of awards, with one more round to go) is at the Seattle Public Library which will be working with other libraries at the University of Washington, community colleges, and with museums and archival collections in Seattle to highlight ethnicity in Seattle. The project budget is $308,000 which was granted outright. A second example is a project in Oklahoma on the same theme which involves the Oklahoma Department of Libraries, the Oklahoma Library Association, and the Oklahoma University School of Library Science. While not required, many of the funded projects have involved libraries working in partnerships with other institutions such as museums, historical societies, local government agencies, and other libraries. A wide variety of libraries are eligible including public, community college, university and special libraries, state library agencies, and library associations.

The National Science Foundation. Largely as a result of a Task Force report prepared by outside experts in 1977, the National Science Foundation shifted its funding emphasis for information projects. The panel recommended that the "emerging new science," information science, be given priority by establishing a new research program in the Foundation. The panel also recommended that the Division of Science Information (DSI) be dissolved and that its functions, positions, and resources be transferred to other parts of the Foundation. DSI has been replaced by the Division of Information Science and Technology (DIST). While the names of the past and present divisions are similar their mandates are quite different. Under DSI, the Office of Science Information Service treated information science as one of several priorities which also included: user requirements, access improvement, economics of information, and national/international coordination. It was this office that funded, for example, the DIALIB study in California, the Fry/White work on scholarly journals, the ANSI Z39 Committee and the Northeast Academic Science Information Center in New England.

Under DIST, there is the new Information Science Unit (ISU). According to its 1979 program announcement, "Research in Information Science," funding priorities include standards and measures, structures of information, behavioral aspects of information transfer, and infometrics. DIST's awards budget for FY 1979 is $4.5 million which represents a $500,000 decrease compared to $5 million in FY 1978. The Information Science Unit (ISU) will de-emphasize funding general surveys, policy studies and operational support, such as that provided to the ANSI Z39 Committee. Modelling, however, will continue to be of interest as will proposals on the structure of the information industry, research relating to network operations, and the economics of networks (e.g., pricing, optimum size, and the impact of regulation). At this time it is not clear where responsibility for the four other functions which the Task Force felt were of importance will go in the Foundation, namely research and applications, policy analysis, coordination and education. Next to emerge will be the Information Technology Unit, also under DIST. At this time, however, its program has not yet been announced.

Other Divisions in NSF. Applied research continues to be funded in the Division of Intergovernmental Science and Research and Development Incentives, but the tradition has been to fund problem-solving efforts at the state and local level. For example, the Urban Technology System positioned technology agents at the local level to dispense scientific and technical information for problem solving (modeled after the U.S. Department of Agriculture's County Agent program). Unfortunately, libraries have not been recipients of grants from this program.

The Division of Mathematical and Computer Sciences funded a program called "Networking for Science" for several years, but because there were few responses to their solicitations for proposals, they have closed down that program. Successful networking proposals would now be funded by the Special Projects Program. Projects must be research-oriented and advance the state of the art of computing.

Federal Funds: Other Sources

General Revenue Sharing (GRS) was one of the hoped for supplemental funding sources for which libraries have been eligible to apply since its enactment in 1972. Two-thirds of GRS monies go to local governments directly while one-third goes to the states. Over the last five years $30.2 billion was expended at the state and local level of which roughly one percent went to libraries.[17] Those GRS funds that went to libraries were apparently often used by local government as substitutes for other funds that libraries would otherwise have gotten. Indeed according to a recent Brookings study, which was reported on in *Library Journal*:

> There is a strong tendency on the part of relatively hard pressed state and local jurisdictions to devote a greater portion of their revenue sharing monies to substitutive as opposed to new uses.[18]

STATE FUNDS FOR NETWORKS

According to Ruth Patrick's evaluation of Title III, not only has the Act provided the state librarians with unrestricted funds to support interlibrary cooperation, but it has stimulated proposed legislation at the state level. Over one-third of the 56 state and territorial library agencies reported that LSCA Title III produced specific changes in state legislation which will facilitate multitype library cooperation, and 76 percent of the states said they actively participated in intrastate and multistate library networks in 1976.[19] At the time of the Patrick report, however, only two states had actually funded legislation similar to LSCA III.[20]

While no precise figures are yet available on state funding patterns to networks, Glyn Evans has made some rough calculations using figures appearing in the *ASLA Report on Interlibrary Cooperation*, 1978 edition.[21] In calendar 1978, it appears that state libraries spent roughly $6.5 million for interlibrary cooperation. Just short of $3 million came from state support and the remainder from LSCA Titles III and I, and other sources. In addition, state libraries expended roughly $1.3 million on Interlibrary Cooperation Communication Devices/Service Networks such as WATS lines, credit cards, telefacsimile and teletype. Mr. Evans excluded reported costs of on-line computer terminals (e.g., OCLC terminals) from this estimate.

LOCAL FUNDS FOR NETWORKS

Very little can be said about how much local money is going to networks, again because of the lack of statistics. We know that in the case of public libraries, over 75 percent of funding came from local sources in FY 1974,[22] and that municipal libraries received nearly 83 percent of their funding from local government in 1977.[23] One suspects that networks, and particularly multitype and/or multistate networks, would be unlikely to receive local funds.

FOUNDATION FUNDS FOR NETWORKS [24]

Over the last few years, community and corporate foundations have provided libraries with grants for a range of activities. In 1977 libraries received 1.2 percent of the $2.1 billion given annually by private foundations, or $25 million worth of grants. A total of 311 separate grants were made to libraries, most were under $50,000.

Every category of library received some foundation support in 1977, with the academic libraries receiving the most (71 grants) and school libraries receiving the least (one grant). Networks or cooperative activities received roughly 15 grants mainly from foundations with a national focus, such as the Council on

Library Resources (CLR), Mellon, Sloan, and Kellogg. One sizable grant of $172,800 came from the Bush Foundation in Minnesota and was awarded to the Minnesota Consortium of Seminary Faculties to computerize their cataloging. The two most notable sources of foundation funds for network activities have been CLR and Kellogg.

The Council on Library Resources (CLR)

CLR had $1.2 million total revenues in 1978. Funds came largely from outside foundation support. Since its inception in 1956, it has served as a conduit for other foundations' support of libraries. Ford has provided a great deal of funds for the Council over the years. In 1978 all but $41,000 came from Ford ($500,000), Mellon ($200,000), Carnegie ($329,397), the National Science Foundation ($20,121) and a combined $83,853 for planning the much discussed national periodicals center (money has come from Carnegie, the Commonwealth Fund, the Lilly Endowment, Ford, Hewlett, Mellon, Rockefeller and Sloan foundations).

The Council has funded an impressive array of network projects including the design, implementation and service expansion of MEDLARS (Medical Literature Analysis and Retrieval System), MARC (MAchine Readable Cataloging), SLICE (Southwestern Library Interstate Cooperative Endeavor), NELINET (New England Library Information Network), SOLINET (Southeastern Library Network), MINITEX (Minnesota Interlibrary Telecommunications Exchange), Project Intrex, OCLC (Ohio College Library Center), BALLOTS, CONSER (Conversion of Serials), WICHE (Western Interstate Commission for Higher Education) and the University of Chicago's Library Data Management System. Since 1976 it has also provided funds for the Network Advisory Committee and the Network Technical Architecture Group for the meetings run by the Library of Congress to shape the emerging national network.[25] It has also been concerned with professional education, particularly to improve the caliber of academic librarianship. In 1978, under the new leadership of Warren J. Haas, formerly University Librarian, Columbia University Libraries, CLR is clearly moving towards the development of a national library network. Mr. Haas has stated that existing resources and institutions will be incorporated into the new Bibliographic Services Development Program (BSDP) which is perceived as "... a cooperative effort involving the Library of Congress and other national libraries, existing operational networks, a number of research libraries, professional organizations, and many individuals."[26] Funds now exceeding $5 million are being provided by NEH (as mentioned above) and seven foundations to explore ways of coordinating the existing actors. The focus of the BSDP appears to be on coordinating bibliographic control by using established standards and authority systems, and on developing links among the existing nodes of the emerging network. Since the Council has long been closely allied with the academic research libraries in the U.S., it will be interesting to see just how much of its resources are spent on nonresearch library nodes and whether the foundation support going to the BSDP and the NPC draw foundation funds away from other types of library projects or stimulate increased foundation funds.

The Kellogg Foundation

The Kellogg Foundation in Battle Creek, Michigan is one of the largest foundations in the country. It has taken an extraordinary interest in library networks. In its 1976 annual report, it stated that it would support "computerized technical services to academic, public and library systems to increase staff productivity, decrease unit costs, and improve services for library users." In 1976, Kellogg provided $4.25 million for this purpose so that "libraries would be more effective in serving library patrons." $2.4 million went to 300 small private liberal arts colleges across the country so that they could buy/lease terminals. $1.5 million went to publicly-funded libraries in Michigan to enhance the Michigan Library Network, and OCLC received $399,319 to develop a mechanism for linking up with other on-line systems in law, medicine, etc. In 1977, Kellogg provided another $1.2 million, going largely for the same purpose, with some additional emphasis on staff training and promotion of the new service. 1978 funding is down to about $65,000 mainly for the small private liberal arts colleges. Kellogg has demonstrated real imagination—it is to be hoped that other foundations will follow suit.

Other Foundations

While there are other foundations funding a few network projects, there is a possibility of increasing this funding base if the network is willing to invest the time and effort in grantsmanship. Stephen Seward feels that community foundations are a promising source of funding for libraries because they must make grants within their community and have a board that represents the community in order to receive maximum tax advantages.[27] While networks that are regional in scope are unlikely to secure funds from community foundations, individual libraries that wish to participate in a network venture might try.

CONCLUSION

The discussion above highlights the paucity of outside funds for network development regardless of source. It also underscores the breadth of past library legislation which has allowed a good deal of flexibility in developing library services. This flexibility has allowed "random innovation"[28] to occur.

Kathleen Molz raises some hard questions in her book, *Federal Policy and Library Support*. She asks 1) whether the federal government should be expected to continue with basic subsidies to libraries and 2) whether "random innovation" is desirable or whether tighter guidelines should be drawn that identify the "federal-aid beneficiaries, rather than federal-aid benefits." The networks need to be able to address these questions both in terms of their own operation and in the context of the national network. The extent to which networks receive current federal funds will not only depend on how much funding is available but also on the national, state, and local level of commitment to networks.

NCLIS, in its 1975 *Goals for Action*, envisioned that "the Federal Government would force no library or information service to join the (nationwide) network, but it would provide technical inducements and funding incentives to state governments and the private sector to strengthen their ability to affiliate."[29] While we do not have national data that tells us to what extent federal funds have stimulated state and private support, we do know according to Ruth Patrick's report (cited earlier) that only two states had enacted Title III-like legislation as of FY 1976. We also know that just a few foundations awarded grants to networks, and then principally to the largest, most visible ones. Regrettably, we cannot cite examples of private sector support of network development unless discounts for high volume use of telecommunications are counted. It would appear that Glyn Evans' words concerning the need for financial self-sufficiency will apply to most networks in the forseeable future.

NOTES

1. Allen Kent et al., "Behavioral Implications" (Working Paper V), "The Economics of Information Transfer Using Resource Sharing Networks—Network Functions," Draft Final Report to the National Science Foundation, January 24, 1979, p. 7. Professor Kent's draft final report has been extremely helpful in the development of this paper. The library community should look forward to the completion of this study.
2. Marcelee Gralapp quoted by Karl Nyren, "Investing in Federal Network Services: How Far Can We Go?" *Library Journal* 101: 1395 (June 15, 1976).
3. When Frank Schick completes the analysis of the National Center for Education Statistics' recent "Survey of Library Networks and Cooperative Library Organizations 1977-78," we ought to have a better sense of how and in what proportion networks are raising and spending money. Results should be available by the end of the year.
4. Ruth Patrick, Joseph Casey, and Carol Novalis, *A Study of Library Cooperatives, Networks and Demonstration Projects, Volume I: Findings and Recommendations.* Prepared for the Office of Planning, Budgeting, and Evaluation, USOE Contract No. 300-76-0464. (Silver Spring, Maryland: Applied Management Sciences, March 31, 1978), p. 9.2.
5. The Council for Computerized Library Networks conducts an annual survey of its members which reports some figures, although Charles H. Stevens of SOLINET and the coordinator of the survey cautioned that figures could be misconstrued.
6. Glyn T. Evans, Director of the SUNY Network, in a telephone call, March 22, 1979.
7. Calculation based on figures reported by Stephen Seward, "Analysis of Foundation Grants to Libraries, 1977," in *The Bowker Annual,* 23rd ed.; p. 183.
8. Lee G. Burchinal, "Impact of On-Line Systems on National Information Policy and on Local, State, and Regional Planning," paper delivered at the Pittsburgh Conference on the On-Line Revolution in Libraries, November 14-16, 1977, p. 12.
9. Figures cited in this discussion come from two sources: The *ALA Washington Newsletter,* January 29, 1979; and *The Bowker Annual,* 23rd ed., pp. 111-56.
10. Patrick et al., "Study of Library Cooperatives," p. 9.2.
11. *Ibid.,* p. 9.6.
12. Joseph F. Shubert, "The Impact of the Federal Library Services and Construction Act," *Library Trends* 24:38 (July 1975).

13. Patrick et al., "Study of Library Cooperatives," p. 9.7.
14. The study is being conducted by Edwin H. Dowlin at Applied Management Sciences in Silver Spring, Maryland.
15. Figures cited in this discussion are drawn from issues of the *ALA Washington Newsletter*, and from essays by Eileen D. Cooke and Carol C. Henderson, in *The Bowker Annual*, 23rd ed., pp. 157-67. Supplementary information was provided in telephone conversations with Margaret Child and Nancy Bolt at NEH and with Helene Ebenfield at NSF during the week of March 19, 1979.
16. Lawrence E. Leonard and Ann M. Erteschuk compilers, *Federal Programs for Libraries: A Directory* (Washington, D.C.: U.S. Office of Education, August 1978), p. 64.
17. Art Goetz, "General Revenue Sharing: The Last Hope of Public Libraries for a Federal Pot of Gold," *American Libraries* 9:286 (May 1978).
18. Richard P. Nathan and Charles F. Adams, Jr., *Revenue Sharing: the Second Round* (Washington, D.C.: The Brookings Institution, 1977), p. 29, quoted in John M. Cohn, "Federal Aid and Local Spending: Stimulation vs. Substitution," *Library Journal* 104:459 (February 15, 1979). For other discussions see the following NCLIS reports: *Evaluation of the Effectiveness of Federal Funding of Public Libraries* (December 1976) and *Improving State Aid to Public Libraries* (February 1977).
19. Patrick, et al., "Study of Library Cooperatives," p. 12.6.
20. *Ibid.*, p. 9.7.
21. Glyn T. Evans, telephone conversation of March 22, 1979.
22. Helen M. Eckard, *Survey of Public Libraries: LIBGIS I, 1974* (Washington, D.C.: U.S. Department of Health, Education, and Welfare, National Center for Education Statistics, 1978), p. 42.
23. Barbara M. Robinson, "Municipal Library Services," *Urban Data Service Report*, Vol. 10, No. 6 (Washington, D.C.: International City Management Association; June, 1978), p. 2.
24. Figures for this section come from *The Bowker Annual*, 23rd ed., and appear in Seward, "Analysis of Foundation Grants," pp. 183-208, and Nancy E. Gwinn, "Council on Library Resources," pp. 168-78.
25. A recent report by Lawrence Buckland and Bill Basinski discusses "The Role of the Library of Congress in the Evolving National Network." Available from GPO (LC 78-10712).
26. "The Bibliographic Services Development Program," *Council on Library Resources Recent Developments* (February 1979), p. 2.
27. Seward, "Analysis of Foundation Grants," p. 183.
28. Alice M. Rivlin as quoted by R. Kathleen Molz, *Federal Policy and Library Support* (Cambridge, Mass.: The MIT Press, 1976), p. 109.
29. U.S. National Commission on Libraries and Information science, *Toward A National Program for Library and Information Services: Goal for Action* (Washington, D.C.: Government Printing Office, 1975), p. 49.

PART V

Network Users and Services

Warp, Woof and Loom: Networks, Users, and Information Systems

Blanche Woolls, Associate Professor
Graduate School of Library and Information
  Sciences
University of Pittsburgh
Pittsburgh, Pennsylvania

INTRODUCTION

When I discussed this presentation I was given three charges. First, point out critical issues concerning network users; second, watch the number of footnotes; third, don't speak in Academese. The latter two are difficult. In Academia, where I live, quality is often determined by the number of footnotes and academic veracity is established by how well you speak Academese.

As my resume documents, you'll know I was a fine arts major and I do know how to weave. Today I plan to weave a cloth, although networking may more nearly resemble a patchwork quilt. I'm a user of networks, both directly and indirectly. For this project I used, directly, one of the more simple forms of networking—I called the librarian at the Indiana Department of Public Instruction. Any materials I needed that were not available in that library would be located and sent on to me. For the past six months my office has been located 50 feet from the seven OCLC terminals in the Indiana Cooperative Library Services Authority (INCOLSA) environs and my indirect contact with the personnel in this operation has extended my horizons into the world of the network provider.

THE NETWORK PROVIDER

The warp of my loom, those long threads which make up the base of the weaving, represent the network providers. If one were to give each type of network provider a unique color, we might have more colors than the rainbow. It will be necessary for us to establish a common definition of network. Networks are difficult to define and even more difficult to divide into specific types. Each division reflects the decision processes of the divider which may or may not be agreeable divisions with the divider's best friend.

My first division would be those networks that offer contracted services for their own products. They make use of computers to generate data bases and serve their users from company computers. From the standpoint of the user, they cost. Color them red. Network providers charge for their services, passing the costs of the initiation and continuance of the services onto the users (e.g., OCLC/WLN/RLIN). In some cases they make a profit on the total operation (e.g., SDC, Lockheed).

The second group of networks also contract to provide services to their members. These providers access the data bases and services generated by the "red" networks and provide this information at a shared cost. Color them blue. Since these networks do buy the service from other sources, they must pay for what they purchase. They must then charge the user for their services or be subsidized by some other funding agency. For some users, these services cost; for others, they appear to be free; still others use central funds to pay partial costs.

While these networks may utilize computers, they do not generate the original data base or other services offered, although they may add to the data bases or provide additional or auxiliary services. The "blue" networks usually represent a region or a state (INCOLSA), but they may expand beyond a single state to a collection of states or areas (SOLINET). Other "blue" networks may serve a single type of library. From the standpoint of the user services may be "free", but utilization is limited to a special clientele. Many of these overlap. For example, MERMLS and PALINET serve a similar geographic area, but one serves only health-related agencies while the other is multi-type, encompassing public, academic and special libraries.

The next type of network provides services which are not tied into an outside data base or nationwide bibliographic or information retrieval service. While they provide a wide range of services, the services they offer might be considered by some computerized network providers as much less sophisticated. Called "cooperatives" by many, they are more likely to appear to be free of charge to the user. Color them green. These networks provide interlibrary loan, shared human resources, shared periodical resources, shared book processing and on and on.

My final type of network is one providing a single service to a special clientele. Color it yellow. Examples of these often exist in education. One frequent service of a "yellow" network is that of the 16mm film library which may serve a cluster of school districts or public library districts. These may or may not be free to the member libraries and may or may not be free to the ultimate user. Individual school teachers seldom pay rental fees for these films, but their school may be billed for the service. The films may be circulated to the member public libraries who pay the fee, but which do not charge the library user.

Where are the networks? A partial list of existing networks is presented in White's background paper in this book. While nationwide networks, providing fee-based services, offer the potential of service to users throughout the U.S., access is obviously restricted to those local agencies that can pay for the services and that have the technological capability of utilizing the service. If network access requires a telephone, a telephone must be in the proximity of the user. Certainly a library would hesitate to join a film consortium if it did not own 16mm projectors.

What are the networks providing? Networks originated, as both Chait and Stevens have described, from a tradition of cooperation which existed because, early on, librarians recognized that their collections would not be self-sufficient for their users and that they could not stand alone. The potential of automation coupled with the necessity of reducing the high costs of certain automated processes added to the already attractive possibilities of sharing.

Networks grew into sophisticated systems because the time was right. It was time to share cataloging, and MARC was there. Creative thinkers, librarians, and information scientists decided to utilize this data base. Only creative thinkers, aware of the extended possibilities of utilizing bibliographic data bases, could have opened the door to interlibrary loan potential and elegant circulation systems.

Other networks have provided such shared resources as film collections, specialized personnel who may work with children or senior citizens, public relations activities, and staff development. Services vary with the size and complexity of the network staff and the staffs of the member libraries.

Less intricate networks have shared collections through interlibrary loan. The installation of TWX systems in public libraries gave persons going to or calling their local public library an opportunity to place requests into a system with some central collection point—either the state library or a university library in the state. Materials were then available from a variety of locations. In some instances, very complicated procedures existed between the user and the use.

When I was a doctoral student at Indiana University, a group of us did an extensive study of the interlibrary loan system at the university library as a part of our systems analysis class. At that time, anyone in the state with a driver's license could walk into the main library and make an interlibrary loan request. That is, anyone except students at Indiana University. The Interlibrary Loan Office was willing to borrow materials, but students had to have their applications signed by the faculty member sponsoring the research. For undergraduate students, the application for an interlibrary loan was initiated by the instructor. The advanced degree people—masters students and doctoral students—were required to state the topic of their research or the purpose of their study, and then have the form signed by the professor who had initiated the research in the first place.

Professors apparently didn't want to discuss every anticipated research need with the students and, in self defense, they left stacks of signed forms (often with stamped signatures) in easily accessible spots. During our systems project, we signed a fictitious name to one request and the request was honored. This pointed out that this restrictive system was not only annoying, but impractical to enforce. After we made our final report, some eight years ago, the policy was changed immediately.

How are the networks providing services and with what success? In a recent talk to the Special Library Association in Indianapolis, Melvin Day, Director of the National Technical Information Service (NTIS), described the philosophy by which

Japan regulates consumer product manufacturing. The Japanese government determined that it would concentrate its industrial research and development funds on electronics, specifically on television. When they had cornered that market in the world, they then turned to the manufacture of automobiles.

Applying this model to networks, how many providers have concentrated on a single service which may be useful to a large portion of the user population? Many have patched together a quilt of service, each of which may be utilized by a few select clients. How many network providers have assessed the need for their service to their users? *Exactly which network services are to be offered to whom is a critical issue from the standpoint of the user.*

No one is questioning the value of networks. The literature is replete with arguments about the scarcity of human and material resources, the need to save dollars and to halt duplication of collections and other efforts, and the need to make operations more efficient (which might increase cost, but would also increase output). However, no network exists simply for the sake of existing—networks can only be held together by the network user.

USERS

Users are those threads that are woven through the services offered by a network. My users come in three primary colors— red, yellow, and blue. "Red" represents the professional user, "yellow" the nonprofessional user, and "blue" the potential user or the current nonuser. While I have placed them into distinct color categories, they, like the networks, do not fit comfortably into distinct niches. Some professional users may make nonprofessional use of networks and some nonprofessional users may be unaware that the information they sought was secured for them through a network and may consider themselves nonusers of networks.

Professional users are those persons who utilize services secured through the network for business or professional reasons. The professional users are divided into two categories—the job-specific and the research-related. The nonprofessional user is someone seeking information for self-satisfaction rather than job-specific or research-related business.

Job-specific users utilize the networks and they are paid a

salary to do so. It is a part of their daily job. Network developers may generate the data base. They may process the data base or use the product of the data base. Other job-specific users access the data bases for bibliographic information. These users may sit in front of a terminal for eight hours utilizing and inputting cataloging information. The terminal or the TWX may be used to facilitate interlibrary loan requests and these requests may be executed with little concern for the reason for the request or the ultimate use put to the material being located. Job-related users may also be reference librarians who hope to secure information for their clientele. Some may manage extensive search services while other reference librarians may develop policies for network building. A job-specific user who is planning a workshop will access the network for the human expertise available there. The world can easily identify the job-specific network user. It may even be a part of the job title.

The world may not so readily recognize research-related users. Research-related usage may be a more individual approach to the network than job-related usage. Research-related users are the consumers of information for both personal and societal reasons. Researchers need the information and will be personally involved in the success or failure of that utilization. The success of a search depends upon the data bases available, the cost, help, and support of the persons in charge of the system. These factors affect the degree to which the system will be potentially utilized. Research-related users of data bases, interlibrary loan, and other information retrieval schemes are found in universities, businesses, doctors' and lawyers' offices, and laboratories. Again, their utilization may go unrecognized. Unless one wins a Nobel Prize for research, the network user may not receive any personal recognition of that use. On the other hand, the information accessed through the network may be transformed into a cure for cancer.

The nonprofessional user wishes some information and has little or no interest in the mechanics which happen to secure that information. This user walks into the library for information and may not know whether or not the information is available in that library and may not, in fact, expect to find any particular amount of information.

This brings us to another description of users—the aware versus the unaware users. While job-related users are aware of the networks, the research-related user may not be. The researcher who may at the time of one search be an aware user, may at another time be unaware—especially if the topic was passed on to a graduate assistant or a librarian. The resulting documents may have been secured through searching *Reader's Guide*, a data base, or through a mechanized interlibrary loan transaction.

It is even less likely that the nonprofessional user will be an aware user. Let's say that the question asked by a nonprofessional user is answered. Little thought is given by the user to the steps which were required to answer the question or, ultimately, where the information was located. The prisoner in the state prison may not be terribly interested in the fact that a book of poetry is cataloged—much less that the cataloging information was put into the system by IPL (symbol for Purdue University on OCLC) or that 29 other libraries have utilized the original cataloging record.

Being aware is not really important from the standpoint of getting information, but it is important from the standpoint of securing public support for funding. Most people are unaware of the general reference possibilities of their libraries—in schools, public, academic or special—for they don't know what's there. Occasionally we are overlooked by fellow professionals. Once a librarian from the Chicago Public Library admitted calling the *Chicago Tribune* to ask the foods editor to locate a specific recipe only to find out later that the editor called the Chicago Public Library to get the information. If job-related users as well as others are unaware of network potential, *this is a critical issue.*

The public is perhaps more aware that systems exist in the world outside the information community. But even here, they care little that a hotel is a member of the International Reservations Company. They are only concerned in knowing if a room is available in Poughkeepsie or Padua or Prague for the night of July 7. At the present time such services are apparently free. That is, any costs are added indirectly into the cost of your room or airline ticket or other charge. Network service costs have been indirect in many cases. If users must become aware of these costs, they must see them as acceptable. Unfortunately, if the trend to charge user fees for information searches continues and expands, an increasing number of users will become aware that the search was on-line, because the fee will be assessed when the search results are picked up at the library.

Users may also be separated into the technologcially educated versus the accidental. The accidental user is the unaware person who makes accidental use of the network. When the librarian suggests the use of an interlibrary loan which will mean a slight delay in securing the materials, the accidental user is minimally educated. When the possibility of the use of a data base occurs, the librarian may have to explain the necessity of charging a fee. At this time the accidental user may suddenly become more than minimally educated.

Some users are aware that a service exists, but this may be a minimally educated user. A more sophisticated user may have been taught how to use a terminal and may be aware of the possibilities of utilizing a network for a specific data base or the possibility of an interlibrary loan from a specific source.

Educated users in the job-related category may have been educated in a variety of ways and may have a wide variety of levels of sophistication. Some users are trained on the job and receive instruction on the utilization of their terminal. Some users may have been educated through workshops with some form of continuing education credit. If the workshop is provided by network staff, their education has become a service of the network. Other users may have been trained as part of their professional library courses or may have returned to the academic setting for updating in network utilization. Others attend special conferences such as those sponsored by LITA on the closing of the catalog.

The topic of education of users will be expanded later in the presentation. However, one can wonder how much information about the logistics of the network is really necessary even for the job-related user. Is the user really interested in the size of a data base or is the user more interested in getting a response from that data base? Even a data base as large as OCLC with its 5 million records will have failed if the record the librarian in Podunk needs is not yet available. Another failure results from concentration on print materials and the exclusion or limited network access to other media. More projects concentrating on input of media records into networks such as the Indiana Department of Education/INCOLSA project are needed.[1]

Some studies have pointed out that research users seem to be more satisfied if they get more responses to their search, although these responses do not necessarily need to be relevant. Kobelski found that 100 percent of the students surveyed were satisfied with an on-line bibliographic search if the search generated over 100 citations, even though 40-49 of those citations generated were designated as relevant.[2] No one asked if they were useful, merely relevant. This is where we need to start asking, "what is *useful?*" and, perhaps, "what do you do with the materials which are not useful?" If anyone knows of a study that determines how many documents are too many documents, I would be interested in knowing about it.

Where do users access networks? Users are mere humans and will utilize networks in the most easily accessible spot. This spot may be a school library, a public library, the academic library, or the library in their company or hospital. *Potential of access to the network is a critical issue.* Access potential may reduce or expand the user's ability to utilize a network.

One continual debate of where information is to be located for one particular user group began in the late 19th century and still rages today: where should children find information? The May 1, 1979 *Library Journal* editorial made some suggestions concerning duplication of collections and effort. The solution suggested was that services be offered in one agency—either the school library or the public library—but not both, thus reducing the implied waste of funds in the cancelled agency. This latest proposal suggests that librarians "define and develop the combinations" of "efficient, economical and comprehensive library service for children and young adults."[3] However this may not mean merging agencies or collapsing one in favor of the other. Certainly if children were deprived of either the school or the public library, not only would one avenue of information be closed, but one potential network access point would be eliminated.

In discussing user access points one must recognize the differences and similarity of these libraries. As mentioned earlier, access points do impinge upon the capability of users to participate. For nine months of the year, five days of most weeks, school libraries serving 43 million students and staffed by 62,700 professional librarians[4] are potential access points. The school librarians represent the largest number of professional librarians and serve one of the largest potential clienteles in the United States. The fly in the ointment is that not all students have access to a school library. While many schools have a library room, it is often managed by a paraprofessional or a volunteer. In other instances, one professional may serve five or ten buildings. Keith Doms recently told me that he may have to assign roving teams to keep his Philadelphia Free Library branches open, but this "roving librarian" method of providing services has long been an accepted procedure for school libraries.

Students in schools provide a captive audience for their librarians. That is, many students are brought into the school library as part of their course requirements. They may be assigned there for a study hall. These situations do not present an optimum condition for encouraging the development of library use skills.

Another factor also characterizes this type of library. Managers of school library media programs have been reluctant to share their collections. Perhaps this is because collections were so small and the development of services and collections in schools (especially elementary schools) with professional staff assigned is so recent. Indeed, they have been so protective that they hesitate to share resources even with the children in the school. I once visited a school where children came to the library for an assigned period of 20 minutes each day. Each child took a book off the shelf, started reading where they had left their unique marker the day before. At the end of the time they returned the book to the shelf and marched back to their classrooms. This was a few years ago, but a good friend has just placed his children in a school with some 1000 elementary children and a school library with over 6000 volumes. His children can take only two books for two weeks (when a first grader devours a book a night) and then only if the student has returned the two books checked out from the previous visit. A librarian who thinks this service is adequate would certainly believe children's needs could be satisfied within the school library and would have trouble even visualizing the potential of network services. If one adds to this the widespread adult belief that students under 18 years of age have very simple information needs and that extension of resources would be unnecessary for all but the very gifted, you have a climate less than conducive to networking.

Public libraries pose a different problem. While public libraries theoretically serve the entire population of the country, there are areas of the country unserved by the public library. Chait tells us that the number of unserved Americans is five to ten million. Public librarians have a policy that permits clientele to check out as many items as they want, with the possible exception of films. Quite often the loan period in which materials may be used is a month. However, some limits are placed on the collection for some persons within the library's clientele, usually these restrictions relate to use of materials by children. In a recent study, children were asked what they would change about the public library. Children registered these kinds of complaints: "I'm in the sixth grade and I can't get a grown-up card till ninth, but I need grown-up books for my reports. Change the grade to seventh for a grown-up card!" and "Let the teenagers check out anything they want to."[5]

Certainly public librarians in recent years have launched concentrated efforts to attract their missing clientele, and they have been very willing to participate in cooperative ventures. They have also gained direct access to their governing boards and have been able to move such projects forward with minimal interference by layers of bureaucracy.

Contrast the small school library collection and the small public library collection with the academic libraries which seemingly have unlimited collections—hundreds of thousands to millions of volumes, and, according to some studies, including one done in my own home institution, mostly unused. Academic librarians are well-trained and well-experienced in permitting materials to circulate, at least to the faculty. Many professors have 1000 volume libraries in their offices, all checked out of the campus library over a period of 20 years. If they are history professors, the number of library materials unused in their offices may exceed 2000 volumes.

Academic librarians accepted early on the need to share their resources and have been willing to share in cooperative endeavors. Their claim to the research function has permitted them to collect esoteric materials and to store them for years under the research rubric while public libraries, with their "popular" reading function, have had to purchase a different type of material and have been more likely to weed their collections.

Special libraries and special librarians, as Roman and Day pointed out in their background paper in this book, are located in a wide variety of settings and therefore serve a wide variety of clientele for very special needs. Some of these special libraries are in academic settings and come under the administration of the academic institution. Others may be located in profit-making enterprises and are at the mercy of company policy. Certainly the formula for Coca-Cola would not be placed on a telefacsimile terminal. Their collections may seem to be too special for general interest. The major problem that special libraries cause users is just finding out where they are and what they have. They are additionally elusive because special librarians have their own national professional library associations.

When can users utilize networks? Certainly the research users and the nonprofessional users may have little choice of where or when a network can be utilized. At times the job-related user is also stymied. Early in my work at INCOLSA, before I was granted my card to the building and a key for my office door, I had to rely on someone else to let me into my work area. Two people were there by 8:00 A.M. The reason—at that time one could do author searches on the OCLC terminal only between 7:00 and 9:00 A.M., and 5:00 and 10:00 P.M. If a user's search requires a terminal and the user doesn't have one at home or the office, the search must be geared to the hours when the telephone is answered, the hours the building which houses an access terminal is open, the hours the computer is functioning and, if the searcher has minimal education in retrieval, the hours an assistant is available to place the search on the terminal. If you were a user in some of the more rural areas of the United States, your library might be open two afternoons a week during the warm months.

THE USER'S WANTS AND NEEDS

In preparing for this conference, I asked one of the computerized network directors to suggest a name of a potential conference participant from one of that network's member libraries. I was questioned as to why we wanted to invite such a participant to this conference since this person's level of understanding would be limited on the issues of networking. My response was that we were interested in the network from a member library's viewpoint. The response from the director was, "Why?"

Few answers to questions about network users or nonusers can be found in the literature today. We have a great deal about users of information in general, but little about network users specifically. The literature also has a great deal about what networks offer and, occasionally, what users get, but not very often can you locate information that confirms that *what users get is what they want*. This is a critical issue—the service, not the material.

Perhaps in the beginning, network users weren't sophisticated enough or educated enough to be able to say what they wanted, but they have became more knowledgeable and better educated in recent years. Are they even asked what they need? Who sets the priorities for network services? Do advisory committees advise network directors or do they appear at meetings to rubber stamp the agenda? The committee's main function then becomes to help determine whom to ask to implement the presented plans. Have the advisory committee members really polled the other users?

One must also determine how well the network is serving the user. Admittedly, this is difficult. One often gets complaints, seldom compliments. Catalogers, long noted for their unwillingness to accept anyone else's cataloging copy (and their own only after three day's meditation) are not suddenly going to be more agreeable to catalog copy just because it is coming out of a machine. Also, the bibliographers who yearn for or need to see the real article can't accept a photocopy, much less a telefacsimile. Can you electronically share a print of the Mona Lisa?

What data bases are needed for users? Have we really considered the user in adding data bases? One researcher sent a questionnaire to ten libraries who had subscribed to the *New York Times Information Bank*. Their rationale for subscribing was:

- enhancement of reference service
- interest in greater use of computerized information retrieval
- advancement of the library's image[6]

Even granting the efficacy of those reasons, whose image is being enhanced in the eyes of whom? Was it to keep up with the Joneses? Has the *New York Times* done that good a selling job to librarians? Only two of the ten libraries allowed users direct access to the terminals. Access would require a minimum of 30 minutes instruction to two hours training. Others felt two hours was an insufficient time to train.

The number of uses reported was nine per day, four per day, 30 per week, and two searches per day. The average rate of success in retrieving adequate information (whatever "adequate" is) was 70-80 percent. The study does not compare time spent in manual versus automated searches. One must also consider the comment by the librarian who responded, "If the correct search term is used with the terminal, then automatic access is definitely better. However, if the user must take time finding the correct search terms then the two methods (automated and manual) become equal in speed and ease."[7]

The research-related and nonprofessional users are at the mercy of highly complex systems: the growth of the number of data bases and the technology of the processing of that data. These users do not know that greater amounts of data are available to them. Reference librarians and other job-related users are themselves overwhelmed with the growing amounts of data and the variety of configurations in which that data are found. Perhaps the research-related or nonprofessional user is as satisfied with what can be located alone at the card catalog as most librarians are satisfied to serve the number of patrons they currently serve.

It's now time to consider the blue color—the nonuser. When this paper was in its infancy, it occurred to me that perhaps I might give you the total number of potential network users by age groups if everyone in the United States decided to access a network. I started with the estimated United States population:

under 5	15,236,000
5-13	32,227,000
14-17	16,781,000
18-21	16,798,000
22-24	11,551,000
25-34	32,990,000
35-44	23,480,000
45-54	23,382,000
55-64	20,395,000
over 65	23,494,000
Total	216,334,000[8]

Then I added nonimmigrants: travelers on business and pleasure as well as students:

from Europe	2,451,000
Asia	1,461,000
America	3,750,000
Africa	130,000
Australia	210,000
other	35,000
Total	8,037,000[9]

To get the grand total:

$$216,334,000$$
$$\underline{8,037,000}$$
$$224,371,000 \text{ potential users of networks.}$$

If one subtracts the under five-year-olds (although I hate the implications in doing that), you have a total of 209,135,000 total potential users.

Marvelous statistics, but we do not serve all of these and why not? The big argument is that, even if we wished to, collections, facilities and staff are too limited, not to mention the funds to keep up all of the above. Maybe the present situation as described by Chait is enough. Maybe missing five to six million people with no service is not bad, or the fact that 50 percent of the population never comes to the public library. However, one must wonder in a nation with the information resources at its disposal that:

approximately 20 percent of the adult population has *no* knowledge about any national issue one would care to name, and frequently, the proportion is as high as 40 percent. Moreover, these same people tend to lack information on employment opportunities, good health and dietary practices, consumer affairs, educational opportunities and almost every type of information related to the satisfaction of basic human needs. Depending upon the measures one cares to use, somewhere between twenty and forty million Americans fall into this group.[10]

This must be a critical issue when you discuss expanding networks to provide the potential of access to all.

Current public library users, whether or not they are network users, are certainly educated. One study done in 1971 reported that public library users are the equivalent of graduates of junior college while nonusers have less than a high school education. One-third of the users had at least a college degree in comparison with four percent who are nonusers. Over half of the nonusers do not have a high school education compared to only 16 percent of the users.[11] In a recent study of one large metropolitan library, the percentage of users with college educations was even higher.[12]

Before we leave the statistics concerning population, it's important that we consider that fewer babies are being born and people are living longer, which is skewing the user age groups to which we offer services. The drop in school enrollments has turned the public school system to seeking activities for the adult learner. Within the kindergarten through grade twelve population, the initiation of programs for the gifted has increased the needs for expanded research potential at all levels. These two emphases may increase network utilization of information sources.

The scramble by institutions of higher education to attract tuition-paying customers has led them to plan continuing education programs which will encourage not only the young adult, but the middle and older adult as well, to return for retreading. Universities have launched programs to attract business executives to seminars and workshops. These experiences might introduce the potential of data bases to this population. Elderhostel programs are luring the senior citizen to college for short periods and perhaps to increased library utilization.

Public libraries are beginning to reach out to the senior citizen with special programming, with expanded large print book collections, with programs for the housebound older adult, and with bookmobile stops and programs in nursing homes. These may also generate information network utilization.

The fact that so little information on networking exists makes it easy to suggest that research on the network user is needed. But what research? Maybe it is time to identify our information providers and users, to establish a common ground. In a conference held three years ago, it was suggested that "The United States has now become an 'information society' with over 50 percent of the Gross National Product being derived from goods and services related to information."[13] These conference attendees were mostly information scientists, and they divided the information society into four compartments for study as to jobs performed by information professionals in the field. The divisions were: 1) business/industrial organizations, 2) nonprofit organizations, 3) educational organizations, and 4) federal government. I have no quarrel with the compartments. My confusion comes with the elaboration of those compartments. For example, the list makes no reference to the potential of information professionals in the public library community where there are 36,000 professionals.[14] Under nonprofit organizations the proceedings mention a "breakdown by type of activity— 'hospitals,' etc."[15] and under educational organizations "higher and secondary schools" are described as "providing a concise universe."[16] This denies the existence of the 36,000 public librarians and the large number of information professionals serving the 33 million children between the ages of five and thirteen. Since both agencies serve users, we thus have a few missing from the so-called universe of information professionals listed.

AREAS FOR RESEARCH

I would like to point out five areas in need of research. First, *we must locate information professionals and their clientele and establish a common ground for their identification.* A second research area is identification of user needs. Martyn reported in 1974 that:

> Although, for years, practical information workers had been supplying documentary information and conducting searches for members of their parent organizations, there were, until the fifties virtually no attempts to categorize user needs and to relate them to definable characteristics of the users themselves.[17]

What are the user characteristics? Network directors should attempt to discover exactly who their users are and what motivated the use or the lack or use of the network. In education there are film libraries with computers to book films. Statistics can be generated as to the dates films are sent to a building, and it is simple to discover which teachers are using films. One can even generalize about why the football coach uses more films on Fridays in the fall than during the remainder of the year. But are we finding out why some teachers do not use the film collection? Is the delivery system bad? Is the collection inadequate? Is the teacher unaware of the potential of this service? Is there a lack of communication?

Is the academic library user a professor researching for a project proposal, the doctoral student for a dissertation? Have they really discovered all there is to know about their subject? Could the network have been more effectively searched? If the project was funded, was the research information secured through the network a part of the reason for its success?

User needs research must be reported back to the users and potential users, especially findings related to cost factors. Is the local public librarian or the school librarian really aware of what it costs to catalog a book as opposed to the costs of shared cataloging through a network?

Thirdly, research is needed into the attitudes of librarians and information specialists toward networking. Attitude research is fraught with problems, but needs to be done. Sara Fine has recently completed an extensive study on resistance to technological innovation[18] by the librarian who is the link or transfer point between many networks and many users. She wondered if the fear of losing access and autonomy was real, or whether those often-given reasons for resistance to joining networks might not be a manifestation of resistance to technology. For instance, she found that 86 percent of the administrators in her sample answered that they thought a national network would be highly favorable but only 53 percent thought this would happen in the next ten years. Is this resistance to technology? Could something considered to be so highly favorable to so many, yet so unlikely to only half, be interpreted as lip service? Is the advocacy of the national network their way of saying "yes" to something they'd rather not see materialize?

A fourth research area is that of determining what happens to a user when the regular information source is cut off: when the company closes the library, when the school system furloughs the school librarians, when the public library closes branch libraries and halts bookmobile service, and when the academic library materials budget will not cover the cost of periodical subscription renewals. This is very difficult research. Most librarians could only conduct *ex post facto* analyses because most have not kept the proper utilization records to determine what they have done so they could legitimately demonstrate the impact of the loss.

The fifth research need is marketing research. What is the most effective way to sell network potential to potential network users—which package, which commercial, which billboard?

THE CRITICAL ISSUES

There are undoubtedly other research areas which need to be addressed, but we must now turn to look at the critical issues. When we consider the future of networks, two themes emerge. The first has to do with the services offered by the network in relation to the user. Which network services are to be offered? Are the services the user gets the services the user wants? What choice of access to networks does the user have? Is the network placing unnecessary stumbling blocks to utilization?

The second critical issue has to do with the potential network user who is unaware of network possibilities. Why are these persons unaware? Are we hiding our lights under bushels or are we off target in what we are providing? Perhaps what users really need is not just books and bibliographic access, but access to information on job availability or a poison antidote. What data bases might be available if we cooperated with the health department or the unemployment office or with the high school's career profile data bases or with all post-high school training institutions? What about a combined data base that would include information or requirements for admission to the educational institution, length of time to complete any given program or course of study, the costs for training, availability of housing in the vicinity of the campus, any financial assistance available, degrees or certificates and licenses awarded with some prediction of the potential for employment in those fields after graduation?

Is lack of choice of access to a network the problem? Networks open only to research libraries or only to adults may be ignoring a potential audience. It is a little like the network provider selecting exactly which data bases to establish and how much data to include in the base. Choosing the data, the services or the audience with no needs assessment may find a network offering an unpopular service to very few takers. Unless networks have a Sugar Daddy, they are better off providing what people want to a wide audience and deleting those services which users may only need at some rare future moment.

How do networks change the services they offer? Once you have determined a need to add or delete, what is the procedure? Are the systems so rigid they merely perpetuate themselves, or are they built with the possibility for change?

Are the networks placing unnecessary stumbling blocks to the network user? Mooer hypothesizes that "An information retrieval system will tend *not* to be used whenever it is more painful and troublesome for a customer to have information than for him not to have it."[19] Mooer goes on to say that "having information is painful and troublesome"[20] because it means once you have the information you must do something with it. If we increase this problem by our restrictions to access we may kill the information seeking behavior in all but the stalwart or those driven by teachers and professors to write reports or papers.

What about the nonprofessional user? If 40 percent of the population lacks information related to the satisfaction of basic human needs, do we leave this up to traditional school and the public library service or do we try to entice these persons into making use of network data base services?

How do we teach what we offer? Do we leave it up to the IBM salespersons who want to sell their mini-computers? Is there a lack of training of trainers? Are network staff forced into training whether they want to or not? Are they successful teachers? Are too many of our college faculty members teaching from the book and not from experience to complement the theory?

SOLUTIONS

Obviously solutions mandate some improvement plan and most people equate improvement (as home improvements) with extensive expenditures of funds. Since this seems unlikely in today's tight money market, may I make some do-it-yourself suggestions? If we are going to improve utilization from the current level we must improve both parts, the networks and the users, but we must become more aware of the part in between. Somewhere along the way we have to expand from this dichotomy of network and user and see if we can analyze what goes on between them. The part in between is made up of the go-betweens, the links, not terminals. The part in between is made up of people—the school, public, academic or special librarians—who can make or break the system. Once the market research has been completed on how to sell the networks to the research-related and the nonprofessional users, it needs to be tested on your middlepersons—all of them—maybe those who have been overlooked in the past—the rural librarian who works two afternoons a week and the school librarians who travel between five or more buildings. Unless you must hire an outside expert to do this selling job, you and your staffs should be able to accomplish it with a little communication time.

Perhaps it is a blatant assumption that it is important to improve utilization. Are we so underutilized that we yearn for activities to keep us busy? Maybe, but we must be doing a less than top selling job or we wouldn't be getting decreased funding as we are. Improved utilization may mean new clientele and we certainly could use a new crop of network advocates.

IMPROVING THE NETWORK

Obviously, in improving the networks, the technological improvements must be in the hands of those who understand the technology and some of this must be done by those who are capable of dreaming for the future. Technological innovation may be for the select few, but utilization of networks will only improve if all network providers stay aware of user needs and try to meet these needs. Providers must also evaluate the degree of success in meeting these established needs.

Let's hold out helping hands. The federal government spends $100 billion annually "to provide services in areas such as health rehabilitation, employment, income, maintenance, nutrition, and education."[21] Let's don't volunteer to take over these services, even though that's been the American way of life. Let's volunteer to do what we do well—provide information and technology to them. Let's volunteer to assist them in return for information about their services which would be of use to our clientele. Our nonprofessional users need information about educational programs and potential professional growth opportunities, career possibilities, social organizations, and cultural opportunities. Relevant information is available from these various information agencies.

Consolidation is always difficult. It never happens easily. It's a question of turf. I have survived one school consolidation and can still recommend consolidation. Let's discuss how to *share the turf.* Consider what happens to the user in southeastern Pennsylvania who is interested in health related information. This user has a variety of networks to choose. The first two were mentioned earlier: MERMLS and PALINET. MERMLS serves all of Pennsylvania and Delaware in the health related professions including academic libraries with health school branches. PALINET, the network providing OCLC services, serves the multitype libraries. There is also the Tri-State College Network (TCLC) which is open to academic libraries in the 50 mile radius of Philadelphia. One medical school is a member of TCLC. The Consortium for Health Information and Library Services has public libraries, colleges, state institutions, hospitals, the State

Department of Health and several special libraries. This consortium covers Delaware County and Chester County, Pennsylvania. And then there are the district libraries linking the state library and the local public libraries, and the intermediate units linking the State Department of Education and the local education agencies. All of these "networks" exist independently in eastern Pennsylvania.

What if once upon a time one network user said to another, "You know we are duplicating services. I'll give up mine." Maybe with this attitude, you could help build quality control into the consolidated product and help develop performance standards. It might also cause a reaction like the Japanese gift giver—if you receive a gift you are responsible for giving a gift in return which is nicer, bigger, better than the one you got. No one could predict where this might end. And it might not cost that many dollars.

IMPROVING THE USER

Perhaps the lack of potential users is not a problem to solve today, but the education of research users and the continuing education of job-related users is. Educational opportunities must be expanded. How can we do this and not add to our dollar burdens? Encourage library schools to change their curriculum? That's not as difficult as you might think. All you need to say is, "I'd encourage my technician to get an MLS at your school if you offered anything worthwhile in networking, resource sharing, technology and other subjects." Be aware of what library schools offer. Make suggestions for joint continuing education projects. They would love it. A first course might be Acronyms 101. That's a language somewhat similar to Academese and equally difficult to translate.

We must develop easy training devices for our youth. Youth are the least resistant to technology, but they must develop library use skills at an early age and a desire to access other sources than the one immediately available to them. This is where your school librarians and children's librarians in public libraries have become so very important, for they and they alone can do this. Certainly if output is going to be on microform, negative film, or the negative image on the RLIN or OCLC terminal, give young children this negative image—white on black or green on black—at an early age, and they won't hate it as much as most adults do.

We should develop easy training devices, perhaps programmed instruction manuals or computer-assisted instruction programs for the job-related and research users—with add-ons for our youth. My suggestion is to put information into pinball machines—lights flashing, flippers flipping—for junior and senior high schools. Tell Mattel to develop a network game.

Everyone everywhere needs patience—nonprofessional users and professional users. Patience allows us to wait in line at the gas station and allows us to wait for the information from the network rather than demanding it from our local collection immediately.

Let's combine efforts to make all users aware of the contents of the various data bases, the methods to search the data bases, and the technology needed to access them. Let's protect the right of ordinary people to data-base access.

I'm ready to cut the cloth from the loom. My woven cloth is ready. Your weaving might look different from mine, but both will be worn in the twentieth century. Let's hope we have an Emperor with real clothes.

NOTES

1. Phyllis Land, "Demonstration of Cooperative Development of a Machine Readable Non-Print Media Data Base for School Library Media Centers" (Submitted by Division of Instructional Media, Indiana Department of Public Instruction, Indianapolis, Indiana to HEA Title II, Library Research and Demonstration Program).
2. Pamela Kobelski and Jean Trumbore, "Student Use of Online Bibliographic Services," *The Journal of Academic Librarianship* 4: 17 (March 1978).
3. John Berry, "Editorial: School/Public Library Services," *Library Journal* 104:989 (May 1, 1979).
4. Boyd Ladd, *National Inventory of Library Needs, 1975: Resources Needed for Public and Academic Libraries and Public School Library/Media Centers* (Washington: National Commission on Libraries and Information Science, 1977), p. 15.
5. Blanche Woolls, *Library Service in the District of Columbia 1978* (Washington: District of Columbia Public Library, 1978), p. 59.
6. Rhoda Garoogian, "Library Use of the New York Times Information Bank: A Preliminary Survey," RQ 16:59 (Fall 1967).
7. *Ibid.*, p. 62.
8. U.S. Bureau of the Census, *Statistical Abstract of the United States 1978*, 99th ed. (Washington: U.S. Bureau of the Census, 1978), p. 29.
9. *Ibid.*, p. 93.

10. Allen Hershfield, "Information Counselors," in P. Atherton, ed., *A Symposium: Humanization of Knowledge in the Social Sciences* (Syracuse, N.Y.: Syracuse University Press, 1972), p. 29.
11. Ray L. Carpenter, "The Public Library Patron," *Library Journal* 104:348 (February 1, 1979).
12. Woolls, "Library Service in District of Columbia," p. 52.
13. *Manpower Requirements for the Information Profession: Conference Proceedings* (Pittsburgh: University of Pittsburgh, 1976), p. 5.
14. Ladd, "National Inventory of Library Needs," p. 16.
15. *Manpower Requirements*, p. 16.
16. *Ibid.*, p. 17.
17. John Martyn, "Information Needs and Uses," in Carlos A. Cuadra, ed., *Annual Review of Information Science and Technology*, Vol. 9 (Washington: American Society of Information Science, 1974), p. 3.
18. Sara Fine, *Resistance to Technological Innovation in Libraries. Final Report* (Washington: U.S. Department of Health, Education and Welfare, Office of Education, Office of Libraries and Learning Resources, 1979).
19. Calvin N. Mooers, "Editorial: Mooers' Law or, Why Some Retrieval Systems Are Used and Others Are Not," *American Documentation* 11:204 (July 1960).
20. *Information and Referral for People Needing Human Services—A Complex System That Should Be Improved* (Report to the Congress by the Comptroller General of the United States, March 20, 1978), p. i.

The Role of
the Public Library
in Networking

William Chait, Director Emeritus
Dayton and Montgomery County Public
Library
Dayton, Ohio

Traditionally, public librarians have attempted to reach their entire clientele. This has made it necessary for public librarians to use a major portion of their energies to extend services to the nonlibrary user—both within their jurisdictions and outside. They have had a commitment toward larger units of service within the library, the development of county libraries, and the expansion of outreach services. Beginning at the end of the 19th century and continuing until today, public librarians have struggled to obtain community support and funding to extend their existing city services to smaller communities and to unincorporated areas that had few, if any, library services. It took an unusual profession to develop bookmobile services more than half a century ago when most public services were still institution bound. The public library's often limited resources were further stretched to give services to students and to faculties of schools and colleges when the lack of adequate support meant that library needs were not met on campus.

Robert D. Leigh noted the public librarian's commitment in 1950 in his book, *The Public Library in the United States*:

THE LIBRARY FAITH Throughout the years librarians have

transformed their concept of function into a dynamic faith. This faith has sustained the men and women who have built and operated American public, as well as university and research, libraries and the men of wealth and political position who have provided for their financial and legal support. It consists in a belief in the virtue of the printed word, especially of the book, the reading of which is held to be good in itself or from its reading flows that which is good.[1]

It was this "Library Faith" that started 1) the development of public library standards, 2) the campaign for legislation which resulted in the Library Services Act in 1956, and a decade later, 3) the Library Services and Construction Act (LSCA), and 4) the development of a variety of public library systems. State librarians, working with public libraries, assumed the leadership role for developing interlibrary loan arrangements, arranging the exchange of information, providing bulk book loans, offering staff development programs and other cooperative activities. While this started long before federal funds became available to accelerate and multiply library cooperation and systems, federal LSCA funds were the great stimulus to the development of systems and networks among public libraries and among public and other types of libraries.

Systems were developed in a variety of patterns. In some states the resource libraries for systems made up of small public libraries were the local college or university libraries; in others, the state library was the major resource. When librarians started working together under the stimulus of federal funds, public and academic librarians, and in some cases school librarians, found that they had a unity of purpose and that they could supplement and enrich each other's collections.

More than a decade ago, this writer made his first application for an LSCA Title I grant for a cooperative program. This enabled the Dayton and Montgomery County Public Library to work with about 30 academic and special libraries as well as with another public library. The product of this grant was a Union List of Serials of the libraries of the Miami Valley. Just a few months ago, an LSCA grant was awarded for the publishing of the 6th edition of this Union List, and to expand it to include many libraries in the Cincinnati area and a few from northern Kentucky. This serials list represents the holdings of 68 libraries. Currently, the Dayton and Montgomery County Public Library is investigating the possibility of developing and installing a computerized circulation system which would include another public library system and three academic libraries.

The definition of networks is given by the National Commission on Libraries and Information Science (NCLIS):

> Two or more libraries and/or other organizations engaged in a common pattern of information exchange, through communications, for some functional purpose. A network usually consists of a formal arrangement whereby materials, information and services provided by a variety of types of libraries and/or other organizations are made available to all potential users.[2]

If we accept this definition, any observer or student of public library development in the 20th century must conclude that public libraries have been in the forefront of the development of networks. They are an important part of many of the existing networks and must play a leading role in the future development of a true national network.

Alphonse F. Trezza, in his article on networks in the 1976 *ALA Yearbook* quotes the goal of networking as expressed by NCLIS:

> To eventually provide every individual in the United States with equal opportunity of access to that part of the total information resource which will satisfy the individual's educational, working, cultural and leisure-time needs and interests, regardless of the individual's location, social or physical condition or level of intellectual achievement.[3]

The only way that this goal can be achieved through libraries, is by making the public libraries the local nodes of the national network. Keeping this in perspective we turn to two recent publications: NCLIS's *Our Nation's Libraries, An Inventory of Resources and Needs*[4] and ALA's *A Perspective on Libraries*.[5] We learn from these that there are 8304 public libraries in the United States with a total of approximately 14,000 main libraries and branches. These public libraries serve about 200 million people. Yet, another 5 to 10 million people have no public library service. While the total annual expenditures by public libraries is $1 billion, 70 percent of all public libraries spend less than $50,000 a year and 50 percent spend less than $16,000 a year. The yearly circulation in public libraries is over one billion volumes. Another study tells us about users.

The 1978 study conducted for the American Library Association by the Gallup Organization indicates that about 51 percent of Americans aged 18 and over have visited the public library in the last year. This underutilization of public libraries may have led R. Kathleen Molz to comment:

> It is the essential dilemma inherent in the current plight of the public library that networking, which seems to hold promise for new revenue support from government, will tend, however unintentional that process may be, to exacerbate the distinction between the haves and the have-nots of this country. Committed library users will tend to make use of the network for further enrichment; conversely it will remain valueless to nonusers of local nodes of service, such as public libraries.[6]

Accepting this caveat, we recognize that networks must remain a part of the public library movement. W. Boyd Rayward describes networks as one of four major contemporary forces for change:

> The fourth major force for change is the contemporary trend toward the formation of networks and systems and larger units of service. ... In sum, there is a far reaching, fragmented, but powerful movement that has been gathering force in the last decade or so toward the integration of certain bibliographic resources and library services locally, regionally, by state, by multi-state region, and nationally through networks, consortia, cooperatives, councils, and systems that cut across traditional jurisdictions.[7]

Networks are a necessary component of public library services. They benefit not only the public library as an institution but also the users of the public libraries. This institution faces constantly increasing demands, in quantity and in variety, as well as an increasing universe of library materials which have to be obtained with dollars that are shrinking rapidly due to inflation. The current mood of taxpayers to decrease spending will not improve this situation. No longer is it possible to obtain new buildings and larger book budgets merely by showing the need to the appropriating bodies or the individual taxpayer who must vote levies. NCLIS puts it very well in *Our Nation's Libraries*:

> Today's Libraries Operate in a Time of Paradoxical Change —The volume of knowledge is growing at an increasing rate. —The creative use of new technology and the linking of libraries through networks is

making all knowledge more accessible. —Severe inflation reduces the value of a fixed library budget.

At the same time our political climate is one of slow-growth, no-growth, and (in some communities) major cut-backs in funding for public services.[8]

Networks can help in this situation. The library user can be told that, while the local library does not have the material or information he or she seeks, this material or information will be forthcoming from a local, state or regional network. Further, the librarian who assists the user may be upgraded in skills by the training services of a network or may have access to a computerized data base through network services or rate benefits. The user may come to the library because of network public relations through the development of regional TV spots or other professionally prepared messages to interest the public in library services.

The public library user also benefits, both directly and indirectly, from the librarys' involvement with such network activities as OCLC. Of the 1914 participating members in OCLC, 34 state libraries, 212 public libraries and 10 processing centers serving public libraries are benefiting from OCLC services. Among these services are almost 5 million bibliographic records in a data base available on a user terminal. Public library users benefit indirectly through the materials cataloged using this data base. A more direct use may be through an interlibrary loan librarian who may locate a potential source of the material for a user. Before 1979 is over, OCLC will furnish direct interlibrary loan services. Other services are being investigated and researched for future implementation. Similar benefits are available to library users through other networks such as the Washington Library Network (WLN).

Another indirect benefit to the library user, but a direct benefit to the libraries is the reduction of costs for some services provided through the network. Frederick G. Kilgour, Executive Director of OCLC, has frequently stated that one of the basic objectives of OCLC is to contain the rate of increase of library costs for cataloging. In the January, 1979 issue of *SONAC Forum*, Kilgour is also quoted as saying that, "the economic viability of libraries is the main question facing us today." Every public library administrator who has faced inflationary pressures and found that OCLC charges have not risen appreciates this fact and waits eagerly for new OCLC services which will keep the rate of rise at more reasonable levels. The library user as a taxpayer benefits from any funds saved in that it makes funds available for other library materials and services.

This writer recently served as a building consultant for a moderate-sized independent public library with a collection of 180,000 volumes. The library authorities refuse to belong to a network for the usual reasons: 1) it will take away their independence, 2) the networks will try to tell them how to run the library; 3) they don't know how much it will cost and if the networks raise their fees they will be locked in; 4) the next thing you know the networks will abolish the library board. It was pointed out that they were considering a building addition which would cost $500,000 to $1 million in order to house a collection which was growing at a rapid rate. The fear of discarding books and periodicals, although seldom used, exists because the library attempts to meet all users' needs by itself. The final recommendation was made that this library should join the regional system, remove about one-third of its collection and use the system to satisfy public demand rather than try to stand alone. It was further recommended that the library join its state network for access to OCLC rather than continue to operate a costly technical processes department which has a very wasteful computer installation.

The public libraries that need networks most are the 70 percent which spend less than $50,000 a year and, even more, the 50 percent which spend less than $16,000 a year. Many of these are members of networks and their users are benefiting from the resources of the networks. It is difficult to estimate how quickly the library described in the previous paragraph and thousands of others will give up their insularity and will be willing to pay their fair share for the services received from networks.

In working with the regional networks in Ohio, this writer has observed that many of the small public libraries are willing to participate as long as the state pays the bill. The future of network development depends on the availability of state and federal funds to support them. Should this support be reduced, the local libraries should be committed to picking up their portion of the cost.

Public libraries with a dedication to good management and cost containment will continue to support networks. Other public libraries will have to be made aware that they cannot stand alone and that the rate of increase in costs can be lessened by participation in networks. Certainly, increased service potential exists for all libraries.

The network concept will continue to develop and grow. The growth and development of networks for public libraries working with each other and other types of libraries may depend on two things. The first is how successful librarians and trustees are in obtaining more state and federal funds. According to ALA's *A Perspective on Libraries*, local taxes make up 82 percent, state government 13 percent, and federal government 5 percent of public library support.[9] The second is the realization that technology must be utilized to keep public library service economically viable. The technological development through minicomputers and microcomputers is an example of a new technology being considered by public librarians.

Fortunately, there are a large number of public librarians and public library trustees who have lost their fear of destruction of the local autonomy. These persons are leaders in the formation of multitype library systems. Moreover, they have learned that they are asked to contribute to the governance of the systems and networks. Cost effectiveness skills developed in administration at the local level, have been applied to the development of new services and new and larger networks. Public libraries can continue their commitment to larger units of service and to the expansion of services through their contribution to, and utilization of, networks. It is inevitable that they will continue their leadership and participation in "formal arrangements whereby materials, information and services provided by a variety of types of libraries and/or other organizations are made available to all potential users."[10]

NOTES

1. Robert D. Leigh, *The Public Library in the United States* (New York: Columbia University Press, 1950), p. 12.
2. National Commission on Libraries and Information Science, *Toward a National Program for Library and Information Services: Goals for Action* (Washington, D.C.: U.S. Govt. Print. Off., 1975), p. 82.
3. *The ALA Yearbook, 1976 Centennial Edition* (Chicago: American Library Association, 1976), p. 249.
4. National Commission on Libraries and Information Science, *Our*

Nation's Libraries: An Inventory of Resources and Needs (Washington, D.C.: U.S. Govt. Print. Off., 1978).

5. American Library Association, *A Perspective on Libraries: Facts, Figures and Opinions About Libraries and Reading* (Chicago: American Library Association, n.d.).
6. R. Kathleen Molz, "The Financial Setting of the Public Library," *Library Quarterly* 48:416-31 (October 1978).
7. W. Boyd Rayward, "Introduction: The Public Library—a Perspective and Some Questions," *Library Quarterly* 48:383-392 (October 1978).
8. National Commission on Libraries and Information Science, *Our Nation's Libraries*, p. 5.
9. American Library Association, p. 3.
10. National Commission on Libraries and Information Science, *Toward a National Program*, p. 82.

The Role of the Special Library in Networking

Mary Ann Roman, Librarian
Barnes, Hickam, Pantzer & Boyd
Indianapolis, Indiana

Heather Day, Librarian
Lilly Endowment Library
Indianapolis, Indiana

The role of the special library in networking is not easy to define. This is due to the wide diversity of libraries that might be termed "special" and because of the various types of networks to which special libraries might belong. Special libraries may be located in profit-making corporations, nonprofit organizations, law firms, or industrial plants, and they may offer the full contingent of library services to a select clientele. They may be found on large, academic campuses where they house specialized collections. Or they may be information centers organized to serve the needs of municipal, state, or federal employees. This paper will discuss the role of the special library in networking from a relatively broad perspective. However, the term "networking" is being limited to diverse, autonomous information sources which are linked in a *formal* relationship, provide increased access to materials and services from other libraries (often with the aid of a computer, though not necessarily), and achieve exploratory, developmental, or operational status.[1]

Special librarians have long had informal links among themselves for obtaining the information they need. In fact, they are often characterized as being especially aggressive in their attempts to acquire information for their clientele as quickly and as efficiently as possible.[2] So the question might arise, "why would special libraries want to join formalized library networks?"

This question is simple to answer for "single-type" networks— i.e., those that specialize in one type of function or that unite libraries whose collections focus on one particular area. For instance, special libraries that need access to such computerized bibliographic data bases as OCLC, RLIN, or WLN often have to join computerized library networks such as NELINET (New England), SOLINET (Southeast), or AMIGOS (Southwest) to receive data base and other computerized services. These regional networks negotiate shared costs among their members, provide staff training on the use of the data bases, define system requirements, and generally help the individual libraries to take full advantage of the computer technology available.

In the case of special subject networks, such as the Twin Cities Biomedical Consortium which brings together hospital and other medical libraries, the benefits to participating libraries are fairly obvious. Benefits might include a union list of serials in their specific subject area, or on-line searching of data banks such as Medline—services that might not be affordable for the individual library alone.

But what can special libraries gain from joining multitype, multipurpose networks—i.e., networks opened to all types of libraries for the coordination of many types of library activities? In the results of a survey of networking practices in special and academic libraries, Murphy found that respondents in the special libraries benefited most from: 1) expanded interlibrary loan services, 2) photocopying services, 3) union lists and catalogs, 4) reciprocal borrowing privileges, and 5) reference services (in that order).[3] The ber. ?fits that special libraries receive from networks vary with the highly diverse offerings of the various networks. However, the five activities mentioned above appear to be offered by most multitype networks. Murphy also found that perceived priorities of special librarians for network activities are: centralized resource and storage centers, clearinghouses, and assigned subject specialization in acquisitions.

Other possible benefits to special libraries from multitype networks include delivery services of loaned materials, joint purchasing of materials, exchange of materials, newsletters, continuing education, cataloging support, microfilming, joint research projects, and so on. The list could go on as librarians find more, sometimes unique, ways for their libraries to benefit from cooperation. Having all types of libraries in a network extends these possibilities for cooperation even further.

Networking has also provided the opportunity for special librarians, many of whom feel professionally isolated in a one- to two-person library, to have worthwhile interaction with other librarians. In this way, old stereotypes of the limitations of other types of libraries are often broken down. Special librarians may find that academic, public, and school libraries have materials and services that could benefit their institutions, or they may find that they have something to learn from other librarians who work in different settings.

The primary contribution that special libraries render by joining a network, whether it be on a local, regional, or national level, is the strength that these libraries with highly specialized collections bring into the system. Access to these in-depth research collections is made available to other network members through contractual agreements. Coupled with this access, the network can retrieve the information through the talents of a trained specialist, the special librarian.

Also, the leadership role of special librarians should not be overlooked. By organizing, participating, and conducting continuing education programs in which they share their specialized talents, they contribute to the ongoing education of librarians.

A basic function of any library organization is its ability to represent the needs of the entire library community. A network provides the ideal environment for an exchange of ideas among all types of libraries. School, public, academic, and special libraries all exist to provide information to their respective clientele. However, libraries often need to interact with each other to provide the best service possible at the most reasonable cost.

But will the benefits of networking always outweigh the cost? Trezza believes that "fear and funding," in that order, are the two most serious barriers to development of library networks in general.[4] Fear often surrounds the issue of local autonomy: will the library have to give up some of its own operating procedures to be able to participate in a network? Or there is fear of overuse of the collection: will outsiders descend in hordes upon the materials which were originally supposed to be confined to a limited clientele? Also, special librarians and management sometimes fear that library networks will request proprietary materials from their libraries. Copyright issues may be another cause for concern. However, these fears or concerns have been demonstrated by the operation of library networks to be largely unfounded. Membership of special libraries in networks of all kinds continues to grow rapidly.[5] Networks have not been known for asking libraries or institutions to change internal policies to suit them. Nor have small, special collections been overwhelmed with requests for materials. And the requests are almost always for published materials, not proprietary.[6]

Funding may perhaps be a more valid constraint to a library's participation in networking. The funding base of many localized library networks has been insecure because they were begun, and often still survive, on LSCA funds. Librarians often fear that once federal money is no longer available, the network will either dissolve or will begin to charge its members higher rates than they can afford. However, the latter situation is unlikely to happen, especially if the members are all serving on the governing board and working together to find mutually acceptable solutions to the funding dilemma.

Another constraint to special library membership in a network is that library staff members may be expected to spend more time attending network meetings than they can afford. In such cases, unless management is convinced of the benefits of formalized interlibrary cooperation, the librarians will not be able to take full advantage of membership in a network, nor will they be able to join other librarians in contributing the time and/or expertise necessary to ensure the continued success of the network.

Special librarians and management need to examine the record of special library participation in all types of library networks. Then they must determine objectively whether or not participation in a network will be of sufficient benefit to the institution. Once a special library is in a network, the librarians need to be committed to supporting that network and to seeing that it works to the advantage of all the members.

It is important for special librarians to become involved and to seek out memberships for their libraries in networks at the local level, for it is at this level that they have the greatest opportunity for communicating the limitations and capabilities of their unique situations. At this stage they have the opportunity of drafting bylaws, participating in writing contracts, and involving themselves in the overall structure of the network. By their nature, networks lend themselves to a "bottom-up" involvement, following a pattern from local, to regional, to national participation. Through this "bottom-up" involvement, special librarians can avoid, or possibly eliminate, some of the barriers discussed earlier which restrain special libraries from joining networks.

As existing networks expand their services, special libraries have little choice but to join—that is, if they are to keep in stride with the information explosion.

NOTES

1. Marcy Murphy, "Networking Practices and Priorities of Special and Academic Libraries: A Comparison," Occasional Paper No. 126 (Urbana: University of Illinois Graduate School of Library Science, December 1976), p. 5.
2. Edward Strable, "The Illinois Experience: Special Libraries," in Beth Hamilton and William Ernst, eds., Multitype Library Cooperation (New York: Bowker, 1977), p. 139.
3. Murphy, "Networking Practices and Priorities," p. 10.
4. Alphonse Trezza, "Fear and Funding," Library Journal, 99:3174 (December 15, 1974).
5. Murphy, "Networking Practices and Priorities," p. 11.
6. Strable, "The Illinois Experience: Special Libraries," p. 142.

The Role of the Academic Library in Networking

Richard De Gennaro
Director of Libraries
University of Pennsylvania Libraries
Philadelphia, Pennsylvania

THE CONTRIBUTION OF ACADEMIC LIBRARIES TO NETWORKS

Academic libraries were at the forefront in the development and implementation of early computer-based systems in libraries in the 1960s. Out of these crude systems grew the much more sophisticated and effective on-line systems of the 1970s which made the bibliographic utilities and networks possible. Academic libraries were the pioneers; they supplied the leadership and the entreprenurial drive. Their staffs contributed enormous amounts of time and effort to the organization, planning, implementation, and governance of the networks. Out of their budgets came the funds needed to develop and operate the expensive on-line utility systems.

Our brief experience with these bibliographic utilities in recent years is teaching us that successful library cooperation and resource-sharing depend in large part on the effective use of on-line computer and communications technology. Before on-line systems came to the library world in 1971, there were numerous library consortia and cooperatives in every region of the country, but few had any significant record of accomplishment. Today, those that have their own on-line systems or those that broker the on-line systems have a sense of purpose and a record of accomplishment, and those that do not are usually vainly struggling to make their resource-sharing and other cooperative programs work.

OCLC, Inc. started out in the late 1960s as a statewide consortium of college and university libraries in Ohio. Its present extraordinary success is due largely to the efforts of its academic librarian-director, Frederick G. Kilgour, and to countless other academic librarians throughout the country.

In the early 1970s, a number of regional consortia of academic libraries were either formed especially for, or adopted as their purpose, the replication of the successful OCLC on-line system. Included among others were NELINET, PALINET, PRLC, SOLINET, AMIGOS, and SUNY-OCLC. When OCLC demonstrated a willingness and a capacity to serve the needs of the members of these academic library consortia in utility-like fashion, the regional consortia set aside the idea of replication and became instead regional service centers devoted mainly to brokering shared OCLC cataloging services.

The BALLOTS utility, now called the Research Libraries Information Network (RLIN) of the Research Libraries Group (RLG), is also the creation of academic librarians. The UTLAS network in Canada is an outgrowth and expansion of the University of Toronto Library Automation System. The Washington Library Network (WLN) is a notable exception to this list of networks that were formed by academic libraries. WLN was formed by the Washington State Library and is a state agency. Nevertheless, it owes much of its success to the strong support of its academic library members.

Academic libraries were not only instrumental in the formation of networks, they also contribute a substantial percentage of the bibliographic entries in the network data bases. Their payments constitute a substantial percentage of the revenues, and their collections carry the bulk of the burden of interlibrary loan.

THE BENEFITS OF NETWORKS
TO ACADEMIC LIBRARIES

If academic libraries are the principal contributors to networks, they and their users are also the principal beneficiaries.

The larger the library, the greater the contribution and the greater the benefits.

Networking enables academic libraries to share the development and use of sophisticated on-line computer technology without incurring the full burden of development and operational costs. The use of these systems enables libraries—particularly the larger libraries—to significantly reduce their cataloging and technical processing costs. Network participation permits academic libraries to gain timely and efficient access to information about bibliographic resources in other libraries through powerful on-line search capabilities. It also permits more rapid and effective resource-sharing via on-line, interlibrary loan systems.

This increased speed of access and the increased confidence in the availability of resources held elsewhere in the network enables libraries to gain increased flexibility in the spending of their book and journal funds. It permits them to spend their funds on the books and journals that are most used and most needed by their local clientele, and to rely on other libraries for lesser-used materials.

In the next few years, as libraries prepare to cope with the complex and expensive consequences of the adoption of AACR 2 and closed card catalogs, they will rely heavily on their networks to ease the pain and expense of the transition that is being experienced. When academic libraries joined together to form computer-based networks in the early 1970s, they created a structure for effectively pooling their financial and intellectual resources, and for developing a new and powerful library technology based on sophisticated computer and communications technologies. The implementation of this new electronic technology in nearly 2000 libraries during a single decade has made change in libraries a way of life. Its effects will multiply and accelerate, and will lead to a sweeping transformation of libraries in the next decade.

CONSTRAINTS TO BELONGING TO NETWORKS

Network membership can involve a heavy commitment of the time of key members of a library's staff—this is particularly true when the network is in its early, formative stage, as many of the regional networks were in the early and mid-1970s. Cooperation does not come easy, as anyone who has ever been involved in the numerous and interminable meetings of bylaws committees and governing boards will readily testify. Indeed, the use of staff time and creative energy is a significant hidden cost of network participation and when it is used for networking, other equally, or even more valuable, opportunities may be lost.

Network participation can cost a library some of its local autonomy in decisionmaking and management, particularly in collecting policies, service priorities, and budgetary flexibility. Moreover, the library can become totally dependent on what may be a distant, and sometimes fragile, unresponsive, or unwieldy organization which is subject to the full range of financial, managerial, political, and technical problems. In a crisis, a member library may find it hard to take rapid and decisive steps to solve its own local problems.

Another constraint of network participation is that rapidly accelerating advances in computer and communications technology may make some network systems obsolete. If that happens, organizational inertia, and political and financial pressures could make it difficult for a library to withdraw and join another network, or to implement alternative local systems. Finally, there is the ever-present danger that overselling the benefits of network membership may raise the expectations of academic administrators for unrealistically high cost savings, and thus provide them with a rationale for reducing budgetary support for libraries.

PROGNOSIS FOR THE FUTURE

During the late 1960s and early 1970s when our concept of a national network was forming, computing was going toward ever-larger, more powerful, and more expensive main frames. Our experience with the Chicago, Stanford, and New York Public Library systems taught us that library systems needed large and expensive computers, too large and expensive for any single library to afford by itself. We found that the cost of developing, implementing, and operating computer-based library systems was beyond what even the largest academic libraries could afford. Thus we turned to sharing computing power and system development through utility-type networking.

The central bibliographic utility will probably continue to

predominate during the next several years. But parallel with it there will be a growing movement toward distributed computer networks in regions, as well as stand-alone systems in individual libraries. This distribution of computing capability will be made possible by the rapidly increasing power and declining cost of computer hardware and communications capabilities, and by the availability of dependable and transferable network software systems. For instance, WLN has already led the way with the apparently successful transfer and implementation of its system to Australia. These regional and local systems will presumably be connected to, and make use of, the massive data bases that will be maintained by the utilities. These central data bases may function like electronic versions of the National Union Catalog and the Union List of Serials and they will serve as sources for bibliographic data, for reference, location, inter-library communication, and various other purposes.

Academic libraries will continue to play the major role in fostering and supporting these and other advances in networking in the future as they have in the past.

The Role of School Media Programs in Library Networks

Richard Sorensen, School Library Supervisor
State of Wisconsin/Department of Public
*   Instruction*
Madison, Wisconsin

The National Commission on Libraries and Information Science recently published *The Role of the School Library Media Program in Networking*, a report of the Commission's Task Force on the Role of the School Library Media Program in the National Program. This paper will summarize the concepts and recommendations that were developed in greater detail in that report, which is available for $2.75 from the United States Government Printing Office (Stock #052-003-00622-7). The full report was also reprinted in the Winter, 1979 issue of *School Media Quarterly*.

The role of the school media program in library networks is one of active participation in all stages of their development, operation, and governance. The rationale behind this complete involvement is threefold: 1) the information needs of the schools' clientele are important, 2) these needs cannot be met without a library network, and 3) school media programs have much to offer the other libraries in a network.

This paper will state those needs, explain their importance, and give examples of the school's potential contributions. In addition, it will describe some of the barriers that impede the full participation of schools and make practical suggestions for removing the barriers.

IMPORTANCE OF THE SCHOOL-BASED USER'S NEEDS

Twenty-three of every 100 persons in the United States are students in elementary or secondary schools. Add to that the number of teachers, administrators, and other personnel associated with schools and you have well over a quarter of this country's population, for whom the school media program is the primary and most efficient point of access to informational resources. Secondly, today's students are tomorrow's users and producers of information. As students, they are at the most impressionable years of their lives. They are learning now how information is organized and made available in our society. They are forming attitudes now about the role of libraries in managing the informational resources of our nation. It is important that they see the best possible image libraries have to offer.

THE SCHOOL'S NEED FOR A LIBRARY NETWORK

How can membership in a library network benefit students or other school-based users? First, the network increases access to a wide range of materials, and schools need access to a great number and variety of resources. The scope of the typical school curriculum is nearly universal, and good teachers reach beyond the written curriculum into other areas of inquiry to build learning experiences on the students' natural curiosity and individual interests. Students learn at different rates and in varying personal styles. Second, students cannot leave school during the day to visit other libraries. Since many students are bussed to and from school, their opportunities to use other collections are further limited. Although it takes an ample collection of print and audiovisual materials to provide enough variety for project and research assignments that accommodate the diverse ability levels and learning styles found in every school, the majority of public and private school collections fall below the standards set by the American Association of School

Librarians and the Association for Educational Communications and Technology.[1] School media centers therefore attempt to provide a basic core of most frequently needed materials. For the rest, the school media specialist must reach beyond the walls of the school building. In the past, only those schools in large districts that had strong central collections and delivery systems or those located next door to large public or academic libraries could provide these supplementary resources effectively. Today, library networks promise an efficient and affordable extended access to every school, regardless of size or location.

But school media programs should serve teachers and other school staff in addition to students. The information needs of teachers are also substantial. The extended access afforded by a library network often includes computer searches of educational and other data bases that can bring abstracts or the full text of relevant documents to the educator at the worksite. The resources of teacher preparation institutions and other specialized agencies are made known through library directories. Network sponsored union lists of periodicals, audiovisual materials, and other specialized resources cut searching time to a minimum, encouraging the serious teacher to invest time in the search for the best materials or the most reliable information. Cooperative indexes of local community resources—speakers, specialists, sites, events, agencies, and others—point out additional resources for creative teachers.

Administrators, counselors, special teachers, and other school staff require data on such varied topics as population trends, curriculum design, educational research, new legislation, job opportunities, and developments in their own and related fields. Library networks can bring this information within reach.

School media specialists too are served in these ways and in others by library networks. For example, networks provide shared services such as centralized cataloging, processing and ordering of materials, and repair of equipment. They can provide joint book and audiovisual examination centers, cooperative collection building, joint programming for common users, and continuing education for library staff. Some of these services could simply not be provided by the school's financial resources alone. In addition, the social contact provided by a library network helps school media specialists cope with the professional isolation they suffer as specialists in the education profession.

Finally, in some instances, school media centers may be the only libraries to which residents of remote communities have reasonable access. In these cases, the network enables the school to provide the general public of that community with a local point of entry into the public information systems they help to support.

THE SCHOOL'S CONTRIBUTIONS TO A LIBRARY NETWORK

In 1967, librarians in northeastern Wisconsin formed a council of school, public, academic, and special libraries to promote cooperation. In developing a union list of serials a few years later, it was found that each of the 20 school media center members had at least one, but frequently many, unique titles to contribute.[2]

But a unique title is not the only potential benefit a school and its media program hold for a library network. Schools own specialized materials, equipment, services, and human resources needed by other kinds of libraries and their clientele.

Materials

Schools have long been forerunners in acquiring and organizing a wide range of audiovisual materials, many of which are useful beyond the range of the elementary or secondary curriculum. These include the following:

- Recordings: spoken word, musical, foreign language, historical, and others, in both disc and tape
- Films, 16mm and 8mm, and videotapes, whose objectives range from developing aesthetic literacies to acquiring specific skills and understandings
- Locally produced materials that present the history, description, local color, or character of the area
- Slides, photographs, study prints, drawings, maps, globes, charts, models and other representations
- Realia ranging from working beehives to preserved specimens

A school's career education program frequently leads to development of a broad collection of employment information giving accurate and timely information on opportunities, requirements, and wages. Many school districts are on-line with career information data bases giving up-to-the-minute salary and job market information.

High interest, low reading level materials provide interesting materials for adults with marginal literacy, and collections of literary classics in both English and foreign languages provide materials useful to the general adult reader.

Equipment

In addition to materials, school media centers have substantial inventories of listening, viewing, projection, and production equipment. While instructional equipment is usually the last item to be loaned freely to nonstudents or faculty members, the school's equipment can function as backup equipment when another library's projector or record player is temporarily out of commission. Schools commonly allow other libraries and community agencies to use their production equipment for limited jobs or they provide production services for the cost of supplies.

Services

Some school districts have developed sophisticated centralized processing services and can take on other libraries as customers to the economic benefit of both parties. School repair services too can sometimes add customers without overtaxing their capabilities. Sometimes they even realize the benefits of economy of scale.

Schools frequently host exhibits of materials so that teachers can select from first hand examination. These exhibits can easily be turned into common selection opportunities for young adult and children's librarians, teacher educators, and parents of the community.

School districts often have interschool delivery systems. Sometimes these can accommodate stops at additional agencies or become the basis of a cooperative library delivery system.

Human Resources

Perhaps the school's most significant contribution is its opportunity to train future users of libraries and information services.

Media specialists and teachers can provide students with understandings that will enable them to be efficient and productive users of the nation's informational resources. A frequently overlooked and under-used resource is the teacher. The personal expertise of experienced faculty members covers a broad range of topics and teachers are most often eager to share their special knowledge with the adult members of the community.

FIVE BARRIERS TO SCHOOL PARTICIPATION, AND WAYS TO OVERCOME THEM

Although school media programs have much to offer other libraries, and their users have much to gain from library networks, schools are perhaps the least involved (in proportion to their numbers) in formal network membership and activities. Why?

At least five factors, actually five groups of related factors, have been identified as the barriers that keep schools and their media specialists from taking an active role in library networks. The first of these, and perhaps the most potent of the groups, is the group known as *psychological factors.*

Psychological factors are largely fears: fear by public, academic, and special librarians that the users of school media programs will cause an intolerable drain on their resources; fear by school media specialists that membership will reduce their own program's autonomy; fear that networking will take too much time and effort; fear of hidden costs; fear of the new and untried.

Some of the fears are justified. Networking is *not* free. It does take time to request a journal for a young scholar, to put a filmstrip in the mail to another library. But allowing these fears to justify continuing insularity is allowing a psychological barrier to get in the way of improving service.

The most effective way to allay fears of any kind is to replace them with knowledge. A large, multifaceted public information effort, sponsored by local, area, state, regional, and national groups and supported by persons who have had experience with library networks is a necessary means to replace fears about networking with knowledge. The Indianapolis Conference on Networking for Networkers is an important first step in this direction. The American Association of School Librarians' work with other associations in setting up a clearinghouse that will collect and disseminate information on the involvement of schools in library networks is another. These national level efforts will help, but fears reside in individuals. The local level must be reached. State libraries and departments of education can structure inservice education opportunities for practicing professionals to learn about and discuss the issue. But local associations, district media program directors, and multitype library organizations must make the concrete moves and provide the experiences that will bring librarians of every ilk together to replace anonymity with acquaintance, suspicion with knowledge, and fears with enthusiasm. And individuals can learn about the concepts from the current literature, discover what others are doing, analyze their programs for "shareable" materials and services, set up or participate in "get to know you" experiences, explore cooperative agreements with other libraries, and test out resource sharing on a limited scale.

The second group of barriers is known as *political and legal factors*. School districts are separated from one another by boundaries that rarely are harmonious with city, town, village, or county lines. If they are, then vocational school or college jurisdictions are incongruent with them. Some state laws and local ordinances leave unclear or appear to deny the legality of resource-sharing agreements. Federal funding programs sometimes restrict the use of funded materials to certain target groups. Some states have not yet clearly assigned to a specific agency the responsibility for planning and coordinating interlibrary cooperation. Local institutions, themselves, are often so caught up in the red tape of bureaucratic procedures that the responsible parties cannot make decisions expeditiously. In schools, for example, the director of the media center must go through a principal, an assistant superintendent, a superintendent, a school board, and sometimes an additional fiscal control board before committing the media center to a cooperative venture. Finally, the flow of information has not been helped or expedited by the provisions of the 1978 revision of the Copyright Law.

Legal and political barriers must also be dealt with at all levels. Agencies administering funds can promote the cause of networks by establishing liberal guidelines for using the materials and services they make possible. State and national agencies, aided by professional associations, can screen existing regulations for barriers, identify model legislation, clearly assign responsibility for statewide coordination and development of networks, provide consultative services to groups exploring resource sharing, and exercise active leadership in promoting library networks. School district media personnel can study actual needs, examine existing policies and procedures, and build in the capability to make agreements with other libraries that permit the practical and efficient interchange of school district materials and services.

The third group is known as *funding factors*. School budgets typically do not have an expenditure category for interlibrary loan transactions or for staff time charged to borrowing, lending, mailing, or photocopying. Even if they did, the true costs of networking are hard to compute ahead of time and difficult to trace in ordinary accounting systems. Furthermore, the costs vary considerably, depending on the total available resources (staff, materials, space, equipment, time) and on access to communication technology with the network area. The current scarcity of funding for all tax supported institutions complicates the situation.

To overcome these limitations, influential leadership and the visible productivity of schools and libraries are necessary more than ever. The supporting public must be shown the value of today's and tomorrow's libraries. It is necessary for each participating member of a network to operate from a basis of strength, so that the differences between net borrowers and net lenders will not be unmanageable.

The collections of participating libraries should be built up to meet or exceed established standards. Schools and libraries should also begin to allocate funds within their total budgets specifically to networking. This would include not only the actual costs of interlibrary loans, but the costs of planning, evaluation, and development of the network. Today's "networkers" are in the best position to provide the reliable cost estimates needed by others who are contemplating a move that will bring the services of a library network to their users. These costs should be determined and made known. Networkers should also provide examples of cooperative activities that require little or no funding, and they should list those that effect a cost reduction. Finally, state and national governments can help the cause of networking by providing initial and continuing financial grants to help groups develop networks and share resources.

The fourth barrier is *communication factors*. Although networking implies communication, some school media centers and small public libraries still lack a telephone. Very few schools use automated cataloging, processing, circulation, serials control, and interlibrary loan systems. However, the need for access to bibliographic information and rapid referral of requests is usually more sharply felt by students than by users of other libraries.

To overcome communication barriers, the basic links must be in place. Individual institutions must provide telephones and other ordinary tools of communication. Studies that show the importance of advanced communication technology in improving the flow of information and materials should be undertaken by national agencies such as the National Commission on Libraries and Information Science and the National Institute for Education. These national agencies and their state level counterparts should also provide models and guidelines for technology so that compatibility and interconnection are assured. Regional, state, and area level groups of librarians can develop data bases listing resources. Local librarians and media specialists can share what communications equipment, systems, or technology they have and improve existing systems to answer the needs of an expanded group of users.

The fifth group of barriers has to do with *planning*. The time for large initial grants to experiment with the library network idea has passed, and the results of the grand experiments must guide our planning for the future. However, evaluative studies, guidelines, models—specifically those that assess the role and functioning of school media programs in library networks—are not readily available. Wide geographic separation of potential planners on the local scene also inhibits good planning. Planning is further inhibited by what might be called psychological or social distance, where a great difference in size of building, collection, staff, or the scope of authority among members of a network planning committee creates an inequality of rank that makes it difficult for the planners to operate as equals. Sometimes, planning is short-circuited by the quick and easy establishment of a network that excludes one or more libraries on the basis of type, size, source of funding, or some other characteristic. Once such a network is established, it is sometimes hard to alter the established patterns of cooperation and interchange, and newly admitted members (often schools) bear the stigma of "second class" or "afterthought."

A key to solving these problems is insuring that representatives of school media centers and all types of libraries are included in network planning teams at all levels, including state network coordinating units. These coordinating units can collect and disseminate information on statewide network development and on the results of network attempts. They can provide information on planning groups, consultants, contact persons, visitation sites, and the success or failure of networks locally or nationally. These coordinating units can recommend uniform guidelines for contracts, compensation plans, governance structures, and others. Individuals, through state and national associations, can develop a useful body of information by documenting experiences; publicizing agreements, contracts, and cost data; and contributing conclusions drawn from evaluations of library networks, particularly those that enjoy the active participation of school media programs.

CONCLUSION

The role of the school media program in library networks is one of active and full participation in planning, governance, and activities. The benefits to the users of the school media program as well as the school's contributions to the library network are many and significant.

There are numerous factors that create barriers to early and effective participation by school media programs, but through the efforts of a number of responsible agencies, associations, and groups, these barriers can be weakened and overcome.

In the last analysis, *individuals*, working alone or as members of the various organizations, must make the concrete moves that will bring about the plans, the guidelines, the organizations, and the body of literature that will guide and promote effective network development. Individuals must extend the invitations to others and participate in the variety of experiences that will replace ignorance and fear with knowledge and enthusiasm. Individuals, whether they are school media specialists or librarians by any other name, must recognize the value of making every library, information agency, or media center an effective point of access to the total information resource.

NOTES

1. American Association of School Libraries and Association for Educational Communication and Technology, *Media Programs District and School* (Chicago: American Library Association; Washington: Association for Educational Communication Technology, 1975).
2. "Report of the Coordinator—1976," (unpublished report to North Eastern Wisconsin Intertype Libraries, University of Wisconsin, Greenbay, Wisconsin, 1976).

Cooperatives and Networks: A Preliminary Survey and Suggested Sources of Information

Brenda White, Teaching Fellow
University of Pittsburgh
Graduate School of Library
and Information Sciences
Pittsburgh, Pennsylvania

This paper provides a preliminary compilation of information about existing cooperatives and networks and their services. There are currently two major sources of information on cooperatives and networks. The first is the ASLA Report on Interlibrary Cooperation, now in its second edition, published by the Association of State Library Agencies.[1] This report provides a state-by-state description of cooperative activites. The second source is the Knowledge Industry Publications, Inc.'s *Library Networks* by Susan Martin now in its third edition (1978-79). It concentrates on networks providing computer-based services.

The U.S. Office of Education is in the process of compiling statistics of networks. A preliminary survey was field tested and the final survey forms were distributed in early 1979.

Another survey of networks has been undertaken as part of the U.S. National Science Foundation's grant for a network study made to the Graduate School of Library and Information Sciences at the University of Pittsburgh. While some persons such as Raynard Swank[2] emphasize computer capabilities as an essential element of networks, others accept "a group of libraries, not limited as to type, which identifies a set of common needs and then compacts together to meet these needs."[3] Networks chosen for the Pittsburgh study more accurately reflect this definintion than Swank's.

The information about networks used in this paper is based on the Pittsburgh data. During this study existing networks were identified through literature searches. The identified networks were requested by letter to send data regarding development, operations, membership, governance, finance and services. Responses were received from 189 U.S. networks. The information submitted from the networks included a narrative description (as requested by the letter); other data such as newsletters, annual reports, articles and other materials were also received.

Services offered by the networks were analyzed and reduced to 11 general categories. These are technical services, acquisitions/collection development, circulation, reference/bibliographic searching/information retrieval, serials control, interlibrary loan/materials duplication, delivery services, storage and preservation, resource sharing, publicity, and continuing education. The range of services within each category will be described in the following section. Brief descriptions of services, cited by network, follow to illustrate the range of services; data have been taken from survey responses; no judgments concerning those services have been made or are implied.

SERVICES OF NETWORKS

Technical Services

This service encompasses shared cataloging including members' access through the network data bases such as OCLC and RLIN, card production, shelf lists, translations, printing of brochures and other publicity materials, and cooperative supply purchases. For example, Suffolk Cooperative Library System in New York, maintains a central processing facility, and three others maintain statistical records for member libraries. The Southwest Missouri Library Network indexes Missouri materials.

Acquisitions/Collection Development

Cooperative acquisitions development is provided by several networks. The Southwest Academic Library Consortium members voluntarily participate in collection development, and a state plan for serials acquisition has been developed by the Health Science Library and Information Cooperative of Maine. San Gabriel Community College Library Cooperative in California has developed a program for mutual notification of purchase or intent to purchase materials, and the New York Metropolitan Reference and Research Library Agency has a Cooperative Acquisitions Program.

Circulation

A number of groups have developed procedures for reciprocal borrowing privileges. Some provide an Info Pass to a patron whose request cannot be filled at the local library. The pass permits the patron to borrow from another library within the system. The Info Pass is most often usable only once. Among the systems using the Info Pass concept are Berrien Library Consortium of Michigan and the Tri-County Library Council of Wisconsin. Others have developed a library card accepted in all member libraries. One such example is the TBL card of the Trail Blazer Library System of Louisiana.

Reference/Bibliographic Searching/Information Retrieval

About one-half of the networks surveyed reported reference as a service to members. This service included ready reference service, verification of bibliographic entries, on-line searching of data bases and provision of union lists. The union lists were for local areas, regions or nationwide; covered books, and audiovisual or serial collections. The technology used varied widely: telephone and mail requests, teletype, two-way radio and computer links. Examples of specialized information available included vocation and career information (Oregon Career Information Systems), foundation information (Consortium of Foundation Libraries) and current awareness services.

Serials Control

A need for system sharing of periodical resources has led to the development of location tools, especially by local networks.

Among those describing such activites as part of their services are the Atlanta Health Sciences Libraries Consortium and the Southwestern Connecticut Library System. Some networks provide records of holdings, including issues available, in order to maintain the usefulness of the collection and union lists. A project for a nationwide, on-line union list of serials system is underway through the joint efforts of the Indiana University Libraries and OCLC, Inc.; the project is an outgrowth of the Union List Project at the INCOLSA network.

Interlibrary Loan/Materials Duplication

Interlibrary loan, lending of materials from one library to another, is a service offered by 109 of the networks surveyed. Of these networks, more than one-half were local in scope. Regional, state, and nationwide networks serve generally as locators of materials and also as sources of last resort for materials not otherwise available. In the interlibrary loan function, materials themselves may be loaned or copies may be provided. Although it is more usual for libraries to provide photocopies or, in some cases, microfilm copies of the materials, other forms are sometimes utilized. The Library of Congress, National Library Service for the Blind and Physically Handicapped, provides copies of materials in braille and as sound recordings. The Metropolitan Cooperative Library System in the Los Angeles area provides cassette duplication, and a patent copying service is provided by the Rochester Regional Research Library Council.

Document/Information Delivery

Delivery of materials may be by courier (Kansas City Library Network, Inc.), by system-owned vans, by commercial carriers such as United Parcel Service or Greyhound, or by mail. The Mideastern Ohio Library Organization features a Mail-a-Book program which provides service to patrons who would be otherwise unable to receive library services. The Interlibrary Delivery Service of Pennsylvania combines system-owned vans and Greyhound to move materials throughout the state. Telefacsimile is the delivery method used by some networks; an example is the QWIP telefacsimile system used by the Greater Cincinnati Library Consortium.

Storage/Preservation

Although the problems of preservation and storage of materials are becoming more and more pressing, few networks address this area directly. Among those who do are the Health Science Library and Information Cooperative of Maine whose services include a standard storage plan for serials, and the Pacific Northwest Bibliographic Center which microfilms records. The Research Libraries Group, Inc. lists preservation as one of its goals. The Medical Library Center of New York maintains a book and periodical depository. The Universal Serials Book Exchange provides for the recycling of materials unwanted by the owners.

Resource Sharing

This service was mentioned most often by networks covering smaller geographic areas. Sharing resources may be through informal arrangements or such activities as joint audiovisual collections (Coastal Bend Consortium in Texas), regional collections and film collections (Central Association of Libraries in California). The Southeastern Wisconsin Health Science Library Consortium is one of many which maintains locator lists, this one of reference books. The Mountain Valley Library System uses a telephone network for resource sharing. The Long Island Library Resources Council, Inc. has established a gift exchange program. Referral of members to resource people and/or consultation is provided by some networks to their members to help with specific needs and problems. The Bell Laboratories Library Network, the Pacific Coast Forest Research Information Network, and the Midcontinental Regional Medical Library Program are among those offering this service.

Communications/Publicity

Communications refers to those activities that are intended to keep network members informed of each other's activities. Publicity refers to activities aimed at reaching beyond network members, either to other libraries or to patrons of the member libraries, informing them of network services intended for patrons. Among communication activities of the networks are the publication of directories such as the Illinois based Department of Dental Health and Developmental Disabilities Library Services Consortium's "Directory of DMHDD Library Services Personnel." The Clinical Neurology Information Center in Nebraska publishes an index to neurology literature, and other networks publish union lists, newsletters, and brochures.

SERVICES CODE KEY

The following lists of networks and cooperatives have been coded to indicate the services offered. These services correspond to the 11 categories used in the Pittsburgh Study and briefly described above. These lists of networks are based on respondents to the Pittsburgh study; therefore, the list is not exhaustive and should be used in conjunction with the other sources mentioned earlier. A few networks for which service data was unavailable are included; these are not coded.

1. cataloging/technical services
2. acquisition/collection development
3. circulation
4. reference/bibliographic searching/information retrieval
5. serials control
6. interlibrary loan/materials duplication
7. document delivery/information delivery
8. storage/preservation
9. resource sharing
10. communications/publicity
11. continuing education

A PARTIAL LIST OF
LOCAL NETWORKS AND COOPERATIVES

California

Bay Area Reference Center—4, 10, 11
Central Association of Libraries—6, 7, 9
Cooperative Information Network—6, 11
Libraries of Orange County Network—4, 6, 10, 11
Medical Library Consortium of Santa Clara County—4, 6
Metropolitan Cooperative Library System—1, 6, 7, 9, 11
Mountain Valley Library System—9
North State Cooperative Library System—1, 4, 7, 11

STATE AND REGIONAL COOPERATIVES AND NETWORKS

Alaska

Alaska Library Network—4

California

California Library Authority for Systems and Services—1, 4, 5, 8, 10, 11

California State Universities and College Academic Library System—4

Consortium for International Development Information Network—4, 9

Pacific Coast Forest Research Information Network—4, 7, 9

Sierra Libraries Information Consortium—6

Southern California Answering Network—4

Colorado

Bibliographic Center for Research

State Wide Reference Network

Connecticut

Connecticut Association of Health Science Libraries—5, 6, 10

Florida

Florida Library Information Network—4, 6

Georgia

Georgia Library Information Network—4, 6

Southeastern Library Network

Hawaii

Community College Film Consortium—9

Idaho

Health Information Retrieval Center

Illinois

Department of Mental Health and Development Disabilities Library Services Consortium—5, 10

Midwest Health Science Library Network—6

Indiana

Indiana Cooperative Library Services Authority—1, 4, 5, 9, 10, 11
Indiana Information Retrieval System—4

Iowa

Iowa Library Information Teletype Exchange—4, 6
Iowa Network for Obtaining Resource Materials for Schools—4, 9

Kansas

Kansas Information Circuit—4, 6

Louisiana

Louisiana-Mississippi Microforms Network—4, 6
Trail Blazer Library System—4, 6, 7, 11

Maryland

Maryland Academic Libraries Automated Processing Center—4, 6, 9

Massachusetts

New England Library Information Network—1, 6, 10

Michigan

Kentucky-Ohio-Michigan Regional Medical Library—4, 6
Michigan Library Consortium—4, 6
Midwest Region Library Network—4

Minnesota

Minnesota Department of Public Welfare Library Consortia
Minnesota Interlibrary Telecommunications Exchange—4, 5, 6

Montana

Montana Information Network Exchange—4

Nebraska

Clinical Neurology Information Center—1
Intermountain Union List of Serials—5
Midcontinental Regional Medical Library Program—4, 7, 9, 11
Nebraska Library Telecommunications Network—6

New Jersey

Medical Resources Consortium of New Jersey—5, 6, 9, 11
New Jersey Library Network—6

Virgin Islands

Virgin Islands Library and Information Network—2, 4, 6, 11

Virginia

Virginia Medical Information System

Washington

Pacific Northwest Bibliographic Center—4, 6, 7, 9, 10, 11
Pacific Northwest Health Sciences Library Network
Western Forestry Network

Washington, D.C.

Interlibrary Users Association—9

Wisconsin

Water Resources National Information Network—4
Wisconsin Library Consortium—4, 11

NATIONAL NETWORKS

OCLC, Inc., Columbus, Ohio—1, 2, 4, 5, 6, 9, 10, 11
    Clientele: open
Research Libraries Group, Inc.—Research Libraries Information Network, Palo Alto, California—1, 2, 4, 6, 7, 8, 9, 10
    Clientele: members of ARL
Washington Library Network, Olympia, Washington—1, 2, 3, 4, 5, 6
    Clientele: open

OTHER NETWORKS AND COOPERATIVES

Bell Laboratories Library Network, Murray Hill, New Jersey—4, 6
    Clientele: closed
Center for Research Libraries, Chicago, Illinois—9
    Clientele: closed
Consortium of Foundation Libraries, New York—4
    Clientele: open
Consortium of University Film Centers, Illinois—9
    Clientele: closed (institutions)
Drug Abuse Communications Network, New York—4, 10
    Clientele: open
Educational Resources Information Center, Washington, D.C.—4
    Clientele: closed (clearinghouses)

Health Education Network, Inc., Columbus, Ohio—9
  Clientele: closed (institutions)
Library of Congress, National Library Service for the Blind and
  Physically Handicapped, Washington, D.C.—4, 9
  Clientele: open
NASA Library Network—1, 4
  Clientele: closed
National Agricultural Library—7
  Clientele: hierarchical access
National Library of Medicine—4, 6
  Clientele: hierarchical access
Oceanic and Atmospheric Sciences Information System, Rockville,
  Maryland—4, 9
  Clientele: closed
Rockwell International Technical Information Processing System,
  Downey, California—4
  Clientele: closed (company divisions)
3M Library Systems, Reading, Massachusetts—4
  Clientele: open
U.S. National Bureau of Standards—4, 10
  Clientele: closed (data evaluation centers)
Universal Serials Book Exchange—9
  Clientele: open
Veterans Administration Library Network—4, 6
  Clientele: closed
Water Resources Scientific Information Center—4
  Clientele: open

NOTES

1. ASLA Interlibrary Cooperation Committee. *The ASLA Report on Interlibrary Cooperation 1978*, 2nd ed. (Chicago: Association of State Library Agencies, 1978).
2. Quoted in E.E. Olson, Russell Shank and Harold A. Olsen, "Library and Information Networks," in *Annual Review of Information Science and Technology*, Vol. 7:280 (Washington, D.C.: ASIS, 1972).
3. MIDLNET Symposium, 1st, Oakland University, Rochester, Michigan, 1976. *Report of the First MIDLNET Symposium on the Role of Local Consortia, State Networks, and Regional Networks in the Emerging National Library Network*, T. John Metz, comp. (Greenbay, Wisc.: Midwest Region Library Network, 1976), p. 5.
4. Allen Kent et al., "The Economics of Information Transfer: Using Resource Sharing Networks—Network Functions," (Draft Final Report to the National Science Foundation, January 24, 1979).

APPENDIXES

Appendix A: Part 1

Critical Issues Submitted by Conference Participants

Three small group sessions were held during the Conference to allow more informal participation and discussion of issues. Groups could reinforce issues presented by Conference speakers, take an opposing view, suggest additional issues, or just register comments as they saw fit. The output from these   sions relating to critical issues is presented below without editing.

Access Issues

How to achieve improved information flow to the public with equality of access to information?

The library profession—technology is moving faster than we are. What we have to discuss is availability of information, access.

How to control access—lay public should not have access to medical information.

What happens to libraries if a patron can do his/her own searching at home?

If you are going to retrieve information rather than artifacts, i.e., data rather than location of books, costs go up. How badly will researchers want information and how willing will researchers be to pay? Will only those people who can't afford information elsewhere go to the public library?

All libraries do not have access to networking services.

Public access to information—natural evolution of networks does not seem to be producing an improved opportunity for public access to information resources. How can we improve representation of end users interests in networking, i.e., reference and referral services and public interest of data bases, e.g., which gas stations are open today?

Education for Networking Issues

Many librarians, boards, legislators and other officials have not yet recognized the value of networks. In some cases there is fear and suspicion of networks and their needs for funding. Need for education for all concerned.

How to increase public awareness of networks for network use?

How to diffuse appropriate knowledge of network use (capabilities) throughout a library staff?

Funding Issues

Libraries are autonomous, with autonomous governance structures. Networks should exist as free marketplace agencies. *Any* agency should be able to request funds from *any* funding organization; however, in a marketplace, funding may not be required.

Need for greater federal assistance. Networks want it to develop their services; state library agencies feel it should be channeled through them; so do individual libraries. How does the library community feel federal assistance should be channeled? What is the appropriate umbrella and who's standing under it?

Education of administrators and the public.

Financial/attitudinal—especially with those places who conduct bake sales to fund libraries.

Federal funds to finance network development.

The issue is how to best articulate the value(s) of networks and networking so as to justify adequate allocation of resources.

A major issue is funding policy: free vs. fee services—all free? a balance? governmental subsidy by grants and/or "information stamps"?

Governance/Management Issues

How are the roles of local, intrastate, interstate, multistate, and national networking activities to be coordinated?

How are policies to be formulated at levels up to national level?

National Information Policy Issues

Libraries and library networkers must not allow the Communication Act of 1934 to be replaced without providing appropriate input.

There is no necessity for and there is danger inherent in establishing and implementing a national information policy.

To identify with greater clarity the role of the federal government in supporting/encouraging the maintenance/growth of library networks in an existing system that is and should be developed from the bottom up. Recognizing the requirement of balancing the need for competition and diversity with the need for more generalized or wide-scale access to network services from a wide diversity of users through libraries of many kinds and sizes throughout the country.

The federal government as an information supplier—consistent federal policy on access to and dissemination of federally produced information resources and significant federal library resources.

How can the federal government play a role in stimulating library networking and help assure the free flow of public information while not interfering with open, innovative competition?

Is it feasible to formulate a single national information policy?

National information policies will need to be defined in relation to balancing the public and private good.

The continual discussion of a national information policy precludes discussion of much more important issues such as the constituencies of networks which are neither well-defined nor adequately publicized.

Copyright constraints must be considered.

National Library Network Issues

There are the basic components of a national bibliographic network in place; an umbrella organization on the national level is not needed. The competitive economic environment should determine the vendors without a national agency. There are other concerns which may require coordination at the national level: standards, preservation, data base maintenance and communications.

Why a national network? We need to define what we mean by a national network. We lack a shared vision. We need to define networks as they relate the local needs and their constituents.

National coordination through cooperation by involved libraries and networks. There is a generally perceived need for establishment of national standards, or guidelines, without sacrificing initiative and innovation on the part of those who have developed networks and consortia on a local, state and regional level. Incompatibilities should be addressed in order to assure efficiency and avoid redundancy.

A national system should not be developed at the expense of the individual and local systems.

Assuming that the federal government does not direct network services, what role should it play in networking? Research and development grants? Supportive funding for cooperative library network services? Regulation of tariffs on telecommunications facilities? Management of a library and information services telecommunications network?

Everyone defines national network in a different way. Networking may be coming from the grass roots, but we have to interconnect.

There seems to be an emerging need for a National Information Network linking together existing systems and services. The basic question seems to be what structure will the network take:

- superimposed from above (federal level)
- constructed out of or around existing networks (OCLC, WLN, RLIN)
- built from the bottom-up through meeting local needs first and then developing the technology for linkage.

Each approach has its advantages and disadvantages, but since each is dependent on funding from some source (flow-through federal funds in many instances) effort will continue to be dissipated until consensus can be reached on which approach is the "best" (most acceptable/least objectionable).

Can one [national] data base be all issues to all people? One [national] service to meet needs of all?

Private Sector Issues

Need to recognize the existence of the private sector, i.e., Baker & Taylor, Brodart, etc.

Research Issues

Research is needed in the following areas:

- patron needs and library (as user) needs regarding services of networks, or potential services
- how networks can better serve special user needs (e.g., law, music, fine arts, etc.)
- how to provide adequate funding
- how to minimize the strings attached to funding

Services Issues

Cooperative library development is more than networking. Need to focus more on services than on mechanisms. Misinterpretations of COSLA position statement.

More efficient delivery services to multitype libraries for all users.

Appropriate research and development for the improved delivery of information and library materials to users.

Technology and Standards Issues

Need interface between circulation system and bibliographic.

Lack of standard technology within the local and regional library networks which causes incompatibility on the national level.

The need for the individual, as well as the individual library, to be able to manipulate the network to satisfy his own needs.

How can libraries keep up with the technology that affects their very existence (cable TV, Viewdata)?

One of the critical issues is the pressing need for standards—widespread implementation of those in being; development and application of those that are missing. Those of concern deal with standards for cataloging, format for transmission and data content designation. Also, standards for application level communications protocol need to be tested.

The security of computer information.

Compatibility should not be pushed at the expense of creativity and developmental progress.

User Issues

The end user is the most important ingredient in the network and is forgotten in network development and services. Networks have developed to provide services which may not be perceived as benefiting the end user or were not designed to benefit end users, but rather to benefit librarians. In information transfer we need to look at what is being delivered—quality question. Is it worthwhile producing catalog cards that lead people to information that is out of date or insufficient.

We must be better prepared to compete better in the public service arena.

An efficient and equitable delivery of cost effective library and information service to the consumer public will best be reached through an evolutionary free marketplace development while there is a need to reallocate resources and force attention to specific problem solving. The public good will not be served by a single federal agency.

How to provide users with direct (easily mediated) access to the data bases in libraries (networks).

To what extent is library planning based on user needs? Proposition 13 is the effect of library problems, not the cause.

Appendix A:
Part 2

Summary of a Debate
Between Roderick G. Swartz
and Glyn T. Evans

A topic of continuing interest is the relationship between state library agencies and cooperatively governed library networks and the appropriate role of each in library development. Conference participants were treated to a traditional debate between Roderick G. Swartz, State Librarian, Washington State Library and Glyn T. Evans, Director of Library Services, State University of New York, the organization which manages the cooperative computer-based network in New York State. Moderating was Joseph Rhodes, House of Representatives, Commonwealth of Pennsylvania.

Words on paper cannot recapture the flavor of the debate, but each debater has submitted a summary of his major points.

Question:

State-level networking should evolve principally from the state library agency rather than the cooperatively governed member library network.

Affirmative: Roderick G. Swartz

My comments are based on the assumption that networking—i.e., a full-service network with computer and telecommunications support—is not a passing fad, but a new way of doing business.

1. If the state library is directly involved in the networking process, you have a direct contact with a stable financial, economic, and social source of energy—i.e., state government.
2. If we are in the business of "changing the way we do business," you need a change agent or catalyst. The state library has been in this business for a number of years, witness the growth of regional public library systems during the 50's and 60's and therefore should be able to apply change agent skills to current developments.

342

3. If you accept a full-service network backed by technology, you need the active involvement of an agency which can help change occur. A cooperative may provide bibliographic utility services, but an established statewide library program is required to develop a full-service network.

4. If networking is to succeed, it must have political and economic support from the national program level down into the most elementary grass roots level. The state library has long been the library agency which "sells" new concepts to the smaller and more rural areas of the country. To gain legislative support for library programs, you need this kind of local-regional support system.

5. Even regional, i.e., multistate systems, must be state-based to function well. This is a typical pattern in the West. All regional or multistate ventures gain their political, financial and program direction from a state-based policy group.

6. Soft money of any nature—foundations, federal grants or otherwise—is helpful, but if networking is to be permanent, rather than experimental, there has to be a solid formula of local, state and federal public monies in the long run.

In summary, if networking is to be permanent rather than experimental, there has to be a base at local, state and federal levels. Governance should be as broad and inclusive as reasonable, but there must be a focal point for leadership.

Negative: Glyn T. Evans

The activities of state library agencies related to cooperative programs are reported in the *ASLA Handbook of Interlibrary Cooperation.* A careful review reveals that

1. State library agencies make genuine, hard-working efforts to improve library services within their states.

2. They are working in an extremely volatile and difficult fiscal, political and social environment, (which would be almost impossible were it not for the stability of federal—LSCA—funds).

3. There is wide variation in performance, skills, objectives, and intents of each agency.

4. Effort has been concentrated primarily (and properly) on public and, to some extent, school libraries, and interlibrary loan systems.

5. The online revolution in library technology has, with some notable exceptions, bypassed state library agencies.

Online networks, on the other hand:

1. Develop services, in conjunction with their members, on a participative, cooperative, stake-holder basis, which respond to user needs and constraints,

2. Encourage a timely acceptance by libraries of current computer

and communications technology, and national and international bibliographic standards,

3. Create an environment for the most cost efficient and cost effective modes of resource sharing,
4. Provide equalization and consistency of funding for operations and, particularly research and development shared among all participants and utilities,
5. Offer fiscal, social, and political stability, and
6. Have the ability to respond quickly to a volatile, electronically-supported, dynamic future.

Response: Swartz

I disagree with Mr. Evans' contention that state libraries provide an unstable environment for networking. It is a strong environment since it attempts to take into consideration local needs and requirements, thereby creating a more stable, accepted network. Too, state libraries have always been charged with a leadership and development role within a state, even if not all pursue that goal. Governance must involve users of the network, but there also needs to be a leadership focal point such as the state library.

Networking is not just another task—it is a different way of doing business in libraries. Introduction of this approach must be placed at the top of the priority list. Networking needs to be introduced carefully, but completely into libraries. The state library agency has a traditional role as a catalyst, introducing new concepts at the local level. The state library needs to expand this role with regard to networking.

Response: Evans

Networks have grown as they have, almost without subsidy, because they fulfill a vital need. They are proven components of library service which have grown to stability outside the funding and control patterns of rigidly-planned state and federal structuralism, (which is being pressed and dictated at a level not expected in a free, entrepreneurial society). They are a grass roots, bottom-up activity, summing the judgments of all their participants and supporters, who know a good thing when they see one.

The wish to leapfrog into leadership by agencies which have ignored or even opposed online networking development does not appear to offer a massive increase in efficiency sufficient to outweigh the inevitable disruption caused by change.

There is, of course, no single focus for all networking, or all library resource sharing, or all librarianship, or all public service.

Together, online networks, state library agencies, and individual libraries *can* combine their unique skills, talents, and constituencies to provide the best possible service to the most users possible. More, they *must*.

Appendix B

Federal Information Agencies and Networks

Prepared by Conference Staff

This sample of federal information activities and programs illustrates not only the range of federal information interests but also the complexity of modes used by federal agencies.

The source of data was *Federal Information Sources and Systems*. The information provided by Library of Congress (LC), the National Library of Medicine (NLM), and the National Agricultural Library (NAL) was submitted to them for review although time did not allow us to grant this courtesy to the other agencies described. Additional sources of information about federal programs are provided at the end of this section.

MEDICAL LITERATURE ANALYSIS AND RETRIEVAL SYSTEM (MEDLARS II) (NLM)

Purpose

The system assists the advancement of medical and related health sciences through the collection and dissemination of bibliographic and monographic information important to the progress of medicine and health.

Input

The major category of input data comes from approximately 2500 recurring biomedical journals which are indexed nationally and internationally to produce over 22,000 citation records monthly. The journals are indexed for input by in-house personnel, contract personnel, and personnel in foreign countries on a quid-pro-quo agreement with NLM.

The indexed records are processed through or prior to addition to the data bases. Monthly magnetic tapes are received from the following organizations or agencies and are added to the pertinent data bases: National Cancer Institute—NIH, National Bio-sciences Information Services, American Society of Hospital Pharmacists, Environmental Protection Agency, and the Hayes File on Pesticides.

Content

MEDLARS is an information storage and on-line retrieval system that currently services more than 900 on-line international users. The principal subject matter is contained in reference citations to over 9000 biomedical journals from this country and many foreign countries. Some of the data elements in the citation record include title, author, pagination, source, vocabulary medical terms, and abstract. The subject matter is designed to help health professionals find out easily and quickly what has been published on any specific biomedical subject. Records indexed from 1966 forward are included in the data bases. Most of the 18 on-line data bases are updated on a monthly cycle. The major category of data from the biomedical journals (20,000-26,000 records) is accumulated during each month and added to the data bases.

Output

Output from the system includes on-line retrieval listings and screen displays of citations retrieved as a result of searching data bases. Output also can be obtained from batch searching of the files. Batch search results are printed using the high-speed printer. On-line retrieval is available from the system 12-14 hours daily, Monday through Friday. Searching of biomedical bibliographic and monographic information for health practitioners, individuals, and institutions within 28 recurring biomedical publications and catalogs is also accomplished by this system (weekly, monthly, bimonthly). Over 900 biomedical institutions have on-line access to the system. These include institutions in this country, plus Canada, Italy, Mexico, and South Africa. In addition, Australia, Brazil, England, Germany, Japan, and Sweden use NLM's data bases on their computers.

Availability

Output from this system is available to the public. Authorized international on-line users can iterrogate the on-line data bases. Requested batch search output listings are mailed upon request. Publications and catalogs produced by the system can be obtained from GPO.

AGRICULTURE ON-LINE ACCESS (AGRICOLA)
(National Agricultural Library)

Purpose

AGRICOLA (formerly CAIN On-Line) was established in 1973 as an on-line interactive bibliographic search and retrieval service to provide information on publications in the National Agricultural Library to scientists and researchers. It includes a family of data bases created by NAL; CAIN, FNIC, and AGECON (a data base created by the Economic Research Service, USDA).

Input

Data are derived from cataloging-indexing records pertaining to books and journal articles acquired by the National Agricultural Library through purchase from publishers and dealers, gifts from individuals, societies, and other noncommercial sources, and exchange with foreign research organizations and governing bodies.

Content

Records include NAL call numbers, ID number, title of article, language, author, journal title abbreviation, volume, number, pages, date, and type of document. Tapes are up-dated monthly. Geographic coverage is worldwide.

Output

Principal products are the magnetic tapes issued monthly for sale. Derived from the sale tapes are the commercially published Bibliography of Agriculture and the National Agricultural Library Catalog. The tapes are also loaded in several commercial on-line information services which are used for current awareness service and retrospective literature searchers.

Availability

Monthly tapes are for sale; the data base is on-line with Lockheed Information Systems, Systems Development Corporation, and Bibliographic Retrieval Services and can be searched by remote terminal. The data base can be queried onsite at NAL.

LIBRARY OF CONGRESS DATA BASES

Automated Process Information File

Records in this file are preliminary cataloging records, not complete records, for English, Portuguese, and Spanish monographs in the cataloging process at the Library of Congress. Also included in the file are records for monographs—in all languages—that are on order. (4000 preliminary, 9000 order records)

Books

Records in this file are catalog records for English-language books cataloged since 1968, French-language books since 1973, and all roman alphabet languages since 1977. Included also are catalog records contributed by 12 libraries participating in the Cooperative MARC (COMARC) project. (780,000 LC records, 40,000 COMARC)

National Referral Center Resources File

This file contains data on organizations qualified and willing to provide information on a large number of science and technology topics, including the social sciences. Primary sources for file entries include records from the Information Resources Information System (IRIS) and the series *A Directory of Information Resources in the United States*. The information given for an organization usually includes name of resource, mailing address, location, telephone, topics of concern to the organization, holdings of special collections and data bases, publications, and dissemination services.

The file is now available on the U.S. Department of Energy RECON Network, serving DOE offices and major contractors.

Register of Additional Locations

A file of location records, that is, symbols of libraries, for titles listed in the *National Union Catalog*. The file contains records for 1,953,000 titles in more than 14 million locations held by 1100 libraries.

Films

This file contains cataloging records for motion pictures, filmstrips, transparency and slide sets, and other visual items issued since 1972 and cataloged by the Audiovisual Section of the LC Descriptive Cataloging Division. The file contains 45,200 records.

Maps

This file contains 53,900 cataloging records for maps cataloged by the LC Geography and Map Division since 1969. Included are all single and multisheet thematic maps, map sets, and maps treated as serials in all languages.

Motion Pictures

This file contains 1000 records for motion picture footage in the Library's archival collections. A grant from the National Endowment for the Humanities made it possible to catalog the Theodore Roosevelt, Kleine, and Taylor collections, and in the near future the records will be available through the MARC Distribution Service.

Names

This file contains 115,000 name and uniform title authority records created after 1977. The Library is inputting all new name authority records to machine-readable form, and eventually the file will have authority records for all names and uniform titles appearing on MARC bibliographic records.

Serials

This file contains 80,000 records, including all new serial titles cataloged by the Library of Congress since April, 1973 and serial titles created by CONSER that have been validated either by the National Library of Canada or the Library of Congress. Records cover all languages, the majority of the titles having a beginning date of 1970.

Subjects

This file contains 250,000 records for subject authorities that appear in the 8th edition of *Library of Congress Subject Headings* and supplements.

PATENT SEARCH FILES: U.S. PATENT
AND TRADEMARK OFFICE

Purpose

This system is designed to provide a comprehensive collection of U.S. and foreign patents to be used by patent examiners, patent attorneys, and inventors in search of prior art in relation to filing and/or prosecuting patent applications; by individuals seeking a specific patent; and by the general public in search of technical information.

Input

The patents are distributed into two collections. The four million U.S. patents are being issued at the rate of 1500/week by the U.S. Patent Office. The foreign patents and patent documents are regularly received from 52 countries. This is the largest foreign patent collection in the United States and numbers approximately 28 million documents.

Content

The major U.S. patent collection is housed in the Public Search Room in two forms—the classified collection in hardcopy and the numerical collection in microfilm. There are various indexes to provide access to the patents via inventor, assignee, and subject. The foreign patents are located in the Scientific Library, filed by country in order of receipt. These documents are partly in hardcopy, partly on microfilm, and are accessible by date of filing by document number, and to some extent by subject. Small collections arranged in U.S. Patent and Trademark Office. These files are primarily the U.S. patents in a given subject area enriched by foreign patents and nonpatent literature about the same subject.

Output

No reports are issued.

Availability

The Public Search Room is available to the public.

NTIS BIBLIOGRAPHIC DATA FILE
(National Technical Information Service)

Purpose

This file contains bibliographic citations of U.S. Government sponsored research, development, and engineering reports; computer products; and inventions available for licensing. Selected state and local government reports are also included. It is a purpose of NTIS to disseminate to the public information products from U.S. Government agencies.

Input

The sources of the information include over 350 U.S. Government agencies. Most of these reports are available for purchase from NTIS. All others contain availability information in the document citation. These reports cover all disciplines of research including physics, chemistry, biology, medicine, materials, sociology, urban development, engineering, transportation, energy, computer technology, and environmental research.

Content

The file is multidisciplinary and contains summaries of new U.S. Government generated research and development reports, other data and analyses, as well as translations of foreign technical materials. The file consists of more than 550,000 titles. Most items have full bibliographic citations. The file can be searched by report, contract, or accession number; personal or corporate author; title; subject category; or keywords. Corresponding hardcopy products associated with the file are the Government Reports Announcements and Index, Weekly Government Abstracts, Published Searches, and the Directory of Computerized Data Files, Software and Related Technical Reports. Biweekly updates provide material for SDI profiles for the NTIS Selected Research in Microfiche. Output consists of custom searches, printouts, computer tapes and microfiche.

Output

Most citations refer to reports available in paper and microfiche copy. Magnetic tapes, inventions available for licensing, and NTIS subscriptions are also referenced. Government Reports Announcements and Index, a biweekly journal, contains new input to the file in paper copy form.

Availability

The magnetic tape may be leased annually, and tapes back to 1964 may be acquired. Current tapes are shipped biweekly to subscribers. The file is also publicly available through commerical on-line information systems.

CENSUS BUREAU POPULATION STATISTICS SYSTEM

Purpose

A census of population has been taken every ten years since 1790, the nineteenth being conducted as of April 1, 1970. The census function is described in and authorized by the Constitution and by laws codified as Title 13, U.S. Code. These data are utilized by the Congress, by the executive branch, and by the public generally in the development and evaluation of economic and social programs.

Input

The major decennial censuses provided the basic data input. To update these data, the current population survey is conducted monthly. Interviewers visit a scientifically selected sample of the population to obtain current information on the personal and family characteristics of the population, mobility of the population, income, consumer buying indicators, school enrollment, and other subjects. Also derived from this survey are estimates of employment, unemployment, hours of work, occupation, and earnings. These labor force data are turned over to the Bureau of Labor Statistics, U.S. Department of Labor, for analysis and publication. That agency assumed responsibility for these functions effective July 1, 1959.

Content

Census information includes a wide variety of statistical data about the people and economy of the Nation. Population and housing data presently available include: 1) 1970 Census Summary tapes (First through Sixth Counts); 2) Selected 1970 Census Subject Report Files; 3) 1970 and 1960 Public Use Sample Files; 4) Census Employment Survey; 5) Annual Demographic Files 1968-1974; 6) Voting Supplement; 7) 1970 Census Child Spacing and Fertility Public Use Sample; and 8) Population Estimates File.

Output

Output includes printed reports, computer tapes, and special tabulations. However, catalogs, guides, and directories that are useful in locating information on specific subjects are also produced. The publication program for the 1970 census was completed in December 1973. Estimates of population for postcensal and intercensal dates, as well as projections of the population are prepared from time to time. Special censuses of local areas are taken at the request and expense of the local governments involved. Reports providing estimates and projections of the population of various foreign countries also are published periodically.

Availability

Output, especially that in printed report form, is publicly available and is listed in its various catalogs and indexes. Contact the Census Bureau for specific documents.

LIBRARY GENERAL INFORMATION SURVEY SYSTEM (LIBGIS)
(Dept. H.E.W.)

Purpose

This system in designed to collect, process, analyze, and disseminate data on all types of libraries; on educational broadcasting facilities and program; and occasionally, on museums.

Input

Data are derived from a complete enumeration of federal Government, state agency, and college and university libraries. Sample surveys are taken of public libraries; those in public and nonpublic schools, in state governments, in commerce and industry, museums, and educational broadcasting.

Content

Data include resources, staff, financial statistics, activities, physical facilities, and programs. Data are updated every 2-5 years.

Output

Statistical summaries, analytical reports, magnetic tapes, and special tabulations are produced.

Availability

Reports are publicly available.

EDUCATIONAL RESOURCES INFORMATION CENTER (ERIC)
(Dept. H.E.W.)

Purpose

The Center (ERIC) was established under the Cooperative Research Program (Public Law 83-531), as amended by Public Law 89-10. ERIC is a nationwide decentralized information network for acquiring, selecting, abstracting, indexing, storing, retrieving, and disseminating the most significant and timely education-related reports. It consists of a coordination staff in Washington, D.C., and 16 clearinghouses located at or with professional organizations across the country. These clearinghouses, each responsible for a particular educational area, are an integral part of the ERIC system.

Input

Reports of cooperative research projects, speeches, professional conference proceedings, selected dissertations, and pertinent educational journal literature, are sources of system input.

Content

The educational subject areas are: Career Education; Counseling and Personnel Services; Early Childhood Education; Educational Management; Handicapped and Gifted Children; Higher Education; Information Resources; Junior Colleges; Languages and Linguistics; Reading and Communication Skills; Rural Education and Small Schools; Science, Mathematics, and Environmental Education; Social Studies/Social Science Education; Teacher Education; Tests, Measurement, and Evaluation; and Urban Education.

Output

The major output is Resources in Education, a monthly abstract journal announcing recent report literature related to the field of education.

Availability

The abstract journal is publicly available by subscription from GPO. Most of the documents cited in Resources in Education are made available for purchase at a low cost in microfiche. Paper copy is available at the approximate cost of reproduction.

WATER RESOURCES SCIENTIFIC INFORMATION CENTER (WRSIC) (Dept. Of Interior)

Purpose

The system disseminates scientific and technical information to the water resources community through a variety of services, including a twice-monthly abstracting bulletin, an annual catalog listing of ongoing projects, topical bibliographies, state-of-the-art reviews, and computer searches.

Input

The system contains data from state water resources institutes, water-related U.S. agencies, "centers-of-competence" in universities and elsewhere, secondary abstracting services, and foreign governments on exchange agreements. Input is in the form of abstract-index worksheets executed to WRSIC specification and accompanied by original document.

Content

Content includes abstracted and indexed information dealing with water-related aspects of the life, physical and social sciences, as well as related engineering and legal aspects of the characteristics, conservation, control, use or management of water. It covers 1968 to the present, although earlier permanently valuable works are included. The coverage is worldwide, with English-language material predominating. The printed file is updated semimonthly; the machine-readable counterpart is updated monthly.

Output

Output includes the Abstracting Bulletin (twice monthly, printed and machine-readable/searchable); indexes accompanying abstracting bulletin; special bibliographies (irregularly printed); catalog (annual, printed and machine-readable/searchable); computer searches (on demand, printout); and state-of-the-art reviews.

Availability

The products are publicly available.

COMPUTER-ASSISTED LEGAL INFORMATION STORAGE
AND RETRIEVAL (JURIS) (Dept. of Justice)

Purpose

Since 1970 the Department has been developing its own computerized legal research system (JURIS) for use by attorneys of the legal divisions and U.S. Attorneys Offices. The system provides fast, comprehensive, and incisive retrieval of case law, statutory law, and internal Departmental work product. Attorneys use this capability to prepare pleadings, briefs, legal memoranda, and other legal documentation in the normal course of carrying out departmental program responsibilities.

Input

The data base comes from: 1) Case Law-Retrospective materials were keyed initially from reported-decision bound volumes; update materials are now obtained mainly from West Publishing Company as a byproduct of the publication process. 2) Statutory Law—materials are keyed from hardcopy source materials such as United States Code, Public Laws, and CFR titles. 3) Other materials are obtained from a variety of sources such as briefs, legal memoranda, and the like.

Content

Data base records consist of the full text of legal opinions and statutory materials, as well as certain digest materials.

Output

Output consists of citations and listings of cases and full text created on an ad hoc basis by system users.

Availability

Output is not publicly available because of the expense and contractual restrictions on dissemination of data held under license.

NATIONAL CRIME INFORMATION CENTER (NCIC)
(Dept. of Justice)

Purpose

This system provides information, on-line, to criminal justice agencies concerning wanted persons, missing persons, stolen property, and computerized criminal histories.

Input

The central processing unit and data storage devices are located within the FBI headquarters, Washington, D.C. Input and retrieval performed via federal, state, and local computer/terminal interfaces with the FBI computer. Input includes entries, updates, clears, and cancellations, as well as inquiry capability, relating to NCIC records.

Content

NCIC serves criminal justice agencies in the 50 states, the District of

Columbia, Puerto Rico, and Canada. Updates to the NCIC files are performed on a 24-hour-a-day on-line basis. This system contains information on criminal careers and permits users to track arrested subjects through the criminal justice system to assess how well the system works.

Output

Output consists of on-line formatted responses. The output medium is dependent upon capability of computer and terminal equipment accessing the NCIC computer.

Availability

Documented information can be directly accessed by criminal justice agencies and disseminated in accordance with 28 U.S.C. 534 and Public Law 92-544, 86 Stat. 1115.

NATIONAL CRIMINAL JUSTICE REFERENCE SERVICE (NCJRS)
(Dept. of Justice)

Purpose

The service was established by the Law Enforcement Assistance Administration during fiscal year 1973 to collect and disseminate literature of interest to the Nation's law enforcement and criminal justice community. The National Criminal Justice Reference Service System (NCJRSS) is the automated system designed to support the NCJRS.

Input

The primary system input is abstracts of documents on law enforcement and criminal justice. The automated system also maintains information on registered NCJRS users including name, address, classification, category, profile, and mailing list control data.

Content

The integrated data base consists of six files: 1) Documentation Data Base—information (bibliographic information, indexing terms, annotation, and abstract) on all active documents in the NCJRS information system; 2) User File—information on registered NCJRS users (name, address, classification, category, profile, and mailing list control data); 3) Selected Notification Information (SNI) Statistics File—information on the extent to which users have used the SNI service; 4) Thesaurus File—a computer file representing the controlled list of descriptors and their structural interrelationships; 5) LLBC File—information on selected holdings of the libraries at LEAA, Drug Enforcement Administration, Bureau of Prisons, and NCJRS; and 6) JURIS II Data Base—the documentation data base restructured for remote search and retrieval capability.

Output

As selected new documents are entered into the data base, NCJRS employs the user profile to determine which users might be interested in the new document. For each potentially interested user NCJRS produces a card on which appears an abstract of the document along with information pertaining to the source of the document where such information is available. The cards are then mailed to the potential users. NCJRS can query the automated data base mentioned above by communicating a question to a staff of referral specialists. With the assistance of the NCJRSS query capability, the referral specialists will compile a response to the query; depending on the nature of the query, the response may be merely a list of resource materials or it may also include documents.

Availability

The service is available to the public, and its use is encouraged within the criminal justice community. Individuals, organizations, and agencies can register with NCJRS by filling out a registration form. Based on this form, a user profile which specifies a user's area of interest is established.

EXCHANGE VISITOR INFORMATION SYSTEM (EVIS)
(Dept. of State)

Purpose

The system was mandated by the National Security Council Decision Memorandum Number 143, which required the development and operation of a central information system on exchanges from all agencies. The system is designed to collect information on the foreign component of the exchange program. It provides reports on all foreign nationals who are sponsored by Government agencies and/or private organizations/institutions or businesses and permits coordination of the overall exchange visitor program. The system will also provide name lists for a central locator system of exchange visitors. Approximately 60,000 exchange visitors enter the United States yearly.

Input

The primary source of information is the program sponsor through the use of a visa document identified as the DSP-66. These sponsoring agencies and organizations represent Government programs (G Series) such as state, AID, USIA, other U.S. Government agencies, and international organizations and private programs (P Series) broken down by academic institutions, hospitals, nonprofit organizations and businesses. There are about 1800 program sponsors throughout the United States.

Content

Information on each visitor includes: 1) Biographical information—name, sex, birthdate, country of residence, and position (primary occupation at home); 2) program information—type of program (new, extension, transfer of program); program number (which identifies the sponsoring institution); length of program (stay in the United States under program sponsorship); visitor category (student, trainee, etc.); subject/field of activity of visitor while in United States; 3) funding information—sources of financial support to be provided to the visitor and amount(s) of support provided; and 4) program status—date of entry, extension, or transfer (INS stamp-date). At this time there is one complete activity year period automated (July 1, 1974—June 30, 1975). This system currently reports foreign nationals from Western Europe (24 countries), Eastern Europe (7 countries), East Asia (24 countries), Near East and South Asia (26 countries), Latin America (30 countries), and Africa (41 countries). There is no U.S. geographic recording of states beyond identification of program sponsor and its address. It is anticipated that new documents will be input seven times a year, with a possible streamlining to five times a year.

Output

Reports are produced periodically or on an ad hoc basis. Reports are either statistical or biographical. They are either produced on-line or off-line depending on the nature and length of the report. Statistical reports include country analysis; program sponsor types (by various data-fields); field of activity (by country, sponsor, or area); and occupation (by country, sponsor, or area). Name lists include lists by program sponsor, country, and year.

Availability

Reports are publicly available.

FATAL ACCIDENT REPORTING SYSTEM (FARS)
(Dept. of Transportation)

Purpose

This system is designed to collect data for research and analysis of the accident environment. The accident environment includes information about the accident scene, all vehicles, and all persons physically involved in the accident. This information is used to identify problem areas such as conditions which are present in fatal accidents or which contribute to the occurrence of the accident. The information is also used to evaluate the effect of safety counter-measure programs and of improvements to the highways or vehicles. Trends over time or emerging patterns can be detected and their significance analyzed.

Input

FARS is a computerized file which can be easily accessed by means of statistical packages such as Table Producing Language (TPL) and Statistical Package for the Social Sciences (SPSS). Its sources consist of police accident reports, driver's license files, registration files, vital statistics files, and highway department files.

Content

Information on all fatal accidents occurring in the 50 states, the District of Columbia, and Puerto Rico is contained in the file. It contains about 250,000 records for approximately 40,000 fatal accidents. The file is updated monthly until it is complete. The FARS data files are on-line. The FARS data may be accessed by the highway safety community or the public in general through the National Highway Traffic Safety Administration.

Output

Quarterly and annually, FARS 76 Statistical Summaries are issued in hardcopy.

Availability

Reports are for internal use only.

AUDIT MANAGEMENT INFORMATION REPORTING SYSTEM (AMIR) AND AUDIT INFORMATION MANAGEMENT SYSTEM (AIMS) (Dept. of the Treasury)

Purpose

The systems were designed to provide Audit national office and field managers with statistical data to measure examination accomplishments and monitor tax returns in inventory.

Input

The data in the Audit Information Management System (AIMS) data base are derived from input through terminals in the district and service center Audit Divisions.

Content

The data base is updated daily. Tape extractions from the data base are made monthly for the Audit Management Information Reporting System, District Review Reporting System, Service Center Audit Division Reporting System, Discriminant Function Reporting System, and Tax Change Distribution Reporting System. There are over 50 data elements on the extraction tape for each record including name of taxpayer, type of return, tax period, activity code (asset class), source, status, disposal code and date, audit results, examiners grade and series, examination time, examination technique, audit issue code, preparer of return name and EIN, grade of case, type of review and review time, principal issue code, fraud, claim, age of return, and age of claim.

Output

The system produces hardcopy and microfiche reports. The major reports produced under each of the following systems are: Audit Management Information Reporting System-Plan vs. Accomplishments and Inventory of Returns by Status vs. Audit Examination Plan (monthly) ... There is no on-line query capability for statistical data.

Availability

Some statistical output is available to the public in accordance with the Freedom of Information Act; 5 U.S.C. 552; however, output which identifies taxpayers and contains return information is provided from disclosure by 26 U.S.C. 6103 and cannot be made available.

AMATEUR RADIO SERVICE (SHZ)
(Federal Communications Commission)

Purpose

The system is for accurately maintaining an automated data base through validating input data, creating new records, assigning call signs, applying changes to current records, and producing statistical reports. By efficiently executing the above functions, this system is capable of processing applications and issuing licenses.

Input

The data are derived from the Application for Individual Amateur Radio Station and/or Operator License, Form 610, and the Application for Alien Amateur Radio Licensee for Permit to Operate in the United States, Form 610-A.

Content

This system's weekly cycle produces licenses as well as transaction error listings and an update transaction tracking list. Work is continuing on improving the efficiency of this system in order to expedite processing.

Output

Selected reports are generated semiweekly, weekly, monthly, and annually both in hardcopy and microfiche. Generally, the reports reflect amateur licenses and associated call signs and depict both statistical and cumulative data.

Availability

All output is publicly available through the FCC Public Reference Room or NTIS.

NASA LIBRARY NETWORK (NALNET)

Purpose

NALNET is a cooperative effort by the NASA libraries located at headquarters and 11 research centers, to provide expanded and improved products and services while achieving the economies of centralized indexing, cataloging, and computer processing. The network offers direct on-line access for search and identification to a computerized data base of citations to over 180,000 books and 6000 journals located at the various libraries. Products include printed union lists of books and periodical holdings, local book shelflists, catalog cards, and indexed book catalogs on COM. With a broad scope of coverage of publications related to aeronautics and space research, earth resources, energy, and other NASA research and development topics, NALNET is primarily for the use of NASA professionals and libraries; but searches are also made for NASA Industrial Applications Centers to assist in technology spinoff.

Input

The NALNET data bank input consists of bibliographic records of books received by the NASA libraries after 1968, all journal titles and selected citations from the Library of Congress Machine Readable Catalog. Book and journal records of the American Institute of Aeronautics and Astronautics will shortly be incorporated into the network.

Content

NALNET subject content covers the broad interests of NASA research and development, management, data processing, and other aspects of aeronautics and space technology and all the sciences related to space studies or the needs of space exploration, including geology, medicine, engineering, electronics, and biology.

Output

On-line identification and search via CRT display is possible. Computer-printed catalog cards; union book and periodicals listings; local current book accession lists; local book shelflists and surplus lists; and local indexed catalogs are also generated. Searches may be made by title, author, Library of Congress or NASA terms, National Library of Medicine terms, LC card numbers, various classifications, corporate sources, and report numbers.

Availability

Data are primarily for the use of NASA libraries, but searches are made for the NASA Industrial Application Centers to assist in technology spinoff.

RESERVE OFFICERS INFORMATION BANK (ROIB)
(Selective Service System)

Purpose

The system is to provide data on currently assigned officers and warrant officers of the Reserve and National Guard assigned to the Selective Service System and former officers and warrant officers.

Input

The data are compiled from military personnel records as used by the members' parent service, data furnished by the members themselves, and the results of correspondence courses.

Content

This system contains a variety of information relating to selection, placement, and utilization of military personnel. The system also contains information about members such as name, rank, social security account number, date of birth, physical profile, residence and business addresses, and telephone numbers. Information is also recorded on unit of assignment, occupational codes, training, cost factors, efficiency ratings, and mobilization assignments and duties.

Output

ROIB reports fall into eight major categories, with several specific reports within each category: information input, strength reports, mobilization reports, financial reports, inspection reports, exception reports, locator reports, and miscellaneous. All reports are computer printouts. The physical reports are the Monthly Strength Report, the Quarterly Financial Summary, the Quarterly Unit Report, the Quarterly Drill Attendance Report, the Unit Commanders' Reports, the Military Correspondence Course Report, and the Mobilization Locator Roster.

Availability

Information in these records may be used by Agency officials for purposes of review in connection with appointments, assignments, promotions, and determining qualifications of individuals. Information is also exchanged with an officer's parent service upon official request.

SMITHSONIAN SCIENCE INFORMATION EXCHANGE, INC. (SSIE)

Purpose

SSIE operates and maintains a national data base of information on research in progress. The Exchange attempts to provide as comprehensive and timely an information resource as possible in order to assist the Nation's research community in avoiding unwarranted duplication of research, enhancing scientific communication, and improving research management.

Input

Notices of Research Project (NRP) are collected from more than 1300 organizations which support or conduct research. These include all agencies of the federal government as well as major foundations, fundraising organizations, universities, and state and local governments. Some foreign organizations which support research in areas of high national concern, such as cancer and energy, also register their research with SSIE on a regular basis.

Content

Each NRP provides information on "who" is conducting "what" research, "when" and "where" the research is intended to be carried out, and under "whose" support. Project records in the system cover research being conducted in every state in the union. They are updated annually and are retained on file for up to two years after completion. Some 120,000 project descriptions are processed into the data base each year. These cover basic and applied research in all areas of the life, physical, social, behavioral, and engineering sciences. SSIE project descriptions are prepared in most cases by principal investigators. Each NRP contains a brief technical summary of the work to be performed in addition to essential administrative information such as project title; principal and co-investigator names; period covered by the project records; names of performing and supporting organizations; performing organization addresses; and, in some cases, project funding.

Output

SSIE produces published information products in the form of inventories of ongoing research in specific fields of sciences such as cancer research, water resources, and environmental research. Some of these are compiled on an annual basis. All are made available to the public through either the Government Printing Office or the National Technical Information Service. The Exchange offers access to subsets of the data base in magnetic tape form under individual leasing arrangements. SSIE also conducts searches of the file in specific areas, by subject, performing or supporting organization, or any combination of subject and administrative search criteria. These searches are performed for a modest fee. The data base is also available for on-line access through the SDC Search Services offered by the System Development Corporation.

Availability

All SSIE products and services are publicly available at published fees.

FILM-TV INVENTORY AND CATALOG SYSTEM
(United States Information Agency)

Purpose

The Motion Picture and Television Service (IMV) is engaged in supplying films and TV programs to USIA posts throughout the world. Each year about 500 new titles are acquired for distribution. The computer system is designed to collect, inventory, and catalog data concerning these titles and their distribution and to retrieve it in useful listings and catalog formats.

Input

The data contained in the data file are derived from internal sources. Information to update the system is sent to the Computer Services Center (IOA/FD) in two forms—paper tapes from automatic writing machines, which also print the Program Products Orders and Film Shipment Notices, and input forms supplied by IOA/FD on which IMV records details concerning titles, post inventory changes, catalog data, and codes used in the system.

Content

Ten or eleven post inventories are printed out each month so that each post receives an up-to-date listing annually. The inventory shows all titles owned by the post except those of a "dated" or "restricted" nature; that is, all titles for which the post is held accountable. The post is responsible for reporting any changes in its inventory and the reasons for the change. Post catalogs are produced with the same schedule for post inventories. Each post catalog contains all titles in the post inventory except those which have been retired by the Agency. A master catalog, containing all titles available for use abroad, except those which are "dated" or "restricted" is produced annually as soon as possible after the close of the fiscal year. The retired title file is updated annually with titles which the Agency retired during the preceding year.

Output

The system produces 22 hardcopy reports on a monthly, annual, and as-requested basis. Principal reports include the following: Post Inventory Listing, Post Catalog Subject Matter, Listing and Subject, Annual List of "Dated Titles," Retired and TV Inventory, Retired Title Report, Master Catalog Alpha Report, IMV Product Distribution Report, Master Title Report, and IMV Country/Language Tables.

Availability

These are for internal use only.

MONTHLY CATALOG OF UNITED STATES GOVERNMENT PUBLICATIONS (Government Printing Office)

Purpose

This system provides tape for printing the Monthly Catalog of United States Government Publications in accordance with Section 1711, Title 44, United States Code.

Input

Catalog entries are prepared in a standard cataloging format from publications received in the Library Division. The entries are then entered into an on-line computer at the Ohio College Library Center (OCLC), where a tape of input and catalog cards is prepared and mailed.

Content

Each new entry is added to the data base where the information is available to all members subscribing to the OCLC system. Various networks covering hundreds of libraries across the country are members. While the data base is continually being updated by the member libraries, the monthly catalog prepared from the tapes covers only the material input by GPO during the previous month. The data base includes non-Government as well as Government publications. The cataloging follows the Anglo-American Cataloging Rules and Library of Congress main entries. Subjects are derived from Library of Congress Subject Headings.

Output

A monthly catalog is issued in hardcopy only.

Availability

The monthly catalog is sold by GPO to the public as well as distributed free to the depository libraries. The catalog tape records in MARC II format will be available from the Cataloging Distribution Service of the Library of Congress in April, 1977.

BIBLIOGRAPHY

Federal Information Sources and Systems. A Directory Issued by the Comptroller General as of December 31, 1976. 1977 Congressional Sourcebook Series. (Washington, D.C.: U.S. Government Printing Office [1976]).

Fry, Bernard M. *Government Publications: Their Role in the National Program for Library and Information Services.* (Washington, D.C.: National Commission on Libraries and Information Science, 1978).

U.S. Government Organization Manual. (Washington, D.C.: Office of Federal Register, n.d.).

Appendix C

Perceptions of Networking:
A Compilation of Official Resolutions
Relating to Network Issues Adopted by
Delegates at the Pre-White House Conference
on Libraries and Information Services

Jan Alexander, Assistant Executive Director
Indiana Cooperative Library Services
  Authority (INCOLSA)
Indianapolis, Indiana

Debora Shaw, Project Manager
On-Line Union List of Serials Project
Indiana University Libraries
Bloomington, Indiana

INTRODUCTION

The importance of networking to the library community is reflected in the resolutions of the Governors' Conferences on Libraries and Information Services held in preparation for the White House Conference on Libraries and Information Services. The officially adopted resolutions from 37 pre-White House Conferences on Libraries and Information Services* including the conference on Indian Library and Information

*The 37 conferences included: Alaska, Arizona, Connecticut, Delaware, Florida, Georgia, Hawaii, Illinois, Indiana, Iowa, Kansas, Maryland, Massachusetts, Michigan, Minnesota, Mississippi, Montana, Nebraska, Nevada, New Hampshire, New Jersey, New Mexico, New York, North Carolina, North Dakota, Ohio, Oklahoma, Oregon, Pennsylvania, Tennessee, Texas, Virginia, Washington D.C., West Virginia, Wisconsin, Indian Library and Information Services on or Near Reservations.

Services on or Near Reservations were reviewed in preparing this compilation.

Each conference produced at least one resolution that addressed networking at some level, i.e., local, state, or national. In the aggregate, these networking resolutions range from specific, immediate problems and program developments to broader, more philosophical issues that libraries and librarians will face as networks evolve.

In some cases, the resolutions are concerned more with interlibrary cooperation than with networks as a specific instance of such cooperation; these resolutions have been included in this analysis.

METHODOLOGY

For this compilation of networking issues, resolutions relating to cooperation and networking at the local, state, and national level were extracted from the full set of conference resolutions. These resolutions are presented in two groups, national and state/local. Each resolution is identified with the name of the state or territorial conference from which it came.

As will be seen the resolutions vary greatly in style, length, and detail; no attempt was made to edit these into a consistent format, rather, the exact language of each resolution has been preserved.

The resolutions have been grouped under the following broad headings:

National	*State/Local*
National Network Design	Cooperation Between Schools and Other Libraries
Interfacing with a National Network	
Funding	Cooperative Demonstration Projects/Studies
National Information Policy	
Research and Library Technology	Network Establishment
Program Suggestions	New Technology
	Interfacing with a National Network
	Funding
	Potential Network Participants
	Program Suggestions

Since some of the conference reports were distributed in late Spring, 1979, it has not been possible to include all states. The missing resolutions are from: Alabama, Arkansas, California, Colorado, Idaho, Kentucky, Louisiana, Maine, Rhode Island, South Carolina, South Dakota, Utah, Vermont, Washington, Wyoming, Puerto Rico, Guam, and the Virgin Islands.

NATIONAL NETWORKING ISSUES

National Network Design

Several of the conferences adopted resolutions advocating the creation of a national library and information service network. These resolutions identified the following agencies as having some responsibility for the network design and development: The National Commission on Libraries and Information Science, The Library of Congress, Council on Computerized Library Networks, state library agencies, existing state and multistate networks and special advisory committees.

For want of a better term we have called these resolutions relating to national network "design," although, as will be seen, the resolutions tend to be general and not specific with respect to how the network would actually operate.

Connecticut. Be it resolved that with the aid of the federal government and with the utilization of new technology, each state create a basic resource center or regional centers for use by all libraries in the United States to provide universal delivery and borrowing privileges with a goal of forming a national library network.

Delaware. Resolved: The Library of Congress shall be designated as the National Library with the responsibility for a nationwide coordinated information network.

Hawaii. We recommend that the federal government develop and help fund a program for the sharing nationally of library resources within each state, with minimum standards for a state's entry into a national information network, based on criteria requiring formalized communication among that state's libraries, an indication of effective mechanism for sharing of their services and resources, and with procedures to guarantee equitable distribution to all citizens.

Whereas the function of the Library of Congress is to serve the information needs of the U.S. Congress, and

Whereas the Library of Congress has become the National Library by default.

Be It Resolved: That the U.S. Congress recognize the Library of Congress as a National Library through legislation and to direct the national library to assume the role of national leadership (such as bibliographic and cataloging services) and to establish a national computerized data bank service.

Illinois. The Illinois White House Conference recommends that a national library and information services network be developed, utilizing the most advanced technology available, to serve the information needs of citizens by facilitating improved resource sharing.

Indiana. Be It Resolved, That at the White House Conference the following issues be addressed:
- The desirability of a nationwide library video system
- The national library network be developed as a cooperative allowing input from all types of libraries and all regions of the country
- A national effort be made to acquire, care for, and make available for use, the manuscript (unpublished) materials that are important for every locality.

Maryland. Be it resolved that the Congress of the United States formally recognize the role of the Library of Congress as the primary national library of the United States, and that the Congress support, through adequate funding, LC's leadership in such essential initiatives as the national serials program center, the national network and the national preservation program.

Be it resolved that the federal government plan, develop, and implement a nationwide network of library and information service along the lines proposed by the National Commission on Libraries and Information Science, provided that participation in said network is voluntary and does not infringe upon the autonomy of publicly and privately supported libraries and networks within the various states.

Massachusetts. Resolved: That health information be made available to all persons residing in the United States, and further that the National Library of Medicine's Regional Medical Library Network be additionally funded to provide access to health information for all.

Whereas: The bulk of support for library resources is at the local and institutional level, and

Whereas: Given the fact that geographic, institutional and political boundaries mean nothing to the individual seeking information.

Resolved that:
- Systematic research and planning should take place on local, regional, state and national levels for sharing resources and services
- There be adequate federal aid to encourage, support, and sustain intertype library cooperation
- Such cooperation consider existing networks and include an adequate needs assessment to avoid duplication
- Such federal aid should augment and enrich already funded programs at all levels
- Such funding be made available to individual libraries, to state library agencies and to networks themselves

Resolved: The Massachusetts Governor's Conference on Libraries and

Information Services calls for the recognition and affirmation of the role and responsibilities of the Library of Congress as the center for bibliographic control and thus an essential component in an evolving national information network.

New York. Whereas: The State of New York has been one of the leaders in the development of statewide information resources systems;

Strong and unique information resources exist within the state; and

Technical developments could significantly affect the manner in which such information resources could become accessible;

Resolved: That a committee of information specialists and information users recommend the application of technologies to the continuing development of information resources;

That a continuing program of research and development be carried out under the auspices of this committee;

That the State of New York fund investment in the further development and growth of information resource sharing networks; and

That this be undertaken by the state in concert with other states, the federal government, and individual institutions and systems.

Ohio. Provide for increased cooperation between *all* types of libraries and between libraries, community organizations and governmental agencies to share resources, reduce duplication, increase the use of technology to improve services and make them more cost-effective.

Develop a national information network for all types of libraries and information facilities, based on evaluation of present and planned networks, using advanced technology that integrates telecommunications and computers.

Pennsylvania. The Governor's Conference on Libraries and Information Services strongly recommends that the National Commission on Libraries and Information Science be funded by Congress to contract for research in library technology conducive to the efficient operation of a national library and information network; further, that support be given to the specific network of a national periodicals system as planned and approved by the National Commission on Libraries and Information Science and the concept of a national lending library for all types of printed material; and further, that the National Commission on Libraries and Information Science, the Library of Congress, the State and multistate networks, the Council for Computerized Library Networks, the State Library Agencies and the library data base centers actively work together in a cooperative spirit in the planning of the National network.

Tennessee. Whereas, networks increase user access to all types of information, and

Whereas, networking activities at a local community level are of highest importance, including school, business and professional libraries, and

Whereas, a large-scale networking system providing patterns for local development and insuring common standards is deemed a priority, and

Whereas, there is a necessity for a close communication between local and larger networking activities so that local development is consistent with the larger systems and the larger systems are responsive to local needs and priorities, and

Whereas, networking does collectively what we single libraries cannot accomplish independently,

Now, therefore be it resolved that a sharing network shall be developed and enlarged to promote cooperation among all types of libraries of all levels (networks include but are not limited to present systems such as SOLINET, regional libraries, etc.), and

Be it further resolved that volunteer organizations, suitable government units and professional organizations such as the Tennessee Library Association undertake a program of informing and educating potential participants of the networking concept and plans, through the media, etc., and

Be it further resolved that any governing body of network systems encompassing various libraries have representatives on said governing body from libraries of all levels from all sectors.

Texas. Be it resolved that interlibrary cooperation be encouraged among all libraries to provide for the sharing of resources, technology, skills, and evaluation so that the users will have access to any information needed in the most convenient, quick and inexpensive method.

Resolved that the Governor of Texas be requested to appoint an Ad Hoc Committee by Spring, 1979, from a list of names selected by a committee composed of five delegates to the White House Conference chosen by the presiding officer of the Texas Conference on Library and Information Services, to plan for Texas to influence developments related to the national program for Library and Information Service; to fund Texas participation; and to ensure that existing and future cooperative efforts in Texas interface with the national plan.

Florida. Whereas, Congress has affirmed that library and information services adequate to meet the needs of the people of the United States are essential to achieve national goals and to utilize most effectively the Nation's educational resources and by creating a National Commission on Library and Information Services;

Whereas, in accomplishing the purposes of a proposed national plan by NCLIS, the services and needs of all types of libraries need to be considered;

Whereas, many developments are occurring on the national level which will have an impact on library service in Florida; and

Whereas, planning on the local and state level is an essential part of our participation in the national program;

Whereas, the NCLIS has demonstrated the value and need for a national program within which current deficiencies can be corrected and future needs be addressed;

Whereas, the knowledge and experience derived from this Conference is a valuable resource;

Whereas, much information exchange and awareness of needs has resulted from this Conference;

Now, therefore, be it resolved that Florida libraries participate in planning for a national library program; and

Be it further resolved that this Conference generally endorses the Program Objectives of the National Commission and urges immediate funding and implementation.

Be it further resolved that Conference participants commit themselves to support implementation of the goals and objectives of this Conference at the local level; and

Be it further resolved that another Governor's Conference be commenced in five years to assess the progress and needs at that time.

Whereas, there is a need for a federal locus of responsibility for a national network; and

Whereas, there is a need to designate a national library;

Now, therefore, be it resolved that the Library of Congress be designated the National Library with responsibility for a national network with authority to make grants and contracts and to promote standards, but to coordinate policy under the guidance of NCLIS and functioning in a supportive and coordinative as opposed to an authoritarian and regulatory manner.

New Hampshire. Establish a locus of federal responsibility charged with implementing the national network and coordinating the national program under the policy guidance of the National Commission. This agency should have authority to make grants and contracts and to promote standards, but must be supportive and coordinate rather than authoritarian and regulatory.

National Library: That the Library of Congress become the National Library.

Mississippi. That cooperation be encouraged among information networks through coordination with the Library of Congress in order to promote the easy access to information and materials.

Arizona. Resolved, That the federal government support and develop a time-efficient and cost-effective national network of library and information services based on strengthened state resources.

District of Columbia. Formal and systematic channels should be developed to provide cooperation among all library and information services: special, public, academic, school and federal, in order to improve access to all information for all citizens.

Policy Recommendations: At the national level, the USOE or the proposed new Department of Education, as well as state legislatures, are responsible for developing channels of cooperation.

Program Recommendations: At the national level, the USOE or the proposed new Department of Education, as well as state legislatures, should examine legislation to ensure that cooperation is permissible. They should provide incentive through appropriations for cooperation, particularly by increasing funding for LSCA, Title III.

Alaska. Strongly recommends that the National Commission on Libraries and Information Science be funded by the U.S. Congress, and from other sources, to coordinate the formation of an efficient, nonprofit national library network, that the Library of Congress be designated and funded to function as the coordinator/administrator of the national network, and that state library agencies be designated and funded to function as the coordinators for each state's participation in the national network.

Recommends that compatibility of existing regional networks be encouraged in every way possible. Needless research should not be undertaken or duplication inasmuch as the essential technology already exists and research is costly both in time and money.

Every effort should be made to assure that the costs of a national network result in services to individuals needing them and that administrative costs be held to a minimum. The Alaska Conference on Library and Information Services recommends that funding to state library agencies be equally apportioned to the states since expenses associated with densely populated areas are offset by costs associated with remoteness and/or vast geographic areas.

Wisconsin. Proposed Board on Library Development and Networking devises structures for technological network.

Nevada. Resolved, That several regional resource centers be established serving separate regions of the U.S. which will facilitate interlibrary loan, make available little-used materials, and eliminate multiple library purchases of little-used materials; and

Be it resolved further, That initial funding come from the federal government while continuing support could be provided by participating libraries or user fees.

West Virginia.   Resolved that a national bibliographic retrieval system enabling all types of libraries across the country to locate information in other libraries, be established and that funds be made available to make this system work.

Iowa.   Be it resolved that the Iowa Governor's Conference on Libraries recognizes the need for a National Network for sharing of resources and information.

Georgia.   Establish a locus of federal responsibility charged with implementing the national network and coordinating the national program under the policy guidance of the national commission.

Plan, develop and implement a nationwide network of library and information services.

Encourage the implementation of library services networks at the national level.

Interfacing with a National Network

The roles of libraries, of state agencies, and of state and multistate networks in relation to a proposed national network were addressed specifically in resolutions from four conferences.

Minnesota.   Whereas, it is the right of all Minnesota citizens to have access to information they need; and

Whereas it is economically and physically impossible for any one library to contain all information, now, therefore;

Resolved, that the State of Minnesota develop "and fund for all participants a statewide multitype library network with a statewide library catalog and statewide access including borrowing privileges and/or delivery; and, that such network be compatible with national developments.

New York.   Whereas: A healthy economic environment is dependent on industry's ready access to the wealth of technical data found in the state's great libraries;

Communities need information on the availability and location of public and private human services;

Networking is the only way to assure adequate access by individuals to the research resources within the State of New York;

The technologies and techniques utilized in such systems must be shared among information professionals; and

A national library network is under development;

Resolved: The Governor shall establish an interagency committee to plan a New York State bibliographic and delivery network to interface with the national library network using computer and telecommunication technologies.

That a clearinghouse of information on networking be established; and

That legislation enable public agencies to pool their resources in a cooperative information sharing network.

Texas.   Resolved that the Governor of Texas be requested to appoint an Ad Hoc Committee by Spring, 1979, from a list of names selected by a committee composed of five delegates to the White House Conference chosen by the presiding officer of the Texas Conference on Library and Information Services, to plan for Texas to influence developments related to the national program for Library and Information Service; to fund Texas participation; and to ensure that existing and future cooperative efforts in Texas interface with the national plan.

District of Columbia.   Planning and coordination at the local, state, and national levels should be provided to ensure increased awareness of library and information resources.

Additional funding for resource development is a federal responsibility.

Locally, the city government should be responsible for establishing coordination.

At the national level, additional federal funding should be secured for resource development and document delivery, as well as the purchase of needed automation, to facilitate sharing. (LSCA-Title I, ESEA-Title IV-B, HEA-Title II-C.)

At the local level, which is especially important, an office should be established under the Mayor for coordinating the use of information resources.

Network Funding

Several conference resolutions addressed the question of network funding specifically, often recommending some level of federal support for a national library network.

Indiana.   Interaction among all types of libraries for effective sharing of technological development and resources should be strengthened in such ways as:
• Continued funding for existing cooperative networks
• Continued support of network research and development
• Increased communication to the public and the library community about the potential of technology for all types of libraries.

Maryland.   Be it resolved that the federal government and the United States Congress enunciate a clear federal policy of responsibility and appropriate the necessary funds for assisting the states and localities in providing library services adequate to meet the needs of the states, and that the federal government specifically assist states in: multitype network development; cooperative programs among libraries; providing library service for persons with handicapping conditions; and strengthening the state library agency.

Massachusetts. Resolved: That health information be made available to all persons residing in the United States, and further that the National Library of Medicine's Regional Medical Library Network be additionally funded to provide access to health information for all.

Whereas The bulk of support for library resources is at the local and institutional level, and

Whereas Given the fact that geographic, institutional, and political boundaries mean nothing to the individual seeking information,

Resolved that

- Systematic research and planning should take place on local, regional, state, and national levels for sharing resources and services
- There be adequate federal aid to encourage, support and sustain intertype library cooperation
- Such cooperation consider existing networks and include an adequate needs assessment to avoid duplication
- Such federal aid should augment and enrich already funded programs at all levels
- Such funding be made available to individual libraries, to state library agencies and to networks themselves.

Minnesota. Whereas, there are populations currently unserved or underserved by existing library systems,

Passed-Resolved, that it shall be the policy of the federal government to assist the states in the equalization of access to library and information services by the underserved population, and be it further

Resolved, that the greater protion of federal aid for such services be distributed in a block grant to an accountable agency of each state, for distribution in the state according to an approved state-developed equalization plan, and be it further

Resolved, that a lesser portion of the federal funds be designated for the establishment of national coordination of networking systems, research and development, and other functions clearly of a national interest and which local and state libraries are unable to provide.

Florida. Whereas, the possibility for achieving universal access to libraries and information services for all the people throughout the nation is much nearer realization than seemed likely even a decade ago; and

Whereas, computers and computer technology have become essential factors in library service and planning and many libraries already have applied computer technology to their programs; and

Whereas, during the next decade it seems likely that computer services will continue to expand and improve; and

Whereas, at present, the cost of such services is a limiting factor and as a rule must be borne by the user;

Now, therefore, be it resolved that libraries cooperate to fully exploit modern technology through the establishment of networks funded for all types of libraries and information agencies at the federal, state, and local levels.

Mississippi. That libraries receive increased public funding at the local, state, and federal levels to assure continued improvement and free access to library services, with these funds being used for such purposes as:

- cooperation and networking
- salaries
- collections
- accommodations for the physically handicapped
- public relations
- expansions of facilities

That public funding of private, academic, and special libraries for purposes related to cooperation and resource-sharing with public institutions be requested at local, state and national levels.

That libraries be a national priority for at least one year—that $1.00 of federal income tax return be earmarked for libraries.

New Hampshire. That federal financing be secured and relied upon as the principal source of funds for the development of regional and national networks of library and information service.

Arizona. Resolved, That equal access to a basic level of information services for all residents of Arizona should be accomplished through the implementation of the current *Minimum Public Library Standards* as recommended by the Public Library Division of the Arizona State Library Association, including networking and interlibrary loan; and

Resolved, That state and federal funding should be made available to supplement local funding to ensure equal access.

Resolved, That the Congress reinstate LSCA Title II, increase levels of funding for LSCA Titles I-V, and amend Title IV with provision for but not limited to the elderly.

District of Columbia. Networking and other uses of advanced technology should be promoted which will deliver services more efficiently and effectively.

Congress should be responsible when modernizing the provisions of the Federal Communications Act and related statutes.

Congress, when modernizing provisions of the Federal Communications Act and related statutes, should require the electronic common carriers such as telephone, telegraph, and communications satellite companies to provide discount rates for libraries and information services comparable to the library special postal rate.

Adequate federal funding should be assured for libraries and information services to develop, implement, and continue net programs begun with these resources.

Adequate federal funding is the responsibility of the Congress and the White House.

Appropriate groups should lobby the Congress and White House to support full funding of existing library legislation, and to encourage new legislation, such as that which would support the NCLIS recommendation to develop a national network, and which would support special libraries serving nonprofit institutions.

Alaska. Strongly recommends that the National Commission on Libraries and Information Science be funded by the U.S. Congress, and from other sources, to coordinate the formation of an efficient, nonprofit national library network, that the Library of Congress be designated and funded to function as the coordinator/administrator of the national network, and that state library agencies be designated and funded to function as the coordinators for each state's participation in the national network.

Recommends that compatibility of existing regional networks be encouraged in every way possible. Needless research should not be undertaken or duplicated inasmuch as the essential technology already exists and research is costly both in time and money.

Every effort should be made to assure that the costs of a national network result in services to individuals needing them and that administrative costs be held to a minimum. The Alaska Conference on Library and Information Services recommends that funding to state library agencies be equally apportioned to the states since expenses associated with densely populated areas are offset by costs associated with remoteness and/or vast geographic areas.

Wisconsin. Development and funding of national network.

Nevada. Resolved, That several regional resource centers be established serving separate regions of the U.S. which will facilitate interlibrary loan, make available little-used materials, and eliminate multiple library purchases of little-used materials; and

Be it resolved further, That initial funding come from the federal government while continuing support could be provided by participating libraries or user fees.

Kansas. Whereas, Libraries of all types must cooperate to provide optimum services to users, and such cooperation can be achieved through networks; therefore, be it

Resolved, That all library agencies are urged to participate in state, regional, and national networks, and state and federal funding should be provided to encourage such participation.

Oregon. Whereas, there is an information explosion and whereas that information is widely scattered and thus is not available to most people,

Now, therefore, be it resolved that the delegates to the Oregon Governor's Conference on Libraries call upon: U.S. Congress

To take action as follows: to provide funding for implementing a computerized information-sharing network in the United States.

With action to be accomplished by: the next congressional session.

Iowa. Whereas, the National Commission on Libraries is encouraging networking;

Be it resolved that the federal government develop a national policy and appropriate the necessary funds to encourage, support and sustain state library agencies in intertype cooperation and networking.

Georgia. We recommend that the Library of Congress study the method by which the National Library of Medicine encourages cooperation among libraries by providing grants to establish consortia. Perhaps LC should encourage cooperation among libraries stimulating interlibrary loan. We realize an act of Congress would be necessary to provide funds for additional responsibilities.

LSCA could have another title to fund interstate networks for eventual movement into national.

That certain federal funds be allocated for research and development on a national level to lead libraries into the computer age.

Begin a process of working toward providing a computer terminal in each library of whichever type, all connected to a central computer. Funding for this should come from both federal and state funds.

Suggest federal funding for such services as interlibrary loan, SOLINET; state funding for services to local areas such as bookmobiles, special collections.

National Information Policy

The need for a detailed national information policy was expressed in the resolutions from several states.

Maryland. Be it resolved that the federal government develop a national policy and appropriate the necessary funds to encourage, support, and sustain the state library agencies in intertype library cooperation and networking.

New York.   Whereas: Information is essential for all persons;
Increased use of expensive automated bibliographic data bases has led to the charging of fees; and
Budget restrictions have curtailed local library service;
Resolved: That all persons should have free access to information in publicly supported libraries regardless of its format; and
That the National Commission on Libraries and Information Science establish a National Information Policy to support funding for automated bibliographic data delivery systems.

Ohio.   Initiate a national information policy recognizing the existence of a diversity of information services and a need for: A) networks; B) national planning for growth and C) a comprehensive approach to information problems.

Texas.   Whereas, there is no clear locus of responsibility for national policies and programs dealing with one of our nation's greatest resources—information,
Be it resolved that a national library agency be created by Congress to perform such functions as
- establishment of national priorities and policies for library and information services (to include greater accessibility to information and to permit the full development of our intellectual and knowledge potential by coordinating between library and information networks and educating society to the availability of information)
- plan and coordinate programs to implement such policies
- seek funds to carry out these programs
- contract and monitor the expenditure of such funds

Arizona.   Resolved, That there be a national policy established defining the purpose and scope of libraries emphasizing the need for equal access to libraries and information services which express all points of view.
Resolved, That beyond a minimal level of service and collection in rural communities, there is an obligation to provide equal access to all users which should be in the form of a Regional Library System, adequately funded, to provide the additional services needed as a result of the demands placed upon it.

Research and Library Technology

Several conferences addressed the issues of information collection and dissemination regarding research and development of library technology. Responsibility for conducting needed research is also an issue.

Delaware.   Resolved: The federal government should continuously study the development of information storage and retrieval methods and supply this information for the guidance of libraries.

Hawaii. Be it resolved that the ALA Library Technology Report Section and other public and private agencies examine all facets of information retrieval technology and recommend standards for national adoption.

Maryland. Be it resolved that the White House Conference is encouraged to refer to the National Committee on Libraries and Information Services the appropriate information technology issues which may involve interstate and state/federal cooperation.

New York. Whereas, The State of New York has been one of the leaders in the development of statewide information resources systems;
  Strong and unique information resources exist within the state, and
  Technical developments could significantly affect the manner in which such information resources could become accessible;
  Resolved: That a committee of information specialists and information users recommend the applications of technologies to the continuing development of information resources;
  That a continuing program of research and development be carried out under the auspices of this committee;
  That the State of New York fund investments in the further development and growth of information resource sharing networks; and
  That this be undertaken by the state in concert with other states, the federal government, and individual institutions and systems.

North Carolina. Resolved: That U.S. Congress continue to support and fund existing federal library programs and that they receive forward funding. These would include: the Elementary and Secondary Education Act, and that this Act be fully funded; the Higher Education Act, especially increased funding for Titles II-A (College Library Resources) and II-C (Research Libraries); and, the Library Services and Construction Act, especially funding of Title II (Construction).
  Resolved: That the U.S. Congress should continue funding for the Library of Congress services in the area of cataloging, preservation, and technology. Also that the National Science Foundation, the National Library of Medicine, and other federal agencies continue experimental projects investigating the development and application of the new technologies to libraries.

Pennsylvania. The Governor's Conference on Libraries and Information Services strongly recommends that the National Commission on Libraries and Information Science be funded by Congress to contract for research in library technology conducive to the efficient operation of a national library and information network; further, that support be given to the specific network of a national periodicals system as planned and approved by the National Commission on Libraries and Information Science and the concept of a national lending library for all types of printed material; and further, that the National Commission on Libraries and Information Science, the Library of Congress, the state and multistate networks, the Council for Computerized Library Networks, the state library agencies and the library data base centers actively work together in a cooperative spirit in the planning of the National network.

District of Columbia. There is a need for uniform standards of communications technology which will facilitate resource sharing.

Government and the private sector should be responsible for cooperative study of the need for standards.

There is a need for a cooperative effort between government and the private sector to study the need for standards of new technology. The study should take into account the fact that stardards should not be so rigidly enforced that they prevent the participation in newer developments when technology advances.

Technology is needed in order to improve the delivery of services as well as to improve the efficiency of operations.

Professionals from government, private industry, and library and information services should be responsible for forming a coalition to deal with technology issues of mutual concern.

A new, powerful coalition of professionals from government, private industry, and library and information services should be created for the following purposes:
- To coordinate current efforts and programs of existing agencies
- To lobby on behalf of librarians in order to secure funding for new technologies
- To assess existing technology in order to be aware of all new advances
- To assure future development of new technology for all libraries
- To educate library and information service administrators about the existence of the new technologies and encourage their use

Wisconsin. National standards for technology.

Funding for research in library and information technology.

Federal programs for development and utilization of technology be coordinated.

Missouri. Resolved, That in the interest of cost effectiveness, the Missouri Department of Higher Education, in cooperation with the federal government, provide direction to encourage standardization of design of computer software and hardware systems for libraries so that they will be compatible for interlibrary service nationwide.

Georgia. Funding research in utilization of new technology to provide immediate access to information in all media formats.

Program Suggestions

Several resolutions were concerned with potential network program areas. These include not only specific technologies and services, but specific user groups which the network would serve.

Illinois. The Illinois White House Conference recommends that:
• The White House Conference on Library and Information Services designate a special task force on Native American *urban* library needs as well as reservation
• Native American institutions with unique collections should be given financial incentives for making their collections accessible to users other than their primary clientele
• Adequate special services to Native American constituents should be provided, especially the unserved
• The planning of urban Indian library services and flexible delivery systems should involve the collaboration of librarians and lay individuals representing all economic, social and educational segments of the Indian community and community agencies
• Library resources should reflect the specific geographic information needs of various Indian groups, urban as well as reservation
• Outreach programs should be initiated to recruit and finance Indian librarians in urban and reservation areas
• All library materials on Native Americans should document their 20th century accomplishments as well as those of the past
• Monies should be allocated for special workshops for educators in the use of Native American materials
• Native American bilingual materials should be made available in those regions where the groups deem them necessary
• General information banks should contain data on all Indian-White policies as a matter of historical documentation.

Indiana. The Indiana Governor's Conference on Libraries and Information Services shows its concern by resolving that in addition to the strengthening of bibliographic (identification and location) access to information resources, there must also be a corresponding strengthening of the delivery of information resources to library users and that specifically, every effort be made on behalf of library users to encourage liberal regulations and procedures for library photocopying.

Be it resolved, That at the White House Conference the following issues be addressed:
• The desirability of a nationwide library video system

- The national library network be developed as a cooperative allowing input from all types of libraries and all regions of the country
- A national effort be made to acquire, care for, and make available for use, the manuscript (unpublished) materials that are important for every locality

Minnesota. Resolved, That the federal government fund the development of national information services in order to: a) encourage and promote standards; b) make unique and major resource collections available nationwide; c) develop central services for networking; d) explore computer use in networking; e) explore and apply new forms of telecommunications; f) support research and development; and g) foster cooperation with similar national and international programs, as described in the section "Nationwide Network Concept" of the pamphlet *Goals for Action: A Summary*, published by the National Commission on Libraries and Information Science. (pp. 10-11).

Maryland. Be it resolved that the National Commission on Libraries and Information Science recommend policy to support funding to public and other publicly supported libraries for automated bibliographic data delivery systems.

Ohio. Develop regional, multitype library networks that encourage the sharing of resources, the identification of specialized needs, and the provision of effective information and referral services to individual citizens.

Pennsylvania. The Governor's Conference on Libraries and Information Services strongly recommends that the National Commission on Libraries and Information Science be funded by Congress to contract for research in library technology conducive to the efficient operation of a national library and information network; further, that support be given to the specific network of a national periodicals system as planned and approved by the National Commission on Libraries and Information Science and the concept of a national lending library for all types of printed material; and further, that the National Commission on Libraries and Information Science, the Library of Congress, the state and multistate networks, the Council for Computerized Library Networks, the state library agencies and the library data base centers actively work together in a cooperative spirit in the planning of the National network.

Wisconsin. Resolved, That the Congress of the United States adopt a plan for broader interpretation of copyright law for educational purposes.

Establish library rate schedule for telecommunication.

Missouri.   Resolved, That the conference support the establishment of a national periodicals center to be funded by the federal government.

Nebraska.   The federal government, appropriate state library agencies, networks, and local library units should assume added responsibility for facilitating the maximun use of the library resources and services.

In order to provide maximum use of library resources and information services in Nebraska, the following services, among others, should be provided:

- establishment of a statewide library card system; a national library card system should be encouraged
- a community relations person in each network who would promote library services
- utilization of commercial enterprises to facilitate delivery of library services
- expanded telephone services available to library users and libraries
- expanded services to the blind and physically handicapped through a statewide public radio network.

New Jersey.   A free National Library Card . . .

Michigan.   Whereas, Library cooperatives serving all types of libraries should be able to connect with a national information resource for immediate reference service,

Now therefore, be it resolved, that as a step toward a library information network, the experimental and successful Library of Congress hotline project, terminated by Congress for lack of funding on August 31, 1977, be re-established and expanded.

Georgia.   There should be an expansion of document delivery programs, funded by federal and/or state funds. Existing document delivery programs should not be phased out, but should be continued with federal and/or state funds.

STATE AND LOCAL NETWORKING ISSUES

Cooperation Between Schools and Other Libraries
(especially public libraries)

Several of the conferences adopted resolutions advocating cooperation between schools and other libraries. Many of these resolutions stressed cooperation should be between schools and the local public library.

Maryland. Be it resolved that the Governor's Conference on Libraries and Information Services, recognizing the differing primary responsibilities of school and public libraries, recommends and urges the State Superintendent of Schools to encourage the administrators of public libraries and school systems within the same geographic area to initiate cooperative plans in order to provide the fullest utilization of their collective resources throughout the year with special consideration being given to the needs of children and youth.

Wisconsin. Encourage cooperation between school and public libraries.

District of Columbia. It is the responsibility of the District of Columbia Government to increase cooperation between the Public School Libraries, the Public Library, and the libraries of the University of District of Columbia.

At the local level, cooperation should be increased between the Public School Libraries, the Public Library and the libraries of the University of the District of Columbia in order to capitalize on existing resources. Cooperation might extend to centralized processing and purchasing operations. School and public libraries establish formal guidelines to delineate their areas of responsibility to the students and the general population.

Illinois. Quality service to children and youth should include:
- greater school/public library cooperation
- full access to materials
- inclusion of children's and young adult materials in data bases for improved access
- equitable budgeting in public libraries for youth services

Oklahoma. Resolved, That we continue to expand our formal and informal efforts at interlibrary cooperation to provide the maximun educational opportunity for our state's children and that we explore further ideas for cooperation to avoid expensive and unnecessary duplication wherever possible.

Iowa. Whereas library networks covering the State of Iowa are necessary for the effective distribution of library service and materials and;

Whereas no formal network exists for sharing resources among area education agencies nor for sharing with other agencies such as the regional library system serving public libraries, therefore;

Be it resolved that delegates to this Conference strongly endorse state legislation and funding to enable school libraries including area education agency media centers to establish a network system for sharing among the member units and to interface with the regional public library system, such other systems as might be developed within the State, and the proposed national network.

Whereas the state agencies for school and public libraries are separate governmental units and the need exists for a coordinated program of library services;

Therefore be it resolved that the Iowa Governor's Pre-White House Conference on Libraries and Information Services recommends and urges the State Superintendent of Public Instruction and the State Librarian to encourage the administrators of school systems and public libraries within the same geographical area to initiate cooperative plans in order to provide the fullest utilization of their collective resources throughout the year and with special consideration given to the needs of children and youth.

Georgia.   Increased cooperation between public and school libraries, including coordination of summer programs.

Cooperative Demonstration Projects/Studies

Two state conferences recommended that demonstration projects/ studies be undertaken to study the feasibility of cooperation among all types of libraries.

Montana.   Whereas many of the resolutions of this Conference suggest benefits to be gained from cooperation and coordination among and between libraries and other entities; whereas testing and demonstrating the feasibility of improved cooperation and coordination would enhance knowledge of the implications involved in implementation, be it resolved that cooperative demonstration projects between all types of libraries and other specialized private and public organizations within the state be encouraged.

Connecticut.   Be it resolved that the State Library and Cooperative Library Service Units undertake a study to examine the problems encountered by private, academic, and special libraries in providing information services and sharing of resources with the public.

Network Establishment

Several of the conferences adopted resolutions advocating the establishment of statewide networks. The resolutions identified a variety of agencies as having the responsibility for the establishment of state networks. Included were state libraries, state departments of education, and special task forces.

Connecticut.   Be it resolved that the State of Connecticut adopt as a priority commitment the interconnection of existing library and information resources through automation (computerized) networks to be implemented through the six Cooperating Library Service Units.

Be it resolved that a library information network in Connecticut be developed for public and librarian use with particular attention to financial requirements of large urban libraries as statewide resource centers.

Delaware. Resolved: Delaware Division of Libraries shall develop a comprehensive computerized network for information dissemination and retrieval to satisfy the needs of all library users (state).

Hawaii. We recommend that a nonprofit corporation be created, consisting of statewide library-related and lay people to develop and coordinate information-sharing and networking activities of all library resources, to provide equal opportunity of access to public information and materials for the people of Hawaii. An initial demonstration project might well be a statewide union list of serials.

Maryland. Be it resolved that the State of Maryland continue and strengthen its efforts to analyze the development and growth of information resource sharing networks throughout the State emphasizing the aspects of 1) acquisition and 2) communication and dissemination, with particular emphasis on security and privacy considerations, and further that incentives be provided to encourage the cooperation of all affected organizations and institutions, both in the public and private sectors.

Be it resolved that the legal, administrative and fiscal means to support a statewide, multitype library network for the purpose of publicizing and delivering to all potential users the bibliographical/informational resources of the State be investigated and developed by the joint efforts of the State Department of Education and the State.

Be it resolved that the position of the State Library Resource Center be affirmed as essential to the effective functioning of a statewide network and the intent as expressed by the recommendations of the Governor's Committee on Funding of the State Library Resource Center be reexamined by the Maryland Advisory Council with a view toward an adequate formula for funding.

Be it resolved that the Division of Library Development and Services prepare and fund a series of regional programs on networking to be given prior to the White House Conference for the instruction of the general public.

Montana. Local libraries, particularly small rural libraries, are unable to achieve basic library standards because of limited funds. We believe community library services would greatly benefit from cooperation among all tax-supported libraries. Therefore, be it resolved, that legislation be enacted allowing all local government entities, including school districts and other tax-supported libraries, to coordinate or combine expenditures for library services, materials, personnel, hours, and facilities.

New Mexico. The citizens of New Mexico do not have adequate access to information resources within the state or the nation and there is an immediate need for the development of a system to improve the sharing of resources. Therefore, be it resolved that:

- The state of New Mexico support the development of a national system to facilitate the access to information through regional and state networks, working together through adherence to national standards for the exchange of information
- That this matter be addressed at the national level through federal legislation and at the state and regional levels through state legislation
- That the delegates to the New Mexico Conference on Libraries and Information Services urge the State Legislature to immediately pass legislation authorizing and appropriating adequate funds to implement a statewide computerized library system
- That a cost analysis and feasibility study be made on computerized cataloging, microfiche output from data bases and other technological innovations in order to advise small libraries of the efficiencies of these systems
- That the participation of all libraries in the state, regardless of their source of funding, should be assured
- That control remain at the state level, with a representative body at the national level being responsible for coordination and integration of regional and national systems
- That the delegates to the New Mexico Conference on Libraries and Information Services support the development of a national periodicals center

North Dakota. Whereas, library materials are available through a variety of facilities in each area of the state, but many of these facilities do not offer totally adequate resources,

Therefore be it resolved, that voluntary cooperation, coordination and communication among libraries be developed, particularly at community, county and multicounty levels.

Oklahoma. Resolved That the Oklahoma Department of Libraries initiate leadership in establishing a statewide plan which will facilitate cooperative planning and implementation of local and area library services.

Pennsylvania. The Governor's Conference on Libraries and Information Services calls for the establishment within the Department of Education of a Commission on Library Services, appointed by the Governor, to replace and assume the functions of the existing Advisory Council on Library Development. The Commission should establish policy for the State Library Agency and for the coordination of state funded cooperative programs among different types of libraries, but should not impinge on the autonomy or management of a school, special or academic library. The Conference also calls on the Governor and the Legislature to budget and appropriate funds to the State Library Agency sufficient to carry out its responsibility as a major back-up resource for other libraries in the Commonwealth and as an information source for state government, to assure that a responsible planning and evaluation arm of the State Library is established and maintained at an effective level, and to provide specialized consultant services in library technology, children's and young adult services, and academic libraries.

North Carolina. Resolved: That the State of North Carolina create, with separate and additional funding, a statewide information network, with planning and implementation to include: the appointment of a Task Force with representation from all types of libraries at the local, regional and state levels, to address planning and governance of such a network; coordination with other state efforts in resource sharing of materials, personnel and bibliographic data and networking, existing and proposed, and with similar efforts at the national level; identification of services that would be created and/or made cost effective by centralization, computerization and other new technologies; examination of the processes of library funding in North Carolina and the conditions placed on such funding in order that funding policies facilitate cooperation among all types of libraries; and, a plan to provide access at the local community level to major data bases required by citizens in the pursuit of governmental decision making, community affairs, educational opportunities, and other activities.

Arizona. Resolved, That the state support, develop and fund a time efficient, cost-effective statewide network designed to facilitate sharing of library and information services (to include special libraries) for all users based on strengthened local resources needed and regularly used by each community; and that this network should be compatible with a national network resource plan to include provisions for statewide borrowing privileges.

Resolved, That the responsibility for promoting a state network of library and information services, strengthening the existing networks, and training appropriate staff in the use of networking must rest with the Arizona Department of Library, Archives and Public Records.

Alaska. Calls on libraries, school boards, library boards, community college and extension centers, local municipalities, and state and federal agencies to create and strengthen cooperative sharing, placing responsibility for maintenance of publicly funded library equipment and materials on the borrowing library so that artificial barriers are eliminated and all people in the community have reasonable access to public resources.

Delaware. Resolved: Be it resolved that the Governor of Delaware establish a task force to promote cooperation, communication and the sharing of resources among all types of libraries within the state. This task force should be convened no later than March 31, 1979 and should include, but not be limited to, the following groups: library personnel, public officials of the state and local levels of government, representatives of the business, and other lay persons.

Minnesota. Whereas, users are best served when their information needs can be met with local resources, but recognizing that no library can contain all the information needs of its users, be it therefore

Resolved, that the purpose of statewide, multitype networks should be to supplement the holdings of the libraries of the state, recognizing the differing needs of the users of such libraries.

Iowa. Be it resolved that the Iowa legislature assign the task of coordinating, initiating and/or facilitating various cooperative efforts among all types of libraries (public, academic, school, special, private, etc.) to the Iowa State Library Commission.

Further resolved that the State Library Commission shall engage a consultant (individual or firm) of proven effectiveness in large-scale systems design to establish a network offering the greatest variety of services (including but not limited to cataloging, circulation, interlibrary loan) to the largest possible number and types of individual libraries.

Further resolved that an advisory council representative to the entire library community be established to assist the State Library Commission in the development of various cooperative efforts.

Georgia. Cooperation among different types of libraries should be stressed even more than it has been.

Recommend a state "umbrella" for all libraries in the state to further cooperation.

We recognize that a coordinating agency is needed to further cooperation between libraries. However, we are hesitant to recommend such an agency, for fear that a super-agency might drain off funds needed by libraries.

Interfacing with a National Network

The relationship of proposed state networks to the proposed national network was addressed specifically in two state conferences.

Oklahoma. Resolved, That the network(s) coordinated by the Oklahoma Department of Libraries (public, school, special, and university) interact and cooperate with the Biomedical Information Network.

Montana. The potential of automated information systems is recognized as promising. However, the rapid pace of developments in the field of automation (for the purpose of information flow) invite the possibility of unnecessary duplication in the purchase of equipment, in selection of access sites, and in staffing and staff development. In the spirit of capitalizing on the potential and maximizing efficient and effective usage of automated systems by citizens in the future and with the goal of eventually realizing in Montana a network of multipurpose information clearinghouses, be it resolved:

That state agencies, in designing and implementing statewide dissemination systems, consider existing public library networks (e.g., federations) as links to their potential clients.

That the Governor, through the Department of Administration's Communications Bureau, initiate a planning process for an integrated network to serve the state's long range needs.

That the library community (through the State Library and Montana Library Association) actively explore the role of libraries in future automated networking in the state and cause the creation of a Library Technology Advisory Committee to develop a state plan for implementing technology in Montana libraries. The committee should be composed of representatives of the Montana Library Association, the State Library, the six federations, school libraries, the College and University system, community colleges, the private academic libraries, special libraries and including lay representation by geographical area. That such a plan address itself to questions of system compatibility, cost-effectiveness, and special user needs, recognizing the unique demographic and geographic characteristics for the State of Montana. That such a plan result in concrete proposals for legislation for the Legislature convening in 1982.

Funding

Several conference resolutions addressed the question of state network funding. Some level of state support was recommended.

Maryland. Be it resolved that federal, state and local guidelines and funding be developed to provide for the establishment of demonstration models of cooperative relationships between public libraries and school media centers.

Minnesota. Whereas, a statewide multitype library network requires coordination and funding at state levels, now therefore

Resolved, that the conference recommend the legislature provide funds for establishing regional network services.

Whereas, there exists in Minnesota a vast array and quantity of valuable information resources in corporate, health, industry and business that are needed by Minnesota citizens, now therefore be it

Resolved, that enabling legislation at the statewide level be passed to encourage inclusion of corporate, industrial, and business information resources into regional and state resource sharing networks.

Whereas, state monies and federal monies supporting library and information services are currently administered and dispersed by several state agencies and boards, and

Whereas, no overall coordination of planning or program services now exists except through the imperfect and overlapping budgetary process of the legislature,

Resolved, that we urge by consolidation, designation, or creation, the establishment of a strong state agency responsible for the administration of state and federal funds for development programs and for cooperative library and information services and also charged with the development of a statewide plan in establishing priorities, policies and programs, and responsible for coordinating related federal programs on a statewide level.

New Mexico. The citizens of New Mexico do not have adequate access to information resources within the state or the nation and there is an immediate need for the development of a system to improve the sharing of resources. Therefore, be it resolved that:

- The state of New Mexico support the development of a national system to facilitate the access to information through regional and state networks, working together through adherence to national standards for the exchange of information
- that this matter be addressed at the national level through federal legislation and at the state and regional levels through state legislation
- that the delegates to the New Mexico Conference on Libraries and Information Services urge the State Legislature to immediately pass legislation authorizing and appropriating adequate funds to implement a statewide computerized library system
- that a cost analysis and feasibility study be made on computerized cataloging, microfiche output from data bases and other technological innovations in order to advise small libraries of the efficiencies of these systems

- that the participation of all libraries in the state, regardless of their source of funding, should be assured
- that control remain at the state level, with a representative body at the national level being responsible for coordination and integration of regional and national systems
- that the delegates to the New Mexico Conference on Libraries and Information Services support the development of a national periodicals center.

New York. Whereas: School district and public library media centers should share resources and services in an efficient and systematic manner; and

The community as a whole is entitled to maximal access to all library facilities and services supported by public monies;

Resolved: That school media program supervisors, BOCES (Board of Cooperative Education Services), and public libraries join in developing cooperative programs and that state funds be dedicated to plan and put into action such collaborative operations, cost-effectiveness surveys, and mechanisms to monitor benefits to patrons.

Oklahoma. Resolved, That the Oklahoma Legislature provide incentive funding for the encouragement and support of cooperative services.

Wisconsin. Support for recommendations of Task Force on Interlibrary Cooperation and Resource Sharing.

Wisconsin Interlibrary Loan Service funded to provide widest possible access for all citizens.

Adequate/stable funding for state-level resources, e.g., Wisconsin Interlibrary Loan Service, Reference and Loan Library, Milwaukee Public Library.

Georgia. SOLINET should be supported by state funds so that more libraries—especially college and public libraries that could otherwise not afford this service—would be able to join (this is especially important now that the Library of Congress is closing its card catalog).

State law needs to be changed to make it able for funding.

We recommend that funds be made available so that the regional libraries of the state may participate in SOLINET to the advantage of citizens throughout the state.

Recommend that the State legislature fund grants that would enable libraries across the board to acquire electronic equipment to meet needs of library users.

Allow state libraries to cooperate in contracting with computer services (MEDLINE, SOLINET) and to fund a jointly-used position to operate the system.

Legislation to subsidize all types of library networks; interlibrary loans. Example: SOLINET, GLIN; funds to establish new networks; to help libraries join into networks (get terminals to participate in SOLINET, GLIN, or other established networks).

Urge State of Georgia to assume fiscal responsibility for funding for the health services ILL network.

Iowa. Whereas, special libraries in Iowa have valuable collections which can contribute to total library and information services in the state and

Whereas, special libraries are increasingly willing to share their collections and services with other libraries.

Be it resolved that funding be provided throughout the State for purpose of identifying Iowa special libraries and defining their collections and

Be it further resolved that federal and state funding programs recognize the contributions of special libraries by providing fundings for services rendered.

Georgia. GLIN provides an interlibrary sharing of resources that profits citizens, students and scholars throughout the State of Georgia. In view of the many benefits of GLIN the state should provide funding to insure GLIN's continuance and expansion. We recommend that state funding should replace federal funding for GLIN network and should receive state support.

Nonprofit special libraries should be more involved in GLIN and some state funding provided for this, e.g., health, law, etc.

Legislative funding to enable GLIN and other networks to take greater advantage of technological developments.

Increased funding for a building and increased personnel for GLIN. Also increased publicity effort.

Potential Network Participants

Several resolutions addressed the issue of including special libraries in network plans.

Maryland. Be it resolved that all privately supported libraries be encouraged to become members of cooperative networks among publicly supported libraries.

Wisconsin. Health Science libraries included in state networks.

District of Columbia. Federal libraries, as part of the national network, should provide awareness of, and increased access to, their collections.

The Federal Library Committee should be responsible for establishing closer working relationships with other types of libraries.

Nationally, closer working relationships should be established by federal libraries with other types of libraries. The Federal Library Committee should coordinate an effort which would enable the federal libraries to provide increased awareness of access to collections, such as health information from the National Library of Medicine.

Locally, federal libraries should be a part of local resource sharing, since thay are a major element in the library resources of the District of Columbia. Our elected delegates should be allowed to participate in whatever conference is devised for the federal libraries.

New York. Whereas: Special libraries of New York have collections that are important to the research community;

Although over 200 special libraries are members of regional cooperative networks, up to 1000 more are not;

Membership in regional networks would provide mutual benefits to the research community and to the libraries that join them; and

The requirements and fees for special library membership in networks now deny or hinder such participation;

Resolved: That all special libraries in New York State be encouraged to become members of regional cooperative networks, and That the rules and fees governing the admission of special libraries be modified to accomplish this goal.

Indiana. Be it resolved, That library networking in Indiana continue to include all types of libraries and be governed on a cooperative basis, and that the State of Indiana continue to provide funding for statewide cooperative library services which cannot be effectively provided at the local or individual library.

Maryland. Be it resolved that each library in this state develop a statement of definition of function in relation to its place in any existing or planned library network.

Iowa. Whereas, library networks covering the State of Iowa are necessary for the effective distribution of library services, and

Whereas, Iowa has a library network of systems representing some libraries, but not all libraries; therefore,

Be it resolved that delegates to this Conference strongly endorse statewide cooperation to enable all types of libraries (public and private) to establish a system to facilitate participation in regional and statewide resource sharing and participation in the proposed National Network.

Georgia. Expand library networks to include school, institutes and special use.

New Technology

Several conferences addressed the issue of utilizing new technologies in networks. Compatibility and efficiency were also an issue.

Maryland. Be it resolved that the Division of Library Development and Services be directed to prepare and publish guidelines with technical advice on the conversion to modern technology for such library installations as electronic circulation systems and computer-output microfilm catalogs.

Wisconsin. Division for Library Services develop statewide plan to insure compatability and efficiency in use of technology.

North Carolina. Resolved: That the State Library establish a committee to evaluate new technologies and set standards for computer, video, and other hardware, as well as information retrieval systems (software) and micrographics. Further, that this committee should be composed of members with library, information science, and technological backgrounds, and that this committee coordinate its activities with those already in existence (e.g., the Governor's Task Force on Public Telecommunications).

Resolved: That the State Library conduct demonstration projects (i.e., long-term feasibility studies or cost-benefit analyses) that will exemplify the advantages brought by technological advances in the library field to the State of North Carolina. Such projects to include but not limited to: a prototype automated library center; on-line information retrieval; uses of public television; and, uses of cable television.

Georgia. Explore new technology to deliver materials and/or information to patrons at faster rate.

Program suggestions

Several resolutions were concerned with potential network programs.

Maryland. Be it resolved that the Maryland State Board for Higher Education encourage the research libraries of the state to work together to identify areas for responsibility in collection development so that unnecessary duplication of expensive, little-used research material can be avoided.

Minnesota. Whereas: it is impossible for any library/library system to build complete collections in rapidly growing subject fields and in the many formats in which they are available, and:

Whereas, the anticipated inflation of prices for all materials, services, salaries, etc. is ongoing and expected to continue;

Whereas, the information explosion promises astronomical increases in the amount of information produced in the future;

Resolved, that a statewide plan for cooperative collection development be adopted both in terms of existing collections (both within and outside the state) and the identification of needs for subject collections.

Hawaii. That children and young adult materials be included in national data banks and cooperative library networks.

Minnesota. Whereas, it is the right of all Minnesota citizens to have access to information,

Resolved, that the state support the development of a statewide data base for all library materials available to the public in all types of libraries and information agencies in Minnesota.

North Dakota. Whereas, access to computerized data bases would be a great benefit to the citizens of North Dakota;

Therefore be it resolved: The North Dakota Governor's Conference on Libraries and Information Services endorse the provision of this additional service to all citizens of the state through the state library network.

Illinois. Quality service to children and youth should include:
- greater school/public library cooperation
- full access to materials
- inclusion of children's and young adult materials in data bases for improved access
- equitable budgeting in public libraries for youth services.

Georgia. Not every public library should have a terminal, but all would have access via telephone.

Recommend the development of an information retrieval service to which regional libraries would have access via computer terminals, such as the New York Times data base.

Connecticut. Be it resolved that the State of Connecticut continue to expand the interconnection of library and information resources through expansion of the Connecticut library delivery system to include all types of libraries, based on the needs identified by the six Cooperating Library Service Units.

Hawaii. It is recommended that the State with federal assistance in funds

- Support the production of bilingual and nonprint materials to ensure wider participation among library users
- Support programs that conduct grassroots workshops to encourage a wider base of community participation in the selection and production of culture-related materials
- Set up an efficient, easy and speedy network for interlibrary loan of materials.

Illinois. The conference recommends establishing the right of all citizens to easy access to all resources contained in all information centers, which might require:
- universal library card
- information provided by mail delivery, home delivery, visiting librarian, bookmobile, telephone ordering, and home computer terminal
- on-site union catalog and bibliographies
- access to national information data bases
- balanced copyright laws.

Maryland. Be it resolved that the State of Maryland delegation to the White House Conference support research and development concerning the needs for, uses of, and access to information; and continuing interaction between suppliers and users in the application of existing and future technologies and systems to the delivery of library and information services.

Be it resolved that the Division of Library Development and Services assist local educational agencies in developing or furthering the development of effective interlibrary loan programs.

Wisconsin. Improve interlibrary loan for more equal access for all citizens.

North Carolina. Resolved: That interlibrary loan is a basic service in all libraries and should be available to every citizen in the state, and that more expeditious delivery alternatives and coordination of services among regional, county, municipal, special, academic, and school libraries be explored by the State Library.

Georgia. Develop systematic method for dissemination and implementation of research findings.

Implement SOLINET as rapidly as possible in bibliographic service for interlibrary loans.

Establish regional reference networks for all of the libraries in the State of Georgia. This would include school, public and academic libraries.

Accelerate efforts of the profession toward cooperative sharing of resources to avoid a hierarchy that will impede effective services to users.

Statewide information service involving special libraries and referral information.

Connecticut. Be it resolved that adequate regional warehouses be set up to house materials which are removed from libraries to relieve space problems.

North Carolina. Resolved: That consideration be given to the establishment of a state-supported depository for the storage of materials that are used infrequently that would be available for use by all types of libraries, both public and private.

Resolved: That in order to aid programs of preservation and restoration, a statewide cooperative preservation and restoration program be initiated, and that this program be coordinated with national and regional conservation efforts. Also, that the problems of preservation be brought to the attention of the publishing industry in an effort to improve its methods and materials.

Indiana. Procedures for use by the public of library facilities—joint use by interlibrary use card—wherever public funds are utilized.

We recommend the development of a systemwide library card good at all units of the university system (perhaps for a nominal annual fee) entitling the holder to check materials out of any unit of the system and return to any unit.

We recommend the development of a statewide public library card which would give the possessor the privilege to borrow from any library in the state. A fee might be charged for this service.

Be it resolved, that a study commission be established to examine the feasibility of a statewide library video system.

Connecticut. Be it resolved that the statewide telephone reference service known as Library Line have the hours of service and staff restored to at least its 1976/77 level.

Oklahoma. Resolved. That funds should be provided to establish a statewide telephone network to connect information and referral centers to all communities.

Delaware. Resolved: A computerized union catalog should be developed for Delaware, to include all library materials (State).

Hawaii. Whereas a comprehensive listing of all the holdings of all libraries in Hawaii does not exist and Whereas such a listing would be helpful to users of the library system, now, therefore, Be it resolved, that the Office of Library Services prepare a list of the holdings of all the libraries in Hawaii and make such a list, also known as a union catalogue, available in every library.

Resolved that the Governor direct the State Library (system) and the University of Hawaii Library jointly form a Hawaii State Bibliographic Center for the purpose of establishing a union catalogue of all holdings in libraries, public and private, in the State, and to serve as the interlibrary loan agency for borrowing materials within and without the State.

Montana.   Whereas, there is NO comprehensive union catalog of Montana library holdings; and whereas, the Montana State Library should be responsible for creating such a catalog and charged with integrating the catalog with any existing computerized list of Montana and/or regional holdings. Therefore be it resolved that the Montana State Library Commission charge the Montana State Library with the responsibility for creating a union catalog of Montana library holdings, including public, school, academic and special libraries. The catalog should be input into a central data base from Federation headquarters libraries (with such libraries responsible for input of unique materials from its member libraries) and integrated with any existing computerized catalog of Montana and/or regional holdings. Further, be it resolved that the costs of these COM-catalogs be borne proportionally by the sharing libraries according to their use.

Minnesota.   Whereas, there is an increasing recognition of the necessity of sharing resources among all types of libraries; and whereas, the resources of those special libraries which serve for profit businesses and corporations in many instances constitute important resources of a specialized nature which are often unique.

Resolved, that effort be made to identify holdings and/or catalogs of these special libraries in general resource lists compiled or created at all levels (local, state, and federal) and Be it further resolved, that a mechanism be established to facilitate the equitable sharing of these holdings.

Montana.   Whereas, an index of Montana periodical references is needed and would be useful to university, secondary and elementary students, the general public, state elected officials, and employees of state agencies, a Montana periodicals index should be created and made readily available.

Appendix D

Glossary and List of Acronyms
for Library Networking

Prepared for
A Conference on Networks for Networkers

These terms have been selected to help the uninitiated decode network talk; an attempt has been made to have definitions that are useful for the nontechnical reader. Since this is an evolving field, the terminology is not yet settled and definitions are sometimes subject to controversy. Also, some definitions are in use only by some agencies. A major source for this list was "A Glossary for Library Networking" prepared under the supervision of Henriette Avram of the Library of Congress.[1] Definitions taken directly from the glossary are indicated by an asterisk*; definitions in the LC glossary not yet widely accepted but in use by LC in its own network publications have been indicated by an (LC) behind the term.

abstracting and indexing service   a service that prepares abstracts or indexes of journal articles, technical reports, etc., usually for a specific subject area, for regular distribution to subscribers.
access point (also access)   a data element used as a means of entry to a file or record; for example, a title or subject heading. See also: heading.
acronym   a word formed from the initial letter or letters of each word or major word in a compound term, commonly used in the networking and data processing fields. See the list of acronyms at the end of this glossary.
architecture   the technical structure or configuration of a system.
ASCII   American Standard Code for Information Exchange. An eight-level code for data transfer.
asynchronous transmission (also start-stop)   a mode of telecommunications transmission in which each character or small block of data is synchronized. The gap (or the time intervals) between transmitted characters may be of unequal length.

[1]DATAflow System Inc. *A Glossary for Library Networking*. Washington, D.C.: Library of Congress, 1978.

authentication (LC) certification that the data content and content designation of a given bibliographic record have been reviewed by an appropriate center of responsibility and that the record meets the established bibliographic standards of a network.

automatic message switching see: message switching.

authority control 1) the functions involved in establishing, maintaining, and using authority files. 2) a system in which the access points to a file are under control for consistency.

authority file a set of records that identifies the established or authoritative forms for headings or access points for a set of bibliographic records. Authority files include cross references from variants to the preferred forms of headings, and links from earlier to later forms and between broader and narrower terms and related terms.

authority record* a record of an individual heading in an authority file. An authority record may include heading variants, cross references to and from the headings, cataloging notes, historical information, and references to the source of a heading.

batch processing a type of computer processing in which similar operations or problems are stored and put in batches to be processed.

baud a unit of speed whereby signals are transmitted over a communications line. Commonly used to mean "bit per second," but this is true only when the signal is representing only one bit.

bibliographic citation see: citation.

bibliographic control the functions necessary to generate and organize records of library materials for effective retrieval.

bibliographic data* data representing individual bibliographic attributes of an item, typically including descriptive and subject cataloging elements, indexing elements, authority elements, and abstracts.

bibliographic information interchange format see: communications format.

bibliographic item* a uniquely identified work or part of a work.

bibliographic record* a collection of bibliographic data fields treated as one logical entity that describes a specific bibliographic item. See also: cataloging record.

bibliographic service center (LC) an organization that serves as a broker or distributor of computer-based bibliographic (processing) services. A service center gains access to national library network resources through the facilities of a bibliographic utility. It does not necessarily contribute records directly to or maintain portions of the national library network data base.

bibliographic utility (LC) an organization that maintains online bibliographic data bases, enabling it to offer computer-based support to any interested users, including national library network participants. A bibliographic utility will maintain components of the national library network data store and provide a standard interface through which bibliographic service centers and individual national library network participants may gain access to the nationwide network.

bit (derived by contracting the term "binary digit.") the smallest unit of information in the binary system. A bit is represented by a "0" or a "1" (or a "space" or a "mark").

byte a unit of data, generally eight bits.

CATV originally Community Antenna Television, also now used for Cable Television.

COM see: Computer Output Microform.

CPU see: central processing unit.

CRT terminal see: cathode ray tube.

catalog a set of bibliographic records generally under control of authority files which describes the resources of a collection, library, or network. It is the instrument by which bibliographic control is maintained and by which the relationship between individual bibliographic records can be indicated.

cataloging record* a bibliographic record that describes a specific item and relates it to other items described in the file.

cathode ray tube terminal (CRT) an input/output device which uses an electronic vacuum tube (like a television screen) to display data.

center of excellence (LC) an institution with the designated responsibility for collecting, cataloging, and providing bibliographic records for materials in special subject, geographic, or language areas. See also: resource library.

center of responsibility (LC) an organization(s) with designated responsibility for establishing and maintaining the authoritative form of data elements to be used within a network. See also: center of special authorization.

center of special authorization (LC) an organization, other than a center of responsibility, that is empowered to authenticate specific data fields in certain bibliographic records. Authentication by these centers of special authorization can be overriden by decision of a center of responsibility.

central processing unit (CPU) the part of a computer which includes the arithmetic and control unit and the internal memory.

centralized (computer) network* a computer network configuration in which one computer or a group of centrally located computers provides computing power and maintains control of application level programs and telecommunications. See also: decentralized (computer) network.

centralized processing* 1) computer processing in which one computer or a group of centrally located computers provides computing services and maintains network control. 2) a system for ordering library materials, preparing them for use, and preparing cataloging records for them in one library or agency for a group of libraries.

character recognition see OCR.

circuit switching see: line switching.

citation the set of bibliographic data needed for unique identification of an item, e.g., a reference to a journal article.

check digit one or more digits automatically generated from data and carried with the data to check the accuracy of the data in subsequent data transmission and processing operations.

clearinghouse an organization that collects and maintains information in a specialized area, monitors research and development in relevant fields, and provides referral to other relevant information sources.

common carrier regulated industries providing communication services such as telephone, telegraph and data transmission; also used for such regulated industries as trucking and bus lines.

communications carrier see: specialized common carrier.

communications computer* a special purpose computer used to control or format data transmitted between network nodes.

communications controller see: communications computer.

communications format a format for the transmission of machine-readable bibliographic data.

communications network* the physical means for a group of nodes to intercommunicate data.

computer output microform (COM) microform, including microfiche and microfilm in which the data have been generated from machine-readable input processed by the computer.

concentrator a device that connects several circuits which are not all needed at once into a smaller group of circuits to reduce the cost of transmission.

configuration* the arrangement of components or functions within a system.

connect time the actual time during which an input or output device is connected via a telecommunications link to a computer system.

conversion the process of encoding data records into a machine-readable format for computer processing. Retrospective conversion is used to describe this process when applied to a mass conversion of data existing from a previous manual operation, such as a library card catalog.

cooperative a formal or informal arrangement, usually within a relatively small geographic area, whereby libraries collectively agree to share some resource or service; generally used for those arrangements which do not involve large scale computer networks.

current awareness a system for notifying users of current documents which may be of interest to them, generally based on a pre-established, user-interest profile.

data information (e.g., numbers, letters, text) represented in a formal manner so that it can be processed, stored, manipulated, and transmitted by computers and other equipment.

data base (occasionally called data bank or data store) 1) a structured collection of data developed according to uniform standards. 2) an entire set of data available to a computer system.

data base access services see: information retrieval services.

data base management* the control processes for the formatting, inputting, storing, retrieving, modifying, and outputting of data in large computer data files.

data base management system a collection of software to manage the formatting, inputting, storage, processing, and output of data in large computer data files.

data base vendors organizations that provide access to one or more data bases for information retrieval usually through a royalty arrangement with the data base developer.

*data communication** the transfer of data from one point to another over communications channels.

*data element** a defined unit of data within a system.

data field a set of characters treated as a whole and used to store a specific kind of data, such as author information or title information.

*data link** the assemblage of communications equipment and interconnecting circuits that allows data to be exchanged between two or more stations.

data transmission see: data communication.

decentralized input a method of building a data base in which records are created and input to a common data base from cooperating libraries.

*decentralized (computer) network** a computer network configuration in which computing power and/or control functions are distributed over several network nodes. See also: centralized (computer) network.

disc drive or rotary memory a circular, metal plate with magnetic material recorded on both sides continuously rotating for reading or writing by one or more read/write heads mounted on fixed or movable arms.

*distributed (computer) processing** 1) computer processing systems in which the control functions and/or computing functions are shared among several network nodes. 2) a single logical set of processing functions implemented across a number of computers.

*distributed data bases** logically interconnected data bases or portions of data bases (indexes, locations, etc.) that reside in separate physical locations in a network.

distributed network a network configuration in which each node is connected to every other node either directly or through an intermediate node.

document retrieval the process of providing a complete copy of a relevant document (rather than a citation to the document) from a collection of documents.

down-loading capability to alter terminal software remotely from a host computer by transmitting part or all of a program over telecommunications circuits.

down-time the time period when any mechanical or electronic device is out-of-service.

duplex circuit a circuit that allows transmission of data in both directions at the same time.

EBCDIC Extended Binary Coded Decimal Interchange Code, an 8-bit alphanumeric code.

encode to translate data into a code for computer systems; the code must be machine-readable.

facsimile transmission (FAX) a system for transmission of graphic and text images in which images or pages of text are scanned and converted to data which can be transmitted and reconstructed at the receiving equipment and output on some form of paper.

fact retrieval system   a system that provides specific information in response to a search request, e.g., a specific chemical formula, rather than a citation to an information source in which the formula could be found.

field*   a specified set of contiguous characters in a record, used for a particular category of data.

file*   a collection of related records.

front end processor (also front end computer)   a subsidiary computer that performs the control and conversion functions necessary for data transmission between host computers and the communications network. See also: host front end processor, network front end processor.

full-duplex (FDX)   a system capable of transmitting data in two directions simultaneously.

full text storage and retrieval   a system in which the full text or contents of a document (in contrast to just a bibliographic description) is stored, searched, and output.

fully connected network*   a network in which each node is directly connected for communications purposes with every other node.

half-duplex (HDX)   a circuit in which data can be transmitted in both directions but in alternate as opposed to simultaneous transmissions.

hard copy   a printed, human-readable copy of machine output, sometimes also called hard copy output or printout.

hardware   the physical equipment used in information retrieval and data processing systems, such as computers, printers, terminals, etc.

heading*   the form of a name, subject, uniform title, series, etc., used as an access point to a bibliographic record or authority record.

heterogeneous (computer) network*   a network that has dissimilar host computers, such as those of various manufacturers. See also: homogeneous (computer) network.

HFEP   see: host front end processor.

hierarchical (computer) network*   a computer network in which processing and control functions are delegated to several levels of specially suited computers.

holdings data   data sufficient to identify a number of items owned by an organization, where the several items are described jointly by a single bibliographic record, commonly used with respect to serials (volumes, issues, etc.). Not to be used interchangeably with locations data.

homogeneous (computer) network*   a network with similar host computers, such as those of one model of one manufacturer. See also: heterogeneous (computer) network.

host*   a system or subsystem in a network that performs actual processing operations against a data base and with which other network nodes communicate.

host computer   the primary or controlling computer in a network or system.

host front end processor*   a front end computer at a host site. It provides the interface between the host computer and the logical network front end processor. Host front end processor functions encompass message formatting, character conversion, operating system control and input/output supervisor control.

host site*   a network location that receives communications from other network nodes, performs operations on them (via a host computer) and sends communications to other nodes.

Hz   Hertz, the frequency of a wave in cycles per second.

I/O   see: input/output.

informaton retrieval   the process of finding data in a file in response to a query, generally used for systems in which the file is accessed by computer.

information retrieval services   organizations that provide computer systems for automatic retrieval of information from one or more data bases.

input/output   1) the equipment used to enter data into and to produce data from a computer system. 2) the process of entering data or producing data from a computer system.

intelligent terminal   a terminal with hardware containing logic circuits capable of retaining a program enabling the terminal to perform certain processes independently of the computer.

interface*   the point or process that joins two system components. 1) a shared boundary, defined by common physical, signal, and logical characteristics, across which data travel. 2) a device that facilitates interoperation of two systems, as between data communications equipment and data processing equipment or terminal installations. Interfaces between computers and communications systems may be divided into various classes of functions, e.g., physical, electrical, logical, and procedural.

interstate network   see: multistate network.

intrastate network   see: state network.

item   see: bibliographic item.

K   the abbreviation for 1024 (2^{10}) which is used to state the capacity of a computer storage device.

level(s)*   relative position(s) in the hierarchical structure of a system.

library bibliographic component   (LC)   that portion of the national library network encompassing its bibliographic service system and segments of its communications system, and exclusive of the resource library system.

light pen   a pen-shaped device for direct input to a computer by passing the pen over data to be transmitted, also sometimes called a light pencil or a wand reader.

line switching*   a method of handling messages in communications networks in which a circuit path is set up between incoming and outgoing lines. See also: message switching.

link   a communications path or circuit between two nodes or points. See also: interface, data link.

locations data   information appended to a bibliographic record to indicate which libraries own the item in question; generally the library is identified in a coded form such as the Library of Congress National Union Catalog symbol.

MARC   MAchine Readable Cataloging, the communications format for the transmission of machine-readable catalog data developed by the Library of Congress.

MHz megahertz; a unit of frequency equal to one million hertz (a hertz equals one cycle per second).

MICR Magnetic Ink Character Recognition, the machine recognition of characters printed with magnetic ink. See also: OCR.

MIS Management Information System, an information system designed to aid in the performance of management functions.

message 1) a single transmission in one direction, consisting of a header and data. 2) a unit of information transmitted from one node to another on a network.

message delivery system (LC) the communications computers and network front end processors which control the transmission of messages between network hosts, and the telecommunications facilities used for message transmission. See also: message processing system.

message processing system* the host computers and host front end processors in a network that perform operations on network messages. See also: message delivery system.

message switching* a telecommunications technique in which a message is received, stored (usually until the best outgoing line is available), and then re-transmitted toward its destination. No direct connection between the incoming and outgoing lines is set up as in line switching. See also: packet switching.

micro-computer a single chip computer containing processor, memory, and input/output devices.

microsecond one-millionth of a second.

microwave electromagnetic waves in the radio frequency above 890 MHz (mega-hertz).

millesecond one-thousandth of a second.

mini-computer a low-cost, physically small, general-purpose digital computer.

modem* (also called data set), modulator-demodulator: a device that modulates and demodulates digital signals so that they may be transmitted over an analog communications transmission medium, such as a telephone line.

multiplex a method of communication in which a common channel is split into more channels by splitting the frequency into narrower bands, each of which constitutes a channel (frequency division), or by allocating the channel by time (time division).

multiprocessing the simultaneous execution of two (or more) computer programs (sequences of instructions) by a computer or the computer network.

multistate network a network serving two or more states.

multitype network* a network that serves more than one type of organization, such as a library network with both academic and special libraries as participants. This refers to types of network participants and not to geographical coverage.

nanosecond one billionth of a second.

national bibliographic center (LC) an organization that provides bibliographic control at the national level, contributing bibliographic records and authority records to the national library network data base.

national bibliographic control* 1) the systematic and nationally coordinated organization and provision of bibliographic data on all materials available in the nation's libraries. 2) a subsystem of the universal bibliographic control system.

national library and information service network a proposed system to facilitate access to the nation's library and information resources. In one proposed configuration, the network would consist of three coordinated parts: a resource system, a bibliographic service system, and a communications system.

national library network (also nationwide library network) 1) a nationwide network linking libraries. 2) in one proposed system, the library-oriented components of the national library and information service network, in all three of its proposed parts: bibliographic, resource, and communications. The national library network will include the contributors to the national library network data store, and will encompass several hierarchical levels: centers of responsibility, centers of special authorization, bibliographic utilities, and bibliographic service centers, or major resource libraries. In this proposed concept, the national library network is expected to provide services to support the identification of items, the location of items, the transfer of items shared by the network's participants (interlibrary loan), and the acquisition of such items.

natural language refers to human-readable text as opposed to coded text readable by machines.

network 1) two or more organizations engaged in a common pattern of information exchange through telecommunications links. 2) a series of points or nodes connected by communication channels. 3) a cooperative organization formed to provide services to members, generally including computer services and telecommunications.

network coordinating agency (LC) a proposed agency to be responsible for coordinating the development of the library bibliographic component of the national library and information service network.

network front end processor* a front end computer that acts as the interface between the host or the host front end processor and the network. Its responsibilities include the reliable routing of messages to and from the associated host front end processor and the transmission of messages from other network nodes.

network library resource system (LC) one of the three components of a proposed national library and information service network. The resource system will designate responsibility to information facilities for providing access to needed library materials and coordinate support for collection development.

network operations center* a center that controls, manages, and maintains a network.

node used to describe the point at which communications lines join in a network; also used to denote a switching center in a network.

OCR optical character recognition; a process in which data are mechanically scanned and automatically converted to machine-readable form for input to computer systems.

offline a system in which peripheral devices such as input equipment operate independent of the central processor.

online a system in which peripheral devices, such as terminals, are in direct and continuing communication with the central unit.

originating host* 1) the initiator of a network session. 2) the host computer at the source of a message transmitted to a target host in a network.

packet switching* a type of data communications in which small defined blocks of data called packets are independently transmitted from point to point between source and destination, and reassembled into proper sequence at the destination.

port* the communications interface subsystem of a computer, front end computer, or terminal.

post telephone and telegraph (PTT)* government-operated or government-authorized (usually European) common carriers.

profile 1) a description of the subjects, languages, etc. in which a user or group of users is interested to allow selection of potentially relevant items from a file. 2) in OCLC, Inc. and some other systems, used for the stored description of a library's requirements for computer processing, e.g., for automatic printing of catalog cards.

protocol* the conventions used in communicating between nodes and levels in a network, specifically a formal set of conventions governing the format and relative sequencing of message exchanges. (Note: the use of "protocol" for communications conventions between nodes at the same level, and "interface" between nodes at adjacent levels has been suggested.)

PTT see: post telephone and telegraph.

R & D research and development.

real time system* a computer system that receives and processes data, and can utilize the results immediately to guide subsequent processing operations.

record a set of data elements or related items of data which represent a unit of information.

referral center an organization for directing information and data researchers to the appropriate source (library, information, or document center) rather than supplying the data or actual document.

regional network a network with nodes in a defined geographic area. The term is not rigorously defined in that it is now used for two types of networks: those serving a portion or area within a state, or those having participants in two or more states (interstate or multistate).

remote input* a method of input in which data are entered for processing via an input device that has access to a computer through a telecommunications link. See also: decentralized input.

resource library* a library designated as responsible for developing collections in special groups of materials and for providing access to these materials to other libraries.

resource sharing sharing of any resources (bibliographic data, facilities, staff, etc.) among cooperating libraries, but most commonly used to designate sharing of items in the collection.

response time the elapsed time between the completion of an input message at a terminal and the display of the first character of the response.

retrospective conversion see: conversion.

ring network* a computer network in which each computer is connected to two adjacent computers in a circular pattern.

SDI Selective Dissemination of Information, the informing of users (frequently through a computer operation) of new documents received which match their interest profile.

software generally used for computer programs, but also used to refer to everything that is not equipment (hardware).

specialized common carrier* 1) a company authorized by a government agency to provide limited telecommunications services. Examples of specialized common carriers are the value-added networks. 2) the term is also used to connote all those common carriers not covered in the original federal communications legislation.

stand-alone a computer system that can operate independently of other computer systems.

star network* a computer network in which each peripheral network node is connected only to the computer(s) at a single central facility. See also: centralized (computer) network.

state network a network that exists wholly within one state.

subsystem a second, subordinate system which performs in a complementary way to the controlling system.

systems analysis an organized study and analysis of a detailed procedure, method or activity which determines precisely what must be accomplished and how to accomplish it.

tag a character or digit or a series of characters or digits which are attached to a field or a record as a means to identify or to signal the computer of what is coming next.

technical information center an organization that acquires, processes, and disseminates technical information.

telecommunications transmission and reception of data by electromagnetic means, including telegraphy, telephony, data transmission, etc.

teleconferencing 1) the use of telecommunications, such as telephone, radio, or satellite to conduct meetings in which participants are at remote sites. 2) the use of telecommunications and computer systems for conducting meetings by inputting data to a storage device for retrieval at remote locations to allow participants to add comments to the data store.

telefacsimile see: facsimile transmission.

teleprocessing* automated data processing that utilizes telecommunications facilities for data transmission.

TELPAK* commercial telecommunications services using wide-band transmission techniques for multiple channel, high-speed, and video communication.

terminal* 1) a device for entering data into or receiving data from a computer system or computer network. 2) a point in a communications network at which data can either enter or leave.

thesaurus a terminology list to control access points in a file. Generally used with respect to control of subject terms for use in information retrieval systems.

time sharing a method of operation in which a common computer facility is shared by several users during the same time period.

topology the configuration of the links and nodes in a network.

transaction an operational unit of processing at the application level; a complete step of data processing.

union catalog a catalog that describes the contents of physically separate library collections, indicating by means of locations data the libraries in which a given item may be found.

universal bibliographic control (UBC)* an international system for handling bibliographic data that describe bibliographic items produced anywhere in the world.

user profile see: profile.

*value-added network** (VAN) a network operated by a private company that is authorized by a government agency to lease basic communications services from common carriers and specialized common carriers, to augment the services through additional facilities, such as switching centers and store-and-forward devices, and to resell the enhanced service to end users. Telenet and Tymnet are examples of value-added networks.

video-display terminal see: cathode ray tube terminal.

video disc a device shaped like a phonorecord, on which analog signals which represent images are recorded by laser or other technologies, to provide a high recording density, e.g., up to 54,000 frames per disc.

*virtual circuit** a telecommunications path that uses a number of point-to-point circuits connected through switching by communications computers. Data transfer is accomplished by forwarding data in blocks from node to node toward the destination, such that the circuit appears as a single physical transmission path.

*voice-grade line** a telephone line suitable for transmission of speech, digital or analog data, or facsimile, generally with a frequency range of 300 to 3000 cycles per second.

wide area telecommunications service (WATS)* communications service that allows users to use telecommunications facilities for voice or data transmission within specified zones for a flat monthly charge, without regard to the number or length of transmissions.

*wide-band** a communications channel or group of channels with a data capacity greater than that of a voice-grade line.

word processor a system, with a CRT terminal and keyboard, for input and with magnetic cards or magnetic floppy discs for data storage, and a printer for output, used principally for automating office routines such as report preparation, mailing lists, correspondence, etc.

LIST OF ACRONYMS

AMIGOS	AMIGOS Bibliographic Council
ANSI	American National Standards Institute
BALLOTS	Bibliographic Automation of Large Library Operations Systems
BCR	Bibliographic Center for Research
BRS	Bibliographic Retrieval Services
CAPCON	Consortium of Universities of the Washington Metropolitan Area
CCLC	Cooperative College Library Center (Atlanta, Georgia)⸍
ESEA	Elementary and Secondary Education Act
FCC	Federal Communications Commission
FLN	Federal Library Network
FTS	Federal Telecommunications System
HEA	Higher Education Act
ILLINET	Illinois Library Network
INCOLSA	Indiana Cooperative Library Services Authority
LC	Library of Congress
LSCA	Library Services and Construction Act
MEDLINE	MEDLARS (Medical Library Analysis and Retrieval System) On-line
MIDLNET	Midwest Region Library Network
MINITEX	Minnesota Interlibrary Telecommunications Exchange
MLC	Michigan Library Consortium
NAL	National Agricultural Library
NCLIS	National Commission on Libraries and Information Science
NEBASE	Nebraska libraries network, Nebraska State Library Commission
NELINET	no longer an acronym but now the official name; formerly New England Library Information Network.
NLM	National Library of Medicine
NTIS	National Technical Information Service
NPC	National Periodicals Center (proposed)
OCLC, Inc.	no longer an acronym but now the official name; formerly Ohio College Library Center.
OHIONET	the name of the network in Ohio.
ORBIT	On-line Retrieval of Bibliographic Information-Timeshared
PALINET	Pennsylvania Area Library Network
PRLC	Pittsburgh Regional Library Center
RLG	Research Libraries Group, Inc.
RLIN	Research Libraries Information Network
SDC	Systems Development Corporation
SOLINET	Southeastern Library Network
STAIRS	Storage and Information Retrieval System
SUNY	State University of New York
USOE	United States Office of Education
WILS	Wisconsin Interlibrary Loan Service
WLN	Washington Library Network
Z-39	ANSI networking committee

INDEX

Compiled by
Sanford Berman, Head Cataloger
Hennepin County Library
Edina, Minnesota

419